Gary & Edie Reger

THE
SICILIAN VESPERS

CHARLES OF ANJOU

THE
SICILIAN VESPERS

A HISTORY OF THE MEDITERRANEAN WORLD
IN THE LATER THIRTEENTH CENTURY

BY

STEVEN RUNCIMAN

CAMBRIDGE
AT THE UNIVERSITY PRESS
1958

PUBLISHED BY

THE SYNDICS OF THE CAMBRIDGE UNIVERSITY PRESS

Bentley House, 200 Euston Road, London, N.W. 1
American Branch: 32 East 57th Street, New York 22, N.Y.

©

CAMBRIDGE UNIVERSITY PRESS

1958

Printed in Great Britain at the University Press, Cambridge
(Brooke Crutchley, University Printer)

To

GEORGE MACAULAY TREVELYAN

*in admiration, gratitude and
friendship*

CONTENTS

CONTENTS

PLATES

MAPS

PREFACE

The Sicilian Vespers are seldom remembered nowadays. To the average educated man the words only suggest the title of one of Verdi's lesser-known operas. A century and more ago it was different. Their story was thought suitable to inspire the pens of poets and dramatists; and about them a great work of history was written which helped to bring Sicily into the cause of the Italian Risorgimento. It is not to be expected that anyone today will wade through the poetic tragedies of Casimir Delavigne or of Mrs Felicia Hemans; and it is to be hoped that no one will try to learn history from the libretto that Scribe provided for Verdi. That was an unfortunate work. It was commissioned for a gala performance at Paris; and it offended Verdi and the Italians because the traditional hero of the Vespers, John of Procida, appeared as a sly and unprincipled intriguer, the Sicilians because they were treated as both cruel and cowardly, the Austrians because it dealt with a rising of Italians against an occupying power, and the French because the climax of the play was a deserved massacre of their compatriots.

Amari's great *Storia della Guerra del Vespro Siciliano*, first published in 1842, can still be read with pleasure and profit. Amari was a fine and learned historian who scrupulously unearthed all the evidence that he could find and brought it together into a coherent story. But Amari was also a politician. He wished to encourage the Sicilians to rise against the Bourbons by telling them of their successful rising against the House of Anjou. His learning was all directed to this one end, not without success. But his deliberate bias narrowed his vision. There is still room for the story to be told again in its wider European setting.

In fact the story of the massacre of the French at Palermo on 30 March 1282, which is traditionally known as the Sicilian Vespers, is important not because it is just an isolated drama of conspirators and cut-throats, nor because it is just one episode in the epic tragedy of Sicily and her oppressors. The massacre was one of those events in history which altered the fate of nations and of world-wide institutions. To understand its importance we must see it in its international setting. I have therefore tried in this book to tell the whole story of the Mediterranean world in the second half of the thirteenth century with the Vespers as its central point. The canvas is wide; it has to stretch from England to Palestine, from Constantinople to Tunis. It is also crowded with characters; but a historical canvas is necessarily crowded, and readers who are afraid of crowds should keep to the better-ordered lanes of fiction. The story has various themes which unite at this one point. It is the story of a brilliant prince whose arrogance was his undoing. It is the story of a vast conspiracy plotted at Barcelona and at Byzantium. It is the story of the brave, secretive people of Sicily rising against alien domination. It is the story of the gradual suicide of the grandest conception of the Middle Ages, the universal papal monarchy.

There are ample sources on which a history of the Vespers can be based. The period is rich in chroniclers and historians of varying reliability. The archives of the relevant governments have been for the most part well searched and their acts published; though there is still probably much to be found in the unsorted archives of the Kings of Aragon, and some of the Hohenstaufen and Angevin archives of Naples perished in the course of the last war. There are many works by modern historians to which I am deeply indebted. In particular I must mention the recently published work by E. G. Léonard on the Angevins of Naples, which, though necessarily a little summary, is invaluable for its learning and its good sense. E. Jordan's great book on Italy on the eve of the Angevin invasion, published in 1909, leaves the historian of today with nothing further to add on that subject; and his more recent (1939) volume on Germany and Italy in the twelfth and thirteenth centuries is still more remarkable for the succinct clarity with which it presents the essential information. Unfortunately it closes at 1273. The short book by Cartellieri on Peter of Aragon and the Vespers establishes definitely the nature of the Grand Conspiracy, though perhaps he underrates the complicity of Byzantium. His work has been confirmed by the researches of Mlle Wieruszowski. Amongst Italian historians, Amari's still invaluable history has been supplemented by such historians as Carucci, Pontieri and Monti, and the Sicilian co-historians Libertini and Paladino. My indebtedness will appear in my notes, in which, where modern historians have fully covered the ground and themselves mentioned their sources, I have on occasion referred only to the modern work.

I have myself attempted to visit personally the sites where the more important episodes in the story took place; and I should like to thank my friends in Italy and Sicily who have facilitated my journeys. I should also like to thank the Syndics and staff of the Cambridge University Press for their habitual courtesy and kindness.

STEVEN RUNCIMAN

LONDON
1957

*Figures in the text refer to notes
beginning on page 294*

SICILY

'Italien ohne Sizilien macht gar kein Bild in der Seele: hier ist der
Schlüssel zu allem.'   GOETHE, *Italienische Reise.*

The island of Sicily lies as a triangle across the centre of the Middle
Sea, dividing it into two and almost forming a bridge that joins
Italy with Africa. Few islands have been better favoured by
nature. Its climate is mild and its scenery beautiful, with rugged
mountains and smiling valleys and plains. Even the frequency of
earthquakes and the ever-present menace of Mount Etna, though
they have borne constant witness to the caprice of natural forces,
have in compensation added to the richness of the soil. Man has
been less kindly to the island. Geography placed it to be an
inevitable battleground between the forces of Europe and Africa
and to be an essential possession for anyone who would rule the
Mediterranean world. Its story is one of invasions, wars and
tumults.[1]

Who the Siculi were who gave their name to the island, and
whether they came from Italy and displaced the older auto-
chthonous Sicani, is a matter for prehistorians to dispute. Sicilian
history begins when the Siculi themselves saw their land invaded
and colonized by the two great seafaring peoples of the ancient
world, the Phoenicians and the Greeks. The Greeks came in about
700 B.C., founding their cities round the coasts of the eastern half
of the island. The Phoenicians had come already, sailing in from
the colonies that they had established in Africa, and occupying the
western half. There were wars between the two peoples, in
which the Greeks held the mastery, though the Phoenicians, with
the great African empire of Carthage to back them, remained a
danger. When they were not fighting the Phoenicians, the Greek
city-states settled down to the endemic pastime of petty wars

between each other and petty revolutions. Syracuse was the chief city, particularly renowned for having driven off the Athenian expedition; and now and then a Tyrant of Syracuse, a Hieron or a Dionysius, would establish a rule that for a few years kept peace and order. Despite the troubles it was a happy time. The Greeks had introduced the olive and the vine. Cornfields covered the great central plain, from whose meadows the God of the Underworld carried off the daughter of the Corn-Goddess. Flocks were plentiful on the hillsides. The gay and innocent lives of the peasants have been immortalized in the idylls of Theocritus. Yet, even so, man was beginning to rob the island of its wealth. The cities, both Greek and Phoenician, had their ships for war and for merchandise; and the forest trees began to fall under the axes of the ship-builders. And while Corydon sported with Amaryllis in the shade, their goats devoured the saplings that might have renewed the forests. Erosion and desiccation were started. Soil was washed off the mountains; and the pleasant rills which watered the valleys began to be replaced by courses down which torrents poured in winter but which lay bare and dry under the summer sun.

The Idyllic Age did not last for long; for Sicily from its geographical position was inevitably involved in the great wars between Rome and Carthage. By 200 B.C. the whole island was under the domination of Rome. The Romans treated the island considerately: they needed the corn that it grew to feed their enormous capital city. There were bad periods. The islanders suffered under the exactions of the Governor Verres, against whom Cicero thundered; and they were involved in the wars of Sextus Pompey against the central Government. Before then their fields were devastated by the revolts of the slaves, mostly former prisoners of war, whom the Romans had settled in the island soon after their conquest. But the writers of Rome have little to say about Sicily. We must assume that their silence is testimony to a quiet prosperity. The island was now essentially Greek. Its inhabitants, whether of Greek, Phoenician or Sicul origin, spoke Greek, though the Roman government officials used Latin as well and official pronouncements were made in both languages. At the same time a certain number of Latin-speaking colonists from Italy were introduced.

The decline of the Roman Empire and its extinction in the West brought new troubles to the island. A storm in the Straits of Messina saved it from invasion by Alaric and the Visigoths; but soon afterwards it was raided and for a time occupied by the Vandals, operating from Carthage. It was reunited to Italy under Odoacer and after him Theodoric the Ostrogoth, both of whom treated it with solicitous consideration; for the Vandals blocked the export of corn from Africa, and all Italy was dependent for its bread upon the cornfields of Sicily. But, even though both rulers were careful not to upset the Sicilians by allowing Gothic or other barbarian settlers into the island, their rule was not popular. When the Emperor Justinian sent an army from Constantinople to restore Sicily to the Empire before proceeding to the conquest of Italy from the Ostrogoths, his troops were everywhere welcomed, and the Ostrogothic garrisons retired without attempting to oppose them. Before the war in Italy ended, the Ostrogoths raided the island, but, unlike Italy itself, it escaped serious devastation.[1]

There followed a brief period of quiet, during which, however, it seems that the anopheles mosquito made its appearance in the island, with the curse of malaria; and in many low-lying districts the population began to dwindle. In the middle of the seventh century trouble started again. The Muslims by now had conquered Syria and Egypt; and as they planned to extend their empire westward, Sicily was an obvious objective. Their first raid on the island took place in 652; but it was not until they conquered the African shores opposite, in the early years of the eighth century, that the pressure became acute. Meanwhile there had been a moment when it seemed that Sicily might become the

3

centre of a reconstituted Empire. The Emperor Constans, despairing of holding the East against Islam, planned to move his capital back from Constantinople to Old Rome. When that proved to be impracticable, he settled at Syracuse. But his officials were horrified by his abandonment of Constantinople; and one day in 668, when he was taking a bath, a courtier struck him fatally on the head with a soap-dish. On his death the government returned to the Bosphorus.[1]

During the eighth century the Byzantine Emperors managed to keep hold of Sicily. There were one or two local revolts, inspired by the dislike of the islanders for the iconoclastic policy of the Isaurian Emperors. But at the same time the Greek elements in the island were strengthened. There was no attempt to introduce iconoclasm into the island; and many image-worshippers from the East took refuge there; while the Emperors in the course of their quarrel with the Roman Church, as well as for administrative convenience, transferred the province ecclesiastically from Rome, to which it had belonged, to Constantinople. In the ninth century Muslim invasions began in earnest from Africa. Their excuse was the revolt of a local governor, Euphemius, who proclaimed himself Emperor and called in the Arabs to help him. The invaders landed in the island in 827. Euphemius was murdered soon afterwards; but the Arabs did not leave. In 831 they captured Panormus, or Palermo, which they renamed al-Madinah and made their centre. Their progress was slow, except in the west of the island, the old Phoenician area, where the Greek influence was smallest. But in 842 they captured Messina and in 857 or 858 Cefalù. Two years later they established themselves in the centre of the island by storming, with the aid of a traitor, the almost impregnable fortress of Enna, or Castrogiovanni. The Emperors did their best to rescue the island; but the Imperial fleet had been allowed to decay under the Isaurians and only now, too late, was being revived. Their efforts preserved southern Italy, which the Arabs had also invaded; but when the Byzantine capital

4

of Sicily, Syracuse, fell to the enemy in 878, they abandoned the island. Taormina held out till 902, and a few villages on the slopes of Mount Etna a little longer; but by the end of the eighth century the island was effectively under Arab control.[1]

The Arabs brought a new vitality into Sicilian life. They introduced the lemon and the orange, the cotton-plant and the sugar-cane, though in return they completed the slow work of the goats by an extravagant destruction of the forests. They were great traders; under their rule Palermo became an international market where merchants from the Christian Italian cities were as welcome as Muslim merchants from Africa and the East. Many colonists, Arab and African, followed their armies into the island, particularly into its eastern half; but the Christians were very little disturbed. Indeed, financially they were probably better off than under the Byzantines; for the taxes were not so high, and they were not removed from their farms and villages to serve in the army. But there were numerous petty wars. At first the Arab emirs paid allegiance to the Aghlabite rulers of Africa; but when the Aghlabites were succeeded by the heterodox Fatimids and Zirids, the Sicilian princes declared their independence and began to fight against each other and against the attempts of the Africans to reconquer them. Early in the eleventh century the Byzantines sent an expedition to recover the island which for a time had some success and was only thwarted by the distraction of the Norman invasions of Byzantine Italy.[2]

In 1060 the Normans decided upon the conquest of Sicily. They had already overrun most of southern Italy and saw that to make an efficient kingdom out of it they must also control Sicily. But, while their conquests in Italy had been made by a group of barons under the leadership of Robert Guiscard of Hauteville, with the help of allies amongst the Lombard lords living there, Sicily was conquered by the unaided efforts of Robert Guiscard and his youngest brother, Roger. In consequence it was a slow business; for the Hautevilles did not command many troops of their own, and Guiscard was continually distracted by trouble on the mainland, while Roger, who did most of the work, often had no more than a hundred knights serving under him. But they were welcomed by the Christian population, and were helped by disunion amongst the Muslims. The three emirs of Trapani, Palermo and Girgenti, who divided the control of the island between them, were bitterly jealous of each other. It was the alliance of Ibn ath-Thimnah of Palermo which enabled the Normans to establish a foothold in the island. They captured Messina in 1061. Their first attempt to take Palermo in 1064, soon after Ibn ath-Thimnah's death, was a failure; but in 1068 they defeated an army sent by the Zirids of Africa to relieve the island, and thenceforward their progress was slow but steady. With the capture of Syracuse in 1085 and Butera and Noto in 1088 and 1091 the conquest of the island was complete. So long as Robert Guiscard lived he claimed a share in the island and suzerain rights over his brother; but Roger held the title of Count of Sicily and controlled the government of the island and of the Calabrian peninsula. After Guiscard's death in 1085 his heirs were too weak to assert their rights; and Count Roger ruled as an independent sovereign, under the ultimate suzerainty of the Pope, who had granted to the Norman princes authority to make their Mediterranean conquests.

Roger died in 1101 and was succeeded by his eight-year-old son, Simon, under the regency of the Dowager Countess, Adelaide of Savona. Simon died two years later and was succeeded by his brother Roger II, who was also aged eight at the time of his accession. Adelaide continued to act as regent till 1112, when Roger was seventeen, and she herself was lured into a disastrous marriage with the divorced King of Jerusalem, Baldwin I.

Roger II inherited all the ability and ambition of his family. He was determined to make Sicily a power of international importance which should dominate the Mediterranean. His attempts to control the central narrows of the Mediterranean by a permanent occupation of the Tunisian coast opposite to Sicily were unsuccessful; but his object was achieved by the conquest of Malta and the creation of a formidable fleet. In 1127 the ruler of Norman Italy, William I, Duke of Apulia, Guiscard's grandson, died. In spite of the opposition of the Papacy and the legal rights of the Prince of Antioch, another grandson of Guiscard's, Roger secured the Italian inheritance. In 1130 he took the title of King of Sicily and on Christmas Day that year was crowned in the cathedral of Palermo. During the remaining twenty-four years of his reign Roger built up his kingdom to be a formidable factor in European politics. He constantly quarrelled with the Pope and with the Western Emperor, neither of whom approved of his increasing power. He made several profitable attacks on Byzantine territory; and he kept the Muslims in Tunisia in permanent awe of him. At the same time he was strict and efficient in the government of his own dominions and strenuously encouraged their commercial prosperity.

His son William I, who reigned from 1154 to 1166, continued his policy, though he was more constant in his support of the Papacy, which was in difficulties owing to the menacing power of the Emperor Frederick Barbarossa. William I, owing to his own severity and the unpopularity of his ministers, has received the surname of 'the Bad'; and he did indeed provoke several revolts among his subjects, in Sicily as well as on the mainland. But the justice and competence of his government were generally admitted. His son, William II, after a difficult minority, had a more tranquil reign and was honoured with the surname of 'the Good' and, according to Dante, a place in Paradise after his death. But in the main he followed the same course as his father and grandfather. He died in 1189.

The rule of these three great Norman kings is generally regarded as the golden age in Sicilian history. For nearly a century the island was the centre of a lively and prosperous kingdom. The kings preferred it to their mainland possessions. Palermo was their capital and their favourite residence. Indeed, neither

William I or William II often emerged from their palace there, where they led lives more reminiscent of a Muslim sultan than of a medieval Christian prince, amid a ceremonial consciously copied from the hieratic style of Byzantium. Their actual system of government was based on feudal lines. This was necessary for their mainland territory, where, owing to the circumstances of the conquest, there were a number of great baronies held loosely under the crown, and the kings had to make a continuous effort to have their authority recognized. In Sicily, however, where Count Roger had had few lords to help him in his conquest, not many fiefs were distributed, and they were all small. The ruler kept most of the island as his royal demesne. Under the Byzantines and the Muslims the towns and villages of the island had been almost all free communities, directly under the government. As the King took over so much of the island himself, the change into a more feudal pattern was barely noticed. But it was to lead to misery and resentment in the future. The actual administration of the island and, as far as possible, of the mainland, was centralized under the King's Curia, which was a curious synthesis of feudal, Byzantine and Muslim systems. The titles of the officials were many of them Arabic or Greek. The provincial government was not allowed to fall into the hands of the local nobility but was conducted by functionaries appointed by the Curia. With rare exceptions, none of the vassals, though they enjoyed other regular feudal rights, was allowed to try criminal cases. The towns and cities were all administered by royal nominees.

Several languages were spoken in the Kingdom. On the mainland, except in Calabria, a form of Italian had come into general use; but in the island most of the population spoke Greek, with large colonies of Arabic-speaking Muslims and a few Jewish colonies. The Court spoke Norman-French, and there was a growing number of officials and of immigrants from the mainland who spoke French or Italian. Laws and decrees were issued in Latin, Greek and Arabic. The Muslims had their own law-courts where Koranic law was used; Byzantine law was kept on for the Greeks. The Muslims were allowed to worship freely in their mosques. There had been at first an attempt to force Latin Christianity on the Greeks, but it was soon abandoned. Services continued to be held according to the Greek rite; but the Greek clergy had to recognize the supreme authority of the Latin hierarchy. As the new ruling class belonged to the Latin Church there was a steady movement towards Latin Christianity, which began to have an effect on the spoken language. The kings kept tight control over the whole Church. They had acquired from the Papacy the right to be permanent apostolic legates; they proclaimed themselves to be 'crowned by God', and it was sacrilege to question their laws or judgements. But the Pope claimed, and was generally admitted, to be ultimate overlord of the Kingdom.

The most remarkable feature of the Norman government was the success with which it brought harmony to the diverse elements in Sicily. Such plots and rebellions as took place were the work of the imported aristocracy. The ordinary Sicilian accepted with gratitude a rule which might be strict and paternalist, but which gave him better justice and more prosperity than his ancestors had known for generations. The kings encouraged trade and industry. They built up and subsidized a large merchant marine. In the course of a raid on Greece, Roger II kidnapped trained silk-weavers to improve the nascent silk-factories in the island. Artists from many countries and traditions were given patronage. The great churches of Norman Sicily perfectly illustrate the civilization that was developing. There you find Norman architects employing Greek and Muslim masons and Byzantine structural devices, Arabic decorators and Byzantine mosaic-artists, who were training a school of local mosaicists, and the whole integrated into a style that is harmonious and unique. At the Court, Arab sempstresses embroidered for the king Christian texts in Arabic lettering on his ceremonial robes. Court officials included men of such diverse origin as the

Greek-born Admiral, George of Antioch, or the English-born Richard Palmer, Bishop of Syracuse, or the Hungarian Gentile who became Bishop of Girgenti. Arab voyagers, such as Ibn Jubayr, were deeply impressed by the contentment of the King's Muslim subjects. Ibn Jubayr remarked in particular on the hospitals and almshouses provided by Muslims and Christians alike; and he noted with interest that the Christian women of the island followed the fashions of Muslim women; they wore veils and abbas when they went out of doors, and never stopped talking.[1]

There was thus in Sicily by the close of the twelfth century a population composed of hereditarily opposed elements living together in peace and moving towards a genuine national sentiment. The Norman kings, ambitious and unscrupulous though they were, must be given credit for this extraordinary achievement. But the golden age did not last for long. The royal family itself began to die out. When William II died in 1189, his heir was his father's half-sister, Roger II's posthumous daughter Constance, who had been married four years before, at the age of thirty-one, to the eldest son of the Western Emperor Frederick Barbarossa, Henry of Hohenstaufen, a boy eleven years her junior. Henry and Constance claimed the inheritance, to which Constance's rights had been admitted by a parliament at the time of her betrothal. But both in Sicily and on the mainland, all classes disliked the idea of a German king. After a certain intrigue the crown passed to Tancred, Count of Lecce, the bastard son of Roger II's eldest son, who had died unmarried while his father was still alive. Henry was too busy in Germany as regent for his father, who had just left on the Third Crusade, on which he was to die next year, to march south and secure the Sicilian inheritance.

Tancred's reign was unquiet. The nobility were jealous of him; the Muslims revolted against him. He had imprisoned his predecessor's widow, Joanna of England; and the arrival of her brother, Richard Cœur-de-Lion, in Sicily on his way to the Crusade, added to his embarrassment, which was not lessened by the simultaneous arrival of the King of France. Tancred managed eventually to secure the friendship of Richard and a promise of an alliance against Henry and Constance, but it was of little use to him, for it offended the French king, and the English army passed on to the Crusade. In 1191 Henry entered Italy and was crowned Emperor at Rome. He proceeded south as far as Naples and Salerno, where he left the Empress Constance. He then was forced to retire; and Constance fell into Tancred's hands. But, on the Pope's orders, she was soon released. The Emperor was not able to return to the attack till 1194. Early that year Tancred died, leaving his throne to his infant son William III and the regency to his widow, Queen Sibylla. When Henry, who had by now established himself securely in Germany, approached at the head of a great army, resistance seemed impossible. Sibylla surrendered on terms which were not kept. She was imprisoned, and many of her supporters were cruelly put to death; and the child-king disappeared into obscurity.[1]

Henry was crowned King of Sicily at Palermo on Christmas Day, 1194. Constance was not present; she was detained at the little town of Jesi in Apulia awaiting the birth of a child. As she was aged forty and for nine years her marriage had been childless, she was determined that there should be no doubt about her baby's authenticity. A company of no less than nineteen cardinals and bishops was crowded into a tent in the market-square of Jesi, where on 26 December she gave birth to a son who was christened Frederick.[2]

The harshness of Henry's government soon made him hated, even more in Sicily than on the Italian mainland. He was a cold, brilliant man, whose ambition to establish his autocratic authority over the whole of Germany and Italy from the North Sea to the African straits and to turn it into the hereditary possession of his house, was very nearly successful. But the Sicilians, who till recently had been governed by local princes considerate of their interests, had no wish to be dragged along in this Imperial train.

He hoped to placate them by leaving the Sicilian-born Empress as regent of the island and its mainland territory; but Constance was regarded merely as his tool. The government was dominated by a German seneschal, Markward of Anweiler, and its power ensured by German troops. Constance protested in vain. In 1197, when Henry revisited the Kingdom, there was a plot to murder him; and it seems that both Constance and the Pope were privy to it. Henry was warned in time and reacted with greater severity than before. There was a general sigh of relief when he died a few months later from a sudden attack of dysentery, at Messina on 28 September 1197.[1]

His death did not bring peace to the island. The widowed Empress took over the government, dismissing all the Germans and surrounding herself with native ministers. But her authority was insecure. Fortunately she found an energetic friend and adviser in a new Pope, elected in January 1198, Innocent III. She herself was already in poor health and was nervous for the future of her little son. She made a will which set up a Council of Regency to administer the Kingdom, but placed the child himself under the guardianship of the Pope. Frederick, at the age of three and a half, was formally crowned king at Palermo in May 1198. Six months later Constance died.[2]

The years of Frederick's minority were turbulent and unhappy for both the Kingdom and the young king. Innocent, as suzerain of the Kingdom and guardian of the king, tried vainly to control the government. There were endless intrigues and petty wars between the chancellor and chief regent, Walter of Palear, and the ex-Seneschal Markward and another German, Diepold of Vohburg, to whom Henry had given the lordship of Salerno. One of Tancred's daughters escaped from captivity; and her husband, Walter of Brienne, was given by the Pope large estates in Apulia and became the chief Papal military agent in the Kingdom, without, however, abandoning his wife's claim to the throne. The Pisans and the Genoese fought with each other along the coasts, particularly round Syracuse, which the latter had occupied. Fortunately for the Kingdom, Markward died from a badly performed operation for stone in 1201, and Walter of Brienne of wounds in 1205. Walter of Palear and Diepold submitted to the Pope, who sent his own nephew, Gerard, Cardinal of Sant' Adriano, as papal legate to superintend the government. For the next two years this government ran more smoothly, with only a savage Muslim revolt in the island and perpetual brigandage by German adventurers on the mainland to suppress.[1]

In December 1208 Frederick attained the age of fourteen, and his minority officially ended. He took over a greatly impoverished kingdom. The royal demesne had almost disappeared. The Pope had given away vast estates from it; various lords had occupied lands from which they could not be dislodged. It was only by gifts from the cities that Frederick received enough money to begin his government. The Pope, who had received by Constance's will the annual sum of just over a thousand ounces of gold as recompense for his guardianship of the King, as well as all his expenses for the defence of the realm, claimed that he had spent another 12,800 gold ounces on keeping order in the island. Frederick began his reign with that debt round his neck.

Under Frederick the island recovered something of its former glory. He loved it above all his other possessions. He had been brought up in the palace at Palermo, with its lovely gardens; and he would always say in later days that it was there alone where he felt himself to be at home. His Court was centred there; his children were born there. But in fact he was seldom there himself. He had too many interests to distract him. As time went on he visited the island less and less, preferring, when he had time to spare, to retire to one of his castles or hunting-boxes on the mainland, in Apulia. He provided Sicily with a just and orderly government. He reformed its laws so as to stamp out corruption, in public as in private affairs. He expelled the Genoese who had been exploiting the island from their colony at Syracuse. But he was obliged to use force to establish his rule. He was not popular. The Sicilians remembered him as the son of the cruel German, Henry. They saw him diverted by his ambitions in northern Italy and away beyond the Alps. They felt no sympathy when he was crowned Emperor in 1220. Though he left his wife, Constance of Aragon, as his regent in Sicily, she commanded no loyalty there. There was a terrible famine in 1212. The Saracens in the island, under the leadership of a brigand soldier, Morabit, rose in revolt; and ten years passed before the revolt was crushed and Morabit hanged at Palermo. The whole Muslim population was then rounded up and transplanted to the mainland, to the north of Apulia. It was only after these campaigns in 1222 and 1223 that the nobles, many of whom had risen in private rebellions, were crushed and their lands confiscated to rebuild the royal demesne.

Frederick had been vigorous but ruthless. The reformed laws that he issued were just, but they were imposed autocratically. Moreover, to support his wars men were conscripted into his armies and high taxes raised to support them. After he had established order his despotism was benevolent. He encouraged trade and industry, as his Norman ancestors had done. He founded new cities; he welcomed useful immigrants. He issued a stable coinage; he lowered import duties. He saw that justice was within reach of all his subjects, and he provided for their education at the great new university which he founded at Naples. His rule provided the island with peace and prosperity, in spite of the high taxation and the drain on manpower. But to the Sicilians it was not the same as in Norman times. Then Sicily had been the heart of a self-contained kingdom. It was from Palermo that the mainland provinces had been governed; and the Norman kings, for all their ambition, had remained essentially kings of Sicily. Now the King of Sicily was also Emperor and ruler of northern Italy. Even in the Sicilian kingdom he did not seem to favour the island more than the mainland. He tried to introduce uniformity between the two portions; and, indeed, his military needs made him concentrate more on the mainland than on the island. His incessant quarrels with the Pope troubled the pious islanders, especially as he was never able to acquire the legateship and the legal control of the Sicilian Church, which the Norman kings had exercised. The population was still mainly Greek, though the Latin element was increasing, and the converts from Islam who had remained in the island when the Muslims were transplanted seem to have identified themselves with the Latins. But in spite of the diversity a Sicilian national consciousness was arising, based on a smouldering resentment. Sicily, after a brief brilliant period of independence, saw itself dragged unwillingly into the quagmire of European politics. So long as the magnificent Emperor lived all might be well, for his government was good and his heart was known to be in Sicily, even if his actions seemed sometimes to disprove it. But no one could tell what might not happen under a lesser ruler, if the proud spirit of the Sicilians was not given the respect and consideration that it felt to be its due.[1]

CHAPTER I

THE DEATH OF ANTICHRIST

On a January day early in 1251 a messenger came to Lyons, where Pope Innocent IV was living in exile from Rome. He had travelled as fast as the winter weather would allow, to bring great news. Three weeks before, on 13 December 1250, the Emperor Frederick II had died of a sudden fever at Castel Fiorentino, in southern Italy. To the Pope in his excitement it seemed that all the troubles of the Church were now ended. Antichrist had perished; the race of vipers had lost its leader. 'Let the heavens rejoice', he wrote at once to the Faithful in Sicily. 'Let the earth be filled with gladness. For the fall of the tyrant has changed the thunderbolts and tempests that God Almighty held over your heads into gentle zephyrs and fecund dews.' His joy was shared by his friends and followers throughout Europe. It seemed to them that the hour was come, when the enemy forces were mourning their prince, to strike at them and crush them into nothingness. In a message that the papal legate, Gregory of Montelunzo, sent to the people of Milan destruction was urged with a vindictive glee that showed little of Christian charity.[1]

It is easy to understand the Pope's pleasure; for the Papacy in all its long history had never met an adversary so formidable as Frederick II of Hohenstaufen. He had been Emperor and head of the most splendid family in Germany. From his mother he had inherited the Kingdom of Sicily, with its Italian lands that stretched from the tip of the peninsula to the very outskirts of Rome. His grandfather, Frederick Barbarossa, had enjoyed greater glamour and renown than any Emperor since Charlemagne. His father, Henry VI, had been even abler and far more ruthless. Had he lived longer he might have secured the imperial throne as the hereditary possession of the House of Hohenstaufen. The

Papacy had fought against them both; their conception of Imperial power could never be reconciled with the Papal conception of a world theocracy dominated by the heir of Saint Peter. With Barbarossa a truce had been reached. Henry VI, with his wife's kingdom of Sicily to add to his strength, seemed near to victory when death prematurely removed him. His son Frederick was a little child, far too young to sit on the Imperial throne, over which rival claimants fought, reducing the Empire to chaos. The Papacy triumphed, under the magnificent figure of Innocent III. But Innocent, for all the plenitude of his power, feared to let the Empire disintegrate. Henry's widow, Constance of Sicily, died soon after her husband; and when, to ensure her son's safety, she left him under the guardianship of the Pope, Innocent made a grave mistake. Trusting on the boy's gratitude, he put forward his claims to the Imperial inheritance. Frederick II was crowned King of Germany in 1215, when he was twenty-one, and Emperor three years later.

Pope Innocent died in 1216. He never knew of the trouble that his ward was to cause the Church. His successor, Honorius III, who had been Frederick's tutor, soon found the young Emperor to be unaffected by his ecclesiastical upbringing or by any ties of gratitude to the Papacy. Frederick had promised, in return for his Imperial coronation, to pass the Sicilian throne on to his own infant son and to go on a Crusade. He showed no intention of fulfilling the first promise and no haste in fulfilling the second. Honorius was a kindly man who was loth to think ill of his former pupil; he reproachfully let Frederick go his own way. But he died in 1227; and his successor, Gregory IX, would allow no further compromise. He distrusted and disliked Frederick. He protested vainly against the Emperor's retention of Sicily; he excommunicated him for not going on the Crusade, and ex-communicated him again when he went. Frederick's success in the Holy Land, where he recovered Jerusalem for Christendom, was not disinterested; for he had married the heiress of the Kingdom of Jerusalem; nor were its results solidly based, as the barons of Outremer clearly saw. He cleverly took advantage of momentary weakness among the Muslims to secure an arrangement which could in fact easily be upset at the first revival of Muslim power. But his achievement won him respect in Europe; and when he returned there to find his Italian territory invaded by Papal armies, he gained general sympathy. The attack by the Pope himself on the lands of an absent Crusader shocked Christian opinion. Even Saint Louis, King of France, was horrified. And when the Pope next preached a Holy War against the Emperor it seemed that the whole idea of the Holy War had become ridiculous. But the Pope was implacable. The struggle lasted on bitterly throughout his pontificate and was maintained by his successors.

In material strength the Pope was no match for the Empire. The Papacy depended on the willing support of the Faithful. The Pope had the advantage of the vast, well-planned ecclesiastical organization of which he was head; but he could not count on the obedience of all his bishops, nor on the regular receipt of the tithes and taxes due to him. He had no armies of his own, apart from levies drawn from the papal estates. He could call on the sympathy of the Guelf factions throughout the cities of Italy; but they were everywhere too busily engaged in fighting their Ghibelline rivals to help him in his wider schemes. Even his own diocese of Rome was often unfaithful to him. The Romans liked to govern themselves and to appoint their own officials and senators. Many a Pope had to spend half his reign in exile.

The advantage lay mainly with the Emperor; but his power was never quite as real as it appeared. He had not the control either of Germany or of northern Italy that his grandfather had possessed. During the years that followed Henry VI's death, the princes in Germany and the cities of Italy had acquired an independence that Barbarossa would never have tolerated. In Germany Frederick II had to bribe the princes to support him by allowing them further rights. In Italy he had to make use of local notables of imperialist sympathies rather than of his own imperial officials. In the course of his reign there emerged in most Italian cities an imperialist party usually called Ghibelline, after the Hohenstaufen castle of Weibeling, in opposition to the papalist party, usually called Guelf, after the Welf Saxon dynasty which the Popes had supported against the Hohenstaufen. The Pope by now had become merely the head of the Guelf faction in Italy; and similarly the Emperor had become merely the head of the Ghibelline faction. This, far more than in the Pope's case, represented an abdication of power. Frederick never commanded a large army. The German princes grudged him troops; and he could not afford to denude his own properties there. The Ghibellines in Italy only thought of fighting the local Guelfs. He was mainly dependent on troops raised in his own southern kingdom. His army never numbered more than fifteen thousand men, of whom few were trained soldiers. The militia of a small Italian city, such as Parma or Brescia, operating from behind the shelter of its walls, could hold him up for months. He might be Emperor and King of Germany, Burgundy, Sicily and Jerusalem; but his high titles had far too little physical power to support them.

The contest was, however, not so much one of material strength as one of prestige and public opinion. Frederick II had on his side the glamour that still clung to the name of the Roman Empire. Medieval man, weary of the troubles that beset him, looked back with longing to the days of ancient Rome, that great world-dominion whose rulers had built the roads that still were used and the drains and aqueducts that were falling into disrepair. He yearned for an Emperor who would revive that lost glory. Charlemagne had almost done so, and, more recently, Frederick Barbarossa. Frederick II inherited with his title the respect and hope that men still attached to the Imperial idea. He was himself well aware of it. It was his aim to make his nominal title a reality, to be Caesar, the heir of Constantine and Justinian as well as of

Charlemagne. Brought up in Sicily, where his Norman ancestors had modelled their Court with Imperial Byzantium in their minds, he sought for such power as the Byzantine Emperors enjoyed, as God's viceroys on earth, deferential indeed to the Holy Church but ultimately supreme under Heaven. The Imperial crown had never graced a more brilliant head. Intellectually Frederick was amongst the most remarkable men of his time. He was a gifted linguist, fluent in French, German and Italian, Latin, Greek and Arabic. He was learned in law, in medicine and in natural history, and he interested himself in philosophy. Though physically un-distinguished, with his short stout figure, his red hair and red face and his myopic eyes, he could if he chose fascinate anyone with the charm and quickness of his wit. His qualities ought to have helped his cause; but he was the victim of his own brilliance. The Emperor for whom people looked was a traditional, paternal figure, in the mould of Barbarossa and of Charlemagne, not a man who had no patience with the conventions of the feudal world. Frederick despised fools and derided sententious piety. He loved to startle men by the audacity of his thought. He had no regard for the susceptibilities of others; and his belief in his high mission led him to cast aside the standards of honour that were held in his time. He was self-indulgent and he had a streak of cruelty in him. His harem at Palermo was notorious; and he kept immured there, in contemptuous neglect, the unfortunate young princesses whom in turn he married. His legitimate sons, who were of a more conventional type, found him a harsh and inconsiderate father. He had loyal admirers, but very few friends. The world in general regarded him with suspicion. His fellow-monarchs, who were ready to sympathize with him against the Papacy, were repelled by his amorality and his blasphemy. To his enemies, horrified by the richness of his intellect and the fearless-ness of his irreverence, he was the embodiment of Antichrist.[1]

None of the Popes who fought against him was of so remarkable a calibre. Honorius III was an amiable but rather feckless man.

Gregory IX and Innocent IV were sterner and abler, both of them indefatigable servants of the Church, but neither with any great breadth or originality of mind. The Papacy, however, was less dependent on the personality of its tenant than was the Empire. The Empire embodied a vague nostalgic idea that could only be realized under a wise, respected and powerful Emperor. Its constitution and its organization were formless and insufficiently defined. The Papacy had been buttressed by generations of Church lawyers and thinkers. It was carefully organized to reach throughout Christendom. Its rights and its claims were clearly laid down. Frederick might with truth doubt the authenticity of the Donation of Constantine; but in that uncritical age there were few who shared his doubts. The Pope as the heir of Saint Peter could maintain that his office had been instituted by Christ and that it raised him, poor mortal though he might be, above the sphere of fallible mankind. The Emperor's office, for all its glamour, had no such holy pedigree. His coronation might elevate him over other men, but he remained a sinful man; and it was the Pope who was empowered to perform the crowning. Both in the efficiency of its organization and in its mystical prestige the Papacy was stronger than the Empire. But it ran the risk of over-reaching itself. The Church was ill-served by its servants. There were increasing complaints about the worldliness of the priesthood and its avarice, indolence and self-indulgence. Religion still flourished among the laity, but the clergy no longer gave a lead. There were saints still, but they were seldom to be found on the bishops' benches. Rather, they were humble folk, men like Francis of Assisi, on whose activities the ecclesiastical authorities looked with some suspicion. Even though the Popes themselves showed a personal integrity that commanded respect, their cause was damaged by the instruments that they used. The fact that their dominion depended on spiritual rather than on material strength tempted them to be too lavish in wielding spiritual weapons. Pope Gregory VII had humbled the King of Germany at Canossa by the power of excommunication; but it had been diplomatic considerations that had persuaded Henry IV to submit. Even Pope Innocent III's triumphs had been in the main due to his sense of political timing. Excommunication, which has no physical sanction, can only be effective when the moral case is absolutely clear. The same is true of the Holy War. There the promise of spiritual rewards was not enough unless the cause had a strong moral appeal. Otherwise material inducements also were needed. Urban II launched the First Crusade in an atmosphere of genuine religious enthusiasm; but most of the Crusaders went eastward with the additional hope of sharing in the fabled wealth of the Orient. The Crusaders whom Innocent III sent out against the Albigensian heretics were hard, ambitious men frankly out for personal gain; and Innocent, for all his authority, could not prevent the Knights of the Fourth Crusade from disobeying his orders and seeking a more profitable enterprise than the failing cause of Christendom in Palestine. When Gregory IX and Innocent IV preached the Holy War against the Emperor, not only were men's consciences troubled but they saw no profit in it. The Papacy seemed to be using the Holy War merely for its own political ends, which were ends that many good Christians did not desire.[1]

The Popes must not be judged too harshly. They saw clearly enough that if the ideal of the Hildebrandine theocracy, which was no mean ideal, was to be realized, foes like Frederick II must at all costs be overcome. But in truth they did not need thus to overplay their hand. The Empire had already lost the battle. The gap between its ideal and its real position was greater even than the Papacy's; and it was even less able to sustain a long struggle. The personal brilliance of Frederick II gave it a last terrible appearance of splendour; but he had been able to do nothing to save it. The true danger to the Popes was not what they had feared. It was not that the Empire might triumph, but that in destroying the Empire the Papacy itself might commit suicide.

A wise spectator might have seen that the day of the old international Empire was over. The longing of mankind for the tranquillity and peace that one universal state should produce had not faded; nor will it ever fade. But the difficulties of achieving unity were now more obvious. Racial needs and traditions were pulling centrifugally; poor communications had created too many barriers. New and smaller units were forming, based on the practical demands of geography. The Emperor, despite his oecumenical title, was merely the king of the lands of middle Europe, and a king whose authority was dependent on a super-imposed idea, unlike his brothers of France or England, whose power was firmly rooted in reality. The Empire was to find its most eloquent advocates during the next century; but they preached a lost cause. The future lay with national kingdoms.

The Western Empire was not alone in its decline. All over the world the Empires of the early Middle Ages had fallen or were falling. Byzantium, the legitimate heir of Rome, where Roman law, Greek language and culture and the Holy Orthodox Church had bound people of many races into a single unit with the city that Constantine had founded as its centre, had survived for nine centuries as the one true supra-national Christian state. But unending attacks from enemies on every front had diminished its extent, and social and economic troubles had sapped its energies. The Turks had broken into Asia Minor. The Normans from southern Italy and Sicily kept up a running threat on the European provinces. Slav nationalism had led the peoples of the Balkans into revolt. In 1204 Constantinople itself, in a moment of particular weakness, had succumbed to an alliance between the Venetians and knights pledged to go on the Fourth Crusade. The Latin Empire that the Crusaders set up was an Empire only in name. The Empire in exile set up by the Byzantines at Nicaea was less an empire than a national kingdom where the Greek and Orthodox world could find refuge and plan revenge. There was no more unity in eastern Europe; and Constantinople itself, which till recently had seemed to be the sacrosanct capital of an enduring Empire, had become a plaything in international politics.[1]

Amongst the Muslims the Abbasid Caliphate, the ancient rival of Byzantium, was close to its end. Its authority, undermined by its Turkish mercenaries, had long since been only nominal; and though in the middle of the thirteenth century the last of the Caliphs, al-Mustasim, enjoyed a few years of independence, he was soon, in 1258, to perish with half a million of his subjects, in the holocaust of the Mongol sack of Baghdad. Of the rival dynasties that claimed the Caliphate, the Ommayads of Spain had been extinct for centuries, and the last Fatimid of Egypt had been dethroned in 1171 by Saladin. Saladin and his Ayubite kinsfolk had almost succeeded in giving unity to the Muslims; but, for all their brilliance, they were only a family of Kurdish adventurers, with no Imperial prestige behind them. In 1250, the very year of Frederick II's death, the last Ayubite Sultan had been murdered; and Egypt passed into the power of a military clique, the officers of the Turkish-born Mameluk regiment. Amongst the many local states into which the Muslim world had now disintegrated, the Mameluk Sultanate of Egypt was the most vigorous and ambitious.[2]

Even in furthest Asia the same process was happening. In China the brilliant Sung Empire, long past its prime, was tottering truncated to its final extinction in 1279. To the south of China the Empire of the Khmers, which had united Indo-China under the monarchs of Angkor, was falling and had only a few more decades to run. In all the world only one great Imperial dominion seemed to be flourishing; and it was so strange and terrible that it fitted into no known category. The Mongol Empire was vaster in its extent and more ruthless in its methods than any that the world had yet seen. Yet even that Empire soon felt the spirit of the time. Within a century of the death of its founder Jenghiz Khan, each branch of his dynasty had acquired the religion and culture of the people which it governed, and the Great Khan at Karakorum was no longer the overlord of them all.[1]

With the whole world moving in such a direction, men would soon begin to ask themselves whether the Papacy itself could survive as the grand universal theocracy envisaged by Gregory VII and Innocent III. The Popes had undermined the power of the Hohenstaufen, whose last great leader now was dead. But when the Hohenstaufen Empire had crashed to the ground, what would they erect in its place? In their preoccupation with the Empire had they not neglected the kingdoms of the West? In Italy, on whose control their physical power depended, could they themselves provide a government that would work, or must they call upon other agents, who in the end might do still deadlier harm to their cause?

CHAPTER II

THE HOHENSTAUFEN INHERITANCE

The Emperor Frederick had been three times married. His first wife, Constance of Aragon, was chosen for him by Pope Innocent III. She was many years older than he and was already the widow of a king of Hungary. She died in 1222, leaving one child, Henry, who as a child was appointed King of the Romans and given the government of Germany. But Henry disliked his father and disapproved of his policy. After many intrigues and quarrels he was deprived of his authority in 1234 and died obscurely from a riding accident in 1242. His marriage with Margaret of Austria had produced two sons, Henry, whom Frederick for a time seems to have recognized as his heir for the Sicilian kingdom but who probably died before his grandfather, and Frederick, who lived a little longer. Frederick's second marriage was with the heiress of Jerusalem, Yolanda (or Isabella) of Brienne. She died in childbirth in 1228, leaving an infant son, Conrad, who at the age of seven days became lawful King of Jerusalem. In 1234 Frederick married his third wife, Isabella of England, sister of King Henry III. She too predeceased her husband and left one son, also called Henry. Frederick had also several illegitimate children. The most attractive of these bastards was the son of a woman of Cremona, a boy called Enzo who enjoyed the title of King of Sardinia. Only a few months before Frederick's death Enzo was taken prisoner in a battle with the Bolognese and spent the rest of his life in captivity. The Emperor's own favourites were his two children by Bianca Lancia, of the family of the Counts of Loreto. Bianca's daughter Constance was married as a child, to the horror of the Pope, to the schismatic Emperor of Nicaea, a man in late middle age who made his bride miserable by openly preferring one of her ladies-in-waiting. Bianca's son, Manfred, who claimed to have been legitimized, was at the time of his father's death a handsome youth of eighteen. Another bastard, Frederick, surnamed of Antioch, who had been born during the Emperor's Crusade, was now Imperial vicar in northern Italy.[1]

In his will the Emperor bequeathed the Kingdom of Sicily to his elder legitimate son, Conrad, to whom it was due by hereditary right. Conrad was already King of the Romans, elected heir to the Imperial title. The younger son, Henry, was to be given the Kingdom of Burgundy or that of Jerusalem. This was an empty gift; for the Kingdom of Burgundy, which had come into the Hohenstaufen through Frederick I's wife, was now little more than a title carrying some shadowy feudal rights; while the Kingdom of Jerusalem was already Conrad's and not Frederick's to bequeath, and the legalistic barons of Outremer would never agree to the transference of the throne without their consent to a prince who was not of their blood royal. If Conrad died without issue, Henry was to succeed to the German and Sicilian lands of the family. Of the Emperor's bastard sons, neither Enzo in his prison nor Frederick of Antioch was mentioned in the will; but Manfred was given a great appanage in southern Italy, as Prince of Taranto, and was appointed *balio* or governor of all Italy till Conrad should come and set up his own administration; and he was put into the succession for the Kingdom of Sicily—the Regnum, without qualification, as the Italian chroniclers now called it—should the legitimate line die out.[2]

In the main the Emperor's wishes were carried out. In the distant Kingdom of Jerusalem his death made no difference. The barons there, who had resented and rejected his attempts to govern them, continued to recognize Conrad as their legitimate king and in his absence entrusted the regency to the next adult heir according to hereditary right, King Henry I of Cyprus, while the actual government was at the moment exercised by Saint Louis of France, who was still in the East after his tragic Egyptian Crusade.[3] In Europe Pope Innocent IV's exultation on the death of Antichrist was shown to be premature. Conrad, who was in Germany at the time, was able to restore sufficient order there to cross the Alps southward in January 1251. The anti-king, William of Holland, whom the Pope had appointed three years before, was restricted to his own lands on the lower Rhine. The great papal champion, Archbishop Siegfried of Mainz, had died in 1249; and his successor, Archbishop Christian, showed a peaceable disposition which the Pope thought most unsuitable in a hierarch. He was, indeed, deposed on papal orders later in 1251. For the moment Conrad's regent, his father-in-law, Duke Otto of Bavaria, was in control of the country. His authority was challenged in 1252, when a diet at Frankfurt confirmed William of Holland's title as King of the Romans, at the instigation of Conrad, Archbishop of Cologne; but by the beginning of 1254 William had quarrelled with all three of the Archbishop-Electors of Mainz, Cologne and Trier; and the papal cause declined again.[1]

Nor did things go much better for the Pope in Italy. He had returned there in April 1251, a few months after Conrad's arrival, and established himself at Perugia. But both he and Conrad found that the northern Italian cities were too busily occupied by their own local Guelf and Ghibelline quarrels to take any interest in the larger issue between the Papacy and the Hohenstaufen. It was impossible for either side to work out a correlated policy. Conrad himself spent the summer in Istria and northern Lombardy, growing more and more suspicious of the aid given to the Hohenstaufen cause by his half-brother Manfred's uncle, Manfred Lancia, and his kin. In the southern kingdom Sicily was kept loyal to Conrad by Peter Ruffo, who had been established there as governor for the late Emperor's grandson, Henry. On the mainland the young Manfred, as *balio*, had shown remarkable energy in suppressing a revolt of the nobility and cities of the Terra di Lavoro, the ancient Campania, which had broken out in the spring of 1251. By the autumn the rebels had been severely crushed, though the cities of Naples and Capua still held out. But Manfred's vigour had an element of self-seeking which disquieted Conrad. Manfred had tried to secure control of Sicily by sending another of his uncles, Galvano Lancia, to replace Peter Ruffo, whose loyalty to the legitimate Hohenstaufen was unshaken; and Conrad's chief advisers, the Seneschal Berthold of Hohenburg, who commanded his German troops in Italy, and the chamberlain, John the Moor, who commanded the late Emperor's Saracen regiments and controlled his treasure, both distrusted the Lancias. Berthold had helped Manfred to suppress the rebellion in the Terra di Lavoro, and had even joined him in an abortive negotiation with the Pope, undertaken without Conrad's knowledge. But he then visited Conrad in Istria, and the information that he brought fanned the king's resentment.[1]

In January 1252 Conrad sailed down the Adriatic and landed at Siponto, in northern Apulia, near to Foggia, where John the Moor and the Saracen troops were concentrated. Manfred submitted to him, but was deprived of part of his appanage; and the grants of land that he had made to his Lancia uncles were annulled. Peter Ruffo was confirmed as Vicar of Sicily and Calabria. Conrad spent the rest of the year in dealing with the rebellion in the Terra di Lavoro, which had flared up again. He was successful, though it was not till the following year that Capua and Naples at last submitted. Meanwhile he started negotiations with the Pope. He was now in a strong position. Pope Innocent was still held up in northern Italy. The city of Rome, which had recently been misgoverned by quarrelling factions of nobles, formed itself into a popular commune on the north Italian model, and elected as its Podestà, or Senator, a Bolognese lawyer with Hohenstaufen sympathies, Brancaleone degli Andalò, who was given almost autocratic powers and exercised them with justice and austerity. In the Lombard cities the Ghibellines were triumphing over the Guelfs; and though in Tuscany the Guelfs were gaining ground, they were in no position to give the Pope positive aid.[2]

Innocent, however, was implacable in his policy. He could not hope to drive Conrad out of southern Italy, but he was determined that the Sicilian kingdom and Germany should no longer be united. Conrad, who needed papal support or at least papal neutrality if his control of Germany was to be maintained, was ready to make any concession but that. The negotiations were doomed to fail. For a time the Pope thought to solve the problem by giving the Sicilian crown to Conrad's half-brother Henry, together with the hand of one of his nieces; and Henry was suspected of having listened with interest to the proposal. But nothing came of it. Conrad and his supporters would never accept such a scheme. When Henry died at the age of eighteen in December 1253, rumour, encouraged by the Pope, accused his brother of having poisoned him. The senator Brancaleone tried to prevent an irrevocable breach between Innocent and Conrad; but in January 1254 Conrad publicly accused the Pope of usurpation and heresy and in February Innocent retorted by excommunicating Conrad.[1]

War was inevitable; and Conrad was in the better position. The Pope's attempt to preach a new Crusade against the Hohenstaufen was ill-received. In France the Queen-Regent Blanche threatened to confiscate the lands of anyone who obeyed his call. In Germany the papal agents were openly derided.[2] Conrad's army was in good condition. His treasury was full owing to heavy taxes that he had raised in his Italian dominions. It seemed that he might succeed, as his father had never done, in destroying the Pope's influence throughout Italy; and he was already planning to march northward to restore order north of the Alps. We may doubt now whether in fact he could ever have put the clock back so far as to restore the Hohenstaufen Empire. But he was never given the chance. In April 1254 he fell ill of a fever at his camp at Lavello, on the borders of Apulia. He was only twenty-six, but he was already worn out. He struggled bravely for life, but in vain. On 21 May he died surrounded by his Saracen soldiers.[3]

Once again Pope Innocent could exult over the disaster that had overtaken the race of vipers, and with better cause than on Frederick's death four years before. There was now only one legitimate prince of the hated family living, Conrad's two-year-old son Conrad II, whom the world called Conradin, a child living in southern Germany with his mother, Elizabeth of Bavaria. King Conrad on his deathbed knew how slender the boy's chances would be. He had no hopes of his succession in Germany, but at least Conradin was rightful King of Sicily and King of Jerusalem. The lawyers in Outremer recognized the second title. So long as Conradin lived the government of the Kingdom of Jerusalem was conducted in his name. But it was certain that he would never go there nor wish to risk losing his European heritage by so doing. The Sicilian kingdom was a different matter. The dying king named as his *balio* there Berthold of Hohenburg, whom he trusted, with Peter Ruffo to continue the government of Sicily and Calabria under him. Then, in a desperate appeal for chivalry, he recommended his son to the protection of the Pope.[1]

The Pope was unmoved; nor did the people of the Kingdom feel much interest in a child that they had never seen. Instead, some of them began to fix their hopes on the brilliant figure of Manfred, and others toyed with a suggestion made by the Pope that the cities and their surroundings should form free communes under the suzerainty of the Church. With his opponents divided, Innocent, who had proposed to offer the Sicilian crown to some foreign prince, decided that he could take over the kingdom himself. The *balio* Berthold was in a dilemma. He could count on Peter Ruffo; but Peter was faced with a communal movement in the island and could send him no help. He could count, too, on John the Moor; but John could no longer control the Saracen troops under his command, who were being wooed by Manfred's friends. Most of the other supporters of the Hohenstaufen were passing over also to Manfred. Pope Innocent hurried southward to Anagni. In despair Berthold sent Manfred to negotiate with him there. Innocent agreed that Conradin's rights should be considered when he at last came of age, but in the meantime the Papacy must have possession of the Kingdom. Berthold was ready to agree; for he saw no other means for safeguarding Conradin's future. But he could not carry his party with him, and he was running short of money to pay his troops. He resigned as *balio*, and Manfred took his place.[1]

Manfred, however, was no more powerful than Berthold. In September 1254 the Pope moved to the borders of the Kingdom at San Germano. Three weeks later Manfred accepted the terms that Innocent offered him. The Kingdom was to pass under papal control, saving the future adjudication on Conradin's rights. Manfred was to recover his full appanage of Taranto, and his uncles the lands that Conrad had confiscated. Manfred was also to be Vicar for the mainland provinces with the exception of the Terra di Lavoro.[2]

Neither Innocent nor Manfred intended to abide by the arrangement. At first there was outward amity. When the Pope crossed the river Garigliano into the Kingdom on 11 October Manfred came to meet him and walked beside him leading his horse. But meanwhile the Pope's nephew, Cardinal William dei Fieschi, led the papal army southward, demanding oaths of allegiance which omitted all reference to Conradin; and the Pope offered to Peter Ruffo, to secure his support, the Vicariate over Sicily and Calabria, though the latter province geographically belonged to Manfred's vicariate. Then, when Manfred arrived with the Pope at Teano, he found that his lands on Monte Gargano had been occupied by a papal nominee, Borello of Anglona. He rode out to consult Berthold, who was moving up from Apulia, and was waylaid by Borello, who tried to murder him but fell himself in the skirmish. Berthold passed him on the road and submitted to the Pope at Capua, on 19 October. Manfred rode on to Lucera, where John the Moor and his Saracen troops guarded the royal treasure. Cardinal William and the papal army followed close behind, making also for Lucera and the treasure. Manfred arrived there first on 2 November and found that John had just left to make his submission to the Pope.[1]

Manfred was convinced now that the Pope intended to crush him. Using all his eloquence and charm he persuaded the Saracens in Lucera to hand over the treasure to him and to join him in open revolt. As the news of his action spread, Hohenstaufen supporters from all over Apulia joined him, including many of Berthold's German troops, who had been shocked by the Cardinal's neglect of Conradin's rights. Berthold still recommended negotiation; but on 2 December Manfred had collected a large enough army to attack the German troops that would not join him, defeating them under Berthold's brother Otto, near Foggia. Refugees from the battle fled to the Cardinal's army, which was now stationed at Troia, and caused panic there. The papal soldiers were hirelings whose pay was overdue; for the Cardinal had counted on securing the treasure at Lucera. When they heard of Manfred's victory they melted away; and the Cardinal fled across the winter snows to Ariano. The whole of Apulia passed without further fighting into Manfred's possession.[2]

Pope Innocent was at Naples. He had fallen slightly ill while he was still at Teano, and his illness dragged on during the fortnight that he spent at Capua. He was well enough to make a ceremonial entry into Naples on 27 October, but there he took to his bed. The news of Manfred's success came as a terrible shock to him. On 7 December he died, conscious of the failure of his schemes. He had broken the power of the Hohenstaufens; he had destroyed their union of Germany with Italy beyond any hope of restoration. But he had left one of the hated race as the strongest power in Italy. In a longer perspective he had done even worse. Few Popes had been so constant, so untiring and so courageous in battling for the papal cause; but few had been so unscrupulous, so treacherous and so ready to use spiritual weapons for a wordly end. He had humbled the secular princes, but the methods that he had employed brought no credit to him or to the Church that he governed. He had been a firm and fearless champion of the Papacy, but the Papacy deserved a champion who was a nobler man.[1]

The Cardinals who met in conclave after Innocent's death were aware of his faults and of their dangers. They turned to a prelate who was known for his gentleness and his piety. But Rinaldo Conti, Cardinal-Archbishop of Ostia, who ascended the papal throne five days later as Alexander IV, could not at once abandon Innocent's policy, and he had no policy of his own to substitute for it. He let himself be led by Innocent's advisers, though the cardinal-nephews of the late Pope lost their influence, and papal policy was now decided by a subtle and ambitious Florentine, Cardinal Octavian degli Ubaldini.[2]

The search for a foreign prince to take over the Sicilian kingdom was continued. But the first task was to crush Manfred. The communes in Sicily and southern Italy were won over by the promise that they should be free under papal suzerainty, inconsistent though this promise was with the promises made to candidates for the throne. Manfred found the Apulian towns unwilling to submit to him. Further south, Peter Ruffo was planning to turn his Vicariate of Sicily and Calabria into a hereditary appanage, with its centre at Messina. But he fell between two stools. Manfred, by an ingenious diplomatic intrigue, turned him out of Calabria, while the Sicilian cities declared themselves to be a confederate republic under the Pope. Meanwhile Manfred sent to Germany to the Bavarian court, and by publicly announcing that he recognized Conradin as king, persuaded the boy's uncle and guardian, Duke Louis, to acknowledge him as regent. Berthold of Hohenburg was still at the papal court. In May 1255 he joined Cardinal Octavian in an expedition against Manfred. As usual, the papal army consisted of unreliable mercenaries; and Berthold, finding that Conradin's cause was now championed by Manfred, decided to play the traitor. He revealed all the Cardinal's movements to Manfred and failed to perform his allotted duty of finding supplies for the army. As a result, Manfred was able to blockade the papalists throughout the summer months till they were threatened with starvation. In September Octavian capitulated and made a treaty. Conradin was recognized as king and Manfred as regent, but the Terra di Lavoro and Sicily were annexed to the Papacy. Exiles of both parties, including Berthold and his brothers, were to be restored to their lands. Octavian with his weakened army retired to Anagni, where the Pope was living. Alexander promptly repudiated the treaty; but the harm was done.[1]

Manfred was now supreme in southern Italy. Next year he conquered the Terra di Lavoro, whose inhabitants were tired of war and had lost faith in the Papacy. Then, after securing the murder of Peter Ruffo in exile and after blinding Berthold and his brothers, he sent his uncle Manfred Lancia to conquer Sicily from the Communes. The Sicilian nobility was dissatisfied with the Communal régime; and most of the Sicilians hoped that the rule of a native prince without German connections would mean a return to the golden days of the Normans. By 1257 he was in full control of the island. The time had now come to throw off the pretence of loyalty to the boy in Germany. A rumour began to circulate throughout the south that Conradin had died in Bavaria. Whether Manfred started it or not is unknown, but he hastened to profit by it. On 10 August 1258 he was crowned King of Sicily by the Bishop of Girgenti in the cathedral of Palermo; and the nobles of the island and delegates from the mainland acclaimed him and paid him homage.[2]

Manfred was now aged twenty-six. He was a brilliant and glamorous figure. He had already shown himself to be unscrupulous, treacherous and cruel; but his defects were forgotten in the charm of his personality. He inherited his father's love of learning and interest in the sciences, and the same gift of fascination in his talk, while lacking Frederick's uncomfortable taste for shocking the conventional. In addition he was unusually good-looking. But he was not as great a man as his father. For all his energy in war and in diplomacy, he had a certain indolence over the daily details of administration. He was ready to let his friends and, in particular, his Lancia kinsfolk, do his work for him and soon found himself swayed by them into directions that it would have been wiser to avoid. Had he been content to copy his Norman ancestors and reign in Sicily, keeping control of the southern mainland and restricting his further activities to schemes that would benefit his subjects, he might have founded a lasting dynasty. The Papacy might have reconciled itself to his existence and let him be. But the Lancias came from the north and they had acquired lands in Lombardy. They urged him on to be king not only of Sicily but of all Italy; and Manfred himself, conscious of his Hohenstaufen blood, could never quite forget that his father had been Emperor.[1]

His rule in the southern kingdom was competent. Though he took away the municipal privileges of the towns, he provided them with a just and efficient government. He revived and re-endowed the University of Naples. He founded new cities, such as Manfredonia, under Monte Gargano. But to the Sicilians themselves he was a disappointment. After his coronation he seldom visited the island, preferring to live at Naples or surrounded by his Saracen soldiery at Lucera. The island saw itself becoming once more a mere appendix to the mainland; and as Manfred's policy involved him more and more in the north, and Sicily was robbed of men and money for those distant wars, Sicilian separatism, which was never far below the surface, began to rear its head once more.[2]

It would have been difficult for Manfred to curb his ambition; for the Papacy was unwilling to allow him his success and provoked him into further fighting. For all his easy-going weakness Pope Alexander had formidable assets. He did not have to worry about Germany. No one there, except his Bavarian kinsfolk,

KING MANFRED

bothered about the child Conradin. William of Holland, the anti-king chosen by Innocent IV, had been accepted by the whole country, largely because he was thought to be incompetent and incapable of interfering with the princes. When he died in January 1256 the Electors decided that a foreign prince with no lands in Germany but plenty of money would suit them best. There were two candidates, Richard, Earl of Cornwall, brother of Henry III of England, and Alfonso X, King of Castile. Alfonso had the support of the King of France, Saint Louis, whose personal prestige gave him wide influence, and of the papal court, which was at the moment negotiating with another English prince for the Sicilian throne and thought that one additional throne should suffice the family, and which considered Alfonso to be a better guarantee against any Hohenstaufen revival as he had, through his mother, claims on the Hohenstaufen Duchy of Swabia. Of the seven German Electors four elected Richard in January 1257 and four elected Alfonso in April, the King-Elector of Bohemia having in the meantime changed his mind. Richard, however, managed to have his election confirmed by a coronation at Aachen in May, before Alfonso could set foot in Germany; and by the spring of 1258 he was generally accepted by the Germans. But his position was unsure. He was therefore eager to win the Pope's favour.[1]

In Italy the Pope, enormous though his debts were, persuaded the Guelf bankers of Florence to become his bankers and thus acquired the steady support of that powerful community. As a Roman by birth, Alexander was more acceptable to the Romans than Innocent had been; and in November 1255 they expelled the Senator Brancaleone and admitted the Pope into the city. Many of the Hohenstaufen supporters were alienated from Manfred by his usurpation of the Sicilian throne, and were not satisfied by his declaration, when it was proved that the rumour of Conradin's death was false, that the boy's rights would be reconsidered when he came of age. Conradin's guardian, Louis of Bavaria, gave his support to Richard of Cornwall and was ready to join in his conciliatory moves towards the Papacy.[1]

Manfred was not deterred. In the spring of 1257 a new revolution in Rome restored Brancaleone, who allied himself with Manfred. He was killed next year; and Rome gradually veered back, rather uncertainly, to the papal interest. But meanwhile Manfred had overrun most of the papal lands. In Tuscany he had the support of Siena; and the intrigues of Cardinal Octavian, who saw himself as the mediator between the Ghibellines and the Papacy and tried to force his fellow-Florentines to share his views, helped to weaken Florence; and eventually, in September 1260, the Florentines were defeated with fearful slaughter at Montaperti, in the great massacre that stained the Arbia red. The victory gave Manfred control of central Italy, which he ruled henceforward through Vicars, as though he were already Emperor. Further north he had the support of the strongest and most vigorous despot in Lombardy, the Marquis Oberto Pallavicini, who governed as his Vicar, and the alliance of the Genoese. One by one the Guelf cities were humbled. After the tyrant Ezzelino of Verona, a Ghibelline who had quarrelled with all his neighbours, had been defeated and killed by Pallavicini in 1259, the Vicar managed by a mixture of energy and tact to keep the peace throughout Lombardy. Manfred meanwhile occupied Sardinia, disregarding the rights of his captive brother Enzo to its crown. By 1261 all Italy was subject to Manfred's power; and the Pope was isolated, nervous and powerless, in uncertain possession of Rome and nothing more.[2]

Manfred's ambition soared higher. He had the Empire in his mind, and hoped that some day he would be able to dominate Germany. In the meantime there was another direction in which he could appear as the leader of Latin Christianity.

CHAPTER III

ACROSS THE ADRIATIC

Whoever rules in southern Italy and Sicily must pay regard not only to the peninsula but also to the neighbouring lands across the narrow seas. The Norman Kings had been ambitious to establish some control over Tunis in Africa, and they had been even more eager to spread their power across the Adriatic into the Balkans and the Greek peninsula and islands. Frederick II's cares in central Europe had been too heavy for him to follow their policy. His aim had been to secure allies overseas so that his papal enemies could not raise difficulties for him there. Manfred, as he strengthened himself in Italy, reverted to the Norman tradition. He had no designs on Africa, where the Hafsid emirs of Tunis were well-disposed towards him. But the former Byzantine lands in the Balkans offered scope for his enterprise.

The godless Crusade of 1204 destroyed the Byzantine Empire, but created nothing stable in its place. The Latin Empire set up in Constantinople, the Empire of Romania, quickly declined. Fifty years after its foundation it consisted of no more than the city of Constantinople, of which the Venetians already owned a third, and its immediate suburbs. The Latin Emperor, Baldwin II, spent his days touring round western Europe searching for a protector to keep him on his tottering throne. He had already disposed of the best pieces in the old Byzantine relic-collection to Saint Louis of France to raise a little money. He paid for the expenses of his court by selling the lead from the palace roofs to Italian merchants, and for his foreign journeys by pawning his son and heir to the Venetians. Unless some friend intervened to save him it could only be a few years before his Empire would be extinguished.[1]

After the shock of the fall of Constantinople, the Byzantine

Greeks had revived. Three Greek succession-states had emerged. In the east of the former Byzantine Empire a branch of the great Comnenian dynasty had established itself at Trebizond. But the ruler of Trebizond, though he called himself Emperor and Grand Comnenus and enjoyed great wealth from his silver-mines and from the position of his capital at the end of a lively trade-route from Mongol Asia, could not make more than a nominal claim to be the heir of the old oecumenical empire; his power was too local, being confined to a strip of the Black Sea coast of Anatolia.[1] In Epirus, in the West, a principality was founded by a branch of the Imperial house of the Angeli. In 1224 the Despot of Epirus captured Thessalonica from the Italian dynasty set up there by the Fourth Crusade, and took the title of Emperor.[2] But his chances of taking over Constantinople were challenged by the most vigorous of the succession-states, the Empire of Nicaea, which owed its origin to the energy of Theodore Lascaris, son-in-law of one of the last Byzantine Emperors, Alexius III Angelus. Theodore had gathered round him the leading refugees from Constantinople, including the Orthodox Patriarch, whose presence gave legitimacy to his court. By the time of his death in 1222 Theodore had recovered all the lands lost to the Franks in Asia. His successor, his son-in-law John Vatatzes, was an even abler man, who took from the Latin Emperor all of his lands outside of Constantinople and its suburbs, and who checked the rival Empire of the Angeli by the capture of Thessalonica in 1246. Meanwhile he reformed the administration of his own dominions and kept the Anatolian Turks at bay. When he died in 1254 his dominions stretched from the heart of Asia Minor to Thessaly. It seemed clear that the Empire of Nicaea would soon absorb Constantinople.[3]

But the Angeli, though they had been checked, were not crushed. A bastard prince of the family, Michael II, still ruled as Despot of Epirus over the lands between the Albanian mountains and the Gulf of Corinth; and the Despot Michael was very ready to seek friends among the Franks who might help him to curb the Nicaeans. He had many allies from whom to choose. South of Epirus and Thessaly there were a number of petty Greek, French and Italian lordships, then the rich Duchy of Athens, under the Burgundian family of La Roche, with its capital at Thebes. The whole Peloponnese was held by the Prince of Achaea, William of Villehardouin, who had succeeded his brother Geoffrey II in 1246. Under the Villehardouins the Peloponnese had reached a higher prosperity than ever before in its history; and William, who had been born in the country and spoke Greek as his first language, had some hope of creating an integrated Greco-Frankish state, which would extend beyond the Peloponnese into northern Greece, possibly even to Thessalonica. He himself was not unpopular with his Greek subjects; but many of his Frankish barons were less tactful, and the Latin hierarchs introduced by the Franks continually trampled on the susceptibilities of the Orthodox Church. The Greeks therefore yearned for reunion with a revived Orthodox Empire of Constantinople which would give them back their pride, even though it might damage their pockets; and Prince William viewed the growth of the Empire of Nicaea with alarm. The Latin Emperor was his nominal overlord and had been his pensioner; Geoffrey II had settled a yearly subsidy of close on £10,000 on him. But there is reason to believe that William had some scheme of obtaining the Latin Empire for himself. In any case he was ready to join in any combination against the Nicaeans.[1]

To Manfred, watching from across the Adriatic, the tangled situation seemed full of promise. His father, Frederick II, had been the constant ally of John Vatatzes of Nicaea, to whom he was drawn by their common enmity with the Papacy. Manfred planned a subtler policy. The Latin Empire of Constantinople was very dear to the Pope. Innocent III had disapproved of the Fourth Crusade, but he relished its results. Rome had long been angered by the refusal of the Patriarchate of Constantinople to accept her supremacy. After 1204 the contumacious Greek Patriarch had been replaced by a subservient Latin, and the grateful Pope had taken the Latin Empire under his protection. Now, unless steps were taken quickly, a Greek would probably soon rule again in Constantinople and, still worse, a line of openly schismatic Patriarchs, whom the Franks had been unable to suppress, would return to the patriarchal city. For some time past the Papacy had preached a crusade against the Greeks, but with very little success. To many western Christians a holy war against fellow-Christians, however schismatic, seemed as inappropriate as the similar holy war against the Hohenstaufens. Innocent IV had been furious when Richard of Cornwall had refused in 1240 to give up a crusade planned against the Muslims in Palestine and instead hand over the money raised for the expedition to the defence of Constantinople.[1] Manfred now calculated that if he joined an alliance against the Nicaeans he would emerge as a champion of Latin Christianity, and the Papacy could hardly continue to show venomous hostility against a ruler who was the main support of a policy so dear to it. It may be that Manfred was also moved by personal feelings. His own sister Constance had been married in 1244 to the middle-aged Emperor John Vatatzes and had met with nothing but humiliation at the Nicaean Court. But Manfred, though some years later he arranged for her return to Italy, was not usually over-sensitive to the misfortunes of his relatives. It was of more interest to him that he might be able to obtain, as the price of his alliance against the Nicaeans, a foothold across the Adriatic.[2]

The alliance was organized by Michael of Epirus. His opportunity came with the death of John Vatatzes. John's son, Theodore II, though the best-educated prince of his day, was opinionated and unwise. He alienated his Church by his dogmatism and his nobles by his tyranny. Michael moved cautiously at first. He had agreed that his son and heir Nicephorus should marry Theodore's daughter Maria and, grudgingly, he consented to the fulfilment of the marriage. But when Theodore became involved in a war with the Bulgarians, Michael began to encroach on his territory. Theodore, however, made a profitable peace with the Bulgarians and sent his ablest general, Michael Palaeologus, to invade Epirus. The Nicaean troops marched through the north of the country and captured the great seaport of Durazzo. Michael of Epirus began to change his tune, when suddenly Theodore recalled Palaeologus to Nicaea and disgraced him, and died a few months later, in August 1258, leaving his throne to a boy of six, his son, John IV Lascaris Vatatzes.[1]

With the rival Greek throne in the hands of a child, Michael was free to proceed with his schemes. He had two lovely daughters. One of them, Anna, he gave in marriage to the twice-widowed but childless William of Achaea, with some districts in Thessaly, filched from the Nicaeans, as her dowry. The second, and the lovelier, daughter, Helena, was offered to King Manfred, with her beauty supplemented by a dowry consisting of the island of Corfu and the towns of Butrinto, Avlona and Suboto on the mainland opposite. Manfred, whose first wife, Beatrice of Savoy, had died a year or two previously, leaving him with only a daughter, gladly accepted the tempting offer. He had already occupied some strong points on the Epirote coast; the marriage would legitimize his position. Early in 1259 Helena crossed to Trani and there was married to Manfred. Both of Michael's daughters were happy in their marriages, but neither of his sons-in-law had any genuine desire to help his cause. They joined him in order to prevent the Nicaeans from suppressing the Latin Empire and in order to increase their own dominions at his expense. Michael himself calculated that if his allies helped him to crush the Nicaeans it would be worth his while to sacrifice some of his western lands; for his interests would then lie in the east, where he intended to capture Constantinople.[2]

It was not long before the alliance was called into action. The child-Emperor at Nicaea needed a regent. He had no near kinsfolk, except for a sister hardly older than himself. His mother was dead, and his father had been an only child. There was one man in the Empire who was clearly marked out for the government. This was Michael Palaeologus, who had been its most successful general of recent years. Michael's parents had both belonged to the great family of Palaeologus. His father was descended from the sister-in-law of Alexius I Comnenus, and his mother's grandmother had been the eldest daughter of Alexius III Angelus. His wife, Irene Ducaena, was the grand-niece of John III Vatatzes. But he had no loyalty to the house of Vatatzes. The Emperor Theodore distrusted his ambition and had not only caused him once already to flee for refuge to the Turkish court but had also, after his reinstatement and his victories against Michael of Epirus in 1258, recalled him and disgraced him. So, when the Patriarch Arsenius, acting in the best interests of the state, persuaded the nobles and people of the Empire to entrust him with the regency, giving him the title first of Grand Duke, then of Despot, he had no hesitation on insisting on sharing the Imperial rank with his young cousin. When the time came for the Imperial coronation, he was so sure of the support of the army and all the many enemies of the late Emperor that he forced the unwilling Patriarch to crown him first. The Patriarch tried to make him promise to hand back his authority to the child in twelve years time, when John would be eighteen. He consented, but saw to it that long before that time John would be rendered incapable of ruling. The boy was kept in obscure retirement and in 1262, when he was aged ten, he was deprived of his sight.[1]

The unscrupulousness of his pathway to the throne and his cruelty and disloyalty towards his young colleague have for ever stained the reputation of Michael Palaeologus. Yet, once he had acquired supreme power, he showed himself a just and vigorous ruler, unsparing of himself and generous to his foes, and above all, devoted to the welfare of his Empire. The Latins soon recognized him as an inflexible enemy; and Michael of Epirus was seriously alarmed. The Despot's first action was to invade Macedonia, where he was well received by the Greek population, who seem to have preferred Epirote to Nicaean rule. Then, fearing that Michael Palaeologus would be provoked into making a counter-attack, he summoned the help of his sons-in-law. Michael Palaeologus had little wish to embark on a difficult campaign so soon after his morally dubious accession to the throne. He knew that peace with Michael of Epirus would be impossible to achieve, but he attempted to detach his allies. An ambassador was sent to Achaea, empowered to offer small territorial concessions if need be; but William, who hoped to obtain far more territory out of the war, replied to the embassy with insults. To Manfred the Emperor sent one of his most trusted envoys, Nicephorus Alyattes. Manfred was reminded of his father's old alliance with Nicaea, and he was offered the return of his sister, the Dowager Empress; but Manfred, who equally hoped for great gain out of the war, merely cast the ambassador into prison, where he remained for two years. At the same time, the Emperor wrote to the Pope, hinting that he would work for the reunion of the Churches if Rome would stop the war. Pope Alexander, who was embarrassed by the whole situation, made no answer.[1]

The Emperor Michael's failure to break his enemies' alliance did not cause him undue despair. When the Latin Emperor Baldwin, who was with good reason nervous of William of Achaea's ambitions and who probably believed Michael to be more insecure than in fact he was, wrote to Nicaea offering peace in return for territorial concessions, his envoy was treated with ridicule. Meanwhile Michael's brother, the Sebastocrator John Palaeologus, was sent westwards with as large an army as could be spared, consisting not only of Greek militia but also Slav and Turkish mercenary horsemen and probably a few mercenary knights from the western nations. In the spring of 1259 the Sebastocrator's army marched swiftly into Macedonia. It caught up with the Despot's Epirote forces near Castoria and severely defeated them. The Despot Michael, who had been taken by surprise, retreated into Epirus to await his allies, while the Sebastocrator captured Ochrida and the neighbouring fortresses.

The allies hastened to help the Despot. From Italy Manfred sent four hundred superbly armed and mounted horsemen picked from his German troops, together with some Sicilian infantrymen. They landed at Avlona and joined the Epirote army at Arta. William of Achaea raised a far larger force by applying the feudal levy throughout the Principality. He led it in person, crossing the Gulf of Corinth to Naupactus and joining his allies on the road to Arta. The combined army then moved to Thalassinon, in a district of Thessaly inhabited by Vlach tribesmen. There the Despot was joined by his bastard son John, who had married the Vlach chieftain's daughter and collected all the available Vlach fighting men; and William was joined by detachments from the various Frankish lords of northern Greece and by troops from the Duchy of Athens, whose Duke he had reduced to submission the previous year. The allies then turned northward, confident of victory. They had already begun to realize that their claims for the territory that they were to conquer might overlap; but, in the atmosphere of mutual good will, they decided to draw lots for it.

The opposing armies met on the plain of Pelagonia, at a village called Vorilla Longhos, not far from the town of Monastir. The Via Egnatia, the great highroad from Constantinople and Thessalonica to Durazzo, ran through the plain; and John Palaeologus was waiting there so as to be in touch with his brother, the Emperor, and the East. His instructions were to avoid a head-on collision with the allied army, which was larger than his own, but to try diplomatic means for breaking the alliance. He was successful. What exactly happened is uncertain; the accounts given in the various chronicles differ. For some reason, when the battle was inevitable, a quarrel broke out between the Epirote troops and those of William of Achaea. Palaeologus undoubtedly had his agents in the Epirote camp, ready to play on any dissension that might arise. According to the rumour that was most generally accepted, the Despot's bastard son, John, was angered by the attentions paid to his beautiful Vlach wife by some of the Achaean lords and could get no redress from Prince William. The Epirotes were already nervous of William's ambition; and the Bastard, in his rage, had little difficulty in persuading his father and his brother to desert the Latins. It is likely that John Palaeologus had distributed money among the Epirote commanders; and it is possible that he sent a message promising not to pursue the Epirotes if they retired. Moreover, in the skirmishes that had already taken place the Frankish cavalry had made a poor showing against the light Nicaean horsemen. During the night the Despot and his family and such troops as he could muster slipped out of the allied camp and fled towards Epirus, and when dawn came the rest of the Epirote army melted away. The Achaean troops, with Manfred's contingent, woke up to find their Greek allies vanished. Before they could regroup themselves John Palaeologus fell on them. They made no attempt at resistance but rushed headlong from the field. Many of them were slain, many more captured, including most of the Frankish lords. Prince William himself was taken a few days later hiding in a haystack. He was in disguise, but was recognized by his unusually prominent teeth.[1]

The battle of Pelagonia was a decisive event in the history of the Near East. It ensured the Byzantine reconquest of Constantinople and the end of the Latin Empire; it ensured that the conqueror would be the Emperor of Nicaea and not the Despot of Epirus. And it marked the beginning of the Byzantine recovery of Greece. The Latin Emperor Baldwin, much as he had suspected Prince William, realized that the Emperor Michael's victory was far more ominous. He at once made a desperate appeal to the Pope for help; and he soon decided that his likeliest lay protector was King Manfred. But the Pope and Manfred were occupied by their quarrels with each other. Neither responded to his appeal.

The best that he could do, after Michael had failed to induce a Frankish traitor to open the city gates to him, was to make a truce of a year with Nicaea in August 1260, a truce which each side was ready to break were it convenient. Early in 1261 the Emperor Michael made a treaty with the Genoese at Nymphaeum, granting them privileges throughout his Empire should they help him to recover Constantinople. Venice had been the mainstay of the Latin Empire, and the Venetians and Genoese had recently been indulging in a war in Syrian waters, in which the Genoese had been worsted. Genoa was therefore ready to listen to the Greek Emperor's blandishments. In July 1261 Michael sent one of his generals, Alexius Strategopulus, with a small army to deal with some trouble on the Bulgarian frontier, and told him, as he passed through Thrace, to make a demonstration outside the walls of Constantinople. When Strategopulus approached the city he was met by the head man of the villagers living in the suburbs, who were known as the 'voluntaries' because they served the Greek or the Latin Emperor as they wished. This man told him that most of the Latin garrison of the city had gone off with most of the Venetian ships to try to capture a Greek island in the Black Sea called Daphnusia, about a hundred miles away. He offered to let the Nicaean troops into the city, through an underground passage whose existence he had discovered. On the night of 24 July a few picked men crept in, guided by the 'voluntaries'. They overpowered the men guarding the walls and opened the gates to the army waiting outside. Early in the morning of the 25th Alexius Strategopulus rode into the city, through streets full of Greeks acclaiming the Emperor Michael. The Latin Emperor Baldwin awoke to find his city lost. He hoped to hold the palace of Blachernae and managed to send a message to the Venetian ships sailing back from their unsuccessful assault on Daphnusia. They arrived in the Golden Horn later in the day. But the Greeks set fire to the quays where they were about to land. Amongst the flames and the general confusion their attack was driven off. Baldwin and his suite fled from Blachernae to the old Great Palace and barely had time to row out and join them before they abandoned the attempt. The Venetians, with the surviving Franks and their Emperor, then sailed away disconsolately to the west. The Latin Empire of Romania was ended.

The Emperor Michael was at the village of Meteorium, near Thyatira, nearly two hundred miles away to the south. His sister Eulogia was with him. One of her stewards happened to be on the Bithynian coast, near Constantinople, when he heard the news. He rode as fast as he could through the afternoon and the night, and reported to his mistress early next morning. The Emperor was asleep when she went in to him, crying that Constantinople was his. Half-awake, he could not believe her; and she had to shake him and repeat that Christ had given him Constantinople before he was convinced. He then prepared his journey to the capital. Half-way, at Achyraus, Baldwin's imperial insignia were brought to him. On 4 August he crossed the Sea of Marmora and made his solemn entrance through the Golden Gate, riding along the old imperial processional road down the whole length of the city to the Cathedral of Holy Wisdom, where he gave thanks to God. A few days later he was solemnly crowned there, in the traditional crowning-place of the Emperors, by the Patriarch.[1]

As lord of Constantinople, styling himself the 'second Constantine', Michael Palaeologus was eager to strengthen his hold on Greece. He still kept captive at his court the Prince of Achaea and the other lords who had been taken prisoner at Pelagonia. In the autumn of 1261 he offered to release William of Achaea and his comrades in return for the cession of the three great fortresses of the south-eastern Peloponnese. These were Monemvasia, on a great rock jutting out into the sea with a fine harbour at its foot, which the Franks had only taken fifteen years before: Maina, on the hills behind Cape Matapan: and Mistra, on a spur of Mount Taygetus, dominating Sparta and the plain of the

Eurotas. William agreed; but the terms had to be confirmed by the actual rulers of Frankish Greece. Guy, Duke of Athens, as the senior lord remaining there, summoned a parliament to meet at Nikli. It was known as the Ladies' Parliament, for it was the wives of the captive lords who dominated it. Duke Guy considered the terms too dangerous. But the Princess of Achaea thought otherwise. Though she was a Greek, no one suspected her of disloyalty, for as a princess of Epirus she hated the Nicaean who had taken Constantinople. But she distrusted Guy and she wanted her husband home; and the other ladies agreed with her. The Emperor's offer was accepted. Prince William returned to his lands, bearing a Byzantine title and having sworn on holy relics never to bear arms against the Emperor; and the three key fortresses were handed over to the Emperor's troops.[1]

This marked the height of Michael's successes in Greece. William was soon released of his oath by the Pope and successfully defeated the attempts of the Byzantines to enlarge their territory. Nor would he accept the Emperor's peaceable solution that the Imperial heir, Andronicus, should marry the Prince's elder daughter and heiress. Some decades passed before the Byzantines could make much use of their Peloponnesian fortresses. Nor was Michael Palaeologus more successful in his further attempts on Epirus. Alexius Strategopulus, the conqueror of Constantinople, was sent to invade the province in the autumn of 1261, only to be surrounded and captured, with most of his men, by the Epirotes. The Despot Michael was able to maintain himself in his native territory till his death ten years later.[2]

King Manfred had suffered in prestige from the defeat at Pelagonia and had lost some of his finest fighting men there; and, like all the Latin princes of the time, he had been shocked by the Greek recovery of Constantinople. But in fact neither event had been harmful to his general policy. He had sent his father-in-law somewhat meagre help in comparison with the territory that he had obtained as his wife's dowry, and his losses had not been serious; whereas the Despot's defeat made him more dependent than before on his powerful son-in-law, especially as his other son-in-law, William of Achaea, when he returned from captivity, was not disposed to forgive the Epirotes for the part that they had played at Pelagonia. By the end of 1259 Manfred's troops and officials were in full control of Corfu and of the mainland fortresses opposite to it, including Durazzo, which does not seem to have been originally part of Queen Helena's dowry.[1] Moreover, the Greek capture of Constantinople could be turned to Manfred's advantage. The Papacy had been deeply shocked by the extinction of the Latin Empire. The Pope could not be expected to take violent action against the one prince who seemed in a position to avenge its loss. Manfred was quick to come forward as the champion of the dispossessed Latin Emperor. Baldwin II, on his flight from his lost capital, stopped in Greece to receive the meaningless homage of the few Frankish lords remaining there, who gathered to greet him at the Cadmea at Thebes and on the Acropolis at Athens. He then sailed on to Italy and landed in Apulia. Manfred went himself to meet him and received him with every honour, showering gifts on him and promising him all the aid in his power to restore him to his throne. He confided in his guest about his difficulties with the Papacy and asked for his good offices. He was ready, he said, to lead an attack on Constantinople at his own expense and then, if it were required, to go on to the Holy Land, if only the Pope would grant him his grace and peace, or even just a truce. Baldwin was impressed by Manfred's sincerity and by his wealth. He promised to do all that he could to reconcile Manfred with the Papacy. On leaving Manfred's court he went to see the Pope at Viterbo and gave him the king's message. The Pope refused to give any answer. Baldwin then moved on to France, to visit King Louis; but he found Louis equally unenthusiastic about Manfred, whom he regarded as a usurper and an enemy of the Church.[2]

It was discouraging. But the ex-Emperor remained faithful for many years to come to his friendship with Manfred, partly from a genuine liking for him and partly because there was no one else so well placed to give him aid; while Manfred pursued his plans, so far as Italian affairs gave him the leisure to spare, for a great expedition against Constantinople. He could not believe that Rome would continue to oppose him if he were to perform so noble a service to the Latin cause. In this he sadly misunderstood the temper of the Papacy.

CHAPTER IV

THE SEARCH FOR A KING:
EDMUND OF ENGLAND

Had Pope Alexander IV still been living when Constantinople fell, the Emperor Baldwin's plea for reconciliation between Manfred and the Papacy might not have been unheeded. Alexander was an easy-going man who disliked extreme measures. He had tried to keep complete liberty of action to deal with the Sicilian question, but he had not the least idea what to do with his liberty. He could not safely maintain himself in Rome; he had been forced to watch Manfred win control of most of Italy and become something of a national hero in the peninsula. He had excommunicated Manfred, and, anxious though he had been about the fate of the Latin Empire of Constantinople, he had refused to give his blessing to the Latin-Epirote alliance which had been defeated at Pelagonia. But his actions were negative and led him nowhere. In his uncertainty it is possible that he would have listened to the Emperor Baldwin's pleading. The Cardinal Octavian, whom he admired and often consulted though never trusted, was in favour of a reconciliation with the Hohenstaufen and would have given his support to Baldwin. But Pope Alexander never had to make the decision. He died at Viterbo on 25 May 1261.

With his characteristic indecision Alexander could never make up his mind whom to promote to the rank of Cardinal. At the time of his death the College only numbered eight members. They hastened to meet to elect a successor. But there was no agreement amongst them. For three months they wrangled, unable to find a candidate who could obtain the necessary two-thirds majority. Yet it was essential that a Pope should be found; for the affairs of the Church at this moment desperately needed a guiding hand. At last someone thought of the Patriarch of Jerusalem. He had been in Italy at the time of Alexander's death to transact some business at the papal court, and he had impressed everyone there by his integrity and energy. His name was put forward; and, just as he was preparing to return to his Patriarchate, he found himself on 29 August, rather to his surprise, unanimously elected Pope. He was enthroned six days later, under the name of Urban IV.[1]

Pope Urban was very different from his predecessor. He was a Frenchman, born James Pantaleon, son of a shoe-maker of Troyes. He was already in his sixties and had a long career of ecclesiastical administration behind him. After an excellent education at the cathedral school of Troyes and then the University of Paris, he had spent his earlier life in France and had come to the notice of Pope Innocent IV at the Council of Lyons in 1247. Innocent employed him as legate to do missionary work in the Baltic and subsequently political work in Germany in support of the candidature of William of Holland. In 1255 he had been appointed to the Patriarchate of Jerusalem. Some years passed before he could travel to Palestine, where he found an almost impossible situation, with the barons of Outremer quarrelling with themselves and with the Queen-Regent Plaisance, the Venetians and Genoese conducting open warfare along the coasts, and the military orders jealous of all authority. He had taken decisive action, supporting the Regent against the barons and the Venetians against the Genoese; and it was to secure papal help in curbing the power of the Knights Hospitaller that he had come to Rome in 1261. He was clearly a man of vigour, who would rescue the Papacy from its policy of drift.[2]

Reluctant though he was to leave the problems of Outremer unsolved, the Pope at once concentrated upon action against Manfred in Italy. Manfred was at the height of his power. He dominated the whole of Italy. His marriage with Helena of Epirus had given him a foothold in the Balkans. In 1258 he had made another alliance, even more annoying to the Papacy, when he betrothed his daughter Constance, the only child of his first marriage, to the Infant Peter, son and heir of King James of Aragon. The Aragonese possessed the best navy in the western Mediterranean; and their friendship, combined with his own naval power, gave Manfred the command of the sea. But there was a streak of indolence in Manfred. All seemed to be going so well that he did not trouble to use the vacancy in the Papacy for consolidating his position nor did he take precautions against the activities of the new Pope. Instead, he spent his days at his favourite pastime, hunting in the forests of Basilicata. He hoped that his friend the Emperor Baldwin would look after his interests at the Roman Curia and in France.[1]

He underestimated both the capability of the new Pope and his hatred for the Hohenstaufen. Urban first elected fourteen new cardinals, several of them Frenchmen like himself, to ensure him the support of the College.[2] He then set about restoring control of the papal patrimony. He was not entirely successful. He could not turn the Vico family, friends of Manfred, from their properties at Bieda and Civitavecchia; nor did he ever dominate Rome itself firmly enough to take up residence there, preferring to live at Viterbo or Orvieto. But he recovered a number of estates which had been alienated under his predecessor and generally consolidated his hold of Latium and the Marches. In Tuscany he strengthened his connection with the bankers of Florence and Siena, thus embarrassing the Ghibelline rulers of the two cities; and he managed to detach Pisa from the Ghibelline league. He did not destroy Manfred's hold over the province but he made it less secure. Further north the Papacy regained influence in Lombardy, when Urban appointed a vigorous archbishop, Otto Visconti, to the crucial see of Milan; while the chief Guelf lord, Azzo of Este, who had been in disgrace in Alexander IV's time for flirting with Pallavicini and the Ghibellines, was restored to favour, and his grandson and heir, Obizzo, was soon appointed the head of a reconstituted Guelf league. As in Tuscany, Manfred's lieutenants were not dislodged but their power was somewhat weakened.[1]

The real solution was, however, to dislodge Manfred himself from the main source of his power, southern Italy and Sicily. Any discontent there was fanned by papal agents, who had some success in Sicily itself. The islanders were disappointed in Manfred, who seldom visited them, preferring to concentrate his government and to spend his leisure on the mainland. In 1261, a few months after Manfred's vicar, his cousin Frederick Maletta, had been murdered there, a man called John of Cocleria claimed to be Frederick II, risen from the dead, and gathered a number of partisans around him. The new vicar, Richard Filangieri, had some difficulty in suppressing the revolt.[2] Such discontent encouraged the Pope in his principal scheme, which was to place a candidate of his own upon the Sicilian throne.

According to papal theory the King of Sicily was the Pope's vassal. It was the Pope who had granted the lands of southern Italy and Sicily to the Norman invaders in the eleventh century. Roger II had, it is true, taken the title of king without the Pope's leave, but his title had been confirmed. Frederick II's inheritance of the Sicilian throne had been legal in the eyes of Rome only because the Pope had recognized it; and in 1245 Pope Innocent IV had considered himself well within his rights when he formally deprived Frederick of the Kingdom. But it was easier to declare his deposition than to carry it into effect. It would be necessary to bestow the Sicilian crown upon a prince powerful enough to displace Frederick. Innocent first applied to the Court of France. But Saint Louis, though he personally disapproved of Frederick, nevertheless regarded him as a legitimate monarch whom the Pope had no business to depose. The court of England, which was next approached, was rather more amenable. King Henry III was a vain man who fancied the idea of having another throne in the family. But the obvious candidate was his brother Richard, the Earl of Cornwall; and Richard knew and liked Frederick, who was his brother-in-law and whom he had visited in Sicily when returning from the Holy Land. So long as Frederick lived the Pope could not find a candidate willing to try to oust him. On the Emperor's death Innocent tried again. After considering the possible nomination of Frederick's younger son Henry, he wrote on 3 August 1252 to the King of England, telling him to persuade Richard to accept the Sicilian throne, to be held under the Papacy, to whom it had escheated. But he seems to have had little hope of success; for two days later he wrote a similar letter to King Louis, offering the throne to Louis's youngest brother, Charles, Count of Anjou. Louis himself was still in the Holy Land, after his disastrous crusade in Egypt. The letter was therefore accompanied by one to Louis's next brother, Alfonso, Count of Poitiers, as the senior prince in France, urging him to use his influence on Charles. These letters were entrusted to the papal lawyer, Albert of Parma, who was to deliver the English letter first, and if the answer was unfavourable then those to the French Court.

Richard of Cornwall refused the offer outright. It was, he said, like being offered the moon on condition that one unhooked it from the sky. Charles seems to have hesitated, though only, perhaps, till he could receive instructions from Louis. Louis disliked the idea, as he considered Frederick's son Conrad to be rightful King of Sicily, while the Queen-Mother Blanche who had great influence over her sons was deeply shocked by the Pope's attempt to turn their quarrel with the Hohenstaufen into a Holy War. So Charles, too, refused.[1]

Conrad's death and Manfred's usurpation of power changed the situation. King Louis disliked Manfred as a godless interloper, but he regarded the throne as belonging by right to the young Conradin.[2] Henry of England had no such scruples. Richard was even more uninterested than before, as he was now ambitious to become Emperor and was pouring all his energy and his money into Germany. But Henry had a younger son, Edmund, whom he would like to see a king. The idea of proposing Edmund as a candidate seems to have occurred to Henry immediately after Richard's rejection of the offer, while Conrad was still alive; but meanwhile Albert of Parma had gone to the French court, and it was not till the following autumn that Charles of Anjou, having by then received firm orders from King Louis, definitely sent his refusal to the Pope. In the meantime Henry was troubled about the rights of his nephew, Henry of Hohenstaufen, for whom he had some affection. But Charles finally withdrew his candidature on 30 October 1253 and the young Prince Henry died some six weeks later. At the very end of the year the Pope authorized Albert of Parma to treat again with the English Court. In February 1254 Henry informed Innocent that he was anxious to put forward Edmund's candidature. In March Albert of Parma made a draft agreement with him, which the Pope was to ratify. On 14 May Innocent wrote a series of letters calling Edmund 'King of Sicily' but suggesting certain changes in the contract. Before they were delivered news came of the death of King Conrad, on 11 May; and Albert of Parma, who doubted the whole wisdom of the English candidature, held them back till he could find out what the Pope would now decide.[1]

Albert's prudence was justified. Innocent was unwilling to commit himself at once against the rights of the child Conradin; and he thought that it might be possible to treat with Manfred, who now controlled the southern kingdom. There followed the brief interlude when Innocent came to terms with Manfred in the autumn of 1254. But neither side trusted the other. Eight days after Manfred had welcomed the Pope into the Kingdom, himself holding his bridle as he crossed the river Garigliano, the honeymoon was ended and Manfred had fled to Lucera. Innocent reopened negotiations with England, but a little less positively than before. He would accept Edmund as King of Sicily, but he inserted an equivocal clause referring to Conradin's rights.[2]

The position was still uncertain when Innocent died in December 1254. King Henry of England was now enthusiastic about the Sicilian scheme. He had many years previously vowed to go on a crusade and was steadily taxing his subjects for this purpose. But he had no real wish to go away to the East, nor would it be prudent to leave his rather turbulent kingdom. His piety and his family ambitions would be gratified far more satisfactorily if he used the money for a holy war on behalf of the Church in which a throne for his son would be the reward. Whether the young Edmund, who was only aged eight, had any views is uncertain. It was, however, certain that Henry's subjects did not share his enthusiasm. They resented the taxation imposed on them; but had the money been genuinely devoted for the relief of Christians in the Holy Land and for war against the infidel, they might have borne it without complaint. A holy war against the Hohenstaufen did not have the same appeal. There was no good reason why English money should be spent on a war in Italy to satisfy the personal vanity of the king. The 'Sicilian Business', as the English called it, threatened to shake the power of the English monarchy.[1]

King Henry paid no attention to the grumbling of his subjects. He had already made a treaty with King Alfonso of Castile, who was his rival in Gascony and who had claims through his mother on the Hohenstaufen inheritance. Henry's eldest son, Edward, was betrothed to Alfonso's half-sister Eleanor. There had been a long desultory war between England and France, which was now interrupted by a truce arranged through the Pope's good offices and the desire of Saint Louis to be at peace with his neighbours. In December 1254 Henry paid a visit to Paris, bringing with him his Queen, Eleanor of Provence, who was the sister of the French Queen Margaret. The queens were joined by their mother, the Dowager Countess of Provence, and by their two other sisters, Sanchia, Countess of Cornwall and Beatrice, Countess of Anjou, whose husbands had in turn rejected the Sicilian crown. It was a happy family party, marred only by slight jealousy between the four sisters. Margaret, Eleanor and Sanchia and their mother all showed a certain coldness towards Beatrice, who, though the youngest, had been left the whole Provençal inheritance by the late Count; and the widow and her elder daughters considered themselves cheated out of their rightful share. But the two kings were charmed with each other. While King Henry, who was fond of art, admired the latest buildings in Paris, Louis agreed not to oppose Prince Edmund's candidature.[1]

The candidature was also confirmed by the new Pope, Alexander IV. Innocent IV may have doubted the wisdom of placing a boy of nine upon the Sicilian throne and may have considered that diplomatic use could be made of the rights of Conradin. Alexander was not so subtle. He believed the King of England to be rich and was delighted for him to pay the expenses of the inevitable war against Manfred. Henry was still under a vow to go crusading in the Holy Land and to have set out by Midsummer 1256. At his request the Pope now commuted his vow. Instead, Henry was to send troops to Italy before Michaelmas 1256, and to pay the papal treasury the sum of 135,541 marks. In the autumn of 1255 the Bishop of Bologna arrived from Italy to invest Edmund with the Kingdom in the Pope's name. With the bishop came the papal nuncio, Rostand Masson, whose business it was to see that the money promised by Henry was collected and transmitted to the Pope. Edmund's solemn investiture took place in October. At the same time King Henry promised on oath to carry out the Pope's demands, under penalty of excommunication.

In his pride Henry never realized what he was promising. The sum required by the Pope was far beyond the capacity of England to pay. He had in fact taken over the debts of the Papacy without stopping to think how the money could be raised. His subjects were less blind. The lay magnates refused to give him any assistance, and he could not force them. The clergy were in a weaker position. The Bishop of Hereford, who had been Henry's envoy to the papal court, had already pledged the possessions of a number of English monastic houses as surety for the loans that he had raised from Italian bankers on the Pope's behalf. A tax of one-tenth on all ecclesiastical property for three years, or five if three proved insufficient, was to be raised to redeem the pledged possessions. It was to be collected by papal officials, under Rostand Masson's directions; and any chapter or monastery that would not pay was threatened with interdict and excommunication. The outcry penetrated even through the king's illusions, while Rostand himself began to realize that the money was simply not available. Huge sums were sent to Italy, but the debt still seemed as vast as ever. Michaelmas 1256 passed, and the bulk of the promised gift was still unpaid. Rostand went back to the papal court and returned in March 1257, accompanied by the Archbishop of Messina, with demands for new taxes. Henry received the envoys ceremoniously, together with Edmund, now aged twelve, who was dressed in Apulian robes at the reception. The Sicilian archbishop may have been pleased by the tactful costume of his would-be king; but he cannot have relished the temper of the English notables assembled to meet him. In spite of an eager sermon that he preached to the English bishops reminding them of their duty to their young prince who was his new king, the English bishops grudgingly offered him the sum of £52,000, in place of the new taxes which the Pope demanded, but declared that the consent of the lower clergy must also be obtained; and the lower clergy were not willing to give consent. The lay magnates once again entirely refused to help.

Even King Henry now realized that he had gone too far. In April he suspended all payments to the Pope's agents, saying that he was uncertain whether to proceed with the Sicilian business. At the end of June he appointed commissioners with plenipotentiary powers to go to Paris, to make a permanent peace with King Louis, and thence to Italy, to offer the Pope alternative suggestions. Henry considered that he had a right to milder terms; for the Pope had done nothing to prevent Manfred from securing a tighter hold upon Italy, and a war to dislodge him would now be a far more formidable task. In view of this, the Pope was asked whether it might not be wiser to make peace with Manfred on the basis of a division of the Sicilian Kingdom; or the Papacy might itself raise the money for half the cost of the war in return for half of the kingdom. If that were unacceptable, Henry was prepared to withdraw Edmund's candidature if he were released from all his obligations, and the Pope could seek for another champion. As the commissioners were held up in Paris, these offers were taken on to Rome by Rostand Masson, who had come round to sympathize entirely with the English point of view and had probably himself drafted the letters to the Pope.[1]

Pope Alexander was furious. With the obstinacy of a weak man he was determined not to give way to Henry. Manfred's successes, for which his own inefficiency was largely to blame, made him all the more unwilling to let the English out of his clutches. Rostand was disgraced. He was allowed to return to England; but the Pope's answer was entrusted to a new legate, the notary Arlotus. Alexander made one small concession; Henry need not pay the remainder of the promised money, which was rather more than half of the sum originally mentioned, till the summer of 1258. In the meantime the English envoys were to go surety for loans to cover part of what was due. Henry was further ordered to make peace with France and to come to Sicily with not fewer than 8500 armed men by 1 March 1259. The archbishops and bishops were to be responsible for collecting money in each diocese, and Henry was to secure a contribution from his lay subjects. Were these conditions not fulfilled Henry would be excommunicated and the country placed under an interdict.

In April 1258 Henry summoned his lay and ecclesiastical magnates and informed them of the Pope's terms. Their reaction was sharp. A few days later a company of the leading lay lords met together and swore to support each other. Then they rode, fully armed, to the Royal Palace at Westminster, and, leaving their swords at the door, burst in on the king. He saw that he was powerless. Along with his heir, Prince Edward, he swore on the Gospels to follow the advice of his barons. They on their side promised to help him in the Sicilian Business, if the Pope would moderate his terms and if the king brought in constitutional reforms. A parliament was to be held at Oxford in May to discuss the reforms.[1]

The Sicilian Business was now swallowed up into the wider issue between the monarchy and the baronage of England. Henry still kept certain hopes. Indeed, he persuaded himself three years later that if the barons had not interfered in 1258 he might yet have come to a workable agreement with the Pope. His envoys, who succeeded in 1259 in making a peace-treaty with France, ratified the following year, secured the insertion of a clause by which King Louis promised to pay for 500 knights for two years to aid in the Sicilian war. The barons wrote to the Pope offering to do their best to further the scheme, though they made it clear that they were not enthusiastic. They pointed out that they had not been consulted, and they hinted doubts of its practicability. In fact it was obvious now, even to the Pope, that nothing could be expected from England. He had not done badly out of it; he had obtained about 60,000 marks from England, at no cost to himself. Making up his mind for once, he issued a Bull on 18 December 1258 cancelling the grant of the Kingdom of Sicily to Prince Edmund.[2]

The long flirtation with England had done nothing to solve the problem of the Sicilian crown. The Pope had obtained some ready money out of it, but in the meantime Manfred had consolidated his position in Italy. The whole affair was chiefly important for its effect on the internal history of England; for it ushered in the Barons' War and the constitutional quarrels and developments that filled the latter part of King Henry III's reign. It seems preposterous, as we look back on it, that King Henry should ever have thought it possible to place his son on an Italian throne. Neither he nor his country could afford so grandiose a project; and the Pope should have realized far earlier that he was wasting his time. But few medieval monarchs paused to think ahead on financial matters. Henry's own brother Richard, who was reckoned to be among the wisest men of the day, thought himself rich enough to embark upon the still more ambitious scheme of making himself Emperor, and very nearly succeeded. If Henry's subjects had been docile enough to pay for an expeditionary force and if the Pope had been less greedy in his demands for money, Edmund might have found himself King of Sicily. Manfred was not invincible, as the sequel would show; and he was weaker in 1256 than in 1266. The army that conquered him, though it had the advantage of competent leadership, was not particularly large; nor did its organizers spend on it the amount of money that Henry was prepared to afford. If, indeed, both Henry and Pope Alexander had been cleverer men and better able to command the respect of their subjects, they might have achieved their object; and it might well have been to the advantage of Sicily to have had a light link with the distant crown of England instead of a closer link with France. Prince Edmund grew up to be an intelligent and open-hearted prince, well liked by all his vassals. He might have been a good king and have founded a dynasty honestly devoted to the interests of the Sicilians. But he was no doubt lucky to have been spared the complexities of Mediterranean politics and far happier to be Earl of Lancaster than King of Sicily.

The abandonment of the English scheme left the Pope free to find a candidate elsewhere. But, as usual, he was hesitant; and death removed him before he could make up his mind. His successor, Urban IV, had more positive views.

CHAPTER V

THE SEARCH FOR A KING:
CHARLES OF ANJOU

Pope Urban had spent his recent years in the East. He had nothing to do with papal policy in western Europe and came to it with an open mind. As soon as he had time to look into the story of the English candidature for the Sicilian throne, he saw that it was impracticable. King Henry, with his incurable optimism, hoped that the new Pope might reverse Alexander's ultimate decision; but, in spite of his pleading, Urban sent a message in September 1262 confirming that negotiations with England were at an end. He was already looking elsewhere.[1]

He was a Frenchman and his instinct was to seek salvation for the Church from France. King Louis had hitherto been discouraging. But there was no one else to whom he could apply. His dislike of the Hohenstaufen, acquired while he had been legate in Germany, was too great for him to put forward the claims of Conradin against Manfred. There was no other possible candidate in Germany, where Richard of Cornwall, King of the Romans, was fully occupied in trying to maintain control and was far too busy to trouble about Italy, even had the Pope been ready to risk another reunion of the Imperial and Sicilian crowns. Of the other western potentates, King James of Aragon was an adventurer ready to take on any new enterprise; but he had just made an alliance with Manfred. King Alfonso of Castile suggested himself as King of Sicily, but he was still a candidate for the Empire and had won the dislike of the Papacy by seeking to further his Imperial schemes by friendship with the Ghibellines of northern Italy. Only the French Court was left. In the spring of 1262 the notary Albert of Parma was sent once more to Paris to ask King Louis to reconsider his decision and to accept the investiture of the Sicilian Kingdom for a prince of his House.

King Louis was embarrassed. He had promised his support for the English candidature, and, even so, he was uncomfortable about the hereditary rights of Conradin. At the same time he disapproved of Manfred, who was quite certainly a usurper and the enemy of the Church. So strongly did he feel against Manfred that he was ready to break off the engagement of his son Philip with an Aragonese princess when he learnt that her brother had married Manfred's daughter. He only agreed to permit the marriage when James of Aragon promised never to give any armed help to Manfred in his quarrel with the Church. King Louis hesitated for a while. Then, with a suppleness hardly consistent with his saintly reputation, he compromised. He refused the throne of Sicily for himself or any of his sons, but he made no objection when Albert suggested offering it to his brother, Charles, Count of Anjou. Delighted by this concession Albert prepared to set off to Provence, where the Count of Anjou was residing, when new letters from the Pope arrived in Paris, ordering the suspension of the whole affair.[1]

The Pope's change of front was due to the arrival at his court of the ex-Emperor Baldwin. Baldwin had come to Viterbo from visiting Manfred, whom he regarded as the only prince capable of restoring the Latin Empire of Constantinople. It was the Pope's turn to be embarrassed. The recovery of Constantinople was a cause dear to his heart, and he was genuinely sorry for Baldwin. He refused to give a direct answer to the letters from Manfred that the Emperor brought with him. He could not readily bring himself to come to any agreement with the excommunicated usurper: but he did not like to refuse the offer out of hand. It was hardly suitable for the Pope, when Latin Christendom in the East was in peril, to concentrate all his energy on a war in Italy. There was, moreover, not only Constantinople to consider. The crusader states in Syria, where Urban had lived and worked, were threatened by the growth of Mameluk power in Egypt. The defeat of the Mongols by the Mameluks in 1260, which had been welcomed at the time by the knights of Outremer, terrified of the vast Mongol Empire, was now seen to offer a greater and more immediate danger to them. Urban was a man of wide experience. He saw Christendom as a whole. He had to pause to reconsider his policy. Instead of pursuing the offer of Sicily to a French prince, the Pope now wrote round to the Faithful, urging the need of an immediate crusade.[1]

To many it seemed that Manfred's diplomacy had been successful. An English observer wrote home from Viterbo to say that a reconciliation between the Sicilian King and the Papacy was imminent.[2] News reached Constantinople that the Pope had released William of Achaea from the vows of friendship that he had sworn to the Byzantine Emperor; and it was supposed there that this was due to Manfred's intervention. The Emperor feared that a grand alliance of all the West had been organized against him.[3] His anxiety was premature; for Pope Urban had second thoughts. He had sent a message summoning Manfred to appear before him, in person or by proxy, before 1 August 1262, to submit himself to papal judgement. At the end of July Manfred sent envoys to Viterbo, where they were introduced to the Pope by the ex-Emperor Baldwin himself. They asked that Manfred should be allowed a further delay, and obtained a prorogation till 18 November. Urban had meanwhile written to King Louis, to ask for his advice. To Louis, who longed for a crusade against the infidel, the prospect of a peaceful arrangement was attractive. Much as he disapproved of Manfred, his conscience would be satisfied if the Pope forgave him. He wrote to express his approval. But for some reason the letter was delayed. It may be that Louis was still a little perturbed by the sacrifice of Conradin's rights, which the reconciliation with Manfred would involve. It may perhaps be that Charles of Anjou, who was by now interested in the Sicilian offer, managed to hold back his brother's answer.[4]

Urban had still heard nothing from France when Manfred's second embassy reached him early in November. He temporized. Manfred was offered a safe-conduct to come to the papal court, but the terms for the reconciliation were left unstated; and a message was sent to Albert of Parma telling him to continue his negotiations with Charles of Anjou. Finally, at the end of November Urban stated his terms to Manfred. What precisely he demanded is unknown. It seems that he offered to enfeoff Manfred and his heirs with the Sicilian kingdom, without regard to any claims that Conradin might possess. Manfred was probably to pay a large sum down and a yearly tribute to the Holy See. He was also to re-admit into his kingdom the political opponents whom he had exiled and restore to them the lands that he had confiscated from them. It was this last clause that proved unacceptable. Even if Manfred had been willing to abandon lands that he considered necessary for the maintenance of royal power, his officials whom he had rewarded out of the confiscated estates would never consent to their loss. Manfred's court would not allow him to accept the terms. By the time that he had put forward counter-proposals, it was too late. Urban had made up his mind that no good could come out of a reconciliation.[1]

The Pope had to move warily. King Louis was desperately eager for a crusade in the East; and the Emperor Baldwin had moved on to Paris to use his influence with the king. Urban still took action as though the crusade was his first object. Though privately he had begun to wonder whether an agreement with Michael Palaeologus on the basis of Church union might not be more satisfactory than the restoration of the Latin Empire, he officially refused to have anything to do with the Greeks. But he gave Louis to understand that in his opinion no reliance could be placed on Manfred, and if a crusade was to be successful there must be a more faithful son of the Church on the Sicilian throne.[2]

Louis let himself be convinced, in spite of Baldwin's pleading. In May 1263 his brothers, Alfonso of Poitiers and Charles of

Anjou, came to visit him at Paris. He gave Charles permission to resume negotiations with the Papacy. In June Charles's ambassadors reached the Pope. On 17 June Urban gave them a draft treaty for their master; and three days later he wrote to Alfonso of Poitiers, asking for his help in persuading Charles to accept the terms. In July he wrote a friendly letter to the Emperor Michael Palaeologus, and he appointed a new legate to the French and English courts. This was the Archbishop of Cosenza, who belonged to the great Neapolitan family of the Pignatelli, hereditary enemies of the Hohenstaufen. The Archbishop was to tell Henry of England that there could be no more question of Edmund's candidature and to tell Louis of France that he must forget his scruples on behalf of Edmund or of Conradin. The interests of the Church and the crusade required the transfer of the Sicilian throne to Charles.[1]

The Emperor Baldwin, on whom Manfred relied, was desperate. On 2 July he wrote from Paris to Manfred, telling him that the Pope had managed to persuade King Louis that Manfred's attempts at reconciliation with the Papacy were insincere. Baldwin urged Manfred to send a trustworthy envoy to Paris with a message to King Louis assuring him of his good faith, and another to the Queen of France, who, as Baldwin could see, very much disliked the Count of Anjou. Manfred never received the letter. It was intercepted by the Podestà of Rimini, who sent it to the Pope. He read it and sent it back, by the hand of Albert of Parma, to Paris for King Louis to see. Louis was shocked to find that Baldwin, who was his pensioner, was intriguing behind his back. The Duke of Burgundy, whom Baldwin had won over by the promise of the kingdom of Thessalonica when the Latin Empire should be restored, was unable to change the king's mind; nor had Queen Margaret now any influence; for she had already offended the king by her hatred of his brother.[2]

With his brother's permission Charles did not hesitate to accept the instrument of agreement drafted by the Pope. His envoys returned at once to Orvieto, where the Pope was now living, with his written consent to it. On 26 June Urban had signed a Bull promising to observe his side of the bargain. The date on which the treaty was ratified is unknown. By the end of July Charles of Anjou was the accepted champion of the Church.

The terms of the treaty were heavily weighted in the Pope's favour. The new King of Sicily was to give up the position held by the Norman sovereigns of being Apostolic Delegate in his kingdom. He was to have no say in ecclesiastical appointments nor in ecclesiastical jurisdiction. He was not to raise taxes from the clergy, nor was he to exercise the traditional right of kings of enjoying the revenues of a vacant bishopric. Not only was he never to aim at the Imperial throne, but he must never hold any post in Imperial Italy or in the estates of the Papacy. He was not to confiscate the whole or a part of any fief held from the crown or in any way to reduce its value. He was to assure a good administration, such as existed in the days of King William II, the 'Good King William' of tradition, and must not levy excessive taxes. If the Pope chose to depose him, he must not demand the further allegiance of his vassals. In addition, he must take over what remained of the English debt to the Papacy; he must provide the Pope with three hundred knights or ships, whenever they might be required; and he must pay the Papacy a yearly tribute of 10,000 ounces of gold, which was over thirty times more than the Norman kings had paid. In return, the Papacy gave him its Apostolic protection. It allowed him a tithe for three years on the ecclesiastical revenues of France, Provence and the Kingdom of Arles. The Pope undertook to preach a crusade against Manfred; and he promised never to permit the election to the Imperial throne of Conradin or of any other person who might claim the throne of Sicily.[1]

That Charles of Anjou should have accepted such terms showed the measure of his ambition. Gossip attributed his acceptance to the influence of his wife. Beatrice of Provence was jealous of her sisters, who were now the Queens of France, of England and of the Romans. When last they had all met together she had been placed, as a mere countess, at a lower table for banquets, and she bitterly resented it. She, too, would be a queen. But Charles was not a man to concern himself with a woman's whims. His desire for a throne was greater even than hers.[1]

Charles had been born early in 1227, a few months after the death of his father, King Louis VIII, and his childhood was passed in the stormy years when his mother, Blanche of Castile, established her authority over the unwilling nobility of France. Blanche was a proud vigorous woman, too busy over politics to spare much time or much affection on her children. A bond of sentiment united her to her saintly eldest son, Louis IX, whose interests she had guarded so indefatigably, and who rewarded her with an unquestioning deferential devotion. But she seems to have cared little for Charles, who of all her children resembled her most. Saint Louis was as indulgent towards his brothers as his austere, unapproachable nature allowed; but his favourite had been the second, Robert, Count of Artois, a gallant, handsome youth who had died, owing to his own rashness, at the Battle of Mansourah during the crusade in Egypt. Of the two surviving brothers, Alfonso and Charles, Louis preferred Alfonso; and Charles knew it. Alfonso, Count of Poitiers, was a frail valetudinarian, industrious and joyless. He had been married when young to Joanna of Toulouse, the greatest heiress in France; but he seldom resided in his wife's southern lands, preferring to live in or near Paris, while a host of couriers went to and fro carrying his meticulous instructions for the administration of his appanage, every detail of which he personally supervised. He was a just and pious if somewhat avaricious ruler; and the king, his brother, found him a prudent and loyal counsellor. Their only sister, Isabella, retired young from the world into the Convent of Saint Cloud which she founded.

With little family affection to soften him, Charles began as a

71

young man to rely on himself alone. He grew up tall and muscular, with a dark olive skin inherited from his Castilian ancestors and the long nose of the Capetians. He had a healthy, well-disciplined body, with all his mother's energy. He had received a good education and never lost his respect for learning or his personal liking for poetry and the arts. But he had his share of his family's austerity and would always abandon his personal pleasures in pursuit of some higher aim; though, while King Louis's austerity came from his genuine piety, Charles's was an instrument to gratify his longing for power. His piety was in its way genuine, but it chiefly took the form of a belief that he was the chosen instrument of God.[1]

Though his family did not shower love on him they gave him great material gifts. Before he was born his dying father willed him, should he prove to be a boy, the rich appanages of Anjou and Maine. It was not till 1247, when he was twenty, that he was enfeoffed with the two counties; but the previous year his mother and brother arranged for him to marry a great heiress, Beatrice of Provence. Beatrice was the youngest of the four beautiful daughters of Raymond-Berengar IV, Count of Provence and Forcalquier. Of her sisters Margaret had married King Louis in 1234, Eleanor King Henry III of England in 1236, and Sanchia, the loveliest of them all, Richard of Cornwall, future King of the Romans, in 1243. By feudal custom, as there was no son the daughters should have been co-heiresses; but Raymond-Berengar did not wish his lands to be divided and left them all to Beatrice, considering that her sisters had been adequately compensated by ample dowries. Unfortunately the dowries had never been fully paid, and the disinherited sisters felt themselves to have been cheated, particularly Queen Margaret, the eldest, who thenceforward pursued Charles with unquenched hatred. Charles was soon also on bad terms with his mother-in-law, Beatrice of Savoy, who quarrelled with him over her widow's jointure.[2]

Charles was undeterred by the hostility of his wife's family.

She had preferred him to such rivals as Conrad of Hohenstaufen, King of the Romans, and two elderly widowers, King James of Aragon and Count Raymond VII of Toulouse; and he justified her choice. Legally the County of Provence owed allegiance to the Emperor, as part of the old kingdom of Burgundy and Arles. Charles paid no attention to this, nor was Frederick II in a position to assert his rights. But the recent Counts of Provence had themselves been easy-going, leaving the cities and the nobility of the county free to do much as they pleased. Charles was determined to stop all that. When he arrived in Provence, early in 1246, there came with him a host of lawyers and accountants trained at the French court, who at once set about looking into his legal rights and privileges as Count and computing the services and moneys due to him. Their actions aroused the angry opposition of the Provençals. Two of the local nobles, Barral of Les Baux and Boniface of Castellane, organized the malcontents. They were supported by the Dowager Countess, who claimed that her husband's will gave her the entire possession of the County of Forcalquier and the usufruct of his property in Provence, and by the three cities of Marseilles, Arles and Avignon. These were legally not part of the county but Imperial cities, which had developed a communal government on Italian lines; and they foresaw a threat to their independence. When in 1247 Charles went north to receive the investiture of Maine and Anjou the three cities formed a defensive alliance to last for fifty years; and they invited Barral of Les Baux to command their armies.

Charles had promised to go on his brother's crusade and had no time to crush the malcontents. All that he could do was to make a compromise with his mother-in-law, allowing her Forcalquier and a third of the Provençal revenues. After he had sailed with the king from Aigues-Mortes in 1248 the discontent flared up into rebellion. Charles proved himself a gallant soldier on the crusade, but as soon as his brother gave him leave he hastened home again, landing at Aigues-Mortes in October 1250. By a mixture of warlike energy and subtle diplomacy he managed to divide his enemies and crush them one by one. Arles submitted to him in April 1251, and Avignon in May. In June Barral of Les Baux surrendered. Marseilles repulsed his first attack in August, but sued for peace next July. Charles treated the leaders of the revolt with personal leniency, but insisted on his legal rights being clearly and definitively stated and recognized. The Marseillais were allowed to keep their communal autonomy, but recognized him as suzerain. In November 1252 the death of the Queen-Mother Blanche, who had been regent of France in King Louis's absence, called him to Paris; and he assumed the regency jointly with his brother Alfonso. It was at this moment that he had first been offered the crown of Sicily. Alfonso disapproved of the offer, and King Louis wrote from the East to forbid him to accept it. In his disappointment Charles intervened in a civil war in Flanders. By supporting the Countess Margaret in a war against her son, John of Avesnes, he received the County of Hainault and the post of Guardian of Flanders; and he began to pour his troops into the county. King Louis had heard with alarm of the war in Flanders while he was still in the East. When he returned to France in the summer of 1254 he ordered Charles to abandon Hainault. His final judgement, in 1256, gave Flanders to John of Avesnes; but John was to pay homage personally to Charles.

By that time Charles had abandoned hopes of a Flemish dominion. While he had been in the north Provence had been in the charge of able seneschals, helped by the local bishops and by Barral of Les Baux, now his loyal friend. But many of the nobles were still restive, led by Boniface of Castellane. The Dowager Countess was making trouble again. The Marseillais resented the visits of officials insisting on his suzerain rights. Once again Charles divided his enemies and dealt with them one by one. In November 1256, thanks to King Louis's intervention, the Dowager agreed to surrender Forcalquier and her claims on the usufruct of Provence in return for a large sum of cash and a handsome income for the rest of her life. King Louis, reflecting that the turbulent old lady was his mother-in-law also, helped his brother by promising to pay the income himself. This settlement weakened the dissident nobles, who relied on her for financial support. Marseilles had hoped to escape out of Charles's power by alliances made in 1256 with the King of Castile and with Pisa. But Alfonso of Castile was too busily occupied with his pretensions to the Empire to trouble to send them help, while Pisa was involved in an unsuccessful war with Florence. A *coup d'état* was staged by the 'Franciots', as the Provençals called Charles's partisans; and Charles came in person to insist on a new treaty, by which Marseilles kept its judicial and fiscal autonomy but surrendered all political power into the hands of the Count's representatives.[1]

With Provence tamed, Charles extended his power over the frontiers of the county. In 1257 he obtained rights over a few lordships in the lower Alps ceded to him by the Dauphin of Vienne. He also acquired from Raymond of Les Baux, Count of Orange, the rights as regent of the Kingdom of Arles which Frederick II had given to Raymond's father. This cession should have been confirmed by the Emperor; but there was no Emperor on the throne at the time. In 1258 the Count of Ventimiglia, hitherto a vassal of the Republic of Genoa, acknowledged Charles as his suzerain, thus extending his power along the coast as far east as San Remo, and up into the mountains as far as the Tenda Pass. In 1259 a subtle mixture of bribes, promises and military threats gave Charles the lordship of Cuneo, Alba and Cherasco in southern Piedmont; and next year the submission of the lords of Mondovi, Ceva, Biandrate and Saluzzo completed his control of the district. Early in 1262, when Charles had gone north to see to his lands in Anjou, and to discuss with his brother the possible offer of the Sicilian throne, a new revolt flared up in Provence. Boniface of Castellane regrouped the dissident nobles, and the Marseillais rose up against the 'Franciot' officials and ejected them. Genoa promised support to the rebels, and the sons of the King of Aragon waited at Montpellier, ready to add to Charles's embarrassment by intervening. But Barral of Les Baux remained loyal, though his cousin Hugh had joined the revolt. By his influence he kept it from spreading. Charles hurried south. He bought off the Genoese by giving back to them the Ventimiglian coastlands, though he kept the mountain districts inland. He scattered the rebel nobles and marched on Castellane, forcing Boniface and Hugh of Les Baux to flee into exile. He then approached Marseilles. But he was already now negotiating with the Pope about the Sicilian throne and wanted to avoid trouble. When the King of Aragon offered to mediate on behalf of the Marseillais, he accepted the offer. Marseilles was to have its fortifications dismantled and its citizens must surrender their arms. But the city could keep its judicial and fiscal rights and the ringleaders of the revolt were to go unpunished. The remarkable mixture of energy and generosity shown by Charles had its effect. He had no more trouble from Provence for the rest of his life. On the contrary, the Provençals soon realized that they might themselves benefit from his Italian schemes, to which they gave their full support.[1]

A far-sighted Pope might have feared that a man with such a record for vigour and ambition would not prove in the long run subservient enough to be a good champion for the Church. But Pope Urban could not afford to look far ahead. Manfred provided too pressing a danger. A child such as Edmund of England, dependent on a weak unrealistic father, was unsuitable for the task of crushing him, even had King Henry been backed by his countrymen. A man of proven ability was needed; and Urban as a Frenchman preferred that he should be a fellow-Frenchman. It did not occur to him that there might be danger ahead if the domination of the Germans in Italy, against which his predecessors had fought so relentlessly, was to be replaced by the domination of the French. Italy must be rid of Manfred; and Charles was the man for the job, especially as he had the wealth of France to back him, and the support of King Louis, who was the greatest moral force in Europe at the time. Louis himself was never entirely happy about the project. But he agreed that Manfred was a menace to Christendom; and it may be that he felt some guilt at loving Charles less than his other brothers and at having thwarted his ambitions in the past in Flanders. Having made up his mind, he gave Charles all the help that he could.

Charles himself had no qualms, even at the exorbitant terms demanded by the Papacy. He knew that he could adjust them later, to suit his convenience.

CHAPTER VI

THE ANGEVIN INVASION

It was not long before the Papacy discovered what sort of man
it had chosen for its champion. The agreement had been concluded
in June 1263. The city of Rome had passed over to the Guelf
camp early in Urban's pontificate; and though the Pope never
resided there he had appointed nominees to govern the city, a
committee of *boni homines*, who were to exercise the functions
of the senator. It was not an efficient government. There was
still a powerful party of Ghibellines who continued to intrigue
against it. Manfred, as soon as he learnt of Charles's arrangement
with the Pope, decided that Rome was a key-city. His partisans,
led by a certain Peter Romani, proposed that he should be appointed senator. His son-in-law, Peter of Aragon, prepared to
make a pilgrimage to Rome to canvass for him there, or to propose
himself as an alternative candidate. The plot was countered by
a cardinal, Richard Annibaldi, who happened to be in the city.
He persuaded the Guelfs to reply by electing a strong senator
devoted to their interests. On his suggestion, they offered the
senatorship to Charles, who accepted it. By his treaty with the
Papacy Charles was not to hold any office, however small, in any
city of the Empire, however obscure. Now he proposed to take
over the chief secular office in the Imperial metropolis.[1]

Pope Urban was in a quandary. Many of the cardinals declared that he should break off negotiations with Charles. But
Urban did not wish to repudiate Cardinal Annibaldi's work and
risk offending his supporters in Rome. Moreover, he could not
afford now to quarrel with Charles. Manfred, thwarted at Rome,
was marching through the eastern lands of the Roman patrimony
and was determined to force Lucca, the last Guelf city that
remained in Tuscany, to submit to his suzerainty.[2] Urban there-

fore announced his approval of Charles's appointment as a temporary measure.[1] Charles tactfully replied that he would not accept it without the Pope's approval. But he knew the strength of his position; he insisted on a revision of his whole treaty with the Papacy. Negotiations were carried on throughout the autumn of 1263. The Pope put forward new proposals which Charles barely deigned to consider. By the end of the year it seemed that the whole arrangement was to be cancelled. But in the early months of 1264 Manfred's hold on central Italy tightened. Lucca at last submitted to him. Urban found himself encircled. If he did not find help soon, he confessed to his intimates, he would have to retire to France. He capitulated to Charles's demands. In April he submitted to the cardinals the revised terms that he proposed to offer. Many of the cardinals were by now thoroughly dissatisfied with the whole Angevin scheme; so Urban began his address practically with apologies, pointing out that Manfred's successes made Charles's intervention essential. He suggested that Charles should resign the Roman senatorship either at a fixed date or as soon as he had conquered the Sicilian kingdom; Charles could choose which he preferred. The other terms arranged previously with Charles should hold good. The Cardinal of Saint Cecilia, Simon of Brie, a man whom Saint Louis was known to admire, was to be sent to Paris, where Charles now was with his brother, and should tell Louis that if Charles were intransigent over the Roman question, his candidature for the Sicilian throne would be considered as having been cancelled. To supplement Cardinal Simon's efforts, the Cardinal-Bishop of Sabina, Guy Foulquois, who was now legate in England and whom Louis liked, was ordered to join him at Paris.[2]

Charles meanwhile sent counter-proposals. He knew that the Pope was in effect committed to him. He now demanded that the yearly sum to be paid from the conquered kingdom to the Pope should be reduced from 10,000 ounces. He would have to make gifts to his supporters from the conquered kingdom and he did not wish to impoverish it. He wanted it laid down that all his descendants, female as well as male, should be eligible to succeed to the throne. To the clause forbidding Charles or his successors to acquire lands or offices in northern or central Italy he wished the word 'wittingly' to be added. Military or other needs might oblige him to occupy such lands; but he would resign them as soon as the Pope requested him. If Charles or any of his successors became Emperor, the Sicilian throne would be handed over to the next heir, whether male or female. If he himself led the army which was to conquer the kingdom, he alone should decide on its size. Finally, he could not accept a clause by which his subjects could under any circumstances be released from their allegiance to him.[1]

These proposals cannot have pleased the Pope; but he was desperate. A message was sent to the Cardinal of Saint Cecilia to tell him how to act on them. The Cardinal was to make the best bargain that he could over the yearly sum to be sent to Rome, but he must not go below 8000 ounces. On the question of allegiance, the clause could be modified so as not to apply to Charles himself; if that was not enough, Charles's immediate successor could also be excluded from its provisions. Failing that, some sort of counter-guarantee must be demanded. At the last resort the clause could be abandoned. As for the other proposals, the Cardinal was to do what he thought best. That is to say, Urban was ready to yield all along the line, but not without a struggle. The Cardinal of Sabina was to see that the King of England did not make any further trouble over Charles's candidature, while the Archbishop of Cosenza, who was already in France, was to see that Queen Margaret's well-known hatred of Charles did not interfere with the negotiations. It might be necessary to make some adjustment about her claims to Provence. If the negotiations with Charles were successful, the French clergy were to be asked to give their *dîme* for three years to the war against Manfred.[2]

While the Cardinal negotiated at Paris, Manfred took the offensive once more. One of his lieutenants, Jordan of Anglona, the victor of Montaperti, swept through the March of Ancona, capturing its papal governor and establishing a liaison with the Ghibellines in Tuscany. Another, Peter of Vico, operated in the outskirts of Rome. The city was only saved by the appearance there of a Provençal regiment under James of Gantelme, whom Charles had appointed as his vicar. Manfred himself gathered a large army in Campania and was ready to cross the frontier in Peter's support. Pope Urban saw himself surrounded; he even began to fear for his life. There were rumours that Manfred was training assassins to eliminate him. His letters to the Cardinal at Paris were almost hysterical. At any cost Charles must be brought as quickly as possible to Italy.[1]

In such an atmosphere the Cardinal could not hope to make a good bargain. He struggled a little but he had to give way. Charles agreed to give up the Roman senatorship as soon as he became master of the Kingdom, and he agreed that the yearly sum due to the Papacy should be 8000 ounces. All his other proposals were accepted by the Cardinal. In the meantime, though Queen Margaret refused to give up her Provençal claims, she consented to take no action that might prevent her brother-in-law's Sicilian venture. In August the Cardinal reported to the Pope that the negotiations were successfully concluded; and as soon as the news reached him, Urban sent back enthusiastic congratulations. Next, the Cardinal set about persuading the French bishops to give up their *dîmes* for the war. By September they had all given their consent, though, it seems, with a bad grace. Only the clergy of the Venaissin refused. They were, they said, part neither of the Kingdom of France nor of the County of Provence, for which alone the Cardinal had been given legatine powers.[2]

Pope Urban never heard of his legate's final successes. His anxieties in Italy were increasing. At last he suspected that Orvieto itself, where he had resided for most of his pontificate, was turning against him. He decided to retire to Assisi. On 11 September he arrived at Todi, where he fell ill, but he insisted on continuing his journey. When he arrived a few days later at Deruta, travelling in a litter as he could no longer ride, he was clearly dying. The cardinals in his train moved him on to Perugia. He died there on 2 October 1264.[1]

Charles heard of Urban's death with some disquiet. His new arrangement with the Papacy had not been confirmed; a new Pope might repudiate it. He knew that there was opposition to him in the College of Cardinals, and his two chief friends there, the Cardinals of Saint Cecilia and of Sabina, were away in France. Were he no longer to be the accepted champion of the Church his enemies would take heart and revive their activities. He had moved from Paris to Provence, to prepare for the invasion of Italy. There he decided on a deliberate act of severity, to show that no one could trifle with him. The previous summer he had captured the rebel Hugh of Les Baux and had arrested various other friends of Boniface of Castellane and the Dowager Countess, including several rich merchants and the ex-Podestà of Arles, on the grounds that they were in communication with the King of Aragon. They had been in prison for a year, but well treated; for it had been Charles's policy to be lenient to his defeated foes. Now, quite suddenly, he ordered their death. The world should see that his clemency was a matter only of policy, not of weakness. On 24 October they were beheaded outside the Church of Saint Michael at Marseilles, and their possessions were confiscated. Having shown that no one could trifle with him and having incidentally added considerably to his wealth, Charles went on publicly with his preparations for the Italian campaign. The new Pope, whoever he might be, should be in no doubt about his intentions.[2]

Out of the twenty-one members of the Sacred College, eighteen met in conclave at Perugia to elect a new Pope. In the absence of the two cardinals who were still in France and the Cardinal of

Saint Martin who was trying to restore papal order in the March of Ancona and could not leave his post, all three of them supporters of the late Pope's policy, the College was fairly evenly divided between those who favoured Charles and those who opposed him. Manfred began to hope for the election of a Pope with whom he could come to terms. Unlike Charles, who made use of the interregnum to take what measures he pleased without reference to the Papacy, Manfred thought it wise to call off his military offensive. He did not wish to frighten the Conclave and so force them further into Charles's arms; and his indolent nature welcomed a holiday from his recent activity.

The Conclave sat for four months without reaching a decision. Of the course of its deliberations nothing is known, till on 5 February 1265 one of the younger cardinals suggested that the choice should be left to two commissioners, representing the two parties. They decided on the Cardinal of Sabina; and the Conclave accepted their decision. The Cardinal of Sabina was already on his way from France. He arrived at Perugia to find himself Pope-designate, and was enthroned on 15 February, with the name of Clement IV.[1]

The election was far from being a compromise. It showed that the College would have no truck with Manfred and that it had decided that Charles's intervention was inevitable. Manfred's forbearance had been wasted and Charles's open and relentless preparations had made their effect. The new Pope was a remarkable man. He was born Guy Fulquois, the son of a lawyer of Saint-Gilles, in Languedoc. As a young man he had entered the legal service of the Counts of Toulouse. His fortune was made when King Louis's brother Alfonso took over the County. He proved to be the most zealous and efficient advocate of the new dynasty and soon became Alfonso's chief adviser. In 1247 his wife died and he entered the Church. He became Bishop of Le Puy in 1252, Archbishop of Narbonne in 1259, and Cardinal of Sabina in 1261. From 1262 to 1264 he had been legate in England. He now owed his election to his known intimacy with Saint Louis and the royal house of France.[1]

From the outset Pope Clement made it clear that he would follow his predecessor's policy. He kept in constant touch with Charles. During his journey to Perugia he had written to give him advice how to treat the Romans. As Pope his first action was to repeat the formal annulment of Edmund of England's candidature and to authorize Charles to accept the senatorship of Rome without conditions. He begged Charles to hurry to Rome as quickly as possible. The situation there was serious. Gantelme and his Provençals were only just able to hold the city against Peter of Vico, who was now master of the Campagna, up to the city walls.[2]

Charles had used the interregnum in making alliances in northern Italy. He controlled southern Piedmont, and secured the neutrality of the Count of Savoy. He was already allied with the Marquis of Montferrat. In January 1265 he made friends with the Torriani family, who now controlled Milan, Bergamo, Como and Lodi, sending Barral of Les Baux with a troop of cavalry to aid them. Soon afterwards the Este lords of Ferrara offered him a free passage through their lands, in return for help that he sent to enable the Guelfs to recover the control of Emilia. He had been on good terms with Genoa since his retrocession of the Ventimiglian coastlands; and this friendship was helped by a quarrel between the Genoese and Manfred. Seduced by Manfred's agents the Genoese Podestà at Constantinople had entered into a plot to overthrow the Greek Empire. The Emperor Michael discovered it and deprived the Genoese of the privileged position that they held in the Empire through the Treaty of Nymphaeum. To recover their privileges the Genoese had to repudiate any friendship with Manfred. They agreed therefore not to oppose Charles's invasion of Italy, though they would not give him active help nor allow his troops to pass through their territory. The way was prepared for Charles to send an army through

Piedmont and Lombardy; but he still needed money before the campaign could be fully launched.[1]

In the meantime, in answer to the Pope's desperate appeal, he embarked at Marseilles on 10 May with a few hundred cavalrymen and bowmen and sailed cautiously round the coast towards Ostia. It was a stormy voyage; but the bad weather prevented the Sicilian squadron policing the Ligurian Sea from noticing him. He landed at Ostia ten days later and prepared to march on Rome.[2]

Manfred was roused to action. On 24 May he wrote a letter to the Romans, designed to appeal to their pride. In it he frankly stated his claims and ambitions to become Emperor; but, he said, it was for the Romans to choose the Emperor. They had allowed the Papacy to rob them of their due privilege. The letter contained threats as well as flattery. He recalled how his great-grandfather Frederick Barbarossa had forced his way into the rebel city and had crowned himself there. But this strange and ingenuous letter was written too late. On 23 May Charles entered Rome amid the plaudits of the Romans. He took up residence in the papal palace of the Lateran; on receiving a hurt complaint from the Pope, he moved to the senatorial palace on the Capitol.[3]

When he heard that Charles was already at Rome, Manfred affected to be delighted. 'The bird is in the cage', he cried; it would only need a short campaign to encircle him there and force his surrender.[4]

But things did not work out as Manfred hoped. The Romans were delighted with Charles. On 21 June he was formally given the insignia of senator. To please the Pope he now promised again to resign the post once the Kingdom was conquered. One week later, on the 28th, four cardinals, specially accredited by Pope Clement, solemnly invested him with the Kingdom. Henceforward he called himself King of Sicily. Charles's good reception as well as the vigour of his personality soon began to win him support. Peter of Vico, who had been Manfred's chief ally in the Campagna, wavered in his loyalty. It seemed to him that

Charles's was the winning side. On 10 July, after brief negotiations, he made his peace with the Church, promising to renounce all his engagements with Manfred and to swear allegiance to the Papacy. He then took service under Charles and was to prove one of his most energetic captains. A few days later Peter Romani, former head of the Ghibellines inside Rome, followed suit.[1]

Manfred found that words were not enough. He led his army out of the Kingdom through the Abruzzi and past the Fucine lake into the Anio valley. The Pope begged Charles not to risk a pitched battle with inferior forces; but Charles marched out to a strong position on the heights near Tivoli. Manfred advanced to Arsoli, on the Anio some fifteen miles away; but his spies told him that he would get no support in the Campagna, and he did not dare to attack Charles's camp. After a little skirmishing in the valley he withdrew. He then marched northward through the Abruzzi, as though to attack Spoleto, then suddenly, for some reason that is now unknown, gave up the whole campaign and returned to his hunting in Apulia. His withdrawal lost him further friends. Within a month he had lost his hold over the March of Ancona; and his influence was sinking in Tuscany.[2]

Charles had won the first round. He had saved Rome and re-stored the position of the Church in central Italy. He had now to take on the main task of attacking Manfred in his own kingdom. But this required money. A large army had to be equipped and paid. During the late summer months he and the Pope discussed financial details. The obligation of the French Church to pay the *dîme* for the war was reaffirmed, and the recalcitrant county of Venaissin, as well as Hainault and the valley of Aosta, was ordered to contribute. But the money was paid grudgingly and some-times not at all. Clement agreed that Charles's own contribution for the campaign should be reduced; and indeed, though the Countess Beatrice pawned her jewels, Charles could not provide very much. It was necessary to have recourse to the Italian banks.

But the Papacy had been borrowing from the Tuscan banks for many years. The bankers knew that they would never be repaid unless the papal policy succeeded, but that did not make them particularly anxious to lend any more money. The King of France and his brother Alfonso refused to provide any money from their dominions, though the latter in the end offered a short-term loan of 4000 silver marks and 5000 pounds *tournois*. The Pope had hoped that the whole treasure of France would be poured into the enterprise; but any wealth that Saint Louis had to spare was being reserved for a crusade against the infidel. In Rome itself Charles was able to raise less than 50,000 pounds *provinois*, barely enough to pay his expenses for a month. The papal court lent him 20,000 pounds *tournois* as soon as he arrived at Rome. In the course of the summer he obtained, on a papal guarantee, some 16,000 pounds *tournois* from various Florentine and Sienese banking-houses and another 20,000 from them before the winter of 1265. At the same time the Pope raised another 50,000, but only by pledging the treasure and the plate of the papal chapel, while Charles raised 62,000 from Roman bankers by pledging the property, with the Pope's permission, of a number of Roman churches. By the end of the year there was enough money in hand for the campaign. But the negotiations had been wearisome, especially as neither Charles nor the Pope wished to publicize their desperate need for money.[1]

Once again Manfred missed his opportunity. Hoping, no doubt, that his enemies' financial problems would prove insoluble and that his Ghibelline allies in Lombardy, to whom he sent a few troops, would block any invading army, he remained on in Apulia, enjoying his hunting. Charles, however, did not wait for the loans to be completed before he set his army in motion. As soon as he had enough money to pay the troops for a few months, he summoned them to assemble at Lyons on 1 October 1265. Meanwhile the Pope sent a trusted agent, Geoffrey of Beaumont, as his legate to Lombardy, to prepare the way diplomatically, according to Charles's wishes. Clement had not liked Charles's north Italian policy. In particular he resented an alliance with the Este family, who, in spite of their Guelf traditions, had been on bad terms with his predecessors, while the city of Milan was still under an interdict. He would have preferred to restore Guelf influence in Tuscany first and bring the army over the Ligurian Alps, avoiding the lands of the Lombard and Emilian cities, whose rulers he did not trust. But Charles had made his plans and would not change them; nor was there time.[1]

The army that marched from Lyons early in October was a formidable force. The chroniclers spoke of six thousand fully armed horsemen, six hundred mounted bowmen and twenty thousand infantrymen, half of them crossbowmen. These numbers are certainly exaggerated; there were probably slightly fewer cavalry and much fewer foot. Many of the highest French nobility had joined the expedition. The Count of Vendôme was there, and the heirs of the counties of Flanders and Soissons, and Philip of Montfort with his cousin Guy, son of the Earl of Leicester. The nobility of Provence was fully represented, with lords of the House of Les Baux at their head. The commander was Guy of Mello, Bishop of Auxerre. The autumn snows had begun to fall on the high Alps; so, to find an open pass as well as to keep to friendly territory, the army moved down through Provence, then over the Tenda Pass into the lands that Charles controlled in Piedmont and on, through Cuneo, Alba and Asti, into the territory of the Marquis of Montferrat. There its way was blocked. The Pallavicini, still allied to Manfred, controlled the towns of Alessandria, Tortona, Vercelli, Pavia, Piacenza, Cremona and Brescia. Vercelli, to the north, was the weakest link in the chain. As the army swung northwards towards it, a revolution was staged there by the bishop of the town. Charles's army was welcomed within the walls, and soon passed on, leaving a small French garrison behind. From Vercelli Milan was reached without difficulty. There the head of the Torriani family had died a few weeks earlier. His nephew Napoleon, who had succeeded to the family influence, showed the French leaders some coldness at first; but after a delay of only two or three days he came to an understanding with them and even brought his own militia out to accompany them on the next stage of the journey.

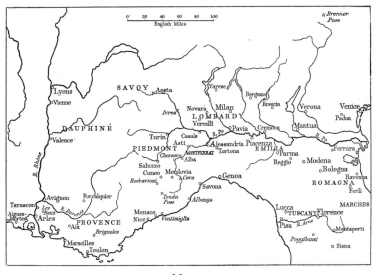

Map 1.

This might have been a difficult stage; for once more the army had to break through the line of Pallavicini fortresses; and Pallavicini himself, with Boso of Dovara, governor of Cremona, was waiting in some strength at Soncino, on the river Oglio. But Pallavicini discovered that the Angevin forces, with their Milanese allies, were far larger than his own. He was, moreover, uncertain of the loyalty of Brescia; and, according to rumour, Boso was given a large bribe by the French to retreat, for which Dante placed him in Hell, to bewail for ever the Frenchmen's gold. The Angevins were able to cross the Oglio further to the north, and to pass close by Brescia, hoping for a revolution there. Pallavicini's garrison was able to hold the town quiet, but could not venture out to oppose the invaders. A half-hearted attempt was made by the Ghibellines to prevent the passage of the river Chiese at Montechiaro. The Milanese militia had now gone home, but Geoffrey of Beaumont was able to send Guelf troops from Mantua to attack Montechiaro in the rear. The town was soon taken; and the army crossed the river into friendly territory at Mantua, controlled by the Este family and their allies. Towards the end of December it crossed the Po and reached Bologna. From there it moved quickly on into the March of Ancona, down the Via Emilia, where the Pope had fresh provisions ready to welcome it. From Ancona it crossed the Apennines, through Spoleto and Terni, and arrived at Rome about 15 January 1266.[1]

The Pope was relieved to learn of its safe arrival. He had been nervous about its passage through Lombardy. As soon as he heard that it had crossed the Po he wrote to congratulate Geoffrey of Beaumont for his zeal but cancelled his legatine authority, saying that the district was too unstable for him to keep a representative there. He did not wish to compromise the Church by taking part in the disreputable quarrels of its local tyrants. Charles was equally relieved; but he had been confident of success. He had already sent for his wife to come by sea to join him. She arrived at the end of December. Charles then asked the Pope to come to Rome to crown them King and Queen of Sicily. Clement refused to leave the security of Perugia; but he sent five cardinals to perform the ceremony in Saint Peter's Church on 6 January 1266. The Countess Beatrice could boast now that she was not inferior in rank to her sisters.[2]

Charles would not allow his army to remain long in Rome. For financial reasons he had to finish the campaign as quickly as possible, and he liked the idea of striking at once, before Manfred expected him, instead of waiting for the usual opening of the campaigning season in the spring. On 20 January he started out from Rome in full force, leaving only a small garrison in the city. He passed down the old Via Latina, through Anagni and Frosinone, to the frontier of the Kingdom at Ceprano on the river Liri. He found the bridge across the river deserted but undestroyed; and the whole army moved safely across. Why no attempt was made to defend the crossing was never known. There were rumours of treachery, which Dante was to immortalize in the *Inferno*.[1]

The news that the Angevin army was approaching Rome had roused Manfred from his lethargy. His spies told him that Charles intended to march straight on to the attack. He hastily gathered together the full army of the Kingdom, and summoned his nephew, Conrad of Antioch, to bring down the troops which he commanded in the Abruzzi and the Marches. When Charles reached the Liri, he was installed at the fortress of Capua with an army about the equal in size to his enemy's. He seems to have hoped that the fortresses along the Liri and the hills of the northern Terra di Lavoro would hold Charles till Conrad of Antioch arrived with his reinforcements. If they fell, Capua and the fortresses along the river Volturno would still guard Naples. He had only to wait to manœuvre Charles into a position from which there would be no escape. Charles's speed and strategy upset his plans. The Angevin army moved steadily onwards, capturing thirty-two castles, including the great double fortress of San Germano, on the hill of Cassino, which fell on 10 February. The small garrisons were discouraged to receive no help from Manfred and made little resistance. Charles was now aware that Manfred's forces were concentrated on the lower Volturno. So from Cassino he suddenly swerved inland, into the Samnite hills, crossing the Volturno in its upper reaches and making his way through Alife and Telese, towards Benevento. When Manfred learnt that his flank had been turned, he left Capua and moved inland, to reach Benevento first.[2]

When the Angevin army on 25 February wound down the mountain pass that led to the city, it saw the enemy in all his strength disposed round the city behind the flooded river Calore. The invaders were discouraged. The passage through the hills in the wintry weather had been arduous. Many pack animals had perished; most of the waggons had been abandoned on the slippery passes; and food was running short. It seemed that Manfred's confident boast that the bird was in the cage was now at last justified. He had only to wait in his strong position for his nephew Conrad to come up with reinforcements and for the Angevins to be forced by hunger either to retreat or to surrender. But Manfred was impatient. He did not feel confident about his subjects' loyalty; he had been shaken by the willingness of so many of his garrisons to yield to the enemy, and he suspected that many of the local barons were wavering. He was not sure when Conrad would arrive; he had just received a reinforcement of 800 German mercenary horse, but could expect no more for the moment. Seeing how wretched Charles's troops appeared to be, he decided to attack at once. Charles, to his delight, as he came down into the plain, saw Manfred's army slowly crossing the river to meet him.

On the morrow, Friday 26 February 1266, the two armies were drawn up for battle. Manfred placed his Saracen troops, archers without defensive armour, in the fore. Behind them, ready to charge when their arrows should have thrown the enemy into disorder, were his best troops, the German cavalry, well mounted and clad in new-fashioned plate armour, and numbering twelve hundred. They were commanded by Giordano Lancia, Manfred's cousin, and Galvano of Anglona. A little way behind them Manfred placed his Italian mercenary horse, mostly Lombard and Tuscan, numbering about a thousand, under the command of his uncle, Galvano Lancia, Prince of Salerno. With them were his two or three hundred light-armed Saracen horse. He himself stayed near the bridgehead with the reserve, the knights and squires of the Kingdom, rather more than a thousand strong. He did not entirely trust them and did not wish to use them till victory seemed assured. With him were his brothers-in-law, Richard, Count of Caserta, and Thomas, Count of Acerra, who were already wavering in their allegiance, his Chamberlain, Manfred Maletta, and his most faithful friend, the Roman Tebaldo Annibaldi.

Charles had a slight advantage in the terrain, which sloped gently towards the river. He also had the advantage that his army was more homogeneous than Manfred's and more reliable. Like Manfred he drew up his men into three cavalry groups, with the infantry, amongst whom were a large proportion of crossbowmen, in front. The first cavalry group consisted of some 900 Provençals, under the command of Hugh of Mirepoix, Marshal of France, and Philip of Montfort. Charles himself commanded the second group, of about 1000, drawn from central France and Languedoc. With them were four hundred Italian Guelf horsemen, under the Florentine Guy Guerra. The Bishop of Auxerre and the Count of Vendôme were with Charles. Behind, as a reserve, were the northern French and the Flemish under Robert of Flanders and the Constable Giles Le Brun.

The battle began with an attack by the Saracen infantry on the French infantry, made before Manfred was ready. When the latter seemed about to give way a detachment of Provençal horsemen charged into the mêlée and scattered the Saracens. Thereupon, again without orders, the German horsemen thundered up the hill, heavy men on heavy horses; and the Provençals began to waver. Charles then ordered his second line to advance. They galloped down into the fighting mass. The Germans were now outnumbered but not beaten. Their plate armour seemed impenetrable, till at last a Frenchman noted that when they raised their arms to strike, their armpits were unprotected. He shouted to his comrades to stab them there. The French closed into the midst of the Germans, in so tight a mass that the German long swords were ineffective but the short sharp daggers of the French could strike home.

The battle might still have been won for Manfred had his second line of cavalry come up quickly. But the Germans had attacked too soon; Galvano Lancia, whose troops had been delayed by the crossing of the river over one narrow bridge, was too far behind. It may be, too, that he had, like all Manfred's captains, faith in the invincibility of the Germans and could not believe that they were beaten. By the time that he had ordered his Lombards and Tuscans to charge, it was too late. They met the victorious Frenchmen head on; and meanwhile Charles had summoned his third line to wheel round to attack them on the flank. The Italians did not wait for them. In spite of all Galvano's efforts they broke and fled. Many were captured, many more were killed. Manfred and his reserve were equally too far behind to intervene in time, if indeed the battle could now have been saved. Barely pausing to exchange his royal surcoat with his friend Tebaldo Annibaldi, he ordered his last line to charge. But the nobles of the Kingdom judged his cause to be hopeless. Led by his brothers-in-law, they rode away from the field. Manfred was left alone with his bodyguard. He might have escaped by flight but he chose otherwise. He plunged into the fight with his faithful retainers by his side. He was soon struck down, with Tebaldo in the royal surcoat next to him. Few of his soldiers survived. The bridge over the Calore was blocked with fugitives; and an armed man could not hope to make his way through the swollen river waters. Moreover, Charles had posted men behind his cavalry whose sole duty was to finish off the wounded. Of the 3600 horsemen in Manfred's army only 600 are said to have escaped.

By evening Charles was master of the battlefield; and the whole Kingdom lay open to him. He rode over the bridge into Benevento; and from there he wrote to the Pope to describe his victory. Amongst his captives, he announced, were Giordano and Bartholomew Lancia. Galvano Lancia was said to be dead. Manfred's fate was still unknown; but as his riderless horse had been found it was assumed that he had perished.[1]

On Sunday 28 February a soldier passed through the camp, leading an ass with a corpse on it and shouting: 'Who wants to buy Manfred?' He was brought before Charles, who told the Count of Caserta and Giordano and Bartholomew Lancia to see if it were really Manfred's. They identified it, Giordano covering his face with his hands and crying: 'Alas, alas, my lord.' Some of the French knights begged that so gallant a soldier should be given a noble funeral. Charles replied that he would gladly have agreed, had Manfred not died excommunicate. But, as he wrote next day to the Pope, when telling him of the arch-enemy's death, he ordered that the body should be buried honourably, though without any religious ceremony. It was laid in a pit at the foot of the bridge of Benevento, and every soldier who passed threw a stone over it till a cairn was erected. It was said later that the Archbishop of Cosenza, on the orders of the Pope himself, exhumed the corpse and buried it again on the banks of the river Liri, just outside the bounds of the Kingdom.[1]

Charles remained at Benevento only long enough to refresh his army. He could not prevent it from sacking the city, although it owed allegiance to the Papacy and not to the Sicilian crown. Summoning his wife from Rome to join him, he marched easily down to Naples. They made their solemn entry there on 7 March, the King on horseback and the Queen in a litter hung with blue velvet.

CHAPTER VII

CONRADIN

'Our dear son Charles', wrote Pope Clement on 6 May 1266, to his legate in England, 'is in peaceful possession of all the Kingdom, having in his power the putrid corpse of that pestilential man, his wife, his children and his treasure.'[1] It was true. After the battle of Benevento there was no more opposition to the conqueror. One by one, even before his troops arrived, the cities sent to tell him of their submission. The Saracens at Lucera, devoted though they had been to Manfred, accepted the new rule without further trouble. Frederick Lancia thought for a time to organize resistance in Calabria, but soon decided that it was hopeless. When Angevin troops crossed into Sicily, under Philip of Montfort, the islanders made no trouble. They had been disappointed by Manfred's lack of interest in them; they felt no regret at his fall. Manfred's navy, which was unbeaten, soon surrendered. Charles had prepared a fleet manned by Marseillais sailors, but he had no need to use it.[2]

Manfred's corpse was still buried at the bridge of Benevento. His wife, Queen Helena, with her one small daughter and Manfred's three bastard sons, was at Lucera when the news came of the disastrous battle. She hurried with the children to Trani, hoping to find a boat to take her across to her father in Epirus. Papal agents, sent to arrest her, were close in pursuit; and as she was waiting in the castle for a boat to be prepared they came up and terrorized the commander of the garrison into betraying her. She and the children were taken to Nocera and imprisoned in the Castello del Parco. She died there in 1271, not yet aged thirty. Her daughter Beatrice was liberated in 1284 and eventually married the Marquis of Saluzzo; but the boys never emerged from prison. One of them was still alive in 1309. Manfred's treasure was handed over at once to the victor by the chamberlain, Manfred Maletta.[1]

One by one Manfred's supporters made their submission. As soon as the victory was complete, Charles showed that he did not intend to be vindictive. Even the members of the Lancia family, after some hesitation, swore homage to him, and were allowed to keep most of their lands. Conrad of Antioch, still unbeaten in the Abruzzi, asked for an armistice. Other friends of Manfred, who had fled or were preparing to flee from the country, were invited to come back under a general amnesty. Amongst those who took advantage of the amnesty was an eminent doctor, John of Procida, who had attended Frederick II in his last illness and had recently cured Cardinal Orsini of a serious complaint. Pope Clement himself recommended him to Charles. Charles was to hear more of him later.[2]

Charles indeed showed remarkable clemency. He had not been able to prevent his army from sacking Benevento; but no other city suffered at all from the excesses of the conquerors. He wished to bring peace and justice to the Kingdom. He was not prepared to reward his Frenchmen and Provençals at the expense of his new subjects. No lands were confiscated except in cases of proven hostility or treachery. His financial officials quickly spread over the land, assessing its resources and seeing that taxes were paid; but the decrees that he issued were almost all concerned with the supervision of their functions, to see that there were no abuses. He ordered that an assembly should meet three times a year to hear complaints against the tax-collectors and to check their accounts. After the rather casual government of Manfred's time it seemed that the country was to settle down now to an orderly and benevolent administration.[3]

But, in spite of its initial tolerance, the new régime was not popular. The new king seemed austere and unapproachable. He had none of the gay affability with which the Hohenstaufen had been able to charm their Italian subjects. Though he liked his

Provençal troubadours and though he showed a sincere interest in learning and the arts, the impression that he made was cold and inhuman. His compatriots, hard though he tried to restrain them, were arrogant and grasping. Moreover, though the taxes were justly levied, they were high and hard to avoid. Charles had debts to repay and needed the money. The southern Italians and the Sicilians would have preferred a more easy-going system, even if it were more corrupt. Manfred had lost favour with his subjects by his curious indolence and by his quarrel with the Church. But they soon remembered him with affection, in contrast with the pious and energetic Charles.[1]

It was not long before complaints reached the Pope. He might boast of the achievements of his dear son Charles, but in fact Charles was quickly becoming less dear to him. He had hoped to control the Kingdom through a grateful and subservient client. But though he poured advice on the King, his admonitions were unheeded. The sack of Benevento had shocked him. He believed, without reason, that Charles was too severe to the Italians who submitted to him and, with more reason, that he was ungenerous in his rewards to his faithful allies in the Church. Charles's methods of taxation particularly annoyed the Pope. He ought, so Clement maintained, to have summoned the bishops, barons and leading townsfolk of the Kingdom to an assembly and told them of his needs, letting them decide what they would contribute. In his vexation Clement began to criticize Charles's person and his household. He was haughty, self-willed and ungrateful, a tool in the hands of his officials, surrounded by a disorderly court. In one bitter letter he complained that Charles was 'neither visible nor audible nor affable nor amiable.'[2]

Nevertheless, little though he relished it, Clement was still dependent on Charles. In May Charles resigned his office of senator of Rome, grudgingly; but he did not wish to break his promise. The Pope soon regretted it; for the Romans thereupon elected two joint senators, Conrad Beltram Monaldeschi and

Luca Savelli, the latter of whom, twenty-two years before, had led a revolt against the Papacy. Their first action was to demand that the Pope and Charles should pay back their debts to the Romans. The Pope answered by denouncing them as thieves and brigands and encouraging plots to overthrow them. The result was not what he expected. Early in 1267 a popular insurrection gave the city into the hands of a prominent Ghibelline, Angelo Capocci. It would have been wiser to have left Charles in control of Rome. But Capocci was prudent. He did not wish to provoke an attack from either Charles or Clement. He did not claim for himself the post of senator but offered it to one of Charles's comrades, the Infant Henry of Castile.[1]

King Alfonso of Castile had two brothers, Frederick and Henry. Both of them had quarrelled with him, finding him unwilling to share any of the royal power with them, and had migrated to lead the lives of adventurers. The Infant Frederick had for a time taken service with the Muslim King of Tunis. He had then passed over to Italy to join Manfred, with whom he was at the battle of Benevento. After escaping from the battlefield, he re-turned to Tunis. The Infant Henry had sought his fortune in France. There he made friends with Charles, who was his first cousin, and lent him large sums of money for the Italian campaign. He expected to be rewarded with the Kingdom of Sardinia or with a duchy in Epirus. But Charles neither paid him back nor seemed in any hurry to gratify his ambitions. It was with resentment in his heart, as Capocci certainly knew, that he accepted the invitation to Rome and was installed as senator, in July 1267.[2]

Saddened by events in Rome, Clement allowed Charles a free hand in northern Italy. Manfred's elimination meant the collapse of Ghibelline power in Lombardy. As early as the end of March 1266 a great Parliament assembled at Milan, where Charles's representatives met representatives from all the great towns of the Po, from Vercelli in the west to Treviso in the east, and from Reggio and Modena, south of the river. All were now

Guelf. Pallavicini still held Cremona and Piacenza; but in June he made his submission to Charles and was obliged to retire to his country estates. Only Verona under its Scaliger lord and Pavia remained independent. The rest of Lombardy was now in the power of Charles and his allies, the Torriani of Milan and the Estensi of Ferrara. His hold over Piedmont was consolidated. The Marquis of Montferrat, alarmed by such a concentration of power, declared a cautious neutrality; he could not risk open hostility. His place in the system of alliances was taken by the Marquis of Saluzzo. Charles's seneschal for Provence, William l'Estandart, was accepted as seneschal for Piedmont and Lombardy. The Pope was not altogether pleased. The Papacy had long distrusted the Torriani and disliked the Estensi; and Charles encircled it as effectively as any Hohenstaufen Emperor had done. But he had no choice.[1]

It was much the same in Tuscany. There the Ghibellines had not been ousted. Florence, it is true, asked for papal protection should Charles wish to attack it. But no other town followed its example. In the autumn of 1266 the Ghibelline League was reconstituted, at an assembly at San Miniato. The chief Ghibelline of Florence, Guy Novello, entered his city in triumph. He was ejected a month later; but the popular government then set up was not reliably Guelf. In January 1267 the Pope thought it necessary to invite Charles to send an army to Tuscany. His troops marched northward at the end of March. On 18 April they entered Florence. The Ghibellines retreated without fighting, never to return. Lucca was entered soon afterwards, and both cities elected Charles to be their Podestà for seven years. Pistoia and Prato followed suit. On 7 May, in spite of the Pope's request that he should remain in the south, Charles himself appeared in Tuscany and made his ceremonious entry into Florence. Only Pisa and Siena still opposed him. He was determined to crush them; but first the Pope summoned him to an interview at Viterbo, where he promised to restrict his rule in Tuscany to three years. He returned to Tuscany at the end of June and laid siege to the great fortress of Poggibonsi, on the road to Siena. For five months he lay before the fortress, which was fiercely defended. It was not till 30 November that it was at last taken by storm. The Pope repeatedly begged him to raise the siege and return to his kingdom, in view of the dangers that were imminent. But he refused to be deflected or to admit defeat.[1]

It was while he was away at Poggibonsi that his wife, Queen Beatrice, died at Nocera, in July 1267. She had enjoyed her royal rank for little more than a year.[2]

The danger that the Pope so feared, which made him condone Charles's policy in northern Italy and long now for his return to the south, was very real by the late summer of 1267. It came from the north. The Papacy, with its concentration of hatred against Manfred, had barely remembered that there was another Hohenstaufen alive in Germany. But the Italian Ghibellines, even when they paid allegiance to Manfred, had not forgotten Conradin. Conradin was now aged fifteen. He had been brought up in Bavaria under the care of his mother Elizabeth, King Conrad's widow, and her second husband, Mainard, Count of Gorizia, while his mother's brothers, Louis and Henry of Bavaria, looked after his political interests. Little was left now of his family's ancient possessions. In Germany part of the Duchy of Swabia accepted the government of his nominees. The barons of Outremer acknowledged him as King of Jerusalem; but had he ever visited his kingdom he would have found his power there strictly circumscribed. But he was a clever, precocious boy, handsome and charming, and deeply conscious of his blood. His mother discouraged his ambitions. She had no wish for him to risk his life on grandiose adventures. But his dearest friend was a boy not much older than himself, his distant cousin Frederick of Baden, lawful heir through his Babenberg mother to the Duchy of Austria, which the King of Bohemia had annexed when he was an infant; and Frederick eagerly supported all his schemes.[3]

The question of Conradin's rights had periodically been opened. The Papacy had occasionally thought of him as a rival to Manfred. Saint Louis had long considered that his claims could not be utterly ignored. In 1260 the Duke of Bavaria had sent two confidential agents to Rome, Conrad Kroff and Conrad Bussarus, apparently to see if Pope Alexander IV, who was not yet committed to Charles of Anjou, would now think of Conradin. While in Rome Bussarus was murdered and Kroff severely wounded, it seems by Manfred's partisans. After the disaster at Montaperti the Florentine Guelfs made momentary advances to the Bavarian court. But, till his death at Benevento, the Ghibellines were committed to Manfred's cause. It was only after the battle that their thoughts turned to Conradin.[1]

In the later months of 1266 the kinsfolk and friends of Manfred, suspicious of the victor's clemency and longing for revenge, began to creep one by one through Italy and over the Alps. The first to arrive at the Bavarian court, in the summer of 1266, was a leading lawyer from Manfred's chancery, Peter of Prezze. He was famed for his mastery of the so-called 'Sicilian' style of writing, which was both pompous and florid but was considered admirable for political manifestos. His pen was now put at Conradin's service. Next came the Capece brothers: Conrad, who had been Manfred's vicar first in the Marches and then in Sicily, and Marino. Their third brother, James, stayed as their agent in Sicily. Soon afterwards Conrad of Antioch, son of Frederick II's bastard Frederick, managed to escape from the prison in which Charles had placed him, together with a fellow-prisoner, John of Mareri, of the family of the lords of Avezzano. They too crossed the Alps to Bavaria. Next came Manfred's own uncles, Galvano and Frederick Lancia, and Manfred's former chamberlain, Manfred Maletta.[2]

The arrival of these partisans, all eager to take vengeance on Charles, could not fail to arouse the spirit of the lion-cub, or the young eagle, as the chroniclers variously called him. Conradin had already begun to send letters to Italy to prepare his partisans.

Now, when so many had rallied to him, he held a diet at Augsburg, in October. There he announced his intention to go to claim the Kingdom of Sicily that was his by right of birth, and he asked his friends and his subjects for their support. But, knowing the risks that he would run, he ordained that were he to die without posterity, his uncles of Bavaria were to inherit all that he possessed. His uncles did their best to dissuade him, but in vain. Carried away by his enthusiasm the diet decided that an expedition would set out for Italy at the end of the following summer to put him on his rightful throne.[1]

Pope Clement was by now well aware both of the flight of the refugees to Bavaria and the ambitions of the young Hohenstaufen prince. On 18 September 1266 he issued an anathema against anyone who should work to elect Conradin to the Imperial crown and anyone who should accompany him on an Italian campaign. Two months later a formal Bull threatened with excommunication and the confiscation of his goods anyone who should admit Conradin's authority or even receive his agents. He had heard that the Florentine Ghibellines were in touch with Conradin. He was sufficiently alarmed to allow Charles a free hand in restoring the Guelf position in northern and central Italy. By the summer of 1267 it seemed that the situation was well under control. There was, it is true, trouble brewing in Sicily itself; and he wished that Charles would give up the attempt to finish off the last centres of Ghibelline resistance in Tuscany and would return to his Kingdom. He did not expect any trouble from across the Alps. On 15 September 1267 he wrote to Charles to say that he did not believe now that Conradin would invade Italy. At that moment Conradin's army was already marching through the Tyrolean valleys towards the Brenner Pass.[2]

Pope Clement's optimism was short-lived. On 17 September he wrote again to Charles, to tell him now that the island of Sicily was in full revolt and that troops had arrived there from

Tunis. At Conradin's behest Conrad Capece had undertaken the dangerous mission of returning to the island, where he had been Manfred's vicar, and rousing it against the Angevins. The Sicilians had not much liked Manfred, but they disliked the attentions of Charles's tax-collectors still more. Capece found a willing response to his intrigues. He then made contact with the Infant Frederick and his fellow-refugees in Tunis. The Tunisian king gave them arms; and they sailed over to help in the revolt. The Pope was also disquieted by the news from Rome. The Infant Henry, as senator, had already aroused his displeasure by occupying various towns in the Campagna and by attacking some of Charles's castles on the frontier. But, though Charles suspected Henry's future intentions, Clement was unwilling to provoke him into open hostility. He could not, he told Charles, organize a revolt in Rome; the Romans were terrified of the senator, and it would cost too much money. He could only suggest Charles made peace with Henry by restoring to him the money that he had borrowed from him in 1266. Charles's suspicions were justified. In mid-October Henry declared himself. He was already in touch with his brother in Sicily. He now received a visit from Galvano Lancia, who came straight from Conradin with a small body of troops. They had made their way swiftly and secretly across Italy and arrived in Rome on 18 October. They entered the city with the eagle banner of the Hohenstaufen proudly flying and were ceremoniously received by the senator. He installed them in the Lateran palace. A few days later a messenger left Rome bearing a letter of welcome from the senator to Conradin, including, as Henry fancied himself as a poet, an exhortation in rather indifferent verse.[1]

Clement was in despair. In the vain hope of winning back Rome he waited for a month before breaking definitely with the senator. It was not till November that he formally denounced him and only the following April that he excommunicated him and all Conradin's supporters in the city. Sicily was now in the hands of the rebels. Only Palermo and Messina were still held by Charles's vicar, and the Saracens at Lucera had joined the revolt, which was spreading into Calabria. But Charles himself insisted on staying in Tuscany. Even when Poggibonsi fell at last, at the end of November, he went on to isolate Siena by the capture of Volterra, then, in January 1268, turned against Pisa. He captured and sacked Porto Pisano, dismantling its walls and interrupting for a time the whole of the Pisan maritime trade. At last, in March, he listened to the Pope's frantic pleading and marched southward from Florence. He paused to visit Clement at Viterbo and to receive investiture from him as Imperial Vicar of Lombardy. Once back in his Kingdom he set out against the Saracen rebels at Lucera, determined to crush them before Conradin should approach.[1]

Conradin, following the time-table that he had made at Augsburg the previous year, left Bavaria in mid-September 1267. His army was not large, numbering probably less than four thousand horsemen, drawn from his own ancestral lands and those of his kinsfolk. There was practically no infantry; and he had not the money to spare for many mercenaries. The men were eager enough; but, with the exception of Frederick of Baden, the German princes on whom the young King relied for support were half-hearted and discouraging. They would accompany him across the Alps, but they would not promise to follow him on rash adventures into the south. His uncles to the last begged him to hold back. His mother, when he bade farewell to her in the castle of Hohenschwangau, could not conceal her fears. But he was determined; and his determination was fanned by the Italians who had joined him. His personal entourage and secretariat was almost exclusively Italian; many of his staff were Sicilians, introduced to him by Peter of Prezze.

Before he left Germany he issued a manifesto, written in Peter of Prezze's most hyperbolic style. In it his rights as the legitimate heir of the Hohenstaufen were proclaimed, the Pope's pretensions were severely trounced, and Manfred himself was denounced as an unscrupulous usurper.[1]

The army moved slowly through the Tyrol and over the Brenner, pausing at Bolzano and at Trent. On 21 October 1267 it arrived at Verona, the great Ghibelline city of the north. There Conradin remained for three months. The reason for his delay is unknown. It may be that he wished to give time for Ghibellines from all over Italy to join him. It may be that he hoped that the revolt of the Sicilians and of the Saracens of Lucera would draw Charles southward and leave all Italy open to him. Or it may be that he hoped that his ally, the Infant Henry, would march northward from Rome. Henry was very active during these months. His agents were working in Tuscany, where Pisa and Siena still defied King Charles. On 1 December the Ghibellines of Tuscany made a solemn treaty with the Senator. Of its three clauses the first announced that the Tuscan League elected Henry as its captain-general for five years. He was to have an annual salary of 10,000 Pisan pounds as well as the pay for 200 Spanish horsemen. In return he was to supply for the Tuscan communes at their expense, whenever they desired it, a force of 2000 horsemen. But the Ghibellines did not entirely trust Henry; they added that, should he break with Conradin, the clause would be invalid. The second clause gave Henry the right to occupy all the Imperial lands in Tuscany, which were not, in fact, the Tuscan League's to offer. Even so, the rights and possessions of the Tuscan cities, including those that were at present Guelf, were carefully reserved. Charles of Anjou was denounced as a public enemy who must be driven from Tuscany. The third clause associated the city of Rome with its senator in the treaty. The Pope vainly declared the treaty null. So long, indeed, as Charles and his army remained in Tuscany, the Ghibellines could do little. But meanwhile Ghibelline soldiers flocked to join Henry in Rome.[2]

Conradin left Verona on 17 January. The Sicilian revolt and the Pope's prayers had not yet persuaded Charles to withdraw from Tuscany. Indeed, Charles was toying with the idea of meeting Conradin in Lombardy, but he did not like to cross the Apennines till he was more sure of the Tuscans. Though Charles's movements were still uncertain Conradin could not afford to wait. The Veronese, friendly though they were, could not be expected to house an army for much longer. The troops themselves were restive. The Duke of Bavaria refused to go further and had already returned home. His example was followed by many lesser German lords, including the most ambitious of them all, Rudolph of Habsburg. The Italian Ghibellines were beginning to show impatience. Conradin had already made one attempt to set out across Lombardy; but a Guelf army had driven him back. Now his movements were unopposed; the Torriani of Milan, who had prepared to challenge him, remained behind their city walls. After a forced march of three days he reached the second great Ghibelline city of the north, Pavia. He paused there for a few weeks, making ready for the next stage, to Pisa. It was at this moment that Charles moved out of Lombardy. Conradin himself, with a few companions, left the army. Thanks to a deliberately blind eye turned on him by the Marquis of Montferrat and the open friendship of the Marquis of Carretto, the husband of one of Frederick II's illegitimate daughters, he was able to cross the Ligurian Alps to Savona, on the coast. From there he sailed in a Pisan boat on 29 March. On 7 April he arrived at Pisa and was received with royal honours. On 2 May he was rejoined by his army. Ably led by Frederick of Baden it had crossed over the Apennines by a pass more westerly than had been expected and had met with no opposition.

At Pisa Conradin received a constant stream of Ghibelline soldiers and Ghibelline gold. In return, acting as though he were Emperor-designate, the young King gave privileges to his faithful allies. Pisa was to receive all the rights that it had ever possessed in the Sicilian Kingdom, as well as the towns of Trapani, Marsala and Salerno and the islands of Ischia and Malta. From Pisa he made an attempt to attack Lucca; but Charles's lieutenant in Tuscany, John of Brayselve, barred his way. He left Pisa on 15 June to march to Siena. Poggibonsi, which had already revolted against its Angevin garrison and sent him the city keys, gave him a warm welcome. On 25 June he arrived at Siena. That same day some of his troops, reconnoitring further east, came upon John of Brayselve as his army was crossing the river Arno at Ponte a Valle, not far from Arezzo. The Frenchmen were taken by surprise and John was captured. Conradin stayed about ten days at Siena. The city was rewarded for its loyalty by the gift of the right to levy tolls and administer justice throughout the district. From Siena the army marched down the old Via Cassia to Rome. The road took them past the walls of Viterbo, where Pope Clement was living. According to the legend the Pope sat at a high window in his palace to watch them pass, muttering hopefully that the lamb was being led to the slaughter.

Conradin's arrival at Rome on 24 July was greeted with scenes of hysterical enthusiasm. Never had the papal city given so tumultuous a welcome to an avowed enemy of the Holy See. Crowds met him singing hymns of praise and flinging flowers before his path. The streets were hung with silks and satins. Everyone was in gala dress. There were games in the Campus Martius and torchlight processions by night. The boy-King, with his beauty and his charm, was treated almost as a god. If the great Guelf nobles were absent, watching cautiously from behind the walls of their castles in the Campagna, no one noticed or cared. The Ghibellines were there in force, their numbers increasing every day; and the senator Henry presided genially over the festivities, assuring the king of his unswerving devotion.[1]

To the Pope at Viterbo the news that came from Rome was bitterly hurtful. Neither he nor his successors for many years could quite forgive the city. They blamed Henry for it most of all. Never again, Clement vowed, should a foreigner be allowed to be senator.[2]

Conradin enjoyed his triumph in Rome for just three weeks. On 14 August full of hope he led his army out to conquer the Kingdom. It had swollen in size. He now commanded about six thousand men, all of them trained horsemen. With banners flying they moved along the Via Valeria, past Tivoli, into the Sabine hills.

When he heard that Conradin was at Rome Charles lifted the siege of Lucera, where he had vainly tried to force the Saracens to surrender, and marched swiftly through the mountains to the neighbourhood of Avezzano, where he arrived on 4 August. He had calculated rightly that Conradin would make for Apulia, through the country round the Fucine Lake, where the chief Lancia estates were situated; for Conradin would naturally seek the districts where he had friends, while the direct road to Naples was well fortified. On 9 August Charles was at Scurcola, where the road between Tagliacozzo and Avezzano crosses the little river Salto. Then he moved north-eastward a few miles and encamped on the hill of Ovindoli, which commanded the only road between Avezzano and Apulia. Conradin could not pass through to Apulia without his knowledge.[1]

Conradin had paused at Vicocaro, a village belonging to the Ghibelline branch of the Orsini, then at the castle of Saracinesco, where Galvano Lancia's daughter, the wife of Conrad of Antioch, entertained him. From there he moved to Carsoli. There the Via Valeria turns south-east over the Monk Bove pass to Tagliacozzo. Conradin knew now that Charles was not far off; so, not wishing to be caught in a narrow valley, he made a sweep to the north, leading his army over a series of mule-paths which brought it down into the valley of the Salto just below Scurcola. He had thus avoided the defiles of Tagliacozzo; but Charles was still in front of him, blocking his way. All that he had gained by the arduous march over the hills was that his army could now fight the decisive battle in a plain, where the heavy German cavalry could be used to some effect.

Conradin established his camp at Scurcola on 22 August 1268. A few hours later Charles and his army arrived and encamped on the other side of the river Salto. When he had learnt of Conradin's route through the hills he had broken his camp at Ovindoli and regrouped his troops at Avezzano, then advanced along the Via Valeria to the river. He knew the plain of Scurcola from having encamped there a fortnight earlier. He was prepared to do battle there. There was a slight indeterminate skirmish between the two vanguards during the afternoon; but both sides wanted to rest, to prepare for the decisive combat on the morrow.

That evening, alarmed perhaps by rumours of spies in the camp, Conradin gave orders that his prisoner, John of Brayselve, whom he had kept with the army, should be summarily put to death. It was against the custom of the time to kill an enemy captured in battle; and Conradin's followers were shocked.

The battle, known in history as the battle of Tagliacozzo, though Tagliacozzo itself lay five miles behind Conradin's lines, began in the morning of Thursday, 23 August. As at Benevento two years before, each army was divided into three corps. Conradin's first corps straddled the road on the west bank of the Salto. It was commanded by the Infant Henry and consisted of his Spanish cavalry and Ghibelline troops from Rome and the Campagna. Behind it was the second corps, made up of the Ghibelline troops from Lombardy and Tuscany and the refugees from the Kingdom, and amongst them a few of the heavy German cavalry. The rest of the German troops were in the reserve corps, under the two boy-princes, Conradin himself and Frederick of Baden. Charles's army was a little smaller, numbering about five thousand cavalrymen in comparison with Conradin's six thousand; but it was composed of veterans who had fought constantly with Charles during the last two years, men whom he knew and trusted. His first corps, consisting of Italian Guelf and Provençal troops, straddled the main road on the east side of the river. Its commander's name is not recorded. The second corps contained the bulk of Charles's French troops, under the Marshal Henry of Cousances. Charles intended that corps to be regarded by the enemy as the reserve; and, as it was usual for the commander-in-chief to stay with the reserve, he gave Henry of Cousances his surcoat to wear and the royal banner to be carried by his standard-bearer. Charles himself, with the actual reserve, nearly a thousand of his best horsemen, remained nearly a mile behind his right flank, hidden from the enemy by the fold of a hill. With him was a veteran soldier just home from a crusade, the Chamberlain of France, Érard of Saint-Valéry. Between the two armies flowed the little river Salto. In the height of summer not much water was flowing; but the dyked banks and the marshy bed made it awkward to cross at places, particularly near the bridge that carried the main road over the stream.

Early in the morning the Infant Henry and his corps rode in good order towards the bridge. In a vain attempt to lull the enemy's suspicions, he ordered his camp-followers to start preparing a camp near the river, as though he did not mean to fight that day. Suddenly, at about nine o'clock, his horsemen sprang into the saddle and charged at the bridge. Charles's first corps was already there to meet them; and his second corps, under Henry of Cousances, moved up behind, to be ready to cross with them over the bridge when the Infant's men should be driven back. In the excitement of the fighting the Frenchmen did not notice that half the Infant's corps had been detached and with Galvano Lancia's corps had moved southward up the river. About half a mile above the bridge the banks flattened and the water widened into a shallow pool, making an easy ford. The Ghibelline troops thundered across and charged down on to the left flank of the Angevin army. Their onslaught was quite unexpected. While Galvano attacked Henry of Cousances on the flank the Italians and Provençals of the first Angevin corps fell back from the bridge, and the Infant was able to cross. It seemed that victory was assured for Conradin. The slaughter among the Angevins was terrible. Henry of

Cousances, mistaken for King Charles, was struck down and the royal banner captured. After his death the remnants of the Angevin army fled from the field. When Conradin and his horsemen rode up to administer the *coup de grâce*, it seemed no longer necessary. The Infant Henry and Galvano were in full pursuit of the fugitives. Some of Galvano's men had turned aside to plunder the Angevin camp, where they were joined by many of Conradin's Germans. The boy-king was left on the battlefield with only a small following.

Charles, lurking in his hiding-place, was appalled by the disaster. He thought for a moment of charging out to rescue his men; but Érard of Saint-Valéry pointed out to him that he was too far off. He would arrive too late and would merely reveal his position. If he waited, the victorious enemy would almost certainly scatter in search of plunder. So he held back until he saw the battlefield empty except for the small group clustered round the Hohenstaufen banners. Then he led his men at full gallop out of their ambush. Conradin's knights had no idea at first that the horsemen galloping across the plain were an undefeated body of the enemy. By the time that they understood what was happening it was too late. They were unprepared and outnumbered. After a fierce struggle Conradin's friends persuaded him to fly while still he could. Together with Frederick of Baden and his personal bodyguard he rode off at full speed along the road to Rome. His standard-bearer was slain on the field and his eagle-banner captured. Most of his knights were slain. Conrad of Antioch, who attempted to rally them, was taken prisoner.

Seeing their king's banner fall, the Germans and the Ghibellines who had been plundering the Angevin camp dispersed and made their escape. But the Infant Henry and Galvano were still in command of an unbeaten army. It seems that Henry as he climbed out of the valley on the road to Apulia in pursuit of his victims, looked back and realized the truth. He turned and regrouped his men, and rode back with them into the plain. His corps was still more numerous than Charles's; but the men and their horses were tired after the long day's fighting; and in the summer heat the Germans in their heavy plate armour suffered more than the French in their chain-mail. Moreover, they had a long way to ride, in full view of the enemy. Charles had time to allow his men to take off their helmets and rest for a while before he drew them up to meet the onset. Even so the Ghibelline ranks were so formidable that Érard of Saint-Valéry counselled a feigned retreat. With Charles's permission he took a company of French horse to the rear, as though he were leaving the field in despair. In spite of Henry's warning the Ghibellines were deceived and broke their ranks, some to pursue Érard and others to attack the King. At first sight the Angevin army seemed to be engulfed; but when Érard swerved back and hand-to-hand fighting began, the Ghibellines faltered. The Infant attempted to detach them and rally them for one more charge. But the horses were exhausted and even the men were too weary to raise their arms to strike. Their efforts flickered out. Soon all whose horses still could carry them had ridden in flight off the field, leaving their comrades to be butchered. After a disastrous opening Charles had won a complete and unequivocal victory.

That night Charles sat down to write to the Pope. With a taste that still jars down the centuries, he began his letter with the words of Esau, taken from the Scriptures. 'Let my father arise', he wrote, 'and eat of his son's venison, that thy soul may bless me.' He then described the battle, passing lightly over its opening stages and minimizing his heavy losses. Triumphantly he ended by saying: 'We have killed such a multitude of the enemy that their defeat at Benevento was nothing in comparison. As we are writing this letter immediately after the battle we cannot yet say whether Conradin and the senator Henry are dead or fugitives. It is certain that the senator's horse was taken, while he fled on foot.'[1]

In fact most of his leading enemies had survived the battle.

Conrad of Antioch was a prisoner in his hands. The Infant Henry, the senator, took refuge in the Convent of San Salvatore, on the road to Rieti. There he was identified and captured. Conradin himself rode to Rome, where he arrived with Frederick of Baden and some fifty knights on 28 August. The senator Henry had left as his deputy in Rome a Ghibelline lord of Urbino, Guy of Montefeltro; but Guy, whose subsequent career as a gallant condottiere was based on a prudent dislike for fallen friends, had already heard of the battle. He refused to receive Conradin and shut the gates of the Capitol in his face. The boy was warned that he had better leave the city, to which Guy was already admitting the Guelfs. Conradin and his company rode back along the Via Valeria, hoping somehow to escape through the mountains and join the rebels in Apulia. At Saracinesco Conrad of Antioch's wife entertained them again, and they found her father, Galvano Lancia, taking refuge there. There they changed their plans; there were too many of Charles's agents guarding the road to the east. Instead, with Galvano, they set out southward across the Campagna to the little sea-port of Astura, in the Pontine marshes, where they hoped to find a boat to take them to Genoa. The local lord, John Frangipane, heard that mysterious strangers had arrived. He sent to arrest them and found that he had in his power Conradin, Frederick of Baden, Galvano Lancia and several of the high Roman Ghibelline nobility. He imprisoned them in a neighbouring castle. A few days later Charles's admiral, Robert of Lavena, arrived with Cardinal Jordan of Terracina, to demand in the names of the King and the Pope that the prisoners should be surrendered to him. They were taken first to Palestrina. There Galvano Lancia was executed as a traitor, with one of his sons and several Italian Ghibellines. Conradin and Frederick of Baden were moved to Naples, to the island Castello dell' Uovo.[1]

Charles felt no mercy. The clemency that he had shown after his victory at Benevento had failed in its purpose. He was not going to be so weak again. Of his prisoners Conrad of Antioch was released, not because he was considered less guilty or traitorous than the others but because his wife held in her dungeons at Saracinesco several important Guelf noblemen, the kinsfolk of cardinals; and she threatened to put them to death unless her husband were restored to her. The Infant Henry was too well-connected to be slain. The courts of France and England both put in pleas on his behalf. But, though his life was spared, he spent twenty-three years in prison. The chief problem was the disposal of Conradin himself.[1]

According to legend, Pope Clement urged the boy's death. The words 'Vita Conradini, mors Caroli: vita Caroli, mors Conradini', were attributed to him. In any case Charles had decided that Conradin must die. He would never be safe on his throne so long as a Hohenstaufen prince lived; and Conradin's boyish charm made him all the more dangerous. But Charles was a legalist. If he were so to outrage the custom of the time by putting a captive enemy prince to death, he must have legal backing. Lawyers were ordered to prepare an indictment against Conradin. His invasion of the Kingdom was branded as an act of robbery and treason. Later apologists of the Angevins have arraigned Conradin as a war-criminal for his execution of John of Brayselve, which had indeed been contrary to the custom of the time; but it was not mentioned and could hardly be dismissed as simple murder. Charles's judges knew what was expected of them. After a short process they pronounced Conradin guilty, and with him his friend Frederick of Baden, whose only crime had been loyalty. Both were sentenced to decapitation. A scaffold was erected on the Campo Moricino in Naples, the site of the present Piazza del Mercato. There, on 29 October 1268, Conradin and Frederick were publicly beheaded, with a number of their followers. It was the only glimpse that the Neapolitans had of the lovely sixteen-year-old boy who might have been their king. They never forgot him.

Conradin's trial and death shocked the conscience of Europe. To Dante, writing half a century later, Conradin was an innocent victim. Even the Pope, glad though he was to see the extinction of the viper's brood, was deeply distressed. The Guelf historian Villani was desperately anxious to free Clement's memory from all suspicion of complicity. To this day Charles is generally condemned, even by Frenchmen eager to excuse one of the ablest of the Sons of France. To the Germans it has always been the greatest crime in history. Centuries later the poet Heine wrote of it with bitterness. But Charles was a realist who believed that the end justified the means. With Conradin dead he thought that he could reign secure.[1]

CHAPTER VIII

KING CHARLES OF SICILY

Two great victories had ensured Charles his kingdom. There were no Hohenstaufen princes left to dispute it with him. Manfred's three young sons were still living, but they were securely held in a Neapolitan prison. In Germany a young Landgrave of Thuringia, Frederick of Misnia, whose mother had been Frederick II's daughter, claimed to be heir of the dynasty and assumed for a time the resounding titles of King of Sicily and Jerusalem; but no one took him very seriously. The King of Castile vaunted from time to time his Hohenstaufen blood; but he had too many other interests to challenge Charles. Moreover his brother, the Infant Henry, was Charles's captive; and, though King Alfonso had no liking for his brother, the family pride of the Castilian House would not allow him to risk the Infant's life. More ominously, Manfred's elder daughter, Constance, was living at Barcelona as the wife to the heir of Aragon; but her old father-in-law, King James, did not include the conquest of Sicily among his many ambitions.[1]

King Charles could settle down to enjoy his kingdom and to plan further conquests. 'King Charles', sang his troubadour, Peter of Castelnau, 'will be lord of the greatest part of the world. It belongs to him and it is fitting for him.'[2] Conradin's execution in no way troubled his conscience. A few days after the boy was beheaded, the town of Trani was bedecked for the King's second marriage. The new Queen of Sicily, Margaret of Burgundy, was not so great an heiress as her predecessor Beatrice had been; but she had a comfortable property in central France, including the cities of Auxerre and Tonnerre and several baronies. Unfortunately the marriage was childless, and on the Queen's death the lands passed back to her own kin. Having thus added to his dominions in France, King Charles set about reaffirming his control of Italy.[1]

Pope Clement's conscience had not been as untroubled as the King's. Exactly one month after Conradin's execution he died at Viterbo, on 29 November 1268. The Ghibellines saw in his death the avenging hand of God; and it seems certain that his last days were darkened by fears for the future.[2] The champion of the Church was showing all too clearly that he did not intend to be its servant. Rome, which the Papacy had determined should never have another foreign senator, returned to Charles's control soon after the battle of Tagliacozzo. On 12 September 1268 he wrote to King Louis to announce that the Romans had unanimously elected him senator for life. The letter was disingenuous. Unanimity had been secured by the exile or flight of the Ghibellines, while later, when the Papacy was in a position to question his tenure, he admitted that the term was in fact for ten years only. He went at once to Rome and spent the last fortnight of September reorganizing its administration. Though a senate of Roman notables was retained to act in an advisory capacity, the Romans were allowed no autonomy. He kept tight hold of the city's finances. Coins were struck in his own names, and the city's revenues were paid into a municipal treasury, the Camera Urbana, whose treasurer he appointed. He organized a police-force, for which he built towers to overawe the fortified palaces of the nobles. He appointed palatine judges to deal with the various branches of the law, and a palatine Chief Justice to hear appeals. A number of regulations ensured the proper revictualment of the city and the exploitation of the Campagna. He even thought of founding a university for the Romans. Charles himself seldom visited Rome again, except for two months in the spring of 1272, when the election of a new Pope and a reorientation of papal policy caused him some concern about the city. His control was exercised through a vicar with full vice-regal powers who held the appointment for one year. Apart from two Neapolitans

Charles regularly appointed a Frenchman to the post. His rule was too authoritarian to be popular; but the average Roman, weary of the factions and riots that had tormented the city since the death of Pope Innocent III half a century before, was grateful for the restoration of order. The statue of Charles which was erected on the Capitol in about the year 1270 was a token of this gratitude.[1]

His task in Rome, and in all Italy, was made easier by the death of Pope Clement. Though the cardinals promptly met at Viterbo to elect a successor, they could not agree amongst themselves. A long series of conclaves was held without any result; for nearly three years the Papacy was vacant. Pope Clement had appointed a number of his compatriots to the College; and these French cardinals blocked the election of an Italian, while the Italian cardinals were determined, in view of Charles's power, not to endure another French Pope. The vacancy was so convenient to Charles that it is hard to doubt that he did his best to prolong it through his influence on the French party; but officially he kept himself clear of the discussions. The absence of a Pope meant that there was no authority that could restrict Charles's power at Rome nor his influence in the papal states in central Italy.[2]

Equally satisfactory for Charles was the vacancy in the Empire. There had been no Emperor since Frederick II's death in 1250. His son Conrad never had secured an Imperial coronation, nor had the anti-King William of Holland, nor yet the subsequent candidates, Richard of Cornwall and Alfonso of Castile. In the absence of an Emperor the Pope had claimed the right to appoint to the Imperial vicariates in Italy; Clement had nominated Charles as Imperial Vicar in Tuscany; and now there was neither Pope nor Emperor to dispute his title. He made full use of it. For some time Charles was too busy in his own Kingdom to visit Tuscany himself; but there was no need for his personal intervention. The Ghibellines had been disconcerted by Conradin's defeat. It was only in their traditional strongholds of Siena and Pisa that they were able to maintain themselves. The other Tuscan cities passed back into Guelf hands. In the spring of 1269 Charles appointed a Frenchman, John Britaud, as his vicar in Tuscany; and on 17 June Britaud and the Florentine Guelfs won a resounding victory over the Sienese at Colle. Siena itself held out against Charles's forces for another year; but in August 1270 it submitted. The Ghibellines were driven out, and the Guelf lords, who had spent their long exile at Florence, took over the city and brought it into the Florentine sphere of influence. It was the end of Sienese greatness. Charles had already brought Pisa to terms. An alliance with the Genoese, who were perpetually jealous of the Pisans, enabled him to isolate Pisa by sea; and by the defeat of Siena it lost its only potential ally by land. In the spring of 1270 the Pisans sued for peace. They were granted gentle terms. They were not obliged to swear allegiance to Charles; they could elect their own Podestà, provided that he was a Guelf and came from a Guelf city; and it was expressly stated that the treaty would come to an end as soon as a new Emperor was crowned, when Charles's Imperial vicariate would automatically end. The treaty was arranged on Charles's behalf by his deputy, Guy of Montfort, the son of Simon, Earl of Leicester. On his father's death in 1265 he had taken refuge with Charles, whom he had accompanied to Italy; and he now was amongst the King's closest friends.

By the end of 1270 all Tuscany was under Charles's control. He was accepted as lord by most of its cities; and the authority of his representative in the province was generally recognized, though his powers varied from place to place. Charles could afford to be easy-going with Tuscany, now that Conradin was dead. So long as he held Piedmont and Lombardy, no invader would penetrate into central Italy. All that was needed was to see that the Guelfs maintained their supremacy there. The Tuscans benefited from his good will, as it enabled their merchants to penetrate his southern kingdom. Tuscan merchants and Tuscan bankers, working in conjunction, from Florence and to a lesser degree from Lucca and Siena, had already captured much of the commerce going to north-west Europe. Now they could extend their operations as far south as Sicily and capture much of the trade from the East, to the detriment of the maritime Italian cities, in particular Genoa, which began to regret its alliance with Charles.[1]

In Piedmont Charles could feel secure. There, in contrast to the rest of Italy, the old feudal families still kept their position. The most prominent of them, the Count of Savoy and the Marquis of Montferrat, were unfriendly towards him; but their attitude made the lesser lords, who preferred a distant suzerain to a powerful neighbour, the more ready to accept his overlordship, and his vassals were so placed as to give him an easy road from Provence into Lombardy.[2]

Lombardy presented a more difficult problem. Conradin's defeat had naturally confirmed the Guelf possession of most of its cities; but Verona and Pavia remained obstinately Ghibelline, while the Guelfs, who had anyhow made no great effort to oppose Conradin, showed some distaste, now that the German danger was over, towards the idea of Angevin domination. The tendency of the times in Lombardy was for the communal organization of the city to be superseded by the rule of a lord; and the new lords, Guelfs though many of them might be, were even less willing than the Communes to admit an active overlord. Charles, however, intended to establish an overlordship throughout northern Italy.

The months that followed Conradin's defeat were filled with petty wars and intrigues. The Ghibellines of Pavia for a while made friends with the Guelf lords of Milan. Pallavicini's attempts to recover Parma and Piacenza led to a series of skirmishes in the course of which he died. Charles was too busy in the south to intervene at first. But in May 1269 he wrote to the municipal chiefs in Parma suggesting that they should lead a vigorous campaign against all Conradin's former supporters; and he followed his letter up with one to the Prior of the Dominicans there, asking him to organize a league of the faithful in Lombardy against the enemies of the Church and against any descendant of Frederick II. He was perhaps afraid that Frederick of Thuringia might seriously contemplate an invasion of Italy. About the same time he announced to all the Lombard cities that he was sending a new seneschal to Lombardy, Walter of La Roche. It seems that the seneschal was not very well received. A few months later, in October, Charles sent the Archbishop of Santa Severina to organize the partisans of the Church; and that same month representatives of all the Lombard cities were summoned to meet Charles's officials at a diet at Cremona. There they were all of them asked openly to admit Charles as their lord. Their reply was far from unanimous. The cities south of the Po, with the exception of Bologna, Alessandria and Tortona, agreed, but Milan and its neighbours flatly refused. One or two of the dissidents consented to take an oath of fidelity to Charles later, in December, but it was clear that Lombardy was no longer prepared to submit to Angevin domination. Nevertheless, Charles continued to appoint seneschals for Lombardy, all of them Frenchmen and none of them in office for long, who threatened any city which appeared insubordinate. In several cities, such as Ivrea, he nominated the Podestà; in others, such as Piacenza or Alessandria, he drew up a list of persons from among whom the citizens might elect their Podestà. But in fact his influence was diminishing; and his use of French officials lost him the general sympathy of the Italians. The growing hatred of the French fortified the resistance of the remaining Ghibelline cities. In Pavia innocent French pilgrims were molested just because of their nationality; and the Dominican convent was sacked because a few of the friars were French.[1]

The Ghibellines, indeed, hoped for help from abroad. In August 1269 Frederick of Thuringia wrote to the Ghibelline leader, Ubertino of Anditò, to announce that he would shortly invade Italy, and in October he informed Pavia that his expedition would consist of four thousand knights and a long list of German barons. During the same summer an agent from Alfonso of Castile, working with the approval of the Infant Peter of Aragon, Manfred's son-in-law, made contact with the Lombard Ghibellines, who responded by sending an ambassador from Pavia to the Castilian court. The Ghibellines hopefully encouraged both Frederick and Alfonso, believing that the former only wanted the Sicilian kingdom and the latter only the Empire, and that their interests would not therefore clash. This was true as regards Frederick and Alfonso; but Peter had joined Alfonso with his wife's claims to Sicily clearly in his mind. However, neither invasion took place. In July 1271 the city of Pavia and the Marquis of Montferrat, who was now openly Ghibelline, induced three Italian cardinals, the most vigorous opponents of the French in the College, to visit Frederick in Germany and ask why he was so late in coming. He replied by nominating a vicar-general to represent him in Italy. But his nominee, the Count of Treffurt, only journeyed as far as Verona. He was well received; but after staying there for a few idle weeks, he returned to Germany. Alfonso of Castile was slightly more active, at least on paper. He proposed sending two thousand knights to Lombardy and suggested a series of complicated alliances, intended to encircle Charles. He even went so far as to marry one of his daughters to William of Montferrat. The marriage took place in Spain in October 1271; and the Marquis returned to Italy with the title of Imperial Vicar. Unfortunately the petty wars that he conducted thenceforward in his father-in-law's name against his Guelf neighbours were uniformly unsuccessful.[1]

Charles had, therefore, no cause to be seriously disquieted by the situation in Lombardy, in spite of the decline in his influence. It was more important for him and for his further ambitions that his own Kingdom should be securely held and exploited to the full. The victory at Tagliacozzo had not ended his troubles there.

Sicily was still in revolt, and the Saracens at Lucera still defied him. But the rebels could not hope for any serious help from abroad now. Indeed, in some of the cities of Apulia and Basilicata, such as Potenza, Gallipoli and Aversa, which had been trembling on the brink of rebellion, the news of Charles's victory incited the citizens loyal to him to massacre all Conradin's known supporters there. Such of the rebels as could escape joined the Saracens at Lucera. That great fortress held out for several months against Charles's generals. It was only in April 1269 that Charles came in person to conduct the siege; and even under his leadership his men could make no effect against its walls. But the blockade was tightened. At last, on 28 August 1269, the garrison was forced by starvation to surrender. The lives of the Saracens were spared; they were merely scattered by families round the King's dominions, and deprived of their arms. But the Christian rebels captured in the fortress were all put to death.[1]

The revolt in Sicily lasted a little longer. Conrad Capece, who commanded the rebels, tried to persuade Frederick of Thuringia to come to his help, but in vain. But he had the support of the islanders; and Charles's general, Thomas of Coucy, could do little more than hold Palermo and Messina. Charles next sent Philip and Guy of Montfort, with reinforcements. They managed to capture the rebel city of Augusta, between Catania and Syracuse, and put it to the sack. The inhabitants who survived the swords of the soldiers were summarily tortured and executed. In August 1269 William l'Estandart was appointed to the Sicilian command; and within a year he had brought the island under control. The Infant Frederick and Frederick Lancia were forced to surrender at Girgenti, but were allowed to make their escape to Tunis. The main rebel army was defeated at Sciacca, the fortress where Conrad Capece had his headquarters. Capece himself fled to the castle of Centuripa, in the centre of the island, but he was captured there in the early spring of 1270. He was taken with his brothers, Marino and James, to Naples, where they were beheaded.[2]

The punishment meted out to the rebels throughout the whole Kingdom was severe, even by the standards of the time. Charles ordered his officials to spare no one who was taken in arms. Those who surrendered must voluntaily submit themselves to the decision of the King, but if they preferred, their cases might be taken before the High Court. But Conradin's fate had shown what the judgement of the Court would always be. In cities where the rebels had been in control, an amnesty was allowed to citizens who had not borne arms against the King; but any Germans, Spaniards or Pisans amongst them had to leave the country at once. Property belonging to the rebels was confiscated. At first their wives were allowed to keep their own estates and goods; but then Charles seems to have suspected that they were sending money to their exiled husbands. Their possessions were therefore sequestered and they were each given an exiguous pension. But exceptions were made; and it was soon decided that widows should have their property returned. These repressive measures were all the more intolerable to the easy-going Italians because they were enforced with meticulous care and because the King's agents were almost all of them Frenchmen. They were remarkably effective. Order was soon restored throughout the Kingdom, even in Sicily. But they left a legacy of bitter hatred in the island.[1]

Nor was Charles's governmental policy of a sort to win the affections of the islanders. He had at first taken over Manfred's administration with very little change. But after Conradin's invasion and the rebellions, he reorganized the Kingdom after the French model and saw to it that the important positions were given to Frenchmen whom he could trust. His followers were rewarded with fiefs. It was done with a show of legality. He refused to recognize that either Manfred or Conrad or Frederick II after his formal deposition by the Pope in 1245 had lawfully been King of Sicily. The grants made by each of them were therefore void. All landowners had to show their title-deeds and prove that their lands had been granted before 1245. Many of the older families had long since lost their deeds or had never had them officially registered; many others' grants had been registered or re-registered under the 'usurpers'. Their lands were therefore forfeited; and these, combined with the lands confiscated from convicted rebels, provided the King with large areas to redistribute. Some 700 Frenchmen and Provençals were given fiefs out of the vacant lands, but Charles saw to it that none of the new fiefs were dangerously large, and he kept much of the land for the royal domain. In order both to keep the French colonists in the Kingdom and to prevent Italians from leaving it to plot abroad, a law was passed empowering the King to confiscate the estates of any feudatory who was absent from the Kingdom for more than one year. At the same time the cities, which had enjoyed municipal autonomy since Byzantine times, were brought into a feudal relationship with the Crown, either directly or through the chief vassals. Royal bailiffs or feudal constables now controlled all their more important activities. Only Naples and a few large cities in the north of the Kingdom preserved a Commune with some degree of political power; but they soon learnt to use their power with discretion.[1]

Charles retained the great offices of state that had existed in his predecessors' time. These officials were the Constable, in charge of the army, and the Admiral, in charge of the navy; the Chief Justice; the Protonotary-Logothete, at the head of the royal secretariat; the Chancellor, who was always a cleric and was chief registrar; the Chamberlain, the treasurer of the Kingdom; and the Seneschal, in charge of the royal domain. In 1259 he sub-divided the Protonotary's office, and after 1272 the Chancellor's office was left vacant and a Vice-Chancellor took charge of his work. Charles added two Marshals to help the Constable in the military administration. Each province was under the control of a Justiciar, who superintended the administration both of the officials on the royal domains and of the vassals; they were in particular responsible for local justice and local tax-collecting. King Charles prided himself on the excellence of the justice that he provided, and, except where political issues were at stake, his pride was justified. A mass of ordinances survive to show how severely officials guilty of oppression or of corruption were punished and how strict were the regulations against murder, banditry and theft and against any attempt to protect criminals. The civil courts also seem to have been efficient and unbiased. It was the duty of the Chief Justice to travel round the country, hearing appeals against the judgements of the provincial courts and complaints against the provincial Justiciar and his judges.[1]

In order to pursue his greater ambitions Charles was eager to exploit the wealth of the Kingdom to the full. His taxes were high. He kept roughly to the system of taxation organized by Frederick II. This included a number of indirect taxes, customs and harbour dues, duties on various raw materials and manufactured goods and on warehousing. But Frederick's main source of revenue had been his *subventio generalis*, a direct tax on property, which had been originally a feudal aid that could be levied in times of crisis for the defence of the realm but which the Emperor had transformed into a regular annual levy, its rate varying according to his immediate needs. His subjects bitterly resented the tax; and on his death-bed Frederick abolished it. When the Pope, in offering the throne to Charles, made it a condition that he should not oppress the Kingdom financially but should return to the system that existed under Good King William, it was this tax in particular that he had in mind. Charles needed money too badly to honour the condition. The sum to be levied from each province was decided yearly. It was for the Justiciar to collect it. After paying and strictly accounting for the expenses of his administration, he sent the rest to the central treasury. In 1277 Charles separated the Treasury from the Chamberlain's office and gave it a fixed seat in the Castello dell' Uovo at Naples. Charles also increased the number of feudal dues to be levied from his vassals; and he added to his income by a penal system in which fines and confiscation of goods were the most usual punishment.

All these taxes weighed heavily on his subjects. But King Charles was well aware that unless he increased their general prosperity the sums that they could raise would diminish. But he believed that the best method was strict state control. Private enterprise was not excluded, but it was hemmed round with regulations. Licences were needed before anything could be imported or exported. Inspectors and tax-collectors examined every detail of economic and commercial life. It is probable that Charles, like so many conquerors of southern Italy, believed the country to be naturally richer than it was and that he underestimated the southerners' individualism and their dislike of working hard for an alien master. Much of his activity was beneficial. He saw that commercial cases were fairly heard and expedited in the courts and gave protection to merchants against his over-zealous officials. He attempted to standardize weights and measures and to reform the coinage. A programme of public works was instituted. Roads were repaired, in particular the main road from Naples through Sulmona and the Abruzzi to Perugia and Florence, and the road from Naples through Benevento to Foggia and the Adriatic. Fairs and markets were founded. Especial care was given to the reconditioning and enlargement of seaports. Manfredonia, which King Manfred had begun, was completed. Barletta and Brindisi were enlarged; and for the latter Charles himself designed a new lighthouse. Improvements were carried out at Naples. The avowed object of these works at the ports was to attract foreign shipping because of the harbour dues that they would pay. Manfredonia in particular was considered likely to provide shelter for boats experiencing contrary weather in the Adriatic. Mining was encouraged. The silver mines on the royal domain at Longobucco in Calabria, opened in 1274, brought the treasury several hundreds of pounds of bullion annually, and the same year a private group was given permission to mine near Reggio, on condition of paying a third of their produce to the state. Charles was interested in agriculture. He introduced Barbary sheep from Africa for the sheep-ranches on the royal domain; and he took trouble to keep the state forests in good condition, chiefly because he needed the wood for ship-building. At the same time he protected the peasants. The bailiffs and foresters of the royal domain were not allowed to encroach on their lands; nor might the tax-collectors foreclose on their farming implements or beasts of burden should they fail to pay their taxes.

The King had other mercantile devices for raising his revenue. He built up a large fleet, and would hire out vessels to traders. He also, to the irritation of the southerners, encouraged merchants and bankers from abroad, particularly from Tuscany, to invade the country. They paid him well for the privilege; and he found them more enterprising and energetic than any of his subjects, with the exception of the Amalfitans. He did not, however, encourage Jews.[1]

In all this intricate administration the king himself took a deep personal interest. Surviving documents show with what care he mastered every detail and himself inspired the innumerable regulations issued by the court. No other medieval ruler, not even his brother King Louis, was so minutely concerned with all the activities of his government. Charles led a restless life, perpetually moving about his kingdom; and all his officials and secretaries had to follow him. This inevitably added to his restlessness, as no town could for long support so large an invasion of functionaries. It was only towards the end of his reign that he began to concentrate the government at Naples and to make of it a real capital. After 1269 he seldom went outside of the Kingdom, apart from several visits to Rome, one to Tuscany, and one to join King Louis's crusade at Tunis; and at the end of his life he revisited France. Except on his way to Tunis he never stopped in Sicily.[2]

Charles's rule was able and efficient. It provided order, justice and some prosperity. But it was never popular with his subjects. Temperamentally they disliked a government that was so meticulous, so pervasive and so authoritarian; and, most of all, they disliked it because it was foreign. Charles mistrusted Italians, particularly after 1258, and he employed as few as possible in responsible posts. All his leading officials were Provençal or French in origin. His high officers of state all came from France or Provence, with the exception of the Protonotary, whose post was vacant from 1269 to 1283. We know the names of 125 provincial Justiciars for the period from 1269 to the end of the reign. Of these only 25 seem to have been Italian. After the Treasury was separated from the Chancellor's office, one of the two treasurers had to be Italian; and there were certainly Italians in the royal secretariat and in lesser legal posts. This was necessary for linguistic reasons. But the King insisted that French should be the language of the government. As he and his chief ministers were all French-speaking, this was natural; but it was not calculated to please the Italians and Sicilians. Nor were they pleased by his bestowal of so many fiefs on Frenchmen nor by his planting of humbler French and Provençal colonists in their midst, such as the community that he settled at Lucera in place of the dispersed Saracens.[1]

If Charles noticed the discontent that his government aroused, he did not deign to pay attention to it. He knew himself to be an excellent administrator, and he seems to have thought that his subjects would be grateful to him because of the order that he established, and that if they showed their discontent by open action his police and his courts could deal with them. He did not forgive the island of Sicily for its long revolt; and it shared little of the benefits of his rule. None of its harbours received the attention given to those of the mainland, and its industries were given small encouragement. The royal estates on the island were well cared for, and the peasants there enjoyed the same protection as elsewhere in the realm. But the islanders were made to feel, more even than under the Hohenstaufen rulers, that they belonged to a mere province whose interests were of no importance in comparison with those of the mainland. It was unwise of Charles to show so little understanding of the Sicilians and of their capacity for remembering wrongs.[1]

Had Charles been dependent on his kingdom alone for his resources he might have been more circumspect. But he gained additional strength and confidence from his possessions outside Italy. In France itself he held the great appanage of Anjou and Maine. These two provinces were organized as a unit with their administration centred at Angers. At their head was a *bailli* appointed by Charles as Count, and under him a Receiver in charge of the central financial bureau. Much of the land consisted of Charles's personal estates and was managed by provosts and chatelains, who were responsible for local order and justice. The vassal lords in the two counties enjoyed the feudal rights usual in France at the time; but Charles's agents closely supervised them, and each of them was recommended to spend at least forty days of the year at Angers, under the *bailli's* eye. Charles was on good terms with the Church in France, but never allowed it to usurp any of his rights as Count. He was a dutiful and correct vassal himself to his brother, King Louis, keeping an agent at Paris to represent his interests. Though he never revisited his County, he was in close touch with all its affairs. Few appointments and no major decisions were made without his authority and a constant stream of couriers flowed between Angers and Paris and his Court in Italy. His second marriage brought him a third of the Counties of Nevers, Auxerre and Tonnerre, together with four small baronies scattered round northern France, Montmirail, Alluyes, Torigny and Brugny. These were administered with the same careful supervision from Italy; though after Charles's death the Dowager Queen Margaret returned to France and took charge of them herself.

The value of these French lands to Charles lay in the income that they brought to him. It has been calculated that his gross receipts from them reached an annual sum that was no less than one-fifth of his whole total receipts from the Italian Kingdom and that his net receipts came to a yearly average of rather more than 6000 gold ounces.[1]

Still more valuable was the County of Provence. Since 1257 Charles had had no trouble with the Provençals. They were now his favourite subjects, to whom he gave the best posts in his dominions; and they were well aware of the advantages of his rule. On his departure to Italy he had left the government of the County in the hands of a trusted friend, Adam of Luzarches, who later became Bishop of Sisteron. Adam was assisted by a seneschal, who was the chief minister and was advised by a council, nominated and frequently reconstituted by Charles himself, by a Chief Justice (the *juge-mage*), a Treasurer, and, later, a fiscal Advocate, together with junior ministers known as *maîtres-rationaux*. The seat of the government was at Aix. The County had been divided into a number of districts known as baileys, under a bailiff. Charles retained the bailiffs, but lessened their power by removing justice from their office and appointing a judge who also controlled finance for each bailey. The towns, all of which he had deprived of their earlier municipal independence, were put under provosts, or *viguiers*, who, like the bailiffs, were each assisted by a judge. Just as he avoided the employment of Italians in the Kingdom, so Charles appointed men from Anjou or Maine, and a few Neapolitans, to the chief executive posts in Provence. When Adam of Luzarches died in 1277, Charles amalgamated the government of Provence with that of the Kingdom, of which it was henceforward treated as a province but with its own peculiar institutions. This was not apparently resented by the Provençals, no doubt because the government of the Kingdom was dominated by their compatriots, while Charles watched with especial personal care over the welfare of the county. He had

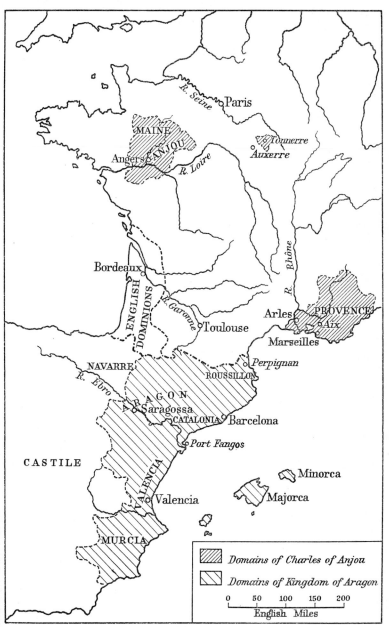

Map 2.

good reason to pay attention to it; for it was his main source of revenue, providing him with a net annual income calculated as being 20,000 lb. of gold. Strictly speaking, Provence formed part of the Empire; but the vacancy in the Empire happily deprived Charles of any suzerain to whom deference had to be paid.[1]

It was Provence that provided Charles with the means which he intended to use to gratify his vast ambitions. With the Hohenstaufen line extinct and with his own dominions ably reorganized, the time had come for Charles, King of Sicily, overlord of most of northern Italy, senator of Rome and Count of Anjou, Maine and Provence, to use his accumulation of wealth and power to build a Mediterranean Empire.

CHAPTER IX

A MEDITERRANEAN EMPIRE

It had long been the aim of the Kings of Sicily to found an Empire over the lands of the Eastern Mediterranean. Robert Guiscard had tried to establish himself east of the Adriatic. His family had supported the First Crusade with Syrian colonies in view. King Roger had contemplated the conquest of Greece. The Emperor Henry VI, King of Sicily in his wife's right, made plans for the annexation of the whole Eastern Empire. Frederick II, though he made no attempt to expand into Greek lands, tried to substantiate his claim to be King of Jerusalem and overlord of Cyprus. Manfred reverted to Guiscard's policy and succeeded in securing a foothold in Corfu and on the mainland opposite. In the meantime the whole question had been amalgamated with the question of the crusade. The Fourth Crusade, in which Constantinople was captured and sacked, had shocked even the Pope. But once the Latin Empire was set up, the Greeks lost what sympathy they had gained in the West by their obstinate refusal to accept the domination and the religion of their conquerors. It seemed henceforward quite legitimate that any war against such schismatics should rank as a crusade. Saint Louis himself, though he thought, with a single-mindedness rare at the time, that the first object of a crusade should still be the liberation of the Holy Places from the infidel, was ready to agree that the strengthening of the Latin Empire and the suppression of the Greek schism would greatly help the main cause. The collapse of the Latin Empire and the reconquest of Constantinople by the Greeks intensified that feeling. Indeed, Manfred, when he offered his full support to the exiled Latin Emperor, hoped thereby to show the world that he was an earnest crusader and so to avert the hostility of the Papacy; and he succeeded for a time in embarrassing the

135

Pope. Had it not been for the certainty that sooner or later he would be attacked in his own kingdom by a papal nominee, he would probably have led an expedition against Constantinople to restore Baldwin II and the Latin Empire.[1]

Charles inherited Manfred's policy. One of his earliest enterprises was to send a small expedition to take over Corfu and the mainland fortresses that had been Queen Helena's dowry. Manfred had entrusted their government to his admiral, Philip Chinardo. When news came of Manfred's death at Benevento, Chinardo carried on the government in his own name. The Despot Michael of Epirus would have liked to recover the lands, now that his daughter was a prisoner in Italy. But he did not feel in a position to try to oust Chinardo. Instead, he saved his face by offering Chinardo the hand of his sister-in-law, a widowed lady of mature years, and announcing that the dowry was now hers. This happy family arrangement did not prevent the Despot from intriguing vigorously against his new brother-in-law and finally arranging for his assassination, so that when Charles's troops arrived, at the end of 1266, there was no serious resistance. Charles, who claimed the territory on the legal ground that as Queen Helena was his prisoner her dowry passed automatically to him, appointed another member of the Chinardo family, Gazzo, as his governor.[2]

But his ambition was not to be satisfied merely with a few islands and cities along the Albanian coast. He aimed at Constantinople. The ex-Emperor Baldwin, who had fixed his hopes on Manfred, had found himself cold-shouldered at the court of France, once Charles's invasion of Italy was under way. He returned disconsolately to Italy. In May 1267 he was with the Pope at Viterbo. Clement arranged for a reconciliation between him and Charles, who interrupted his Tuscan campaign to interview him there. Baldwin was made to pay heavily for the new king's support, but he was in no state to dispute the terms offered to him. These were that he was to confirm Charles's possession of Queen Helena's dower-lands; he was to cede to Charles the suzerainty over the Principality of Achaea and to give him full sovereignty over all the islands of the Aegean, with the exception of those held by Venice and of Lesbos, Chios, Samos and Amorgos, which Baldwin was permitted to retain, and to recompense him with a third of any territory, other than Constantinople itself, which Charles might conquer for him. In addition, his son and heir Philip was to marry Charles's daughter Beatrice, with the stipulation that if Philip died without issue, his rights to the Empire were to pass to Charles himself. In return Charles promised to raise and to maintain for one year an army of two thousand knights destined for the conquest of Constantinople.[1]

Charles was already in touch with Prince William of Achaea, with whom he exchanged ambassadors in February 1267. The Prince was glad to welcome as his new suzerain and protector a powerful and active king in place of the penniless exile for whose upkeep he had been obliged to make generous gifts. Though his wife was the sister of the unfortunate Queen Helena, whatever sisterly feelings she may have had were ignored. As soon as Charles had signed his treaty with Baldwin, he sent a seneschal to represent his suzerain interests at the Achaean court. William, who was alarmed by the recovery of Byzantine power, willingly promised his help for any expedition against the Greek Emperor.[2]

The web of diplomatic alliance did not end there. That same year Charles dispatched an embassy to the court of the Mongol Ilkhan of Persia. The Mongols had been defeated by the Mameluks of Egypt seven years before, at the decisive battle of Ain Jalud, but they still controlled northern Syria and eastern Anatolia, as well as Persia and Iraq. Charles feared that the Byzantines might ally themselves with the Turks and hoped that the Mongols could keep both of them in check. His ambassadors were graciously received and failed in their object. The Ilkhan Abaga, who had recently succeeded his father Hulagu, had no great sympathy with the Franks. Besides, he had married a Byzantine princess, Maria Palaeologina, known to the Mongols as Despina

Khatun and deeply respected by them all.[1] Charles was more successful in seeking an ally in central Europe. The Kingdom of Hungary now stretched from the outskirts of Vienna to the Balkan peninsula. It included Slovenia and Transylvania and most of Croatia, and Dalmatia. Its aged king, Bela IV, had on several occasions invaded Serbia and Bulgaria. The King of Bosnia was his client and son-in-law. He himself had offered a few years previously to lead a crusade against the schismatic Greeks. He would also be a useful ally in central Europe, where his neighbour, the King of Bohemia, seemed to have pretensions to the Imperial crown. Hardly had Charles received the news of the death of his queen, Beatrice of Provence, before he wrote to Bela to ask for the hand of his youngest daughter, Margaret. But this princess had vowed to become a nun; and her parents respected her wishes. It was rumoured that she disfigured herself in order to escape the unwanted marriage. Charles thereupon made another suggestion. The crown prince of Hungary, the future Stephen V, had a son, Ladislas, and a daughter, Maria. Ladislas was to marry Charles's daughter, Isabella, while Charles's eldest son, the future Charles II, who now had the title of Prince of Salerno, should marry Maria. King Bela consented, and the double marriage took place. It was later to give an Angevin dynasty to the Hungarian throne.[2]

These first preparations for the expedition against Constantinople were interrupted by Conradin's entry into Italy. Till the invader was defeated there could be no eastern adventure. Indeed, the Prince of Achaea came in person with 400 horsemen to help Charles against Conradin and was present at Tagliacozzo.

After the victory the scheme was revived, and the alliance between Charles and William of Achaea tightened, in a manner not entirely to the latter's liking. William had no sons but two daughters, the elder of whom, Isabella, he named as his heir. Isabella had been sought in marriage by the Byzantine Emperor Michael Palaeologus for his eldest son Andronicus; and, had the

Franks permitted this peaceful reunion of Achaea with the Empire, the whole history of Greece would have been happier. But Charles thought otherwise. He now demanded Isabella for his second son, Philip; and he insisted on a stipulation similar to that which he had obtained from the ex-Emperor Baldwin: that if the bridegroom died without issue the heritage was to pass to Charles himself. In the case of Baldwin's son the clause was perhaps justifiable; for Baldwin had no other direct heir.[1] But in this case it meant the disinheritance of the lawful heiress, against all feudal precedent. William had to agree, though he resented it; on his deathbed, his son-in-law Philip having already died, he made a secret will in favour of his younger daughter, Margaret.[2]

Charles intended that the expedition against Constantinople should set sail in the summer of 1270. Throughout the spring his ships were being prepared and were mustering in the Adriatic ports. The marriage-contract between Philip and Isabella was signed on 17 June, when the final arrangements with the Franks of Achaea were settled. At Constantinople the Emperor Michael was seriously alarmed. He had repaired the city walls and re-organized his fleet, which, though small, was well equipped. But he knew that the news of the expedition would bring a combination of all his neighbours against him. His only ally in the west was Genoa; and Genoa was now in the hands of its Guelfs, who were friendly with Charles. His agents worked hard there and amongst the Genoese colonies in the east to revive the Ghibelline party, but as yet without success. When he had been threatened by Manfred, he had sought the friendship of the Pope, holding out the one bait that he could offer, the promise that he would do his utmost to secure the reunion of the Church of Constantinople with that of Rome. Pope Urban IV, in his fear of Manfred, gave him some encouragement. But Pope Clement was less amenable; when the menace of Manfred was removed, he saw no reason for treating with the schismatic Emperor.

But, as his mistrust of the victorious Charles grew, he did not entirely turn down the overtures that Michael continued to make. He was particularly pleased when the Patriarch of Constantinople wrote to him in friendly and respectful terms, and when Michael, to show his sincerity, offered to take part in the next crusade to be arranged against the infidel. The Pope felt that he now could dictate terms. His reply to the Emperor's proposals, which he sent on 17 May 1267, insisted that the Greek Church must submit to his authority unconditionally before any political or ecclesiastical discussions could be opened. He probably knew that Michael could not accept such terms. It would cost him his throne; for the Byzantine people, with their pride and their bitter memories of Latin persecution, would need careful coaxing before they would consider reunion. Ten days after dispatching the letter, before it had even reached its destination, Clement presided over the reconciliation between Charles and the Emperor Baldwin at Viterbo.[1]

Conradin's invasion saved the Emperor Michael in 1268; but soon after its failure Pope Clement died; and the vacancy in the Papacy left Michael with no over-riding authority to which he could appeal. But he was well informed about the west; he knew of the piety and prestige of Saint Louis. Two Byzantine embassies followed each other in quick succession to Paris during 1269, conveying vague proposals for the union of the Churches and pointing out how much more satisfactory a voluntary union would be than one imposed by force. It was a prudent move. Louis had no liking for schismatics, and he merely referred the Emperor's suggestion to the College of Cardinals; and they answered the Emperor by repeating the late Pope's conditions.[2] But Louis's attention had been drawn to the urgency of the question. His ambition was to set out once more on a crusade against the infidel, and to do so soon; for his health was beginning to fail. His memory was haunted by the fiasco of his earlier crusade. Now at last conditions at home would permit him to leave the country. But he wanted his brother's help. If Charles was to start at this moment on a campaign against Constantinople, even if it were in the interests of Holy Church, it would handicap his own holier crusade. Messages were sent to Charles to tell him of the views of the King of France.[1]

Charles was put into a quandary. He had a genuine admiration and respect for his brother, and he was well aware of the force of public opinion that Louis commanded. It would never do for the King of Sicily not to join his own brother of France on the crusade. But he was unwilling to abandon his personal eastern venture. In the vain hope that Louis would postpone his expedition he went on with his military and diplomatic preparations against Constantinople. But at the same time he decided that if he was to join in a crusade against the Muslims, it would be against Muslims whose conquest would be of direct advantage to him.

Just across the sea from Sicily lay the domains of Mustansir, King of Tunis. Charles was displeased with him. Since the days of King Roger II, Tunis had agreed to pay a yearly tribute of 34,300 gold besants to the Sicilian king. Mustansir had made the change of dynasty on Manfred's fall an excuse for discontinuing the payment. He had moreover given refuge to Manfred's and Conradin's exiled supporters and had even provided help for the rebels in Sicily. But he was not a bigoted Muslim. The Christian refugees at his court as well as visiting Christian merchants were allowed complete freedom of worship. He permitted the establishment of a Dominican convent in his capital. Indeed, there were rumours that his own conversion was not impossible. Charles skilfully directed King Louis's attention to Tunis. He pointed out how valuable the control of Tunis would be for an attack on Egypt and the Muslim East. He indicated that Mustansir was trembling on the brink of adopting Christianity but was afraid of the opposition of his generals and his imams. A slight show of force would enable him to defy them and make up his mind for himself. It is doubtful whether Charles really believed in the convertibility of the Tunisian king. But it would suit him to have a docile client ruling in Tunis; and it would suit him still better to conquer the country and add it to his Empire. It would give him complete control of the narrows of the Mediterranean and would guarantee him against further trouble in Sicily.[1]

King Louis allowed himself to be persuaded by his brother. The opportunity of capturing a whole country and its king for the Faith roused his enthusiasm, and the strategic argument seemed to him to be sound. Many of his counsellors were less optimistic. Few of them wanted the king to absent himself on a crusade; but if he had to go crusading surely it would be better to go straight to the east, where Christian reinforcements were desperately needed by the hard-pressed knights of Outremer. Several of his most trusted friends, such as his biographer Joinville, refused to accompany the expedition. It was, however, with a formidable army that Louis sailed from Aigues-Mortes on 1 July 1270. With him were his three surviving sons, the wife of his eldest son, his son-in-law, King Tibald of Navarre, and many of the greatest noblemen of France. The Genoese provided the ships that transported most of the troops.

Though a Tunisian expedition was to have its advantages, to the last minute Charles still hoped that Louis might cancel the whole crusade. He knew that many of the king's advisers were against it. It was only when the French army actually set out that he gave up his preparations for his expedition against Constantinople and ordered his ships to proceed instead under his command to Tunis. It took time to sail them round from the Adriatic ports and reassemble them in Sicily. He himself left Naples, where he had spent the early summer, on 8 July. On 13 July he was at Palermo, where he remained for a month, awaiting his ships. On 20 August he was at Trapani, at the extreme west of the island. On the evening of 24 August he set sail at the head of his fleet; and next day he anchored off Tunis, to be greeted by the news that King Louis had died that very morning.

The French army had arrived off Tunis on 17 July. Its landing was unopposed; but King Mustansir showed no haste to come forward and announce his conversion. Instead, he retired into his capital and manned its fortifications. King Louis set up his camp amid the ruins of ancient Carthage; but, in view of Mustansir's hostility, it seemed wiser to postpone a direct attack on Tunis itself till King Charles should arrive with his troops. In the meantime Tunisian skirmishers kept up continual raids on the camp. But far more effective than they were was the African summer. In the sweltering heat, with little knowledge of tropical hygiene to guide them, the French began to sicken with dysentery and typhoid. Soon half the army was stricken, its leaders no less than the humble soldiers. On 3 August the king's second son, John Tristram, who had been born at Damietta twenty years before when his father was held prisoner by the Egyptians, succumbed, to be followed four days later by the papal legate. By now King Louis himself and his eldest son Philip were ill. Philip survived the crisis of his illness; but after three weeks on his sick-bed King Louis died early on 25 August.

Charles's coming saved the French army. His troops were fresh and knew better how to deal with the climate. As soon as the weather grew cooler Charles pressed an attack against the city of Tunis. After the Tunisian army had been defeated in two small battles, and news had come that another crusading army under Prince Edward of England was approaching, Mustansir sued for peace. A treaty was drawn up on 30 October and signed by Mustansir and Charles and his nephew the King of France on 1 November. In it Mustansir agreed to pay all the expenses of the war, one-third of this sum going to Charles, to release all Christian captives held in his dominions, to pay Charles a tribute slightly greater than the tribute previously paid to the Norman kings, to allow Charles's merchants a counter in the city, with the right of free access to and from it and the free exercise of their religion. Finally, all the political refugees in Tunis were to be banished. The treaty was to last for ten years. It was apparently renewed in 1280.[1]

Charles had done so satisfactorily out of the affair that suspicions about his honesty arose among the crusaders. The Christian army could have taken Tunis, they thought; but in that case Charles would have had to share the spoils with the French King, the King of Navarre, the English prince who was on the point of arriving, the Holy See, the Genoese and a number of lords. It was no wonder that he preferred a negotiated peace which gave him the plums. Prince Edward, when he arrived with his cousin Henry of Cornwall early in November, was disappointed to find the fighting over. He sailed on to the Holy Land, after instructing Henry of Cornwall to return with the French army in order to take over the government of Gascony.[2]

In spite of the favourable peace-treaty ill luck still dogged the crusade, even for Charles. Sickness continued in the camp and took off many more victims. The King of Navarre was already ill, and died at Trapani. As the French Army journeyed by land through Calabria the young Queen of France, Isabella of Aragon, fell from her horse and died from her injuries at Cosenza. Charles's own army was depleted through sickness, and a worse disaster befell him from the hand of God. As the crusading fleet sailed northward from Tunis a terrible storm struck it off the west coast of Sicily. Eighteen ships were lost, including some of Charles's best galleys. Many others were severely damaged. It would take many months to repair the losses sufficiently for an expedition to set out against Constantinople.[3]

Charles had also suffered a serious loss in the death of King Louis. He had not always liked Louis's policy nor sympathized with his scruples; in particular he had resented his fatal determination to go crusading. But Louis had been a loyal and affectionate brother upon whom he could rely. The new King of France was a weaker character. Philip III admired his uncle and when he was with him was subject to his influence. But Philip was also devoted to his mother; and Queen Margaret would never forgive Charles for taking the whole Provençal inheritance. As far back as 1263 King Louis found out that she had extracted a vow from Philip never to give Charles any assistance at all. Louis had been furious and forced Philip to retract the vow. But with Louis dead and his young wife dead, when Philip returned to France there was no one there to counteract his mother's hold over him. Charles could no longer count on the support of the French court.[1]

The French army journeyed slowly home by land through Italy; and Charles accompanied his nephew as far as Viterbo. King Louis had been deeply distressed by the inability of the cardinals to elect a new Pope, and King Philip was eager to carry out his father's wishes and end the scandal. Once again Charles must have regretted his relatives' piety. The vacancy in the Papacy suited him well; but clearly it had some time to be filled, and it would never do for him to appear unwilling to help. The two kings remained at Viterbo for most of the month of March 1271. Their efforts with the cardinals came to nothing at the time, but they seem to have persuaded both parties in the College that a compromise was essential. After some months of further wrangling they appointed a subcommittee, which at last agreed on a candidate, Tebaldo Visconti, archdeacon of Liége. He was elected on 1 September 1271.[2]

The Kings' visit to Viterbo was darkened by a tragedy. With the French army was Henry of Cornwall, whom the English called 'of Almain,' the son of Richard, King of the Romans, a young man of promise, whom many saw as likely heir to his father's claims on the Empire. With Charles were Guy and Simon of Montfort, the sons of Simon, Earl of Leicester, who had died as a rebel against the English crown. Henry had been told by Prince Edward to try to negotiate with Charles the release of the Infant Henry, Edward's brother-in-law, and to try to reconcile the Montforts with the English royal family. The Montforts would not abandon their feud with the Plantagenets; and one day, as Henry was worshipping in the church of San Silvestro, Guy crept up behind him and stabbed him to death. Henry had been well liked; and the sacrilegious circumstances of the murder shocked opinion. Though Guy was one of his most active and successful lieutenants, Charles was obliged to repudiate him and dismiss him from his offices and his estates.[1]

The close of the crusade permitted Charles to revert to his East European schemes. The grand expedition against Constantinople had to be postponed; but there was plenty of work to be done. The Despot Michael of Epirus died early in 1271; and his legitimate son Nicephorus I had a hard task in preserving his inheritance from his bastard half-brother, John, who was already lord, or 'Duke', of Neopatras and ruler of the mountain lands between Thessaly and the Gulf of Corinth. Charles took advantage of their wars to extend his possessions in the northern provinces of the Despotate. In February his troops occupied Durazzo, and during the early summer they penetrated far into the Albanian interior. In the following February Charles proclaimed himself King of Albania and appointed Gazzo Chinardo to be his vicar-general, with a judge and a minister of finance to aid him. The kingdom stretched along the coast from the Acroceraunian Cape to Alessio, at the foot of the Montenegrin mountains, with a vague control over the tribes of the interior. Corfu and the cities on the mainland opposite seem to have been governed separately. Except from the strategic point of view Charles gained little from his Balkan possessions. Their revenues barely paid for the upkeep of the administration. The attempt to force Latin Christianity on the inhabitants provoked constant trouble; and even though a Latin was installed as Archbishop of Durazzo he was on permanently bad terms with the Vicar-General. In accordance with his usual policy of never allowing natives to occupy posts in their own provinces, Charles rewarded loyal Neapolitans with appointments in Albania and Corfu. But they served him badly; and the Saracens from Lucera, many of whom he used to garrison the new kingdom, were apt to show more sympathy with the Albanians than with the government.[1]

Nevertheless Charles was now an important factor in Balkan politics. He soon found friends among the neighbouring monarchs who shared his hopes for the destruction of the Empire of Michael Palaeologus. Serbia, immediately to the east of his new kingdom, was ruled by Stephen Uroš I, whose queen, Helena, was the daughter of the ex-Emperor Baldwin and was an eager proselytizer for the Latin Church. East of Serbia was Bulgaria, whose Tsar, Constantine Asen, was married to a sister of the boy-Emperor, John IV, whom Michael Palaeologus had dethroned and blinded. Though the actual interests of their countries differed, both royal ladies encouraged their husbands to take any action that might humiliate the hated Greek Emperor at Constantinople. Charles's envoys were well received at both courts. The Peloponnese was now well under Charles's influence. The marriage of its heiress with his son Philip took place in May 1271, promising him even closer control for the future. Meanwhile Prince William was a dutiful vassal. The other important lord of Frankish Greece, John, Duke of Athens, recognized William as his immediate suzerain and eagerly supported him, though gout prevented him from displaying great activity. Even the Greek Duke of Neopatras, though he was a vehement defender of the Orthodox Church whenever Michael Palaeologus showed signs of flirting with Rome, was on good terms with his Latin neighbours. One of his daughters was married to William of Athens, Duke John's brother and heir, another to the heir of Stephen Uroš and his Latin wife. He was, moreover, interested in the trade of the Gulf of Corinth, for which friendship with the Sicilian king was advisable. It would be easy for Charles to bring together a grand coalition against Constantinople. But he had to move cautiously. He could not tell how the new Pope would act.[2]

CHAPTER X

POPE GREGORY X

Charles's caution was wise. The new Pope could not be ignored. Tebaldo Visconti had been an admirable candidate on whom the cardinals could compromise. He was an Italian, born at Piacenza; but he had spent most of his ecclesiastical life north of the Alps, in the Low Countries, and had not been involved in recent political controversies. At the time of his election he was in the Holy Land. He had gone there at the head of a party of crusaders from the Low Countries, who had accompanied Prince Edward of England's expedition. His election came as a complete surprise to him; and he was unwilling to leave Palestine. His first action as Pope was to send out encyclicals appealing for greater help for crusaders in Syria, and his final sermon, preached at Acre just before he set sail for Italy, was on the text: 'If I forget thee, O Jerusalem, let my right hand forget her cunning.' Throughout his pontificate an Eastern Crusade remained his burning desire.

The new Pope landed in southern Italy in January 1272. King Charles entertained him as he passed through the Kingdom and doubtless tried to discuss politics with him. He passed on to Viterbo, arriving there on 10 February. But he wished his enthronement to take place in Rome. Charles, as senator of Rome, hurried to receive him. He was consecrated on 27 March under the name of Gregory X.[1]

Gregory had had plenty of time in which to consider his policy. Four days after his enthronement he issued a Bull summoning a General Council of the Church to meet in two years' time, on 1 May 1274. It was to discuss three main subjects, Church reform, the union of the Church of Constantinople with that of Rome, and an Eastern Crusade.[2] Charles was not greatly pleased. The question of Church reform did not much concern him, unless it were to lessen his influence over the Church in the Kingdom; and the crusade that he desired was one against Constantinople. Negotiations for the voluntary union of the Churches would oblige him to abandon his desire. But it was difficult for him to protest against so pious a programme. Besides, he needed the Pope's support in Italy. The position of Imperial Vicar in Tuscany had been given him by the last Pope in the absence of an Emperor; and he wished to retain it. The Pope's co-operation was essential if his influence over the Guelfs all over Italy was to be maintained. If, as soon seemed likely, the Pope was to concern himself in finding a new Emperor, Charles must be at hand to look after his interests. Moreover, he had just involved himself in a quarrel with Genoa and he wanted the Pope's sympathy.

Charles's relations with Genoa had never been very good. They had quarrelled long ago over the Ligurian coast-line; and though Genoa had recovered the land that she claimed and in return had not actively opposed Charles's passage into Italy, she had done nothing to help him. Her government was nominally Guelf, but the Ghibellines were not in exile, nor would she ally herself with other Guelf cities. She resented Charles's arrangement with the ex-Emperor Baldwin, as she enjoyed a favoured position with the Byzantines and feared to lose it, expecially as the Treaty signed at Viterbo offered guarantees only to her hated rival, Venice. She had given no help to Conradin; but her leading Ghibellines had ostentatiously gone out to salute him when he put in for a day at Portofino. In August 1269 her government, which was alarmed by the confirmation of Charles's power in Tuscany and was anxious for its trading privileges in the Sicilian Kingdom, at last agreed, in a treaty with Charles, to banish the Ghibellines. In return it was allowed consulates, quarters and tax-relief for its merchants in Charles's ports.

The treaty was short-lived. The Genoese government showed its good will to the French by lending King Louis the ships that he needed for the Tunisian Crusade. When news reached Genoa of the sickness and misery suffered by the crusaders, the Genoese sailors amongst them, public opinion turned against the government. It had been impossible to exile all the Ghibellines; they were too numerous; and their leaders, the Spinola and Doria families, had many friends in the city. On 28 October 1270 the Feast of Saint Simon and Saint Jude, a sudden rising overthrew the government and the Ghibellines returned. Oberto Spinola and Oberto Doria became Captains of the city, with absolute powers, advised by the Ancients of the Commune and the People and by a popular party organization known, from the date of the rising, as the Fortunate Society of the Blessed Apostles Simon and Jude.

The new Ghibelline government did not wish to break with Charles. It carefully kept itself aloof from the Ghibellines of Tuscany and Lombardy. Genoa benefited from the treaty that Charles made with Tunis, since many Genoese who had long been captive there were released. But in the storm which overwhelmed the crusader fleet as it returned from Tunis some Genoese ships were sunk and many more disabled. Charles ungenerously claimed rights of jetsam and of salvage on all the wrecks and damaged ships that were driven on to the Sicilian coast; and Genoa protested in vain. A few months later, when Charles was in Rome for the enthronement of the Pope, Cardinal Ottobuono dei Fieschi, who was in close relations with the Guelfs of Genoa, arranged for the leading Guelf exiles to meet him there. He promised them his help, and they offered him the Captaincy of Genoa when they should be reinstated. News of the pact strengthened the popular support given in Genoa to the Ghibelline government, but it caused alarm. The Captains decided to appeal to the Pope.[1]

Pope Gregory had his hands full. He was a sincere, unprejudiced man whose only aim was the welfare of Christendom. It seems that he did not care for Charles; but he was quite ready to support Charles wherever it seemed to be of advantage to the Church. His beloved nephew, Visdomino dei Visdomini, had worked as a judge for Charles in Provence and had been raised by him to be Archbishop of Aix. The Pope was devoted to Visdomino and made him a cardinal in 1273. Gregory was also willing to employ Provençals, no doubt on Visdomino's recommendation, such as Fulk of Puyricard, one of Charles's most loyal officials, whom he appointed rector of the March of Ancona. He made no attempt to reduce Charles's powers. Charles remained senator of Rome and Imperial Vicar in Tuscany. The excommunication that Clement IV had pronounced against the obstinate Ghibelline cities of Verona, Pavia, Pisa and Siena was confirmed. In western Lombardy Visdomino as papal legate accompanied Charles's troops in his war against William of Montferrat, who had put himself hopelessly in the wrong by mutilating three envoys whom Charles had sent to discuss a truce.[1]

But Gregory had no intention of letting the Papacy appear in any way dependent on Charles; and he was desperately eager to heal the feud between Guelf and Ghibelline which tore nearly every Italian city. It distressed him to find that Visdomino was considered to be Charles's tool; the legate was summoned back to the papal court and kept there, consoled with a cardinal's hat. In May 1273 Gregory tried to arbitrate between the Guelfs and Ghibellines of Florence at a conference held in the dry bed of the river Arno. He arranged that the Ghibellines should hand over the fortresses that they still held in the countryside to the Guelf government and in return would be allowed freely back to the city. When the Guelfs dishonoured the treaty by handing over the fortresses at once to Charles's vicar and continuing to penalize the Ghibellines, Gregory excommunicated the city, proclaiming his sympathy with the Ghibellines. But his main solution was to be the election of a new Emperor. Not only was Germany now in such anarchy that some sort of central power was essential, for the sake of the Church there as well as of the State; but it seemed to him that if there appeared in Italy an Emperor working in cordial amity with the Pope the whole reason for the cleavage between Guelf and Ghibelline must vanish. The difficulty was to find such an Emperor.[1]

Richard of Cornwall, King of the Romans, died in England on 2 April 1272. He had never got over the shock of his son's murder. His death eased the Pope's problem. Although it had long been clear that he would never be Emperor, he had been recognized by the Papacy as King of the Romans, so blocking the way for any other candidate. His old rival, Alfonso of Castile, still called himself King of the Romans and showed signs of once again taking the title seriously. But his policy was to ally himself with the more intransigent Ghibellines in Italy, thus making it impossible for the Pope to consider his claims. Moreover, he had no support now in Germany; and Gregory was determined that the new Emperor, whoever he might be, should be someone who could restore order in Germany. As soon as he heard of Richard's death Alfonso wrote an arrogant letter to the Pope, demanding that his title should be recognized and steps taken to prepare for his Imperial coronation. In return he seems to have been ready to abandon his Ghibelline friends and promise the vicariate of northern Italy to King Charles. Gregory answered with a tactful refusal. It was for the German electors to decide who should be King of the Romans.[2]

In the meantime he urged the electors to meet and perform their duty. It was difficult to find the right candidate. Gregory wanted a strong man but one who would be properly deferential to the Pope. The German princes wanted a weak man who would not restore order at their expense. Neighbouring monarchs had other views. The most imposing candidate was Ottocar II, King of Bohemia. The Kings of Bohemia, as hereditary cup-bearers to the Emperor, ranked among his electors; though certain lawyers objected to it, on the ground that they were not German. But Ottocar was now master of vast German lands, having, partly by conquest and partly by marriage to a lady twice his age, obtained the inheritance of the Babenbergers in Austria and Styria. He had also, as a result of profitable crusades conducted against the heathen Prussians in conjunction with the Teutonic Knights, acquired much of Silesia and its northern marches, so that his dominions stretched almost from the Baltic to the Adriatic. He was on the whole on good terms with the Church, and his family had always disliked the Hohenstaufen. Lately, with the idea of the Empire in his mind, Ottocar had veered round against the Guelfs and had betrothed his daughter to Frederick of Thuringia. Then he switched again, and made friends with King Charles and the Papacy. Gregory was asked to cancel the daughter's betrothal-vows in order that she might be free to marry Charles's eldest grandson. Gregory agreed, and for a time it seemed that Ottocar was his candidate.[1] Charles, however, thought differently. He wanted Ottocar's alliance; but Ottocar as Emperor, with the lands that he already held in Styria and at the head of the Adriatic, would be too powerful in northern Italy. He wrote to his nephew, King Philip of France, to tell him to become a candidate for the Empire. He was, he said, sure that he could persuade the Pope to support him and that the six powerful kings to whom Philip was related would all give their help. It was an ingenious idea. Philip as Emperor would certainly leave the control of Italy to his beloved uncle, for whom his gratitude would be such that he would escape from his mother's baleful influence. But Charles's optimism was almost insane; he entirely misjudged Pope Gregory, and he cannot seriously have thought that the Kings of Castile and Aragon would really have encouraged the candidature of their cousin of France. Philip was tempted by the scheme. In July 1273 he sent an embassy to the Pope to ask for his support. Gregory's answer was tactful but vague. He told the ambassadors that he wished their master nothing but good, but that the whole question needed further consideration; he reminded them that the King of Castile was still in the running.[2]

In fact Gregory had no intention of allowing a foreign king to become Emperor. He even decided against Ottocar of Bohemia, wisely, because the German electors had no intention of choosing him. Of the German princes the most obvious candidate was Henry of Bavaria, the uncle and heir of Conradin. But though he had split up the family inheritance with his brother Louis, who was now Count Palatine, he was too powerful. Nor did he covet the post. His brother, Count Louis, proposed himself. As Count Palatine he was an elector; but his was the only vote that he was likely to obtain. Count Otto of Anhalt was next considered; but he was too much of a nonentity. Finally Frederick, Burgrave of Nuremberg, ancestor of the house of Hohenzollern, suggested Rudolph of Habsburg, Landgrave of Alsace.

Rudolph was a good candidate. He was a man of known experience and known piety, with a tall, rather austere presence and a quiet, courteous manner, now aged fifty-five. His family was traditionally loyal to the Hohenstaufen; and Rudolph himself had been excommunicated more than once for his services to the dynasty; the last occasion was when he accompanied Conradin as far as Verona. He was only a Count of the Empire, not a Prince, but he was rich. His family lands were in north-west Switzerland, where he owned most of the country between the Rhine, the Aar and the Lake of Lucerne; and he had recently inherited the rich County of Kyburg, which comprised roughly the modern Canton of Zürich. In addition he possessed most of Upper Alsace. He was thus personally respected, wealthy and not too powerful. By the summer of 1273 he had emerged as the likeliest candidate in the eyes of the Germans. But the electors were slow in making up their minds. The free cities of the Empire had already announced that they would accept no one who had not received the unanimous vote of the electors; they were determined to have no more uncertainty and anarchy, however much the Princes might enjoy it. In August Gregory wrote sternly to the electors to say that if they did not do their work within a fixed time he would himself nominate the King of the Romans. Rudolph himself won support by promising that, if elected, he would not alienate any of the lands of the Crown without the permission of the Princes.

The Diet was eventually fixed for 29 September 1273. On 11 September the three ecclesiastical electors, the Archbishops of Cologne, Mainz and Trier, issued a manifesto jointly with the Count Palatine that they would accept anyone whom the other electors agreed to nominate. It seems that they were certain that Duke John of Saxony and the Marquis of Brandenburg had decided to support Rudolph. Ottocar of Bohemia still hoped for his own election and refused to vote for anyone else.

He would not come to the Diet in person, but sent the Bishop of Bamberg to represent him, with orders to hinder it as far as possible. The other electors retorted when they met by declaring that the King of Bohemia had no right to be an elector and that the seventh electorship should belong to the Duke of Bavaria. It was thus possible for them to give unanimous approval to Rudolph. He was proclaimed King of the Romans at Frankfurt on 1 October and was crowned at Aachen on 24 October.[1]

Gregory would probably have preferred the election of Ottocar; but, though the Bohemian King wrote to him in angry protest, he accepted the electors' choice with every show of gracious warmth.[2] Some months passed before he gave Rudolph formal recognition; it was not till the following September that he invited Rudolph as King of the Romans to come to Rome for his Imperial coronation. But in the meantime he made it clear that he regarded Rudolph as lawful king, and welcomed his representatives as such at the Council of Lyons.[3]

Rudolph's election aroused great hopes in Germany. They were not entirely fulfilled; but his wise and tactful government succeeded in restoring order in the country and laying the foundations of its prosperity in the next century; while his triumphant war against Ottocar gave him and his descendants control of the Austrian and Styrian provinces which were to be the foundation of Habsburg power in the future. For Charles the election was a diplomatic defeat. The emergence of an active Emperor-elect necessarily undermined his authority in northern Italy and encouraged his enemies. Chief of these at the moment was Genoa. In November 1272 he had provoked war by seizing the goods and the persons of all the Genoese, Guelfs excepted, whom he found within his dominions. The Genoese government appealed to the Pope, who blamed Charles but recommended the Genoese to restore the Guelfs to power. At the same time, eager for his crusade, he tried to make peace between Genoa and Venice, who had been skirmishing with varying violence in eastern waters for the last few decades. The Venetians were willing to reach some sort of understanding. In a frank note to Genoa they pointed out that they both had a dangerous neighbour who would only leave them alone if they worked together. But, though both home governments might have been glad of a reconciliation, their merchants' rivalry in the East was too bitter. Nothing came of the negotiations.[1]

Open hostilities between Charles and the Genoese broke out at the end of 1272. The Genoese held their own. Charles's only success was the temporary occupation of their port of Ajaccio, in Corsica. But in the autumn of 1273 he took more active measures, attacking both from Tuscany and from Piedmont. The Genoese had hitherto refused to seek allies from other Ghibelline cities, in the hope of securing the Pope's sympathy. Gregory had done nothing for them; so at the end of October they entered into a pact with Pavia and Asti, promising to give support to Alfonso of Castile, who was on the point of invading Lombardy in the belated hope of staking his claim as Emperor-elect before any election took place in Germany. Alfonso proved a useless ally; but Genoa was thus involved in the general uprising of the Ghibellines of the north against Charles of Anjou.[2]

The war with Genoa was expensive; and Charles also had the expense of reconditioning his fleet after the Tunisian Crusade. He had not been able to plan a new campaign against Constantinople before Pope Gregory made his wishes about Church reunion known. Gregory knew the East, and he realized, as no one since his great predecessor Urban II had realized, that a really successful crusade would need the willing co-operation of the Eastern christians. It was useless to imagine that a revived Latin Empire would help the cause. Past experience had shown the contrary. But a Greek Empire which had submitted voluntarily to Rome would be a precious ally. Gregory chose his moment well; for the Emperor Michael, with enemies all round, was terrified of an attack from Italy. If the only way by which Charles could be neutralized was submission to Rome, then the policy of religious submission must be seriously considered at Constantinople. Michael was a watchful diplomat. He knew the importance of the papal alliance, but his attempts hitherto to appease Rome had failed. When the new Pope sent him an invitation written in friendly terms to attend a Council for Church reunion, he responded at once, even though Church reunion would mean the humiliation of his own Church. He saw it as the only means for preserving his throne, and he hoped, wrongly, that his people would see that political independence was worth the sacrifice.[1]

Gregory was astute enough to realize that the chief argument at Constantinople in favour of reunion was the dangerous situation of the Empire. He was not therefore going to smooth out all the Emperor's political problems till he had obtained from him a definite declaration in favour of the ecclesiastical supremacy of Rome. That must be made even before delegates from Constantinople could come to discuss the details of the reunion at the General Council. In the meantime Gregory put gentle pressure on the Emperor by forbidding any western state, such as Venice, which wished to enter into a treaty with him, to make more than a temporary arrangement. He hinted, too, that he would not always be able to restrain Charles. But Charles was forbidden to take any hostile action as yet. Instead, he was required to give safe-conducts to any Byzantine ambassador who might pass through his dominions on the way to Rome. The ecclesiastical negotiations lasted throughout 1273. By the end of the year Michael had convinced the Pope of his own sincerity but had openly confessed to him that the idea of union was not popular at Constantinople. Thanks chiefly to the persuasive tact of a Greek-born Franciscan friar, John Parastron, whom both the Pope and the Emperor trusted and whom the Greeks respected because of his gentle and pious demeanour, and to the vigour of the Chartophylax, John Veccus, who had been converted to the cause of union, a synod was induced, despite the opposition of the Patriarch Joseph, to sign a declaration admitting the full primacy of the Roman See, the right of appeals to Rome, and the need for the Pope's name to be mentioned in the liturgy. The theological point of the *filioque* clause in the Creed was not mentioned but was left to be discussed at the Council. This satisfied the Pope for the moment; and a Greek delegation was formally invited to the Council.[1]

All these negotiations were particularly irritating to Charles. He had to obey the Pope's order to stay his hand against Constantinople; his war with Genoa was accompanied with increasing difficulties in northern Italy, and he could not afford a breach with the Papacy. He still hoped that nothing would come of the union. On 15 October 1273 he at last celebrated the marriage between his daughter Beatrice and Philip of Courtenay, son of the ex-Emperor Baldwin, which had been arranged at Viterbo four years previously. A few days later Baldwin died, and Philip assumed the Imperial title. Gregory, when writing to Philip in November to tell him to do nothing to impede the Greek ambassadors, addressed him as Emperor of Constantinople and spoke of Michael as Emperor of the Greeks; but that was a courtesy from which Philip could not derive much hope.[2]

While Charles was forced to be inactive, Michael's diplomatic activities were intensified. The Bulgarian Tsar had lost his wife. In 1272 Michael persuaded him to marry one of his nieces,

Maria Cantacuzena, daughter of his favourite sister Eulogia. Thenceforward tension with Bulgaria lessened, though there was a quarrel over the bride's dowry. Michael had promised the sea-port of Mesembria, then refused to hand it over on the ground that the inhabitants were Greeks and could not be transferred against their will. The Bulgarians retorted by invading the Empire in 1272, and when that failed, by sending an embassy to Charles in 1273, but it led to nothing. With Serbia Michael's attempt to arrange a marriage alliance collapsed, owing to the opposition of the Latin-born queen. But Michael safeguarded himself against trouble in the Balkans by two diplomatic triumphs. The Black Sea steppes beyond the Danube were under the control of a Tartar prince, Nogai, to whom in 1266 Michael had given one of his illegitimate daughters, Euphrosyne; and the alliance with Nogai was now confirmed and renewed. The Bulgarian invasion in 1272 had been quickly checked by an appeal to Nogai, and Bulgaria had learnt its lesson. To keep Serbia in check Michael now made an alliance with Hungary. Charles's friend, King Bela IV, had died in 1270. Stephen V, his son and successor, was married to a lady of the Cuman, or Polovtsian, tribe, heathen nomads who had taken refuge in Hungary from the Tartars; and the queen, though a Christian, seems to have preferred eastern to western Christianity. Her son and her eldest daughter were married to two of Charles's children, and another daughter was married to the heir of Serbia, son of the passionately Latin Queen Helena. But two other daughters were betrothed, apparently at their mother's wish, to Orthodox princes in Ruthenia. The youngest was now offered to Michael's son and heir, Andronicus, and the marriage was sealed with a treaty. King Stephen died in 1272, but his son Ladislas was influenced by his mother rather than by his Angevin wife, and was moreover frightened of Ottocar of Bohemia, whose territorial ambitions were accompanied by eager Latin missions. The alliance with Byzantium was maintained.[1]

Michael could feel secure about the Balkans. His diplomacy in

Greece itself was less successful. Michael Angelus's successor as Despot of Epirus, Nicephorus, was married to a niece of the Emperor, the sister of the Bulgarian Tsaritsa; but though the Despoena Anna was a woman of unscrupulous vigour, her husband was weak and ineffectual. His bastard brother, John, Duke of Neopatras, was a more important figure. The Emperor attempted to control him by marrying one of his nephews, Andronicus Tarchaniotes, to John's daughter and by giving John the title of Sebastocrator. But the ungrateful nephew identified himself with his father-in-law, who paid no regard to Constantinople. Michael had hoped to arrange a Greek alliance against the Latins in Greece. All that he could achieve was a petty war in Euboea, for which he employed a young local adventurer of Vicenzan origin, Licario. Licario proved to be a brilliant commander and gradually conquered the island for the Emperor.[1]

Further west Michael was now in close touch with the Genoese, and through them he had, by the end of 1273, made contact with Alfonso of Castile. Byzantine money seems already to have gone to encourage the Ghibellines in northern Italy.[2]

It was infuriating for Charles that his hands were tied by the Pope and he could do little to counter the Emperor's activity. He could only hope that the projected Church reunion would fail. His treaty with the ex-Emperor Baldwin had stipulated that he would invade the Empire before the summer of 1274. The Pope now forbade him to fulfil it, but gave him permission to prolong the time-limit by another year. By 1275 it would be known whether Michael was really bringing his Church into the Roman fold. It was as well that the Greeks should realize what would happen to them if they stayed out.[3]

In the spring of 1273 Gregory decided to hold his Council at Lyons. He was a little unwilling to leave Italy; but the powers which he wished to interest in the crusade were those that were north of the Alps, and he preferred that a Council should be in a district where Charles would be unable to put any pressure on the delegates. He was not pleased with Charles. He thought that Charles was to blame for his troubles with Genoa. In the autumn of 1272 he was visited by his old friend, Edward of England, who was on his way back from the Holy Land to assume his father's crown. Edward was furious to find that his cousin's murderer, Guy of Montfort, had not been properly punished but was still at large, under the protection of his father-in-law, Hildebrand Aldobrandeschi, the chief Guelf lord of southern Tuscany. It was suspected that he still enjoyed Charles's good will. In June 1273 Gregory left Orvieto, where he had been living, to go to Lyons. It was as he passed through Florence that he attempted to reconcile the Guelfs and Ghibellines there, to have his efforts wrecked after he had left by the Guelfs with the backing of Charles. But he did not want to break with Charles, for he wanted to reward him for not attacking Constantinople and to interest him in a crusade in the Holy Land.[1]

Gregory entered Lyons with an impressive train early in November. He spent the next months in preparing for the Council, writing to all the high prelates of the West summoning them to preliminary meetings where crusading problems could be discussed. He had already obtained a number of memoirs from experts, each suggesting how to make the movement popular once more. He summoned theologians to help him in the arguments that would arise with the Greeks. Amongst them was Thomas Aquinas, who had written a tract on their errors. Thomas was living at the time at Naples, where he was not on very good terms with King Charles. When he fell ill at his niece's castle of Magenza, not far from Naples, men at once suspected Charles's agents of having poisoned him. He continued on his journey, a very sick man, and died at Fossanuova, near Aquino, on 7 March 1274. Dante was convinced of Charles's guilt; but, though Charles may have feared that Thomas would complain of him to the Pope, there is no evidence for supposing that the great doctor's death was not natural.[2]

After three days of fasting the Fourteenth Oecumenical Council was opened at Lyons by Pope Gregory in person on Monday, 7 May 1274. He had invited thirteen kings to be present, those of France, England, Scotland, Norway, Sweden, Hungary, Bohemia, Castile, Aragon, Navarre and Armenia, in addition to Charles of Sicily, whom he knew would not come, and the King of the Romans, whom he did not yet officially recognize, but who was encouraged to send ambassadors. Unfortunately, with one exception, the kings refused the invitation. He did not expect otherwise of those who lived in distant realms; but the King of France, who met him just outside Lyons and escorted him into the city, refused to return for the Council. Edward of England, on whom he particularly relied, snubbed him by arranging for his coronation to take place while the Council would be sitting, thus preventing his leading bishops also from attending. Alfonso of Castile tried to obtain an interview with Gregory on his way to Lyons but would not go there himself. Of the royal personages who did attend, two were unsuccessful claimants to a throne, the titular Latin Emperor Philip and Princess Maria of Antioch, who had pretensions to the throne of Jerusalem. The only crowned monarch was James of Aragon, a swashbuckling old soldier who was genuinely interested in crusading, but who soon came to think the Pope's schemes amateurish and unreal, and who did not much care for the austere atmosphere of the assembled prelates. He soon returned to the arms of his mistress, the Lady Berengaria, having promised nothing; and he died two years later, excommunicated by Gregory for having eloped with the wife of one of his vassals.

The Council dealt first with various matters of Church reform. Most of them merely concerned quarrels between various prelates and abbeys. A few dealt with the laws of excommunication and interdict. One important rule was passed to prevent any further interregnum in the Papacy. On a Pope's death the cardinals were to wait not more than ten days for absent colleagues to arrive.

They were then to meet in conclave, without communicating with the outside world till they had made their choice. The longer they delayed, the more austere their living conditions would be; and they would receive no salaries or emoluments so long as the See remained vacant. Next, the Council discussed the crusade. In the absence of the kings, no practical decisions could be made; and once James of Aragon had left, the whole atmosphere was discouraging. The French king's ambassador, Érard of Saint-Valéry, had already announced, to James's indignation, that he considered a general crusade to be a futile scheme; and his remark had been received not with protests but in silence. All that the Pope could do was to issue new regulations for the collection of tithes to be spent on the crusade, an action which only made the idea of the crusade still more unpopular both to the kings of Europe and to their subjects. He also forbade the Italian maritime cities to sell arms or their raw material to the Saracens, and he ordered that no Christian merchant-ship was to enter a Muslim port during the period of six years. It was impossible to enforce either regulation.

Gregory was a little more successful in his diplomatic dealings. He was determined to restore peace and order in Europe as the preliminary to the crusade. His command to all the monarchs of Europe to cease from wars was not entirely obeyed; but in fact some of the more quarrelsome princes, such as the Spanish kings and Ottocar of Bohemia, did for a while restrain themselves. By himself setting the example he obtained a general recognition of Rudolph of Habsburg as King of the Romans.[1] But his great diplomatic triumph was the submission of the Greek Church.

In spite of growing resentment at Constantinople, the Emperor Michael was determined to accept the Pope's terms. The Patriarch of Constantinople, Joseph, still refused to countenance even the mild formula worked out by John Parastron. In January 1274 Joseph was ordered to retire to the monastery of the Peribleptos. He was told that if the Union failed to be agreed he could emerge again with full Patriarchial powers on condition that he took no disciplinary action against its advocates. If the Union was signed, he could either accept it or resign and remain in the monastery. Meanwhile Michael assured his clergy that there would be no alteration in the rites and that no papal legate or representative should set foot in Constantinople. The Pope had suggested that it would be enough for the Empire and the assembled clergy at Constantinople to declare their adhesion to the Roman Church before special legates sent from Rome. Michael realized that that might cause a riot, and preferred the alternative that he should send a plenipotentiary delegation to Lyons.

The delegation set out at the beginning of March, in two galleys. The first carried the ecclesiastical representatives, the ex-Patriarch Germanus and Theophanes, Metropolitan of Nicaea, and the Emperor's personal ambassador, the logothete George Acropolites. The second contained two other high court officials and a number of secretaries and clerks, as well as the presents destined by the Emperor for the Pope. As the ships rounded Cape Malea they were caught in a storm and the second galley was wrecked on the rocks. All its company and all its contents were lost, except for one sailor. The embassy which arrived at Lyons on 24 June was therefore less brilliant than was intended. Nor was its actual personnel very impressive. George Acropolites was a statesman and scholar of distinction, but of its ecclesiastical leaders, the Metropolitan of Nicaea was a man of no great notability, while Germanus, though he had been Patriarch of Constantinople in 1266, had been removed after a few months owing to his incompetence and indiscretion. It is significant that Michael had not been able to find more deeply respected churchmen to go on the mission.

The embassy was welcomed ceremoniously by the Pope and the cardinals, and handed to the papal secretary three letters, one from the Emperor, one from his eldest son Andronicus, and one from a number of leading Greek archbishops. Five days later, on the Feast of Saint Peter and Saint Paul, they attended a religious service which was partly sung in Greek. During the course of it the Greek clerics joined Uniate Greek bishops from Calabria in singing the creed, including the *filioque* clause, which was thrice repeated. It was noticed that the Metropolitan of Nicaea stopped singing when the word appeared.[1] The formal ceremony of union took place on Friday 6 July. The Pope, expressing his joy at the voluntary return of the Greeks to obedience, first read out in a Latin translation the three letters that he had received. The Emperor's letter contained a declaration of faith in the creed as given at Rome and of belief in the primacy of the Roman Church, to which he offered his obedience. He then asked that the Greek Church might keep to the creed that it had used before the Schism and to its existing ritual, so long as they did not conflict with the commandments of God, the Holy Scriptures, the Councils and the Holy Fathers. His son's letter was couched in the same terms; and the letter of the bishops, after referring to the sincerity of the Emperor's efforts for union, announced their own willingness to pay the Pope all his due as their predecessors before the Schism had done. This last letter was worded with some care; it did not commit its signatories very far. The logothete then, as the Emperor's personal plenipotentiary, swore in his master's name to abandon the Schism, to accept the creed and doctrines of the Roman Church as the one true Church, and to accept the primacy of the Roman Church and to give it all the obedience owing to it. The Pope would have liked a written and signed copy of the oath; but there was none. It may have perished in the shipwreck. When the logothete had repeated the oath, the Pope solemnly intoned the Te Deum and himself preached a sermon, using as text Christ's words in Saint Luke's Gospel: 'With desire I have desired to eat this Passover with you.' Then the creed was sung in Latin and in Greek, with the words 'Qui ex Patre Filioque processit' twice repeated. The Schism was officially ended.[2]

The following Monday the Pope received an embassy that delighted him almost as much as the Greek. The Ilkhan of the

Mongols of Persia sent sixteen ambassadors, who had arrived on 4 July, with instructions to try to arrange an alliance with the Christian nations against the Muslim Mameluks. Gregory gave them every encouragement, and was particularly pleased when one member of the embassy, with two of his suite, asked for and received Christian baptism. But he had nothing more concrete than pious promises to offer the Ilkhan.[1]

Gregory was content with the results of the Council. It is true that nothing definite had been decided about a crusade. But he believed that the Union of the Churches was valuable not only for itself but also because it would facilitate any crusade, opening up again the land-route across Anatolia. Moreover, the kings were a little ashamed of having given him no help. Philip of France took the Cross the following year, and King Rudolph about the same time, in return for the promise of his Imperial coronation. In the meantime the Pope continued his work of pacification. He met Alfonso of Castile in May 1275 at Beaucaire on the border of Provence, and persuaded him both to abandon the title of King of the Romans and his consequent pretensions to be leader of the Ghibellines in Italy. A few months later, in September, he was at Lausanne to meet Rudolph, whom he now formally recognized and for whom he arranged a treaty of friendship with Charles of Anjou. It was to be sealed by the marriage of Charles's eldest grandson, Charles Martel, with Rudolph's daughter Clementia. Rudolph paid for his recognition by virtually resigning all Imperial rights over the Romagna and the Marches.[2]

Charles had already been informed that the Union was completed.

Letters were written on 28 July 1274 to request Charles and the titular Emperor Philip to prolong the truce with Constantinople that they had undertaken to keep, and to the Emperor Michael to tell him to make a truce with Charles. The negotiations were entrusted to Bernard, Abbot of Monte Cassino. He visited Naples and Constantinople and induced both Charles and Michael to commit themselves to a year's truce, beginning on 1 May 1275. The truce was not altogether fair to Charles; for, while it kept him from attacking Constantinople, neither side held it to apply to the Greek peninsula and Albania, where the Byzantines were starting an offensive but where Charles would have preferred to avoid war, counting that the whole would fall to him once he captured the Imperial capital.[1]

It was not such a sacrifice for Charles to agree to the truce at the moment. His war with Genoa had now spread to be a war against a revived Ghibelline League and it was costing him more than he could afford. Gregory was not unsympathetic. When he heard that Charles was about to sell his jewels in order to pay the tribute due to the Holy See, he allowed him to defer payment. He also excommunicated Genoa and her Ghibelline allies, Asti and the Marquis of Montferrat. But he made it clear that he now regarded Rudolph of Habsburg, not Charles, as the proper person to restore order in northern Italy. He wrote to Charles to say that he quite understood that Charles would dislike his policy but on reflection he would see that it was reasonable and right. When Charles asked him to persuade Rudolph to enfeoff him with Piedmont, he transmitted the request but added privately that he was only doing so at Charles's request and that personally he thought it would be a grave mistake to alienate a province of such strategic importance.[2] Nor did he react as strongly as Charles would have wished when his old enemy the Queen-Mother of France made trouble again. As soon as Queen Margaret heard that Rudolph was generally recognized as King of the Romans, she wrote to him, with the concurrence of her sister the Queen-Mother of England, about her old grievance of having been cheated out of the inheritance of Provence. As Provence still officially owned the Emperor as its suzerain, she appealed to him to redress her wrongs. Rudolph, delighted, no doubt, to have his authority over Provence admitted, seems to have gone so far as to promise to invest her with the County. The Pope's efforts to bring Charles and Rudolph together prevented the latter from pursuing this plan; but the Pope sent no form of reproof to the vindictive old Dowager.[1]

The Genoese war was going badly. In October 1274 the situation in Piedmont was serious enough for Charles to appoint his nephew, Robert of Artois, as his Vicar in the province, but Robert had no success. In January 1275 Genoa, Asti and Montferrat, together with Novara, Pavia, Mantua and Verona, swore allegiance to Alfonso of Castile. His retirement from the war in May did not stop their victories. They had already forced Charles's vassal-cities of Vercelli and Alessandria to join their Ghibelline League. During the summer they won the adhesion of Saluzzo and Revello, and while their troops moved freely through Charles's lands in Piedmont the Genoese fleet sacked Trapani in Sicily and the Maltese island of Gozo and made a demonstration in the Bay of Naples itself. The Pope was desperately afraid that the war would spread to Lombardy, where the great city of Milan was growing restive. But he saw that the Emperor-elect was the only person now to reconcile Guelfs with Ghibellines; he wrote to congratulate the Milanese for sending an embassy to Rudolph and he urged the other Lombard cities to do likewise. It is not surprising that he could not sincerely recommend Rudolph to put Charles in charge of Piedmont.[2]

There, in the autumn of 1275, Asti, as chief city of the local Ghibelline League, offered to make peace on the terms that the Ghibellines should keep what they had gained. Charles contemptuously refused the suggestion. A few days later his seneschal, Philip of Lagonesse, suffered a severe defeat and was forced to retire with a shattered army over the Alps to Provence. By the summer of 1276 all that was left of Charles's Piedmontese dominion was the three isolated towns of Cuneo, Cherasco and Savigliano and a few unimportant villages.[3]

In all his dealings with the kings of Europe Gregory had been

THE TOMB OF POPE GREGORY X AT AREZZO

guided by one dominant principle, how best to further the crusade in the Holy Land. If he seemed callous towards Charles's failures in northern Italy and his thwarted ambitions in Greece, it was because he hoped that Charles would then turn his attention to the one direction where aggression would meet with divine approval. He did his best to draw Charles to look that way. One of his few royal visitors at Lyons, Princess Maria of Antioch, came there to seek his support for her claim to the throne of Jerusalem as the successor of Conradin. Though her mother was the younger half-sister of Conradin's great-grandmother, Queen Maria of Jerusalem, she considered herself to be closer to him than the successful claimant for the throne, King Hugh III of Cyprus, who was the grandson of an elder half-sister of Queen Maria. She had put forward her claim before the High Court at Acre as soon as news had reached there of Conradin's death. But the lawyers of Outremer had decided in favour of King Hugh. Only the Templars had supported her. To everyone else a vigorous young man seemed obviously a better candidate than a middle-aged spinster, whatever the legal rights might be.

Gregory while he was in the east may have shown the disappointed princess some sympathy, so that she felt it worth while to come to the Council at Lyons. Her optimism was justified. The Council did not discuss her case; but Gregory gave her his personal approbation, and he persuaded her that it would be wise to sell her claim to King Charles. It was high-handed of the Pope to go against the legal opinion of Outremer and the expressed wishes of its people; nor was it legally at all certain whether the rights to a throne could be bought and sold. But Gregory had probably formed a poor opinion of King Hugh, who, indeed, was to prove himself quite incapable of giving his Kingdom of Jerusalem an orderly government and in 1276 was to retire in despair to his easier Kingdom of Cyprus. But the scheme especially commended itself to the Pope because it offered Charles consolation for his disappointments elsewhere; it would flatter his vanity; and it would give him a serious personal interest in the welfare of the Holy Land, at the same time providing the Kingdom of Jerusalem with a ruler whose ability was beyond question. Maria, who no doubt realized that the throne of Jerusalem was scarcely a comfortable seat, accepted the Pope's advice. The negotiations took some time. Charles was short of ready money, and the princess was not going to sell too cheaply. In the end her need for money proved greater than Charles's. On 18 March 1277 a contract was signed. In return for a thousand pounds of gold and an annuity of four thousand pounds *tournois*, she gave over all her hereditary rights to Charles, who at once took the title of King of Jerusalem.[1]

By that time Pope Gregory was dead. After his meeting with King Rudolph at Lausanne in October 1275 he had moved slowly over the Alps to Milan and thence southward through Bologna to Florence. As he went his secretaries were busily writing letters about the crusade. King after king was told that he could collect the tithes due to the Church if only he would use them for the Holy War; legates were ordered to whip up flagging enthusiasm. In spite of all his disappointments he believed that his dream of a great crusade might yet come true. But while he paused at Florence for Christmas he fell desperately ill. On 1 January 1276 he wrote urgently to Charles, desiring to see him while there still was time. He then was carried in his litter to Arezzo, where he died on 10 January.[2]

Charles was at Rome when he heard of the Pope's death. It is hard to believe that he grieved very bitterly.

CHAPTER XI

THE ANGEVIN REVIVAL

The late Pope's obstinate striving for peace in Europe and a crusade against the infidel had interrupted all King Charles's schemes of conquest. Charles did not want peace in Europe except on his own terms, nor, though he was glad enough to accept the Kingdom of Jerusalem, did he wish to risk its loss by a crusade. Gregory had forbidden him to attack Constantinople; and now the Byzantines were taking the offensive against his possessions and his allies in Greece. His arrogance had involved him in a war with Genoa, and now he was on the defensive in northern Italy; and Gregory's sympathy was cancelled out by his invitation to Rudolph, King of the Romans, to restore order in the province. Charles was determined not to permit the election of any other Pope with such inconvenient ideals.

When Gregory died at Arezzo, Charles was at Rome. According to the procedure laid down at the Council of Lyons, the cardinals assembled at Arezzo, allowing ten days' grace so that absent members of the College should have time to join them. They were conscious of the king's proximity. Their deliberations lasted less than twenty-four hours. On 21 January 1276 they elected a cleric known to enjoy Charles's favour, Peter of Tarentaise, a Dominican born in Savoy, who had been Archbishop of Lyons and now was Cardinal-Bishop of Ostia. He took the name of Innocent V, and went at once to Rome, where he was consecrated on 22 February. Charles escorted him to Rome from Viterbo and was present at the consecration; for the next five months Pope and king remained at Rome, seeing each other constantly.[1]

Charles had reason to be pleased with the new Pope. Innocent at once confirmed him as senator of Rome and as Imperial Vicar of Tuscany. So long as Gregory was alive, King Rudolph had not protested against Charles's Imperial Vicariate; but he considered that the new Pope had no right to appoint to Imperial offices now that there was an Emperor-designate. In protest he sent officials to obtain oaths of allegiance to him in the Romagna, in spite of his promise to the late Pope to regard the Romagna as part of the papal patrimony. Pope Innocent answered sharply. Rudolph was not to come to Italy till the oaths that he had extracted were annulled. Rudolph, who was anxious to come to Rome for his Imperial coronation, understood that he must now make terms with Charles as well as with the Pope. He sent the Bishop of Basle to negotiate with them both.[1]

Innocent next arranged a peace between Charles and the Genoese. It was not a very glorious peace for Charles; for the Ghibellines were left in control of Genoa, and Charles had to give them back the privileges enjoyed by the city in his dominions and such small conquests as he had made. In return they recognized his suzerainty over Ventimiglia. But it left him free to try, in vain, to salvage his possessions in Piedmont, and to strengthen his hold in Tuscany, where alone his arms had recently been successful and Pisa had been humiliated. The peace was signed on 22 June 1276. Four days later Pope Innocent died at Rome.[2]

It was convenient for Charles that the next papal election had to take place at Rome. As was required, the cardinals met ten days later at the Lateran Palace, where Innocent had died. Charles, as senator, was able to surround the Palace with his police, who permitted the cardinals of his own party to communicate freely with the outside world and to receive presents of foodstuffs, while the opposing party was kept enclosed and subjected to the increasing austerities ordered by the Council of Lyons. The policy worked well. After little more than a week, on 11 July, the cardinals elected one of Charles's most faithful friends, the Genoese Cardinal Ottobuono dei Fieschi, who was a passionate Guelf and the nephew of Pope Innocent IV. He proposed to take the name of Adrian V. But he was only a cardinal deacon. Before he had time to be ordained, as a preliminary to his consecration, he fell seriously ill, and died at Viterbo on 18 August.[1]

Charles had followed the Pope-elect to Viterbo and was living nearby, at the castle of Vetralla. But he was not able to put so much pressure on the Conclave that met to elect the new Pope as he had done at Rome. The senior cardinal, John Gaetan Orsini, who was head of the anti-French party, dominated the meeting but tactfully proposed the one cardinal who was neither Italian nor French, the Portuguese John Peter Juliano. His advice was taken. Cardinal Juliano was elected early in September and consecrated as John XXI at Viterbo on 20 September. King Charles came to Viterbo for the consecration and paid him homage for the Kingdom of Sicily.[2]

Pope John was personally well disposed towards Charles. He allowed him to retain the senatorship of Rome and the Vicariate of Tuscany. He obligingly excommunicated Charles's Ghibelline enemies in Piedmont, but at the same time sent envoys to try to arrange a truce for him there. He forbade King Rudolph to come to Italy, as Rudolph's officers were still forcing the cities of the Romagna to recognize him as overlord. He gave his personal approval to the contract, signed on 18 March the following year, by which Maria of Antioch sold Charles her rights to the crown of Jerusalem.[3] But he would do no more. Charles had hoped to revive his power in northern Italy. The victories of his troops over the Pisans in September 1275 and June 1276 had confirmed his hold of Tuscany. Across the Apennines the Guelf cities south of the Po, such as Parma, publicly asserted their devotion to the Church and King Charles.[4] Across the river the tyrant Napoleon della Torre was overthrown in January 1277 by his own subjects. His family had ruled Milan for thirty-six years, but he had himself abandoned their traditional policy of friendship with Charles in order to seek favour from Rudolph. In his place the Milanese gave the lordship to their Archbishop, Otto Visconti.[5]

King Rudolph was unlikely to intervene in Italy for some time to come. Not only had the Pope forbidden his coming, but in June 1276 he was involved in a war against Ottocar of Bohemia. He was victorious; a peace, to be sealed with two marriage-alliances between his and Ottocar's children, was signed in October 1276. By it Ottocar ceded the Babenberg duchies of Austria, Styria, Carinthia and Carniola and acknowledged Rudolph as his overlord for Bohemia and Moravia. It was a great potential increase in strength for Rudolph; but he was fully occupied with the reorganization of his new provinces; and it was soon clear that Ottocar did not mean to keep the peace.[1]

It seemed a favourable moment for Charles. But the Pope would not help him there. Instead, the Archbishop of Milan and the other Guelf leaders in northern Lombardy definitely announced their vassalage to Rudolph. The Papacy wished to keep the door into Italy open to the German king, lest Charles should become too powerful again.[2]

Nor was Pope John more helpful to Charles in his schemes against Constantinople. The Union of the Churches, which had so delighted Pope Gregory X, was not proving as easy to establish as the prelates at the Council of Lyons had hoped. The Emperor Michael was sincere in his desire to carry out his obligations. Unlike most Byzantine Emperors, he had no great personal interest in theology and he thought that the political advantages of the Union far outweighed any ecclesiastical humiliation that his Church might suffer. Few of his subjects agreed with him. Joseph, the Patriarch of Constantinople, refused to have any truck with the Unionists. A synod composed of the Emperor's supporters dethroned him and appointed in his place a distinguished theologian, John Veccus, who had been genuinely convinced of the propriety of union. But Veccus had no followers other than the bishops who had elected him at the Emperor's bidding. Michael's son and heir, Andronicus, dutifully seconded his father; but, as the future showed, his theological studies inclined him against the

Roman Church. In the Palace the opposition was led by the Emperor's sister Eulogia, a forceful widow who had hitherto been Michael's most intimate counsellor. Her daughters were the Bulgarian Tsaritsa and the wife of the Despot of Epirus; and they shared her views. Within the Empire the monasteries, the lesser clergy and the vast majority of the laity were passionately shocked by the idea of union. Only two generations had passed since the Latins had sacked Constantinople. Many men and women still living remembered how harshly the Latin conquerors had treated the Orthodox Church. They still heard stories of persecution in Latin Greece and in Cyprus. It was too much to expect that they would now admit that Rome had been right after all. Observers might well doubt whether the Emperor's Unionist policy could survive.[1]

These doubts were not unknown at the papal court. Indeed, Michael himself hinted to the Pope of his difficulties. A Byzantine embassy which reached Italy just before Gregory X's death begged him to launch a crusade against the infidel at once and meanwhile to excommunicate the Emperor's enemies. There must be something practical to show immediately in its favour if the Union was to be accepted. Innocent V answered that the crusade was indeed imminent, but he shelved the question of excommunication. It would have meant giving offence to King Charles and the Latin princes in Greece. Indeed, under pressure from Charles, Innocent seems to have wavered a little in his attitude towards Constantinople. John XXI reverted to Gregory's policy. He sent a mission, of two bishops and two Dominicans, to Constantinople with letters to the Emperor, asking for a personal declaration of faith from him, and to his son and the Patriarch and clergy generally, enjoining obedience and expressing his friendly interest in them. Michael replied by sending a copy of the oath in favour of union that he had publicly sworn. Andronicus wrote to proclaim his zeal for the Union; and the Patriarch John Veccus and his bishops signed a document reaffirming their faith in the primacy of the Roman See and in the Roman addition of the *filioque* to the creed; but the wording was not as precise as Rome might have wished, and it was rumoured that some of the bishops had refused to sign and their signatures had been forged by an Imperial notary. Pope John was satisfied, and continued to forbid Charles to take steps against Constantinople.[1]

The Pope's insistence on a truce between Charles and the Emperor did not prevent warfare between them in Greece and Albania. It was necessary for the Emperor, if he was to force his religious policy on his reluctant people, to accompany it with military successes and the expansion of the Empire. Knowing that Charles was forbidden to attack him at Constantinople, he had no scruples against attacking Charles in Greece. In the summer of 1274, before his envoys had yet returned from the Council of Lyons, he sent an army into Albania, where it captured the fortress of Berat and the sea-port of Butrinto. In October the Byzantines laid siege to Avlona and to Durazzo, where Charles's Captain-General, Narjot of Toucy, was in residence. The kingdom of Albania seemed on the point of collapse. Reinforcements were hurried across from Italy; and for the moment both cities were saved.[2]

In the spring of 1275 Michael, encouraged by his success, sent an army and a fleet under his brother, the Caesar John, the victor of Pelagonia, to central Greece to crush the bastard Epirote prince, John of Neopatras, and his Latin allies. The campaign against the bastard was a failure. The Byzantine army consisted largely of Cuman and Turkish mercenaries, who offended the local population as well as their Greek fellow-soldiers by sacking monasteries; and the Greek soldiers themselves were unwilling to fight against the Greeks in the bastard's army. The Caesar advanced as far as Neopatras itself, where he found that the enemy had been joined by John, Duke of Athens, with three hundred of the best horsemen of Frankish Greece. In the battle that ensued the Imperial army, though it was vastly superior in numbers, melted away at the first Latin charge. The Caesar was forced to seek refuge with his fleet.

A few days later the Byzantine fleet, under the admiral Alexius Philanthropenus, met a Latin fleet off Demetrias, in the Gulf of Volo. The Latin ships belonged partly to the Venetians and partly to the Latin lords of Euboea, nearly all of Lombard descent. They were armed with wooden towers, which made them look like floating cities, and each ship carried an unusually large complement of fighting-men. At first they were successful in their attack. Philanthropenus was badly wounded and was rowed ashore, while his flagship fell into the enemy's hands and his other ships were driven back with heavy losses on to the coast. At that moment the Caesar John rode up with the survivors of the land battle. They hastily manned the ships and sailed back against the Latin fleet. The Latins were taken by surprise and were easily defeated. All but two of their ships fell into Byzantine hands. But the Caesar did not feel strong enough to follow up his victory. He returned with his troops to Constantinople, where he retired from public life, in shame, he said, at the defeat that he had suffered at Neopatras, but also, perhaps, because he disliked his brother's religious policy.[1]

The battle of Demetrias left the Byzantine fleet in control of the Aegean. When the news arrived, Venetian ambassadors who were at Constantinople to discuss a new treaty with the Emperor hastened to sign one for two years. Next year, in 1276, Michael determined to make a second attempt against central Greece. Once again his land forces were defeated by John of Neopatras. But once again he was triumphant by sea. He employed as his admiral an Italian adventurer from Vicenza, by name Licario. Licario had come as an ambitious young mercenary to Euboea, where he soon won a reputation for brilliance. But he offended the local Lombard lords by seeking to marry a lovely widow far above his station in life. Exiled from Euboea he captured the town of Karystos, which he turned into a successful pirate's nest. He then visited Constantinople and impressed the Emperor by his intelligence. Michael offered him the command of a number of Byzantine troops and ships and the promise that he should hold all Euboea as a fief when he conquered it. The Latins had not recovered from their naval defeat at Demetrias; they could not interrupt Licario's communications with Constantinople nor prevent him from capturing the islands of the Sporades. On Euboea itself he took fortress after fortress. Only the town of Negropont, or Chalkis, the metropolis of the island, held out against him; and the defeat of the Byzantines at Pharsala deprived him of the land reinforcements that he needed. But during an engagement outside the walls he succeeded in taking prisoner the Duke of Athens himself, and many other Latin lords. He brought them in triumph to the Emperor, who rewarded him with a rich Greek wife and the title of admiral. For the next few years he was master of all Euboea, except for Negropont, and regularly raided the lands of his Latin neighbours, pausing only to help the Emperor in a campaign against the Turks. When the Venetians renewed their treaty with the Emperor in 1277, they asked for protection against Licario.[1]

Further south, in the Peloponnese, the Emperor's troops enjoyed a mild success in 1275, when the combined forces of Prince William and the Angevins were defeated at Great Arachova. Their commander, Geoffrey of Bruyères, one of the few Franks whom the Greeks also admired, had died of dysentery just before the battle. The victory enabled the Emperor to consolidate his hold over Laconia, in the south-east of the peninsula.[2]

By 1277 Charles's possessions and influence east of the Adriatic were thus increasingly precarious. He wanted more than ever to avenge himself against the Emperor by leading a huge expedition against Constantinople. It was poor consolation that he could now take over the Kingdom of Jerusalem. On 7 June 1277 Roger of San Severino, Count of Marsico, arrived at Acre with six galleys and presented to the authorities letters signed by Charles, by Maria of Antioch and by Pope John XXI, demanding that the city and kingdom be handed over to him as Charles's representative. The rightful King of Jerusalem, King Hugh of Cyprus, had left Acre in disgust seven months earlier. He had been unable to control the quarrels between the nobility of the kingdom and the merchants of Acre, between the two great Military Orders of the Temple and the Hospital, and between the Venetian and Genoese colonies. It was when his authority had been publicly flouted by the Templars that he retired to Cyprus, leaving his cousin, Balian of Ibelin, as his *bailli*, or viceroy. Balian did not know what to do. The High Court of the kingdom had decided against Maria's claims to the throne, nor, had it endorsed them, would it admit her right to dispose of them without consulting it. But none of the nobles was prepared to resort to arms to protect the rights of a king who had deserted the country. The Order of the Temple, which had long been opposed to Hugh, welcomed Charles's deputy, especially as its Grand Master, William of Beaujeu, was Charles's cousin. This put the Hospitallers against him; but they, like the barons of the High Court, were not eager to fight for an absentee. The Patriarch of Jerusalem, Thomas of Lentino, disliked the Templars but could not act in opposition to the Pope's recommendation. The Venetians, who had temporarily driven the Genoese out of Acre, saw in Charles a potential ally against Constantinople and knew him to be the enemy of the Genoese. They therefore supported his cause. Balian therefore, with a protest, yielded the citadel of Acre to Roger of San Severino. Roger hoisted Charles's banner there and proclaimed him King of Jerusalem, then ordered the barons to come and pay homage to their king's deputy. They hesitated, insisting that King Hugh must first release them of their oaths to him; but when they sent to Hugh to ask for advice, he would not give them any answer. At last Roger grew impatient and announced that he would confiscate the lands of anyone who refused him homage. The barons then submitted.

Charles had won a new kingdom without bloodshed. But it was a worthless kingdom. All that was left of the kingdom founded by the early crusaders was a coastal strip a hundred miles long but never more than ten miles wide, stretching from Mount Carmel to the Dog River, just north of Beirut. To the north of it was another strip, shorter but a little wider, which was the County of Tripoli. But its Count, the ex-Prince Bohemond VII of Antioch, though he at once recognized Charles as King of Jerusalem, refused to regard him as suzerain. There was still a certain revenue to be derived from the kingdom's trade with the interior, so long as peace was maintained; but most of it went to the Italian merchants or to the Military Orders, whose castles dominated the frontier customs houses. The king did not even own any of the fortresses of the kingdom, apart from Acre itself. All that Charles had acquired was the obligation to keep troops in the East, with no profit to his exchequer. His success was only one of prestige.[1]

Nor did the Papacy derive any profit from the transaction. Charles was not going to endanger his new possession by launching any crusade against the infidel. The great power in the Near East was now the Mameluk Sultanate of Egypt. It acquired its hegemony of the Muslim world by its decisive victory over the Mongols at Ain Jalud in 1260. The terrible Sultan Baibars, who had won the throne soon after the battle, had in the last fifteen years conquered all the inland possessions left to the crusaders and had destroyed the old crusader principality of Antioch. The remnants of the kingdom lay at his mercy. But the Mongols, though the battle of Ain Jalud had checked their advance into Palestine and Egypt, were still powerful. The Ilkhan, the Mongol prince who ruled Persia under the distant suzerainty of the Great Khan in Mongolia, controlled all the country between Afghanistan, the Caucasus and the Syrian desert. The Mongols were known to be sympathetic to the Christians and ready to join in any alliance against the Mameluks, as their embassy to the Council of Lyons had shown. To many Christians, including successive Popes, such an alliance seemed to offer salvation. But Charles thought otherwise. The Mongol alliance was particularly advocated by the Genoese, who had a practical monopoly of the Mongol trade in the Black Sea and in northern Syria. It was therefore opposed by the Venetians, and by Charles, who also had no wish to see Genoa enriched. Moreover the Templars, on whom he relied, always favoured an alliance with the Mameluks. They were now the chief bankers in the East, and many of the Muslim lords were their clients. They believed that the Mameluks, if unprovoked, would not upset a state of affairs which was financially convenient to them. Charles's instruction to his officials at Acre was, therefore, to keep the peace with Baibars and to show him every friendliness. He was anxious that the Mameluks should realize that the change of régime at Acre meant them no harm. His motive was not only to preserve his new dominion. The King of Tunis was in touch with Cairo. If he saw that Charles was allied with the Sultan there, he would continue to pay his tribute to Naples regularly; and Charles needed the money.[1]

The only direction in which Charles felt aggressive in the southeast Mediterranean was against King Hugh of Cyprus. Successive Popes had to remind him that he was not authorized to attack the island, to his disappointment, for it would be a rich and profitable prize.[2]

The papal policy thwarted Charles, but he was not pessimistic. He hoped, with reason, that sooner or later the union of the Churches would prove illusory. He calculated that King Rudolph had too many problems in Germany, with enemies such as King Ottocar, to commit himself far in Italy, and that the Papacy would soon realize that he was its most valuable friend. He did not despair of Pope John XXI. But he was quite unprepared for John's sudden death. The Pope had added a new wing to his palace at Viterbo. It was carelessly built. On 12 May 1277 as he lay sleeping in his new bed-chamber the ceiling collapsed on him. He was terribly hurt and died eight days later.

Charles was lying sick in southern Apulia when the Pope died. He could not hurry north, but hoped that a new election would be delayed. One of Pope John's few acts had been to revoke the decrees passed at Lyons which confined the cardinals, with increasing austerity, till they appointed a successor to the Papacy. At the time of the Pope's death only eight of the eleven cardinals in the College were near enough to Viterbo to take part in the election. Four of these were Italians and four Frenchmen. They could not agree between themselves. For six months they bickered, till the citizens of Viterbo in exasperation imprisoned them in the papal palace, and at the same time made it clear that they wished for an Italian. The French cardinals gave way. On 25 November 1277 Cardinal John Gaetan Orsini was elected as Pope, with the title of Nicholas III.[1]

The new Pope was by many years the senior cardinal. He had been given his hat by Innocent IV in 1244. Since then he had led the moderate Guelf anti-French party in the College. He belonged to one of the greatest Roman families; and his loyalty to Rome was only exceeded by his loyalty to his family. Later writers criticized him severely for his nepotism and for the avarice that accompanied it. Dante saw him in the cave of Hell reserved for Simoniacs, repentant of his eagerness to advance and enrich the 'bear-cubs', the scions of the house of Orsini, whose badge was a bear. The historian Villani believed that his whole policy was based on his secret rage against Charles of Anjou. When he offered the hand of one of his nieces to the king for one of his sons or nephews, Charles had replied that the Orsinis were not worthy to mate with the royal Capetian house. The story is unsupported; but it is true that when Nicholas appointed new cardinals a few months after his accession he bestowed one hat upon his brother Jordan and another on his nephew Latino Malabranca, and that he gave the best posts at his disposal to others of his clan. It is probable that his kinsfolk were the only friends that he could trust. To contemporaries Nicholas appeared as a man of irreproachable private morals and wide political views.[1]

He was not, nevertheless, the Pope whom King Charles would have chosen. Charles was now recovering from his illness. It gave him an excuse not to make haste to pay homage to the Pope for the Sicilian Kingdom. It also gave the Pope an excuse to write affectionately to him, inquiring about his health. Each could wait politely to see how the other would behave.[2] Charles was a little uncertain about Nicholas. Within a fortnight of his accession the Pope had written in kindly but firm terms to King Rudolph to tell him to order his officials out of the papal patrimony in the Romagna. The letters of previous Popes had had no effect. Rudolph, who was faced with a new war against Ottocar of Bohemia, complied with the command. Then Nicholas turned to Charles and requested him to resign his post of senator of Rome. He reminded Charles that his appointment in 1268 had been for ten years only. Charles was also to give up the Imperial Vicariate of Tuscany. Things were still going badly for Charles in Piedmont. He could not afford to offend the Pope, who had moreover come to Rome and was firmly established among his friends there. When Nicholas confirmed the excommunication of his enemies in Italy, he agreed to pay homage to the Pope. The interview took place at Rome on 24 May 1278. After the ceremony Charles promised to give up the senatorship and the Vicariate in four months' time. To reward him, Nicholas refused to receive an embassy from the Ghibellines of Lombardy, saying that he was too busy.[3]

Having thus established his authority over Charles and Rudolph, Nicholas set about reconciling them for the peace of Europe. The chief trouble-maker was the Queen-Mother of France. Rudolph had promised her the County of Provence; and, though her son, King Philip, gave her no sympathy now, she had the support of her nephew, King Edward of England. In the summer of 1278 her agents arranged with Rudolph that his eldest son, Hartmann, should marry King Edward's daughter Joanna. Hartmann should then be recognized as his father's successor and, if possible, be crowned King of the Romans as soon as Rudolph was crowned Emperor. If Hartmann's succession to the Empire was doubtful, he and Joanna should be given the Kingdom of Arles and Vienne, including Provence, as an hereditary possession. Both Edward and Rudolph were delighted with the arrangement. In August Rudolph finally defeated Ottocar, at Dürnkrut in Moravia. Ottocar was slain on the battlefield. A month later all the Bohemian nobles had submitted to Rudolph and had accepted him as guardian for Ottocar's young son, Wenceslas, who was his son-in-law. Rudolph was now in a position to advance into Italy or into Provence.[1]

The Pope's reaction was in favour of Charles. Throughout the autumn and winter of 1278 he was in close touch with both Charles and Rudolph, encouraging the former and restraining the latter. Rudolph still hoped for his Imperial coronation, which was more important to him than the Kingdom of Arles. But he did not wish to surrender any rights without proper guarantees. Nicholas had some difficulty in finding terms that he would accept. Charles was more amenable; but he was sensitive about Provence and was determined not to lose it. Nicholas had various schemes in mind. His most cherished plan was that the crown of Germany should be given as an hereditary possession to Rudolph; that Charles should be restricted to southern Italy; that the Kingdom of Arles should go in its entirety to Charles's young grandson Charles Martel when he should marry Rudolph's daughter Clementia; and that northern Italy should be turned into a kingdom and bestowed on the Orsini family. Unfortunately there was no evidence that either the Lombards or the Tuscans wished to be ruled by the Orsini; nor could any Emperor-designate be expected willingly to abandon control of the traditional lands of the Empire south of the Alps.[2]

A settlement was at last reached in the summer of 1279. The rights of the Empire in Italy were admitted and Rudolph was promised his coronation. But he was not to interfere in the Romagna; and it seems that the Papacy was to exercise the Imperial Vicariate in Tuscany. Charles was recognized by Rudolph as Count of Provence, but would do homage to him for the county. The Kingdom of Arles was to be reconstituted, apparently without Provence, and was to be given to Charles's eldest son, Charles, Prince of Salerno, to hold in trust for Charles Martel and Clementia, who were to take it over as soon as their ages were suitable.

There were various points to be settled. Edward of England must not be offended. Fortunately for the peacemakers, the death of Rudolph's son, Hartmann, ended any question of his betrothal to an English princess, while Edward had a number of problems to occupy him within the British Isles. But Edward was not pleased and seems chiefly to have blamed the French court. It was even harder to placate the Queen-Mother of France. Both the Pope and King Rudolph wrote to her in the spring of 1280 to assure her that her claims on Provence were not prejudiced by the treaties. As she received no support from her son, King Philip, she could do nothing in protest. But she intended all the same to see that an Angevin Kingdom of Arles should never be founded.[1]

It was not till May 1280 that the treaty between Charles and Rudolph was signed in a series of letters between the contracting parties. In the meantime Charles had been admirably deferential to the Pope. On 30 August 1278 he wrote to his representatives at Rome to tell them to hand over to the Roman people the fortresses and prisons that they controlled; and he formally gave up his office of senator into the Pope's hands. Nicholas at once secured the appointment of his own brother, Matthew Orsini. At the same time Charles resigned from his Vicariate in Tuscany. In his place Nicholas installed his nephew, Cardinal Malabranca, until there should be an Emperor who could name a new Vicar. Nicholas then called upon Charles to help him to restore order in the Romagna. King Rudolph's officials had left the province; but it was not easy to reduce the Ghibellines. The papal nephew, Bertoldo Orsini, who had been sent as Rector there, was ill-supplied with troops. Charles sent one of his highest officers, William l'Estandart, with three hundred picked horsemen, delighted to have the opportunity of fighting against the Ghibellines at the expense of the Papacy. With this help the Pope recovered control of the country south of the Po, even though the rebels had the support of several Lombard cities including Milan, whose Arch-bishop had passed into the Ghibelline camp.[1] Charles needed the prestige that he thus won; for he had now lost his last possessions in Piedmont. In Tuscany, where he had been obliged by the Pope to abandon his various overlordships, Cardinal Malabranca reversed his policy and returned to Gregory X's. Florence appointed the Pope as its Signor and readmitted the exiled Ghibellines. Several other cities joined in the general reconciliation. King Rudolph, as Emperor-designate, sent his own Vicar there, who was allowed to collect certain dues but was given no political powers.[2]

Charles's deference was not due to any love of the Pope. Neither he nor Nicholas trusted the other very far. But it suited both of them to work together; and the Pope's policy had not in fact weakened Charles. Provence had been saved for him, and he had the prospect of the Kingdom of Arles for his descendants. By reducing his commitments in northern Italy he had greatly improved his finances. He was richer in 1280 than he had been five years earlier. He could once again afford to plan his expedition against Constantinople.[3]

The Pope still forbade the expedition; but the Union of the Churches was going badly. The Pope was beginning to speak in sterner terms to the Emperor Michael. There were signs that a breach might soon occur and Charles be free to proceed with his scheme.

The envoys that Michael had sent to Italy bearing his and his clergy's Declarations of Faith arrived there to find Pope John XXI dead. They deposited their documents with the cardinals and returned home. When Pope Nicholas had time to read the Declarations, he considered them inadequate. Reports had reached him from the Latin colony at Galata, across the Golden Horn, that the churches at Constantinople were not saying the creed in its Roman version, nor in any way altering their ritual. In October 1278 he decided to send an embassy to the Emperor to insist on stricter conformity. He drew up the instructions for his nuncios very carefully. They were to greet the Emperor very cordially, then to remind him sharply that complete unity does not permit of divergences. There were ten points on which he must satisfy them. He and his son must rewrite their Declarations ot Faith, using the exact terms in the creed, as it was laid down at the Council of Lyons. He must make the Patriarch and all the prelates of his Church adhere to the same creed. The word *filioque* must be introduced into the creed in all church services. No part of the Greek ritual was to be retained unless the Holy See considered it to be in accord with the true faith. The nuncios were to visit every main centre in the Empire to see that these instructions were carried out. The Greeks must all ask the nuncios for absolution for their past schism. The nuncios should confess, over the heads of the Greek clergy, anyone who sought confession. The Emperor must ask for a permanent cardinal-legate to reside in the Empire. All opponents of the Union were to be excommunicated. The Patriarch and all the bishops must apply to the Pope for confirmation of their appointments.[1]

These demands went so far beyond the terms arranged at the Council of Lyons that it almost seems as if Nicholas was deliberately trying to wreck the Union. The nuncios, led by Bartholomew, Bishop of Grosseto, set out from Italy in midwinter and arrived at Constantinople in the spring of 1279. Michael was deeply embarrassed when they presented their terms to him. But he sincerely believed that the Union was the right policy, and he did his best to comply with them. He now had almost the whole of his empire against him. Finding persuasion useless he had tried sterner measures to break down the opposition. The ex-Patriarch Joseph had been at first allowed to live in peace in his monastery in Constantinople and was on friendly terms with the new Patriarch John Veccus; but he still refused to subscribe to the Union. He was therefore exiled to a lonely island in the Black Sea. He was at once treated as a martyr, and his following grew. Michael had already offended large sections of the Church in 1266, when he had deposed the Patriarch Arsenius for refusing to absolve him of the blinding of the little Emperor John Vatatzes. Now the Arsenite party united with Joseph's. Prelates and statesmen who spoke against the Union were deprived of their posts. Many of them were imprisoned; others fled into exile, sure of a welcome at the Bulgarian court from the Emperor's sister Eulogia and her daughter the Tsaritsa. In Epirus Eulogia's other son-in-law, the Despot Nicephorus, repudiated the Union and took advantage of its unpopularity to drive Michael's troops out of the town of Butrinto. Further south Duke John of Neopatras, who owed his independence to alliances with his Latin neighbours, came out as the champion of Orthodoxy. He summoned a synod of all the clergy in Greece in 1277, which pronounced the excommunication of the Emperor, the Patriarch and the Pope. It was followed by open rebellion against the Emperor in Macedonia; and when Michael sent troops to reduce the rebels, the army showed such marked sympathy with their cause that he recalled it to Constantinople.

There followed a number of further arrests in the capital. Even members of the Imperial family, including the Emperor's nephews, Andronicus Palaeologus, his brother's son, and Eulogia's son John were imprisoned. Sterner treatment was given to bishops who were suspected of not wholeheartedly accepting the Union. The Emperor's measures only provided his opponents with a list of martyrs and embittered their resistance. The Patriarch John Veccus begged Michael to temper his severity. Michael was furious with him and ordered him to resign from the Patriarchate. But as the papal legates were now expected, his resignation was not publicly announced, to avoid embarrassment.

The legates arrived at Constantinople in the late spring of 1279, after having first met the Emperor at Adrianople, where he had gone to restore order in his mutinous army. He assured them of his personal loyalty to the Union and with his son signed a new Declaration of Faith which embodied the creed of the Council of Lyons. He proved his sincerity by sending them round the prisons, where they could see for themselves how strictly he was punishing the enemies of Union, however high-born. They soon discovered that he had quarrelled with Veccus and wisely insisted that he should be restored to favour. But it was impossible to convince them that the Union was in fact accepted by the Emperor's subjects. Before they met the assembled clergy of the Empire Michael held a secret meeting at which he spoke frankly to his bishops. He told them of the new papal demands, some of which, such as the acceptance of a permanent cardinal-legate, were contrary to Gregory X's promises. He assured them that they need not themselves add an iota to their creed; he would not insist on it, even if it meant a war with all the Italians. But, he said, some concessions were necessary in the present crisis. When the storm is raging, a wise captain does not hesitate to jettison part of the cargo. Great tact must be shown; in hunting you do not alarm your quarry by making too much noise. The Emperor's metaphors were effective. When the legates made their demands to the Church Assembly they were heard courteously and calmly. The bishops then proceeded to draw up a statement on the creed in which the Procession of the Holy Ghost was discussed at enormous length with all the subtle theological verbiage in which the Greek language was rich and which was quite impossible to translate into Latin. It was signed by all the bishops present, though some of the signatures were said to be forged by the Emperor. The Pope's further demands were not mentioned. The

legates were sent back to Rome with this document and the
Emperor's and his son's personal declaration and a number of
verbal promises that the Pope's wishes would be carried out. As
an earnest of the Emperor's good faith he insisted that the legates
should be accompanied by two Greek bishops, Ignatius and
Meletius, who had led the opposition. The Pope was asked to
punish them as he thought best.[1]

Pope Nicholas was not satisfied by his legates' report, but he
took no hostile action against the Emperor. With admirable
wisdom he sent Ignatius and Meletius straight back to Constantinople, saying that they struck him as sincere and virtuous men
who had been falsely accused. He wished to show that he was
not personally unreasonable nor unsympathetic towards the Greeks.
He still forbade Charles to attack the Empire. His forbearance
was perhaps due to handsome gifts of money sent him by Michael.
His avarice was notorious; and it was freely rumoured that
throughout his pontificate Byzantine gold brought to him by the
Emperor's agents had been the main cause of the restraint that he
imposed upon Charles.[2]

But Charles did not have to suffer this restraint for much longer.
On 22 August 1280 Nicholas III died from a sudden heart-attack
at his villa of Soriano, near to Viterbo. The cardinals met at once
at Viterbo to elect a successor. Once again the Italian and French
parties in the College were too evenly balanced. The Italians,
however were divided among themselves, as many of them had
resented the concentration of power in the hands of the Orsini
family. Charles himself remained discreetly in Apulia, but his
agents in Rome and at Viterbo stirred up hostility against the
late Pope's relatives. The conclave dragged on for six months.
Early in the New Year the impatient populace in Viterbo began
to riot against the cardinals. Charles used the disorder as an excuse
to move troops to the town and with the consent of the citizens to
imprison the cardinals in the palace till they should make up their
minds. They were overawed. On 22 February 1281 they elected a

Frenchman, Simon of Brie, Cardinal of Saint Cecilia, who took the title of Martin IV and was enthroned on 23 March at Orvieto.[1]

The new Pope was an old friend of the French royal House. In his early days he had worked at Saint Louis's court. Pope Urban IV had given him his cardinal's hat and had appointed him legate in France, where he had played a part in arranging for Charles's candidature for the Sicilian throne. Of recent years he had led the French faction in the College of Cardinals and was known to be in close touch with Charles. He was a passionate patriot. Of the seven cardinals that he elevated within a month of his enthronement four were Frenchmen, one English and only two Italians. Charles could count on a revolution in papal policy. It was with high expectations that he journeyed northward to greet his new overlord at Orvieto in April.[2]

He was not disappointed. Pope Martin was ready to do his utmost to oblige a fellow-Frenchman. He had no feeling for the dignity of the Holy See as arbiter between the princes of Christendom. He disliked the Germans, and King Rudolph in particular. He distrusted the Italians and had no intention of allowing them to rule themselves. The Christians of the East meant nothing to him except as offering a field for renewed French imperialist expansion. The first result of his meeting with Charles was the King's restoration to the post of senator of Rome. The Orsini family were disgraced. In their place Charles appointed as his pro-senators three Provençals, Philip of Lavena, William l'Estandart and Geoffrey of Dragon. Charles was also invited to send troops and officials to other parts of the papal states. This was necessary, as the change of papal policy had roused the Ghibellines into action. Led by Guy of Montefeltro they organized a revolt, based on the town of Forli. The Pope sent against them Angevin troops under the direction of the papal Vicar, the Provençal canonist, William Durand, with one of Charles's most able soldiers, John of Eppe, as Rector. They laid siege to Forli without much success, but were able to keep the rebellion in check.[3]

In Tuscany Cardinal Malabranca, the late Pope's nephew, was removed, and the peace that he had arranged between Guelfs and Ghibellines collapsed. King Rudolph hastened to appoint a new Imperial Vicar; and his coming encouraged the Ghibellines to rise. Pisa, San Miniato, San Gimignano and Pescia paid him homage, but an attempt to stage a Ghibelline revolution at Siena in July 1281 failed. The Imperial Vicar was not allowed into any of the Guelf towns.[1] With the Pope's encouragement the Tuscan Guelf League re-formed itself early the following year. But Martin made no further overt interference in Tuscan affairs. Further north he could do little to help Charles. A small Angevin army that invaded Piedmont in May 1281 was decisively beaten by the Marquis of Saluzzo at Borgo San Dalmazzo. Thenceforward the only Angevin lands left there were in the upper valley of the river Stura, beneath the Maddalena Pass. But Charles was no longer interested in Piedmont. He had decided that it was of no particular value to his Empire. Had he hoped still to control Lombardy, control of the Piedmontese passes would have been almost essential. But there, too, he had cut his losses. When the two leading members of the Torriani family that had formerly held Milan, Gaston, lord of Lodi, and Raymond, Patriarch of Ravenna, were routed by the Visconti at Vaprio on 25 May 1281 Lombardy passed to the Ghibellines, paying a vague allegiance to King Rudolph.[2]

Little as Charles and the Pope liked Rudolph, they would not quarrel with him; for the scheme to revive the Kingdom of Arles and give it to Charles's family depended on his co-operation. On 24 May 1281 Martin issued a Bull which recorded the arrangements made by his predecessor. The little Habsburg princess Clementia was due now to arrive in Italy to marry Charles's grandson, Charles Martel; and as soon as the marriage between the two children had taken place, the kingdom was to come into being and the bridegroom's father, Charles, Prince of Salerno, was to take over its government. There were many lords in the upper Rhône valley to whom the prospect of the new Angevin dominion was unwelcome. Their resentment was fanned by Charles's indefatigable enemy, the Queen-Mother of France. In the autumn of 1281 Queen Margaret organized an assembly at Troyes. Her son-in-law, Duke Robert of Burgundy, Otho Count of Burgundy and the Franche-Comté, and his stepfather, the old Count of Savoy, John of Belesmes, Archbishop of Lyons, the Count of Champlitte and several lesser lords attended. They made plans to gather together an army to meet at Lyons in May of the next year, when it was expected that the Angevin troops would arrive to take over the kingdom. But outside help was needed. Queen Margaret could get none from her son, King Philip. He was under the influence of his second wife, Maria of Brabant, and his cousin, Robert of Artois, both of whom admired King Charles. He was also annoyed with his mother because of her adoration of her English nephew, King Edward. But King Edward would equally give her no help. He was sympathetic; but he was not going to risk a war with France. King Rudolph, whose approval as suzerain of the kingdom was necessary to her schemes, refused to go back on his treaty with Charles. He was satisfied with a solution that gave his daughter a kingdom and himself, so he hoped, a free hand in northern Italy. By the early spring of 1282 it was clear that the lords who had met so enthusiastically at Troyes were in no position to take action. Instead, a fleet of Angevin ships was assembling at Marseilles, ready to sail up the Rhône and establish the new government.[1]

Charles was now secure in central Italy, with Rome in his hands once more. He had the prospect of a rich kingdom in the Rhône valley to round off his Provençal lands. He was King of Jerusalem and recognized leader of the Latin East. A period of comparative peace had restored his finances. The Pope would do whatever he might wish. The time had come at last for his grand expedition against Constantinople.

Pressed by Charles, Pope Martin did not hesitate to break off the negotiations over Church Union with the Emperor Michael. He had some justification. The report brought back by Pope Nicholas's legates made it clear that the Greeks themselves were unflinchingly opposed to the Union, however sincerely their Emperor might support it. Further news from Constantinople told of bitter debates and riots. The conditions laid down by Pope Nicholas had not been fulfilled. Michael himself still hoped to keep on friendly terms with the Papacy. As soon as he heard of Martin's election he sent two of his Unionist bishops, the metropolitans of Heraclea and Nicaea, to Italy with his congratulations and his assurance of devotion to the Roman See.[1]

When the ambassadors arrived at Orvieto, in November 1281, they were greeted with a chilly disdain. They found King Charles as well as the Pope in residence there. Four months before, on 3 July 1281, Charles and his son-in law, the titular Latin Emperor Philip, had met at Orvieto delegates from the Republic of Venice and, with the Pope's blessing, had signed a treaty 'for the restoration of the Roman Empire usurped by Palaeologus'. A joint expedition was to set out in April 1282. According to the rumour of the time Charles was to provide twenty heavily armed men-of-war, a hundred light galleys, and transports for eight or ten thousand horsemen and their horses and a larger number of infantry. Venice would provide about the same number of galleys and men-of-war. More troops would join the expedition from the Frankish principality of Achaea. The Pisans were told by the Pope to provide ships and agreed, under protest, to send a few. Only Genoa refused to take part in the alliance.[2] When at last the Byzantine bishops were granted an audience with the Pope he thundered at them an angry complaint against their Emperor and all his people and dismissed them with a copy of a Bull which he signed on 18 November. It denounced Michael as a heretic and a fosterer of heresy. It forbade all Christian princes to have any contact or communication with him, and added that unless he submitted and handed over his Empire to the Pope by the following 1 May he would be deposed and considered an out-law.[1]

Secure in the Pope's good graces, Charles and his allies had made no secret of their preparations. Michael was already alarmed; but he had not expected so complete a change in papal policy. When he heard of his excommunication he ordered the commemoration of the Pope's name to be left out of the divine liturgy and he suspended all the measures that he had taken to force Union on his subjects. But, for all his faults, he was a sincere man. He considered himself bound to the policy of Union for the rest of his days, still hoping that some later Pope might show a better understanding. Meanwhile he made his preparations to meet the coming storm.[2]

It had already broken in Albania. There, in 1280, Charles had captured Butrinto from the Despot of Epirus and sent an expedition under one of his most trusted generals, Hugh, called the Red, of Sully, to reoccupy the interior. During the autumn of 1280 this Angevin army drove the Byzantines back to the fortress of Berat. The siege of Berat began at the end of September. Its governor was Michael Angelus, full brother to the bastard John of Neopatras, but the son-in-law of the Emperor and loyal to him. He appealed for help from Constantinople. In answer the Emperor sent as large a force as he could afford under his nephew and commander-in-chief, Michael Tarchaniotes; but it did not reach Albania till February. Meanwhile Charles had sent reinforcements including a number of powerful siege-engines to Sully, with the order that he was to take the city by storm. The tremendous rock on which Berat stands made an assault difficult. Sully preferred to occupy the countryside and starve the garrison into surrender. But he failed to intercept the Byzantine relieving force. It arrived in March 1281 and encamped in a good defensive position across the river Lium at the foot of the citadel. From there it was able to send provisions of food and arms by raft across the stream, and skilled climbers carried them up the rocks into the town. At the end of March a small Angevin body of troops, led by the Marshal of Albania, Polisi, was surprised and annihilated by the Byzantines. A few days later, on 3 April, Sully himself made a reconnaissance towards the Greek camp. Tarchaniotes feigned flight and led him into an ambush. In the skirmish Sully himself, a huge, heavy man, easily distinguished by his flaming red hair, fell from his horse and was captured. More Angevin troops hurried across the river to rescue their leader, but as the soldiers clambered up the bank the Byzantines fell on them and drove them back in panic. Soon the whole Angevin army was in headlong flight towards the sea. The victory not only relieved Berat but gave the Emperor control of the whole interior of Albania and northern Epirus, as far south as Janina. But Charles retained his hold over the coastal towns, from Durazzo to Butrinto and Chimara.[1]

The giant red-haired captive was led in chains through the streets of Constantinople; and Michael was so delighted by his victory that he commissioned a fresco of it to be painted on the walls of his palace.[2] He had little else to cheer him, apart from minor successes in the Peloponnese. Prince William of Achaea died in 1278. By the terms of his treaty with Charles his principality passed to his daughter Isabella and her husband, Charles's son Philip, and Charles took over the government in their name. He sent out as his *bailli* and Vicar-General a Frenchman, Galeran of Ivry. Galeran had been for the last six years seneschal of Sicily, where he had made himself thoroughly disliked. He was not more popular in the Peloponnese. His arrogance offended the local Frankish nobility. He filled the administration with his own personal friends. His troops freely plundered the Greek villages throughout the principality. His only campaign against the Byzantine possessions in the south-east was badly defeated in the defiles of Skorta, in the Taygetus mountains. In 1280 a deputation of Achaean barons went to Naples to insist on Galeran's recall. The next Vicar-General was Philip of Lagonesse, who had been a rather unsuccessful commander in Piedmont. He was more considerate towards the local baronage, but had some difficulty in persuading them to provide troops for the grand expedition against Constantinople. In the meantime the Byzantine lands in the peninsula were left in peace.[1]

Charles was not much better served by his naval commander in Aegean waters, Marco II Sanudo, Duke of Naxos. He used his ships as a pirate fleet and preyed more successfully on Latin shipping than on Greek because the Latins did not expect to be attacked by him. But he was ready to join in the great expedition.[2]

Such successes as Michael's policy enjoyed in Greece were outbalanced by new diplomatic troubles. In Bulgaria his niece, the Tsaritsa Maria, who had been a fierce opponent of his religious policy, had fallen from power in 1279. Her first husband, Constantine Asen, had been badly injured in a riding accident early in 1277. She then had her stepson, his heir, murdered to secure the succession of her own child, Michael; but before the end of the year a popular revolt led by a peasant called Ivailo, whom the Greeks surnamed Lachanas, the 'vegetable-eater', dethroned and killed the crippled Tsar. Maria, after a little hesitation, married Lachanas, raised him to the throne and soon had him under her influence. The Emperor Michael sent an army to replace Ivailo by Constantine Asen's grandson, Ivan Mytses, who had fled to Constantinople. His troops were routed. He then appealed to the chief of the Tartars of the Russian steppes, Nogai, who had married his illegitimate daughter. Nogai invaded Bulgaria. Lachanas was captured early in 1279, and a few months later Maria and her son, Michael Asen, surrendered and were sent to the Emperor. Ivan Mytses Asen was put on the throne and given the hand of Michael's daughter Irene. There was still some unrest in Bulgaria, led by a powerful noble, George Terteri Rakovski. On the Emperor's advice the new tsar offered his own sister to George Terteri, who took the bride and then began at once to intrigue against his brother-in-law. At the same time Ivailo reappeared to reclaim the throne, backed by a Tartar army. The Tsar Ivan fled with his wife to Constantinople to ask for help from his father-in-law; but Michael was shocked by his cowardice and would not receive him. He went on instead to the Tartar court, hoping that Nogai's wife, his sister-in-law, would help him. There he found Ivailo, who had found George Terteri too powerful to attack. Nogai played with both suppliants, then decided to rid himself of both. Ivailo was put to death; but Ivan Asen was warned by his sister-in-law. He returned to Constantinople, where the Emperor relented so far as to give him a place in the Imperial hierarchy. Meanwhile George Terteri, who was well aware of the general diplomatic situation, sent an embassy to Italy to tell Charles that he was ready to make an alliance with him and to hint to the Pope that he might bring the Bulgarian Church under Rome.[1]

All Michael's activities had only resulted in Bulgaria joining his enemies. Serbia had never been a friend. Stephen Uroš I had been dethroned in 1276 by his elder son, Stephen Uroš II Dragutin, with the help of the King of Hungary, his brother-in-law, and possibly the connivance of the Emperor Michael. But Dragutin was a sick man. After resigning once from the throne in favour of his younger brother and returning to it again, he finally abdicated in 1281, and he was compensated by the Hungarian king with a duchy in Bosnia, where he spent the rest of his days vainly persecuting the Bogomils. His brother, Stephen Uroš III Milutin, who succeeded him, was under the influence of his mother Helena, the daughter of the Emperor Baldwin. He reverted to his father's anti-Byzantine policy. Under Dragutin Serbia had been neutral; but Milutin began his reign with a campaign against the Empire; and in the autumn of 1281 he captured the Macedonian fortress of Skoplje, thus threatening the road to the Emperor's Epirote possessions. Milutin was glad to promise his alliance to his uncle, the titular Emperor Philip, and to King Charles.[2]

The Despot of Epirus, liking neither Charles nor Michael, kept as neutral as possible. But his half-brother, John Angelus of

Neopatras, conveniently forgetting his rôle of champion of orthodoxy in 1279, offered his support to the Latin crusade against
Constantinople.[1]

To add to the Emperor's embarrassments war had broken out
along his Asiatic frontier. For most of his reign the Anatolian
Turks beyond the frontier had been quiet. Michael's policy had
been to maintain an alliance with his son-in-law, the Mongol
Ilkhan Abaga. The Mongols were always ready to put pressure
on the Seljuk Sultans of Anatolia. But the Mongol attacks resulted
in the decay of Seljuk authority, especially in the west of the
peninsula, where a number of ambitious local Turkish emirates
grew up, their numbers reinforced by Turkish immigrants who
had been swept along westward in the wave of the first Mongol
invasions. The increase of Mameluk power, and especially the
capture of Antioch by Sultan Baibars in 1268, made the Ilkhan's
control over Anatolia less easy to sustain. In 1277 Baibars had
himself invaded Anatolia and only retired at the approach of a
large Mongol army. The Ilkhan's task was to recover the mastery
of northern Syria from the Mameluks. His last great effort to
drive them back met with disaster at the battle of Homs in the
autumn of 1281. In the meantime the recapture of Constantinople
diverted the main interests of the Byzantines to Europe. The
Asiatic frontier, which the Nicaean Emperors had carefully reorganized, was neglected. The peasant military holdings which
the Nicaeans had set up on the old Byzantine model gave way to
feudalized estates. Taxation rose steeply to pay for the Emperor's
European commitments. When the Turkish tribes began to in-
filtrate over the frontier there was no proper opposition to them.
In the winter of 1280 a combination of Turkish emirs invaded the
Meander valley and laid siege to the city of Tralles, the modern
Aydin, which commanded the lower Meander plain. Michael sent
his son Andronicus against them, but he could not spare many
troops; his main army was marching to the relief of Berat, far
away in Albania. Andronicus was unable to save Tralles. He

spent the whole of 1281 trying to establish a firm frontier north of the Meander, to protect Smyrna and the Lycus valley. It was clear that part of the Byzantine army would have to remain in the district, and thus reduce the forces that could defend the capital.[1]

By the end of 1280 the outlook for the Emperor Michael was sombre. He was entangled in warfare in Asia. In Europe a great alliance of enemy powers encircled him, dominated by the relentless King of Sicily. His religious policy, for which he had forfeited the love of his subjects, had proved an utter failure; the Papacy, which he had hoped would protect him, was goading his enemies on. If the great expedition that King Charles was preparing were indeed hurled against Constantinople, there seemed little chance that he and his Empire would survive. But Michael was not quite at the end of his resources. Byzantine diplomacy was still the best in the world.

Though foes surrounded the Byzantine capital, further afield there were still friends who might help. It was with trepidation but not in entire despair that Michael awaited the spring of 1282, when the Angevin armada was due to sail out from the harbours of Italy.

CHAPTER XII

THE GREAT CONSPIRACY

At the opening of the year 1282 Charles, King of Sicily, Jerusalem and Albania, Count of Provence, Forcalquier, Anjou and Maine, regent of Achaea, overlord of Tunis and senator of Rome, was without doubt the greatest potentate in Europe. In a few weeks his ships were to sail up the Rhône to give his grandson the Kingdom of Arles; in a few weeks a still vaster expedition would be launched against the Christian East, to make him master of the Mediterranean and ruler of an Empire unparalleled since the days of Justinian. Men talked of an ancient prophecy about a certain Charles, descended both from Charlemagne and the House of France, who was to become Emperor of the world and reformer of the whole Christian Church. Everything was ready for the supreme triumph of the Angevin.[1]

But his arrogance blinded his vision. Confident in his power and the support of the Papacy, he forgot that he still had enemies in Europe whose strength he had not tested. He forgot that despite the efficiency of his government many of his subjects detested him and the haughty French officials who carried out his will. He forgot the exiles from his Sicilian kingdom who were sworn to his destruction.

These exiles found a refuge across the sea, at Barcelona, capital of the kingdom of Aragon. Twenty years before, in 1262, King Manfred had married his daughter Constance to the Infant Peter, elder son of the Aragonese king, James I. As though foreseeing the future, Pope Urban and King Louis IX of France had protested against the marriage. But Manfred was still on his throne; his friendship was of value to Aragon. With Manfred slain and Conradin beheaded and Manfred's bastard sons languishing in prison, the Infanta Constance became the heiress of the Hohenstaufen cause in Italy. Her husband was devoted to her and proud of her descent. For some years before he ascended his father's throne his court gave her in her own right the title of queen.[1]

So long as her father-in-law lived, Constance could do little to justify her title. King James was a remarkable man, gallant, boastful and eccentric. He had inherited his throne in 1213, when he was aged five. In his younger days he had by his own energy and enterprise conquered the Balearic Islands and the rich emirate of Valencia from the Moors. When he was nearly sixty he himself led the army which added the emirate of Murcia to his kingdom. He was involved in French politics, as the Counties of Roussillon and Cerdagne formed part of his kingdom, and he had inherited Montpellier from his mother. The Counts of Provence were a cadet branch of his family; and he considered that he should have been consulted on the disposal of the County after the death of his cousin, Raymond-Berengar IV. He only agreed to recognize Charles as Count when Saint Louis offered in exchange to give up the suzerain rights of France over Roussillon and Cerdagne. As he grew older James preferred to spend his time in dalliance with his mistresses. He never quite forgave Charles for his possession of Provence; and he still saw himself as a great crusading king. He was the only monarch to accept Gregory X's invitation to the Council of Lyons, where his mixture of good sense and grandiloquent bombast impressed and exasperated the assembled Fathers. But he was too shrewd and too weary, for all his talk, to involve himself now in a war. He did not, however, discourage his son and his daughter-in-law in their ambitions.[2]

It was after Conradin's defeat that the first distinguished refugees arrived at the Infanta's court at Barcelona. They were led by Roger of Lauria, who had shared her foster-mother with her. With them came officials who had served her grandfather, Frederick II, such as Richard Filangieri. They were followed soon afterwards by the lawyer Henry of Isernia and by the ablest intriguer of them all, the doctor John of Procida.[3]

John of Procida was born at Salerno in 1210. He studied medicine at the famous university of his native city and was given a professorial chair. His talents impressed Frederick II, who gave the university his special patronage; and John soon became the Emperor's personal physician. He was rewarded for his work by the gift of various lands near Naples, including the island of Procida. He attended Frederick in his last illness. On the Emperor's death he reverted to a general medical practice, numbering among his patients Cardinal John Orsini (the future Pope Nicholas III) and King Conrad. He entered Manfred's service when Manfred took over the government of the Kingdom. Manfred was so struck by his ability that he made him Chancellor of the realm. On Manfred's fall he went into retirement. Pope Clement wrote to Charles to recommend John to him for his medical skill; and John was allowed to keep his estates under the amnesty offered by Charles after Benevento. But his loyalty was given to the Hohenstaufen. During the year 1266 he obtained leave to go to Viterbo to arrange for the betrothal of his daughter to the Neapolitan Guelf, Bartholomew Caracciolo, who was in attendance at the papal court. As soon as Conradin's descent into Italy was known he slipped away from Viterbo and joined the Hohenstaufen army. After the disaster at Tagliacozzo he escaped from the battlefield with Manfred Maletta and for a time took refuge at Venice. His estates were confiscated by Charles; and it was popularly supposed that his wife was maltreated, one of his daughters raped and one of his sons killed by the arrogant French knight who came to evict them from their home. John spent the years 1269 and 1270 in Germany, together with his friend, Henry of Isernia, trying to induce Frederick II's grandson, Frederick of Thuringia, to invade Italy and restore the Hohenstaufen. But Frederick was an unsatisfactory candidate, readier to talk than to act. John seems to have lingered some time in southern Germany and the Ghibelline cities of northern Italy. His brother Andrew and his surviving sons were with him. He secured for Andrew a place at the court of the Marquis of Montferrat. Then, some time before 1275, he moved with his sons, Francis and Thomas, to Barcelona. He had decided that Constance of Aragon should avenge her father's family. He was at once taken into the confidence of Constance and her husband and set himself to further their ambitions.[1]

King James of Aragon died in July 1276, after a glorious reign of sixty-three years. He preserved his vigour to the last, and was little troubled by his excommunication by the Pope for his last illicit love-affair. The new king and queen, Peter and Constance, were free to pursue their own policy. They could only move slowly at first. King James had left the Balearic Islands and Roussillon to his younger son, the Infant James, who took the title of King of Majorca and refused for nearly three years to acknowledge his brother as his suzerain. The risk of a fratricidal war was only ended when James of Majorca submitted and took an oath of vassalage in January 1279. Peter also had trouble with the Moors of Andalusia, who made a determined effort to reconquer Murcia. It was not till the end of 1279 that his southern frontier was secure. He was determined to be equally secure on his western frontier, with Castile, before he started on any new adventure. Luck favoured him. The Infant Ferdinand, surnamed of La Cerda, King Alfonso X's eldest son, died in 1275, leaving a widow, Blanche of France, Philip III's sister, and two young sons. Alfonso decided to leave the Castilian throne to his second son, Sancho, rather than risk a long minority. Philip III prepared to march into Castile in defence of his nephews' rights, while the widowed princess, fearing that Sancho had designs against her boys' lives, fled to Aragon. King Peter made them welcome, but refused to allow them to leave his care. So long as they were in his power he had a hostage to use against King Philip and a tool to use against King Alfonso, who soon repented of his decision, and Sancho, who was so impatient to secure the inheritance that in 1281 he openly rebelled against his father. By 1280

Peter of Aragon could count on having no more trouble in Spain. He could give his full attention to Italy.[1]

Legend has made of John of Procida a grand conspirator who journeyed in disguise round the courts of Europe winning adherents to the cause of his master and mistress. Stories of his adventures were in circulation almost within his own lifetime. They survive in vernacular Sicilian chronicles and are echoed in the works of Villani, of Petrarch and of Boccaccio. In fact John's own role was not so adventurous nor so picturesque as his admirers and his enemies imagined, but it was none the less vital. He was at the centre of a vast political conspiracy.[2]

Soon after his accession King Peter nominated John of Procida as Chancellor of Aragon, commending him in the deed of appointment for his learning and his known fidelity to the House of Hohenstaufen.[3] The post gave John control of the king's foreign policy; and he used it, with Peter's full approval, to plan the downfall of the Angevins. Till 1279 he could do little more than keep in touch with King Charles's potential enemies, with the Queen-Mother of France, with Rudolph of Habsburg, with Alfonso of Castile and, above all, with the Ghibellines in Italy. It was only when Peter was secure in Spain that more active work could be done. John was a realist. He saw that allies such as King Rudolph or King Alfonso were not to be trusted; their interests and ambitions were too various. There were only two foreign powers on which he could entirely rely. The Emperor Michael at Constantinople, faced with the perpetual threat of an Angevin invasion, had gone so far as to submit to Rome in his attempt to avert it; and his submission was unavailing. He would welcome an ally whose aim was Charles's destruction. He could not provide naval or military help for the invasion of Angevin lands; he needed his soldiers and his ships to defend his own territory. But his treasury still was full; he could afford to be generous in such a cause. Bound up in alliance with Constantinople was the Republic of Genoa. The Genoese enjoyed special trading privileges throughout the Empire. They had long been on bad terms with Charles of Anjou. If Charles, allied to the Venetians, overran Byzantium, it would mean the end of their commercial domination of the Black Sea. They were rich, and they had a fine fleet.

The plotters began work in earnest in 1279. According to the Sicilian legend it was in that year that John of Procida went secretly to Constantinople. Two Sicilian refugees who were living there told the Emperor of his arrival. Michael received him in private audience and was delighted with him. He remained for three months at the Imperial court; and when he left he was provided with letters from the Emperor to the King of Aragon and the people of Sicily and a generous sum of money. He went to Sicily, disguised as a Franciscan. There he met some of the leading Sicilian barons, headed by Palmieri Abbate, Alaimo of Lentini and Walter of Caltagirone. They told him of their grievances against the Angevin domination and of their despair of ending it. He comforted them and gave them Michael's letter to them, and suggested that they should write an appeal to the King of Aragon, the husband of their lawful queen, to come and rescue them. Having obtained this document he moved on, still in his Franciscan disguise, to see Pope Nicholas III at Viterbo. Their interview took place at the castle of Soriano, close by the city. John had cured Nicholas of a serious illness in his earlier days, and could talk to him as an old and trusted friend. His arguments appealed all the more to the avaricious Pope because they were accompanied by gifts of Byzantine gold. Nicholas was reminded of his grievances against Charles and in particular of the king's refusal to consider the marriage of a papal niece with a prince of the House of France. He let himself be persuaded by his old doctor, and at John's request wrote a letter to King Peter authorizing him to rescue Sicily from its Angevin bondage. John then returned to Barcelona, to report on his activities to King Peter. Peter was at first dubious, but when he saw the letters from the Emperor, the Sicilian nobles and the Pope, he congratulated John with enthusiasm and told him to continue on his work.[1]

In the spring of 1280 John set out again. His first visit was to the Pope at Viterbo. There he obtained definite authority from Nicholas to tell the Sicilians to entrust themselves to King Peter. From Viterbo John went down to the coast and found a Pisan vessel, in which he sailed to Trapani in Sicily. His friends among the barons met him there. He told them of all that he had done and arranged a further meeting with them when he should return from Constantinople. A Venetian boat took him, still in disguise, to Negropont, where he transhipped into a Greek boat for the capital. The Emperor Michael received him again in secret audience and was delighted with his news. He offered the sum of thirty thousand ounces of gold to further the work. After a few days John left Constantinople in a Genoese galley, accompanied by a Byzantine ambassador, Latino Allardi, a Lombard in the Emperor's service. They sailed to Trapani, but on the way they met a Pisan boat, whose crew informed John that Pope Nicholas had just died. John was able to keep the news to himself. His Sicilian friends were waiting for him at Trapani. He persuaded them to come with him and Allardi to Malta, which was, it seems, less efficiently patrolled by King Charles's police. Their conference began well, till the Sicilians heard of the Pope's death. Alaimo of Lentini recommended that the whole enterprise should be called off. John answered sharply that it was too late for that. The next Pope might be as favourable as Nicholas to their cause; and if he were one of Charles's creatures, the Sicilians had resisted greater men than Charles in the past. They were convinced by his words and the sight of the Byzantine gold, and agreed that if King Peter were still willing to support the conspiracy they would co-operate. John and the Ambassador continued on their way to Barcelona. Peter received the ambassador with honour and gratefully accepted his gold, and he gave his approval to John's labours. It was arranged that an expedition for the conquest of

Sicily should be launched as soon as preparations could be completed, probably in the spring of 1282.[1]

It is difficult to know how much truth lies behind the legendary story. Throughout 1279 and 1280, when John was supposed to be on his conspiratorial travels, his signature appears regularly as Chancellor on documents signed in Aragon. It seems improbable that he would have gone to the trouble of arranging for the forging of his signature in order that his absence might remain secret. He was an old man approaching his seventieth year; it is unlikely that he would wander round Europe in disguise. The part assigned to Pope Nicholas is not very convincing. It is certain that he did not much like Charles, and that he was avaricious and would appreciate a gift of money from the Emperor. But his policy was for pacification, the independence of the papal states and the enrichment of the Orsini family. In none of the many papal documents of his time that survive is there any hint that he contemplated removing Charles from the Sicilian throne and replacing him by Peter of Aragon. It was alien to his temperament to risk a general war and the expenses that would undoubtedly follow. His attitude towards Byzantium was sterner than his predecessors'. It is possible that Byzantine gold kept him from breaking off negotiations with Michael altogether and from giving Charles permission to attack the Empire. It is possible, too, that he gave a friendly personal welcome to some emissary of his old doctor, John of Procida, and that the Aragonese party exaggerated the welcome in order to justify their policy. Out of some such incidents the rumour of the Pope's implication arose and Dante could reprove him for the 'ill-gotten coins which incited him against King Charles'.[2]

The legend errs over John's physical activities and the Pope's complicity. But many of its details carry conviction. Though John may have stayed at home, it is probable that someone made the journeys in his name. Their course and the details of the ships in which they were made are too precise to be entirely fictitious.

A contemporary Sicilian document connects John's name with those of the three Sicilian barons whom the legend cites as his accomplices. By 1280 there was certainly some diplomatic contact between the Byzantine and Aragonese courts; and at some time, as the sequel showed, the Emperor Michael made contact with the conspirators in Sicily. It may be that one of John's sons undertook the voyages later credited to his more famous father. We know that his brother Andrew, who was in the service of the Marquis of Montferrat, acted as liaison between Aragon and the Ghibellines of northern Italy. His son Francis may have gone on these longer journeys. It can hardly be doubted that they took place, though the trusted emissary who made them cannot now be identified.[1]

By the end of 1280 King Peter was so far committed to an attack on Sicily that he barely bothered to disguise his intentions. A letter that he wrote in October to the Milanese government, regretting the defeats of his ally of Montferrat, spoke of 'the Day'—'dies illa'—which was not far off, when they would all rejoice. In December he went with his brother, the King of Majorca, to Toulouse to interview King Philip of France about the Castilian question and the fate of the Infants of La Cerda. Philip was accompanied by his cousin, Charles, Prince of Salerno, King Charles's eldest son. Peter made a point of treating the Prince with such chilly disdain that the French were deeply shocked and James of Majorca felt obliged to show the young man especial cordiality to avoid an open quarrel.[2]

The election of a French Pope, Martin IV, early in 1281, did not discourage Peter. Throughout that year, while Charles of Anjou in Italy was preparing his armada for his attack on Constantinople, the Aragonese at Barcelona prepared a fleet of almost equal strength. Charles's expedition was officially said to be a crusade against the infidel; and on that excuse the Pope allowed him the tithes of the Church in Sardinia, an island which Charles and the Pisans disputed and Peter claimed as his own. But Charles himself did not hide the fact that his first objective was the Byzantine capital. The alliance that he made in July, under the Pope's authority, with the titular Emperor Philip and the Venetians, openly stated his claims.[1] Peter was rather more cautious. He too announced that his expedition was a crusade; and he could give good proof of it. Two years before, in 1279, he had taken advantage of a disputed succession to the Tunisian throne after the death of King Mustansir, Saint Louis's old enemy, to secure the succession of his own candidate, Ibrahim Abu Ishak. An expedition under Conrad Lancia installed King Ibrahim, who in return promised Peter a large yearly tribute and the right to open consulates at Tunis and Bougie. At the same time Peter took the governor of Constantine, Ibn Hasan, under his protection. During 1281 the governor quarrelled with the Tunisian king, who prepared to march against him. He appealed to King Peter, hinting that if he were given assistance he would adopt Christianity. It was therefore Peter's duty to rescue the potential convert and his territory from the infidel Tunisians. He had a ready and unexceptionable answer to give when King Philip of France, nervous for his uncle Charles's welfare, sent to ask him about the army and the fleet that he was collecting.[2]

He was franker with his allies. At the end of 1281 a distinguished Genoese sea-captain, Benito Zaccaria, arrived at his court. Benito's brother Martin was a friend of the Emperor Michael, to whom he had in the past lent money and by whom he had been rewarded with the possession of Phocaea and its rich alum-mines. Benito had been visiting him and had gone on to Constantinople; and Michael had appointed him to be his ambassador to Genoa and to Aragon. He brought King Peter the assurance that both the Emperor and the Genoese were eager to help him, an assurance that was backed by gifts of money.[3] About the same time John of Procida wrote to Alfonso of Castile and his sons, knowing their dislike of the Angevins, to tell them that his master's alliance with the Marquis of Montferrat, Alfonso's son-in-law, had been joined by the Florentine Ghibelline chief, Guy Novello. His letters were taken to the Castilian court by Andrew of Procida, who had come from northern Italy with the Ghibelline ambassadors. John spoke openly of the plan to restore the Kingdom of Sicily to its hereditary and rightful owner and suggested that the Castilians might join the alliance. The quarrels between King Alfonso and his son Sancho prevented them from accepting the suggestion.[1]

These diplomatic activities strengthened King Peter's hand. But the main object of the conspiracy was to stir up trouble within King Charles's dominions. Here John of Procida showed his political genius. He came himself from the Italian mainland; but he knew that the mainlanders were not dissatisfied with Charles's government. Charles himself was an able and conscientious ruler. He spent most of his time in or near Naples or in Apulia. There he could supervise the administration and see that his officials were not oppressive. The Neapolitans and the Apulians might resent the high taxation and the the ruthless efficiency of its collection; they might resent the small part that they were allowed in their country's control. But Charles was ready to improve their harbours and their roads and to encourage their fairs. There were also good jobs that loyal Italians could obtain in his other dominions, in Provence or Albania or Palestine. The island of Sicily was in a different position. Charles distrusted the Sicilians, especially after the great revolt at the time of Conradin's invasion. He did practically nothing to help their economy. He never visited the island except when he was on his way to the Tunisian crusade; he never personally supervised its administration. It was run by French justiciars, with Italians from the mainland working under them. There is little doubt that these administrators were haughty, harsh and rapacious and almost certainly corrupt. Taxes were heavy; and only the friends of officials were spared extortion. The Sicilians had, even under Frederick II and Manfred, resented a government based on Naples. To their dislike of the mainlanders was added a hatred of the French, who never bothered

14-2

to learn their language or to respect their customs. They saw themselves now being ruled to enable an alien tyrant make conquests
from which they would have no benefit. The Greek element in
the island was still strong and kept some sympathy with the
Greeks of Byzantium. To be press-ganged into Charles's fleet for
the purpose of conquering Constantinople had no attraction.[1]

Charles was wrong to disregard the Sicilians and John of Procida
right to seek their support. Of all the peoples of Europe they are
the most adept at conspiracy. Their loyalty to the Secret Society
is only equalled by their loyalty to the honour of the family.
They provided a perfect field for John and his fellow-plotters to
cultivate. Their grievances against Angevin rule were real and
intense; they could be trusted to welcome a deliverer. But the
good conspirator works in silence. Apart from the legendary
tales of John's journeys there are no records of the manner in
which the island conspiracy was organized. Everything was done
in secret. It is certain that agents from Aragon were working in
the island. It is certain that arms were smuggled in. It is equally
certain that the conspirators were in close touch with Constantinople, from which they received money with the promise of
more to come, should all go according to the plan.

In the spring of 1282 the whole Mediterranean world knew
that a crisis was near. King Charles was gathering his great fleet
together. In the middle of March his Neapolitan and Provençal
squadrons assembled in the harbour of Messina, ready to set sail
as soon as the order was given. Other squadrons waited in the
ports for Venetian ships to join them. King Charles himself was
at Naples, making the final dispositions for the campaign. It seems
that he planned to hurry across to Apulia and embark there when
the moment came.[2] It could not be long delayed. Three times
already he had been thwarted of his expedition, when King Louis
obliged him to join his crusade, when a storm destroyed his fleet
on its return from that crusade, and when the Pope banned it
during the long-drawn negotiations over the union of the Churches.

Now there was nothing to stop him. The Venetians and the Latins in Greece were about to join him. The Slav monarchs in the Balkans and the Greek princes of Epirus and Thessaly watched eagerly for the chance to share in the destruction of the Byzantine empire. The Emperor Michael himself was near to despair. If once the great Angevin armada reached his shores, only a miracle could save him; and a miracle was needed to keep it from sailing out from Italy. But Michael had his friends.

Charles in his self-confidence ignored those friends of his foe. He was warned by his agents throughout Italy that John of Procida had rallied all the Ghibellines to the support of Aragon. His nephew the King of France told him of the huge Aragonese fleet that was assembled in the Bay of Fangos, at the mouth of the river Ebro. This fleet was officially destined to fight the infidel in Africa; but King Philip knew that there were other aims in view. Charles discounted the rumours. He was too powerful; no one would dare to attack him. He never realized where his greatest danger lay.[1]

The fate of the future was hidden in Sicily. The discontented Sicilians, inflamed by agents from Aragon and enriched by agents from Constantinople, went their secret way plotting rebellion. It was on them that the Emperor Michael placed his reliance. Peter of Aragon might well wish to wait till Charles was fully engaged on his eastern war before venturing on the invasion of Angevin lands. Michael could not afford to wait for so long. The Angevin fleet was to set sail in the first week of April. Something must be done before that date.

CHAPTER XIII

THE VESPERS

Easter fell early in the year 1282, on 29 March. Throughout Holy Week the island of Sicily was outwardly calm. A great Angevin armada lay at anchor in Messina harbour. Royal agents toured the island commandeering all the stores of grain that they could find and rounding up herds of cattle and of pigs, to provide food for the expedition, and horses for the knights to ride, regardless of the peasants' sullen resentment. The Royal Vicar, Herbert of Orléans, governor of the island, was in residence at Messina, in the castle of Mategriffon, the 'terror of the Greeks', which Richard Cœur de Lion had built a century before. In Palermo the justiciar, John of Saint-Rémy, kept the feast in the palace of the Norman kings. None of the French officials and none of the soldiers who commanded the forty-two castles from which the countryside was policed noticed more than the habitual unfriend-liness shown them by the subject race. But amongst the Sicilians themselves as they celebrated the resurrection of Christ with their traditional songs and dancing in the streets, the atmosphere was tense and explosive.[1]

The Church of the Holy Spirit lies about half a mile to the south-east beyond the old city wall of Palermo, on the edge of the little gorge of the river Oreto. It is an austere building, without and within. Its foundation-stone was laid in 1177 by Walter Ophamil, or 'of the Mill', the English-born Archbishop of Palermo, on a day made sinister by an eclipse of the sun. It was the custom of the church to hold a festival on Easter Monday, and on Easter Monday of that year people came crowding as usual from the city and the villages around, to attend the Vesper service.[2]

There was gossiping and singing in the square as everyone

THE CHURCH OF THE VESPERS AT PALERMO

waited for the service to begin. Suddenly a group of French officials appeared to join in the festivities. They were greeted with cold, unfriendly looks, but they insisted on mingling with the crowd. They had drunk well and were carefree; and soon they treated the younger women with a familiarity that outraged the Sicilians. Among them was a sergeant called Drouet, who dragged a young married woman from the crowd and pestered her with his attentions. It was more than her husband could bear. He drew his knife and fell on Drouet, and stabbed him to death. The Frenchmen rushed up to avenge their comrade and suddenly found themselves surrounded by a host of furious Sicilians, all armed with daggers and swords. Not one of the Frenchmen survived. At that moment the bell of the Church of the Holy Spirit and of all the churches of the city began to ring for Vespers.[1]

To the sound of the bells messengers ran through the city calling on the men of Palermo to rise against the oppressor. At once the streets were full of angry armed men, crying 'Death to the French'—'moranu li Franchiski' in their Sicilian dialect.[2] Every Frenchman that they met was struck down. They poured into the inns frequented by the French and the houses where they dwelt, sparing neither man, woman nor child. Sicilian girls who had married Frenchmen perished with their husbands. The rioters broke into the Dominican and Franciscan convents; and all the foreign friars were dragged out and told to pronounce the word 'ciciri', whose sound the French tongue could never accurately reproduce. Anyone who failed in the test was slain. The Justiciar, John of Saint-Rémy, shut himself in the old royal palace; but most of the men of his garrison had been away holiday-making in the town. The few that remained could not hold it for him. He was wounded in the face during a skirmish at the entrance before fleeing with two attendants out of a window through the stables. They found horses and rode at full speed to the castle of Vicari, on the road into the interior. There they were joined by other refugees who had escaped the massacre.[3]

By the next morning some two thousand French men and women lay dead; and the rebels were in complete control of Palermo. Their fury had calmed down sufficiently for them to think of the future. Representatives of each district and each trade met together and proclaimed themselves a Commune, electing as their Captain an eminent knight called Roger Mastrangelo. Three vice-captains were appointed, Henry Baverio, Nicholas of Ortoleva and Nicholas of Ebdemonia, with five counsellors to assist them. The Angevin flag was torn down, and everywhere replaced by the Imperial eagle which Frederick II had allotted as a badge to the city of his childhood. A letter was sent with ambassadors to the Pope asking him to take the new Commune under his protection.[1]

Already news of the rising was spreading throughout the island. Runners hurried out during the fierce Monday night from Palermo to tell all the towns and villages to strike at once, before the oppressor could strike back. On the Tuesday the men of Palermo themselves marched out to destroy the castle of Vicari, where the Justiciar and his friends were taking refuge. The garrison was too small to resist for long; and the Justiciar offered to surrender if he were allowed to go down to the coast and embark for his native Provence. As the negotiations were beginning one of the besiegers fired an arrow at him and shot him dead. It was the signal for a general massacre of everyone inside the castle.[2]

Throughout the week news came of further uprisings and slaughtering of the French. The first town to follow the example of Palermo was Corleone, twenty miles to the south. After killing the French it too proclaimed itself a Commune. On 3 April its captain, Boniface, sent three envoys to Palermo to give the news and to suggest common action. The two Communes decided to send troops in three directions, westwards towards Trapani, southward towards Caltanissetta and eastward towards Messina, to rouse the rest of the island and co-ordinate its efforts. As the rebels approached each district, the French fled or were massacred.

In two towns only they were spared. The Vice-Justiciar of Western Sicily, William Porcelet, who lived at Calatafimi, had won the love of the Sicilians by his benevolence and his justice. He and his family were escorted with honour to Palermo and were allowed to embark for Provence. The town of Sperlinga, in the centre of the island, prided itself on its independence of view. The French garrison there was unharmed and was able to retire safely to Messina.[1]

In Messina there was no rising. The Vicar, Herbert of Orléans, had a strong garrison. The great Angevin fleet was in the harbour. Messina had been the only city in the island to which Charles's government had shown any favour; and its leading family, the Riso, supported his régime. On 13 April, a fortnight after the Vespers, when all the west and centre of the island was in rebel hands, the Commune of Palermo sent a letter to the people of Messina, asking them to join the rebellion. But the Messinese were cautious. With Herbert and his garrison dominating them from the castle of Mategriffon and with the king's ships lying off the quay, they preferred not to commit themselves. Instead, on 15 April a Messinese army troop, under a local knight, William Chiriolo, moved south to the neighbouring city of Taormina, to protect it against the fury of the rebels. At the same time Herbert sent the Messinese noble, Richard Riso, in command of seven local galleys to blockade Palermo harbour and if possible to attack its fortifications. The Palermitans hastened to display the banner of Messina with its cross alongside their banner on the walls, to show that they regarded the Messinese as their brothers; and Richard's sailors refused to fight them. The galleys remained off the harbour maintaining an unenthusiastic and inefficient blockade.[2]

In Messina opinion was swaying round in favour of the revolt. Many of its citizens were also citizens of Palermo who had moved to Messina when it became the administrative centre. Their sympathies were with their native city. Herbert began to lose confidence. He determined to make sure of Taormina and sent a troop of Frenchmen there under a Neapolitan, Micheletto Gatta, to replace the Messinese garrison. William Chiriolo and his men were offended by this lack of trust in them. They came to blows with the French and took them all prisoner. Two or three days later, on 28 April, Messina broke out into revolt. Most of the French had already retired to the castle of Mategriffon; and the massacres were on a smaller scale than at Palermo. Herbert blockaded himself in the castle, but he was obliged to abandon the fleet, which was set on fire and utterly destroyed. The Messinese declared themselves to be a Commune, under the protection of the Holy Church. They elected as their captain Bartholomew Maniscalco, who had played the chief part in organizing the revolt.

That same day three distinguished citizens of Messina arrived back from King Charles's court at Naples. They were Baldwin Mussone, a former judge, and Baldo and Matthew Riso. Mussone at once threw in his lot with the Commune, and Maniscalco resigned the captaincy to him next morning. One of the younger Risos, the doctor Parmenio, tried to persuade his uncles Baldo and Matthew to join the rebellion; but they and the rest of the family remained faithful to Charles and took refuge with Herbert in the castle. They found that Herbert was already giving up the struggle. After a preliminary attack had been made on the castle, he negotiated with Mussone and obtained a safe-conduct for himself and his staff. Two galleys were put at their disposal on condition that they sailed directly to Aigues-Mortes in France and promised never to return to Sicily. Herbert gave his word; but as soon as he was clear of the harbour he ordered the galleys to sail to Catona, just across the Strait. There he found Peter Ruffo, Count of Catanzaro, who was the richest noble in Calabria and loyal to Charles. They assembled troops to prepare for a counter-attack on Messina.

The Chatelain of the castle of Mategriffon, Theobald of Messy, with seventy French sergeants and their wives and children, was allowed similar terms. The whole company was placed in another ship, with orders to sail to Aigues-Mortes. The loyal members of the Riso family were kept as prisoners by the Commune in the castle of Mategriffon, where they were joined by Micheletto Gatta and his Frenchmen, who had been brought up under escort from Taormina. Messengers had already been sent to Palermo to tell of the events at Messina and of the foundation of the sister-Commune; and the Messinese ships still hovering off the port were ordered home. Their commander, Richard Riso, managed to slip away to Calabria. When the vice-commander Nicholas Pancia sailed round into Messina harbour he met the ship carrying the Chatelain Messy and his party. Pancia had already heard that Herbert of Orléans had broken his promise to retire to France and suspected that Messy was about to follow his example. The ship was detained and all its company cast into the sea and drowned.[1]

When order was restored in Messina the Commune elected four counsellors to assist the captain. They were all of them local judges, Raynald of Limogia, Nicholas Saporito, Peter Ansalano and Bartholomew of Neocastro, who later wrote a history of the great events.[2] Next it was decided, significantly, to send news to Constantinople, that the Emperor Michael should know that his chief enemy had been crippled. No doubt he might then in gratitude send more of his gold to the islanders. It was difficult to find a messenger to go on the perilous journey; but a Genoese merchant, Alafranco Cassano, volunteered his services. His nationality would protect him if he were detained by one of Charles's ships. He reached Constantinople a few weeks later and was given an immediate audience with the Emperor. Michael, when he heard the news, gave thanks to God and hastened to add to the autobiographical memoir that he was preparing for his son the significant words: 'Should I dare to claim that I was God's instrument in bringing freedom to the Sicilians, I should only be stating the truth.' His agents and his gold had indeed played their part in planning the uprising; and the uprising had not only freed Sicily; it had also saved his Empire. Charles's great expedition against Constantinople had now to be postponed for ever.[1]

Charles was at Naples when in the first days of April a messenger sent by the Archbishop of Monreale told him of the massacre at Palermo. He was angry; for it meant the postponement of his eastern expedition for a while. But he did not at first take the revolt seriously. It was a local affair, he thought, with which his Vicar, Herbert of Orléans, could deal. He merely ordered the vice-admiral Matthew of Salerno to take four galleys to attack Palermo. The order was given on 8 April; but when Matthew arrived off Palermo he found the Messinese squadron already cruising ineffectually outside the harbour and did not venture to press any attack. When Messina joined in the revolt, the Messinese ships attacked him and captured two of his galleys. He retired with the others to Naples.[2]

It was the rising in Messina and the destruction of his fleet there that brought Charles to realize the seriousness of the rebellion. 'Lord God,' he cried, 'since it has pleased You to ruin my fortune, let me only go down by small steps.' He set about seeing that the steps should be small. The eastern expedition was countermanded. Instead, the ships and men assembled in his Italian ports were summoned to the straits of Messina, and he himself set out to command the force which should reduce the rebel island.[3]

He had the full support of the Pope. When in April an envoy from Palermo arrived at Orvieto to ask the Holy See to take the new Commune under its protection, Pope Martin refused to grant him an audience. The island still hoped that Martin would relent. In the first days of May Messina joined Palermo and the other cities in sending three ambassadors to his court. They came solemnly into his presence before the whole Consistory chanting three times the words: 'Lamb of God, Who bearest the sins of the world, have mercy upon us.' But the Pope replied bitterly repeating three times the words in the Passion, 'Hail, King of the Jews—and they smote Him.' The embassy had no other answer from him.[1] Instead, on 7 May, Ascension Day, he issued a Bull of excommunication against the rebel Sicilians and against anyone who should give them aid. A second Bull excommunicated Michael Palaeologus 'who calls himself Emperor of the Greeks', and a third Guy of Montefeltro and the Ghibellines of northern Italy.[2]

Charles had another sympathetic friend in his nephew King Philip of France. He wrote in April to the French court to inform Philip that active steps might be needed to prevent the revolt from having serious consequences. When Messina rebelled, he wrote again to ask for help against the rebels. In response two of his nephews, Philip's brother Peter, Count of Alençon, and Robert of Artois, prepared to send a party of French nobles to Italy. Charles's son, Charles of Salerno, who was in Provence at the time, was told to go to Paris to arrange for further co-operation with the French court.[3] To King Philip the main danger seemed to come from Aragon. He had already warned Charles to beware of the Aragonese king; and Charles had not heeded him. He was convinced that the great Aragonese fleet assembled in the harbour of Fangos was destined for an attack against Sicily, in spite of all King Peter's protests that he was going crusading in Africa. Before he had heard that Messina was lost to Charles he had sent an embassy to King Peter, who was already with his fleet. It reached Port Fangos on 20 May and gave Peter a letter in which Philip demanded assurances that the fleet would not be used against Charles. If it were, he warned, he would regard it as an hostile act and would send an army against Aragon.[4]

His warning was ineffectual. Peter merely answered that he was, as he had always maintained, preparing for an expedition to Africa. In fact, the Sicilian revolt had taken Peter by surprise. His agents had planned it; but he had counted on Charles's expedition against Constantinople taking place. Then, when the

Sicilian kingdom was bared of its best soldiers, Sicily was to revolt and he would intervene. The Sicilians, abetted by the Byzantine Emperor, had forestalled him. When the news of the massacre at Palermo reached him, he did nothing. It was only after the revolt at Messina and the destruction of Charles's ships there that he decided to act. Even so, he moved cautiously. He would genuinely sail to Africa and fight the Moors there while waiting to see what would happen in Sicily. On 3 June he sailed out of Port Fangos at the head of a great flotilla of men-of-war and transports, heading for the Algerian coast.[1]

To maintain his pretence, he sent a special envoy to the Pope to ask for his blessing for his crusade and for the usual indulgences. Martin was not deceived. He gave a curt reply to the ambassador. The Swiss knight, Otto of Grandson, who was acting as Edward of England's agent at Orvieto, reported on 11 June to his employer that everyone at the papal court expected the King of Aragon to intervene in Sicily.[2]   But Peter was in no hurry. His fleet put in at Port Mahon in Minorca, which was still a Muslim emirate, though tributary to the Aragonese crown. The emir hastened to supply the fleet with generous provisions, but sent a secret messenger to Tunis to warn its king of the expedition. When the fleet arrived at Collo, on the Algerian coast, Peter learnt that his ally, the governor of Constantine, whose detachment from the Tunisian kingdom and whose conversion the expedition was supposed to achieve, had been suddenly attacked by the Tunisians, as a result of the Minorcan message, and had been put to death. His elimination deprived the crusade of its object. But Peter remained on with his soldiers at Collo, conveniently close for watching events in Sicily.[3]

The Sicilians were meanwhile preparing themselves to meet King Charles's counter-attack. Charles did not hurry his preparations. He meant, when he struck, to strike hard and decisively. The ships and men destined for the eastern campaign were gathered together at Catona on the Calabrian shore of the Straits.

Peter of Alençon and Robert of Artois were summoned with their French knights to join the Angevin army. Contingents were diverted from Provence, from the expedition that had been going to sail up the Rhône and refound the Kingdom of Arles. The Guelfs of Florence sent a troop under Count Guy of Battifolle, with the banner of the city and fifty young squires to whom King Charles promised knighthood. Ships were hired from Venice, Pisa and Genoa, to take the place of those that the Messinese had destroyed. It was a formidable army which King Charles himself joined as commander-in-chief on 6 July. Nineteen days later he led it across the Straits and encamped in the vineyards just to the north of Messina.[1]

Pope Martin hoped that the Sicilians would be alarmed into submission without fighting. They still maintained that their Communes were under his protection. On 5 June he had appointed one of his ablest ministers, Cardinal Gerard of Parma, to be his legate in the island with orders to obtain its unconditional surrender.[2] Five days later, to supplement his efforts, King Charles issued a long ordinance reforming the administration of the island. Royal officials were in future forbidden to indulge in any form of extortion; they were not to sequester goods or beasts or commandeer boats without payment, not to force towns and villages to give them gifts nor to imprison citizens on inadequate grounds, nor to annex their lands, crimes which the ordinance admitted to have been committed in the days before the rising.[3] But the promise of these reforms left the Sicilians unmoved. They had suffered too much at the hands of the Angevins, and their pride had been roused. They were ready to fight against odds. Already on 2 June the Messinese had foiled an attempt of the Angevins to land forces at Milazzo, on the north-east coast of the island. Nor was their spirit broken when three weeks later an Angevin detachment effected a landing there and defeated with heavy losses the Messinese militia which tried to drive them back. The only results of their defeat were that the

Messinese broke into the Castle of Mategriffon where the members of the Riso family were imprisoned and dragged them out to death, and that they removed the judge Baldwin Mussone from the office of Captain, judging him to be inefficient and lukewarm. In his place they elected Alaimo of Lentini, one of the three Sicilian nobles who had taken the lead in John of Procida's intrigue. He proved a more vigorous commander, whose only fault was his subservience to his wife, Machalda of Scaletta, an heiress of humble origin and vast ambition.[1] At the moment she was not by his side; she had gone with some of her vassals to Catania, where she had tricked the frightened French garrison into surrendering to her and then had put them to death, taking control of the city herself.[2]

Alaimo worked hard to put the defences of Messina into good order. Foreign volunteers came to swell his forces; there were several Genoese galleys and their crews, regardless that some of their compatriots had been hired by King Charles; there were twelve galleys from Ancona, and, unexpectedly, twelve from Venice, manned by men who disliked King Charles and his policy. The Sicilians had been promised help from Pisa; but the Pisans had just begun a war against Genoa and withdrew the galleys that they were sending. The only Pisans to take part in the Sicilian war were the crews of four galleys hired out to King Charles. They were in the forefront of his forces and made themselves particularly objectionable to the men of Messina. Towards the beginning of August the defenders were joined by fifty Aragonese nobles and their followers, who had left their King's army in Africa as volunteers to help the Sicilian cause.[3]

Charles launched his first serious attack against Messina on 6 August, with an attempt to storm the quarter at the end of the peninsula which protected the harbour. He was driven back with very little loss to the defenders. Two days later his men tried to storm the fortified heights of Capperrina, at the north-west edge of the city, furthest from the sea. After the failure of an attack by daylight, his men returned to the assault after dark, but were discovered and discomfited by the prompt action of two local women, whose names, Dina and Clarentia, are recorded with honour in the chronicles. These successes encouraged the Sicilians. It was an unusually rainy month; and the mud hindered the attack more than the defence. The citizens, women as well as men, took their turns in manning the defences. They sent spies to the enemy camp, notably a Franciscan friar, Bartholomew of Piazza, who had made a thorough inspection of the Angevin army before it crossed the Straits. The city was further encouraged by a report that the Holy Virgin herself had been seen blessing the defence. But Charles was taking his time. His army was large and strong and his fleet greatly outnumbered the Sicilians', and both awaited reinforcements. He tightened his blockade of Messina till the moment should come for the final assault.

During the lull after his first attacks, he sent the papal legate, Cardinal Gerard, into the city. The Messinese gave an honourable welcome to the representative of the Pontiff whom they declared to be their overlord. The Captain, Alaimo, formally offered to place Messina in his hands if the Pope would declare himself Protector of the Commune. The cardinal replied that the Church would give back the city to its faithful son, Charles, to whom the whole island lawfully belonged. Alaimo snatched back the keys of the city which he had handed to Gerard and declared in a loud voice that it was better to die in battle than to submit knowingly to a hated enemy. The cardinal was sent back to the royal camp.

After the failure of the legate's mission Charles pressed on with the attack. On 15 August another attempt was made to storm the wall at Capperrina, but it too failed. The blockade was tightened. The citizens were ready to suffer for their cause, but they were saved from starvation by exceptionally good crops of fruit and vegetables from the allotments within the walls and exceptionally large hauls of fish from the harbour. An attack on the north wall

on 2 September equally failed. On 14 September Charles ordered
a general assault. The fighting that day was fiercer than ever before.
But once again the assailants made no progress; and after two of
the nobles standing by Charles had been killed by a stone hurled
from the walls, he called off the attack and retired to his camp.
From there he wrote to Alaimo to promise him that if he would
surrender and would proclaim Charles in the city, he would be
rewarded with hereditary estates wherever he wished and money
to pay for the expenses of the war. All that Charles asked was
that six citizens of Messina, whom he would choose, should be
handed over for punishment. Every other citizen of Messina
would be pardoned.

Alaimo contemptuously rejected the offer. He and his govern-
ment realized their danger; but they had hopes now of a saviour.
When the Pope through his legate rejected their scheme to turn
Sicily into a group of Communes under the authority of the
Holy See, they understood that they must find another solution
for the island's future. One was at hand.[1]

When King Peter of Aragon sent an embassy to Pope Martin
to ask for papal blessing for his crusade, he had little hope of a
friendly answer. His chief ambassador, the Catalan William of
Castelnou, had instructions to pause on his return journey at
Palermo and to make contact with the rebel leaders there. The
Palermitans knew by now that nothing would make the Pope
desert King Charles's cause. The Sicilians had been unwilling at
first to substitute the rule of one foreign potentate for that of
another. But they could not stand alone. Queen Constance of
Aragon was after all the representative of the House of Hohenstaufen and the ultimate heiress of the great dynasty of kings. Her
husband was near at hand with a splendid armament. Prudence
and legitimacy alike counselled them to accept Peter and Constance as their king and queen. When William of Castelnou sailed
on to join his master at Collo, he brought with him three envoys
from Sicily. One was a Messinese noble called William, who had

been living at Palermo, the other two were judges from Palermo, whose names were unknown.

The Sicilian delegation came before King Peter at the camp at Collo and made obeisance to him, telling him of the plight of their orphan island. The Lady Constance, they said, was their lawful queen to whom the crown should be given, and after her to her sons, the Infants of Aragon. They implored him to come and rescue them and to see that his queen enjoyed her rights. Peter received them honourably but hesitated to commit himself. Four days later a ship arrived bearing two knights and two burghers from Messina, who had slipped through the Angevin blockade. At the same time three other citizens from Messina made their way to Palermo to announce that they were joining in the appeal to King Peter. Peter still affected to be diffident. But he had consulted his army leaders and found them willing to follow him to Sicily. After a due show of modesty he graciously announced that he would accede to the Sicilians' request. He would sail to Sicily and would place his wife upon the throne of her ancestors. He promised the islanders that their liberties should be respected and that all should be as it had been in the days of Good King William. He then sent William of Castelnou once again to the papal court with a careful and pious explanation of his motives.[1]

Towards the end of August the Aragonese camp at Collo was dismantled. For three days the army authorities piled men, horses, arms and provisions into the waiting galleys and transports. The Sicilian ship hurried home to announce to the islanders that its crew had seen King Peter embarking. Some two days later, on 30 August 1282, the great host of Aragon, with the King at its head, disembarked at Trapani. The rebellion in Sicily was now a European war.[2]

CHAPTER XIV

THE DUEL BETWEEN THE KINGS

The massacre at Palermo and the gallant defence of Messina had been achieved by the Sicilians alone. Their rising had been the result of a great conspiracy. It may be that they received arms from Genoa and Aragon; they certainly received gold from Byzantium; but they had fought unaided. Their passionate hatred of the oppressor had given them strength enough so far. The future was less sure. King Charles was checked at Messina but not defeated. He could still expect reinforcements. More ships were due from Venice. The French knights led by the Count of Alençon were gathering together to start out for Italy. The Pope refused to countenance the revolt. If reconquest by the Angevins was to be averted, foreign help must be given; and the King of Aragon, with his wife's hereditary claims and his own army waiting not far away was the man to help the rebels. But King Peter was almost as ambitious as King Charles. Both had built up a system of alliances; and when they clashed the war was on too wide a scale for the interests of Sicily to be remembered for long.

After landing at Trapani King Peter and his army made their way to Palermo, while the fleet followed them round the coast. He arrived at Palermo on 2 September. He would have liked to be crowned King of Sicily at once. But the Archbishop of Palermo was dead, and the Archbishop of Monreale, who was a French partisan, had fled. Peter was therefore merely proclaimed king before the Commune on 4 September. In return he solemnly promised to observe the rights and liberties of the Sicilians as in the days of Good King William. He then summoned all the able-bodied men of Palermo and western Sicily to join his army and march with him to the relief of Messina. A few days later he set out slowly eastward through Nicosia and Troina in the

centre of the island, with his fleet keeping pace with him off the
northern coast. He had already sent two ambassadors, Peter of
Queralt and Roderick of Luna, to King Charles, to tell him to
withdraw from the island.[1]

Charles did not hear of Peter's landing for some days after it
had taken place. Two Carmelite friars saw the Aragonese ambassadors at Nicosia, on the inland road from Palermo to Messina,
and discovered their business. They hurried back to Charles with
their news. The people within Messina as yet knew nothing; and
the general assault which Charles ordered for 14 September was
an attempt to overpower the city before the citizens were aware
that an ally was at hand. The peace-terms offered to Alaimo
immediately after the failure of the assault were similarly an
effort to settle the issue before the Aragonese invasion was known.[2]

King Peter's ambassadors came before King Charles on
16 September. He received them with an ill grace, but did not at
once reply to them. They were told to come back the next day.
They took advantage of their leisure to go as near as possible to
the walls of Messina and shout up that their king was already at
Palermo. They were suspected as agents and no one believed them;
except for the deposed captain, Baldwin Mussone. He slipped
out through the besiegers' lines to join King Peter and gain his
ear before his rival Alaimo. He was stopped by some peasants
and brought back into the city. The citizens' tempers were high.
They wanted to lynch him as a deserter; and Alaimo had to take
him into protective custody, together with a certain Frederick
Falconio, who had been overheard making defeatist remarks.
A judge, Henry of Parisi, and three friends of his were less lucky.
They were suspected of treasonable contact with the enemy and
were summarily executed.[3]

Charles debated with his counsellors before answering the
embassy. He had learnt that Peter's army and particularly his
fleet were formidable. He could not entirely trust his own fleet;
the mercenary crews were unreliable and the Genoese even openly

fraternized with the Sicilians. He had no wish to be caught at Messina, in front of an unconquered city, with his retreat across the Straits threatened. Nor did he wish to risk a pitched battle till his French allies arrived. Among his counsellors Thomas of Acerra took the lead. Thomas was the son of one of Frederick II's bastard daughters and as such was suspect to the Angevins; but Charles was ready to trust him now. He pointed out the military situation. It would be far better, he said, to await reinforcements in a strong position on the mainland shore of the Straits. The Sicilians would soon grow tired of the Aragonese. Then a new descent could be made on the island, preferably at a weaker spot than Messina.[1]

When Charles saw the Aragonese embassy again, on 17 September, he made a long answer rejecting King Peter's claim to Sicily, but indicating that he was prepared to evacuate his forces from the island, though with no guarantee that he would not return some day, without warning. A week later, when he found that his equivocal answer had not kept Peter from slowly advancing on Messina, he began to tranship his army and his war material across into Calabria. By now the Messinese knew of the Aragonese invasion. A Genoese merchant who had himself seen King Peter in the island made his way into Messina and reported the news to Alaimo. There was great rejoicing among the citizens; and when they saw the enemy army preparing to strike camp and to embark they made sorties from their gates. The whole army had not yet left before the first Aragonese troops approached. In the confusion the Angevin commanders managed to get most of their men into the transport ships; but some were left behind and slaughtered and an immense amount of armaments and of baggage was abandoned.[2]

King Peter made his triumphal entry into Messina on 2 October. He had not hurried on his journey from Palermo. Like King Charles, he was unwilling to provoke a pitched battle and wanted to give the Angevin army time to cross to Calabria, so that he could win the whole island without striking a blow. He was none too sure of the temper of the island; but he was well aware that his chief asset in the islanders' eyes was his army and his fleet. He was not prepared as yet to risk damage to either. He had had some disquieting personal experiences. While he was halting at Milazzo, there came to him by night a ragged old man, whose name, he said, was Vitalis dei Giudici of Messina. He had been a devoted friend of King Manfred, on whose fall he had lost everything. Since then he had lived as a beggar; unlike, he added, most of the Sicilian lords, against whose inconstancy he anxiously warned the king. In particular he told him to beware of Alaimo of Lentini, the gallant Captain of Messina, who had already betrayed King Manfred and King Charles in turn. And worse than Alaimo was his wife, Machalda, and her father, James of Scaletta. King Peter answered very properly that his business was to make friends in Sicily and not to offend the Sicilians by suspiciousness and recrimination about the past. The vindictive old man's warning merely made him announce next morning an amnesty to all political offenders.

Next evening he remembered the old man. He intended to spend the night at the village of Santa Lucia, two miles beyond Milazzo. There he found the Lady Machalda waiting for him. He had met her already, two days before, at Randazzo on the northern slopes of Etna, when he had paused to greet a delegation that had come from Messina to tell him that King Charles had left the island; and she had arrived from Catania, bringing with her the keys of the city. She had decided then that the post of Royal Mistress would suit her and tried now to put her scheme into effect. King Peter had an acutely embarrassing evening. He only escaped by talking at immense length of his loyalty to Queen Constance. It was not an argument that the Lady Machalda found attractive. Henceforward her jealousy of the queen was outspoken; and she began to use her influence on her husband, Alaimo, to draw him into intrigues against the House of Aragon.[1]

For the moment Alaimo was unmoved. He welcomed Peter at Messina and put the militia of the city at the king's disposal. The Sicilians and the Aragonese mingled together fraternally, and enthusiastically set out to ravage the Calabrian coast. Charles's retreat had been so hurried that his fleet had not had time to refit. Charles had set up his camp at Reggio, trying to reorganize his forces and awaiting his allies from France. He was in no position to attack the Aragonese before the last squadrons of their fleet arrived in Messina harbour on 9 October. Two days later some Angevin ships tried to slip out of Reggio to sail to Naples. The Aragonese set out in pursuit, whereat Charles ordered his main fleet to attack. It was driven back into Reggio harbour with heavy losses, including two of the galleys hired from Pisa. On 14 October there was a second naval battle, off Nicotera, some thirty miles north of the Straits. The Aragonese, though fewer in numbers, managed to capture twenty-one galleys laden with armaments sailing down from Naples.[1]

King Peter was emboldened by these successes to plan the invasion of the mainland. He was in full control of Sicily and he had, at least for the moment, command of the sea. At the end of October he landed troops near Nicastro, at the narrowest point of central Calabria and occupied the isthmus between the Tyrrhenian Sea and the Gulf of Taranto, thus cutting Reggio and King Charles's army off from the rest of the mainland. It was not a very effective blockade. Charles, Prince of Salerno, with six hundred knights from France, managed to pass through to Reggio early in November, and the Counts of Alençon and Artois followed him a month later. Charles entrusted the defence of the district to two of his best French commanders, Bertrand Artus and Pons of Blanquefort, aided by the chief local Italian baron, Peter Ruffo, Count of Catanzaro. They did their work effectively; and their competence, together with the reinforcements from France, prevented the Aragonese from tightening their hold.[2]

By early winter the war seemed to be in a state of stalemate.

It was still localized; and the next move to break the deadlock would have to be the intervention of other powers. King Peter was particularly anxious to avoid such complications. He had won the first round with the help of the Sicilians. He could count on the support of the Ghibellines of northern and central Italy. Indeed, on the news of the Vespers there had been a short-lived Ghibelline revolution at Perugia; and most of Umbria was now under Ghibelline control. In the villages the hated French Pope was burnt in effigy. On 1 May Guy of Montefeltro with a number of Tuscan and Emilian Ghibellines had ambushed the papal governor of Romagna, the Frenchman John of Eppe, at Forli, and had destroyed most of his army. The Orsini rose in Rome, but were forced to retire to their country castles. Conrad of Antioch, Frederick II's grandson, appeared with an army in the hills behind Tivoli.[1] But though the Ghibellines could embarrass and distract King Peter's enemies, they could not give him much positive assistance. Of his other friends Genoa shared his enmity towards King Charles, even though they had been ready to hire out galleys to the Angevins. But Genoa had too many preoccupations, with her rivalry with Venice over the Eastern trade and her war with Pisa.[2] Peter had a potential ally in the Emperor Michael at Constantinople. But, now that there was no more danger of King Charles leading an expedition against Constantinople, the Byzantines could afford to neglect the West. They had quite enough to occupy them in the Balkan peninsula and in Anatolia. Michael himself was ill and nearing the end of his days. He died on 11 December 1282 satisfied with his life-work. He had restored the Empire to Constantinople and he had averted the counter-attack of the West. His son and successor, Andronicus, was a peaceful and rather incompetent man, whose main interest was theology. His diplomats kept a watchful eye on Italian affairs; and he went so far himself as to marry as his second wife the daughter of the great Ghibelline prince of the north, William of Montferrat. But even if King Peter had wished it, the Empire would not involve itself in a west European war.[1] Peter had only uncertain allies. The Castilian kingdom, over which his retention of the Infants of La Cerda gave him a certain control, was distracted by civil war between King Alfonso and his son King Sancho. Rudolph of Germany was a disappointment to the Ghibellines. He was unwilling to quarrel with the Pope, as he still hoped for an Imperial coronation; and he considered himself bound by his treaty with King Charles, whose eldest grandson was his daughter's husband. King Edward of England was not unfriendly to Peter and was on cool terms with the court of France. But he had enough cares of his own to occupy him. He remained strictly neutral, eager to do anything that would preserve the peace of Europe.[2]

King Charles had firmer allies. The Guelfs of Italy were, it is true, unlikely to be of more use to him than the Ghibellines to his rival; and Venice, though ready enough to join him in a campaign against Constantinople, wanted even less than Genoa to be involved in an Italian war. But the King of France regarded the rising in Sicily almost as a personal injury, an insult to the French nation. He gave his full support to his uncle. When the Prince of Salerno hurried up from Provence to Paris to tell King Philip of the Vespers, he met with every sympathy. Not only were his cousins of Alençon and Artois authorized and encouraged to join the Angevin army, but Philip offered a loan of 15,000 pounds *tournois* for the expenses of the war. The Prince had also been told by his father to try to placate the Queen-Mother Margaret by offering a new and generous settlement of her claims to Provence. Thanks probably to Philip's good offices, the dowager consented to take no active steps against Charles for the moment.[3]

The good will of the French court was very welcome to Charles. But so long as the war was localized in Italy the French could not do much more than send him recruits and lend him money. He could not be sure, in spite of King Philip's warning to King Peter before the Vespers took place, whether the French would be willing to carry the war into Aragon. They might, however, do so if they were urged by the Pope; and in Pope Martin Charles had an even stauncher friend. Martin unhesitatingly identified Charles's cause with his own. Ghibelline successes in and around his own territory only made him the angrier and more determined. He thundered excommunications against his and Charles's enemies, against King Peter, the Emperor Michael, Guy of Montefeltro and the Ghibelline cities of Perugia, Spoleto and Assisi. More practically, he lent money to Charles out of the Church revenues. But in return he had to ask for military aid from Charles to defend his own lands. To him the moral and military issue alike seemed clear. His authority had been flouted by Peter of Aragon and the rebel Sicilians. It was the duty of all good Christians to come together and crush them both.[1]

If Charles did not entirely share the Pope's point of view, it was because of finance. Wars were growing expensive. A king could no longer count on feudal levies coming ready armed at his bidding. Most soldiers now expected to be paid and to be provided with arms. Armaments were costly, as were ships, whether they were built for naval purposes or hired. Wars, moreover, were apt to interrupt trade and so reduce the tolls and customs dues that formed a large part of the state revenue. Neither Peter nor Charles wanted the cost of a long war. Peter was comparatively poor. Aragon was not a rich country; and its nobles had constitutional privileges which controlled the extent of the taxes which the king could raise. His dominions included such prosperous merchant cities as Barcelona and Narbonne; but the merchants, too, had their rights and were not over-eager to help finance a war whose effect on foreign trade could not be foreseen. Peter raised what taxes he could and supplemented his income by tribute paid by Muslim princes in southern Spain or Africa. He feared the expense of a long and widespread war. Charles had a larger income. He had fiscal control of his dominions and taxed them heavily. But it was clear that excessive taxation created unrest.

With the loss of Sicily he could no longer count on the tribute that the King of Tunis had hitherto sent him. His grandiose foreign policy had always been costly, and he had largely paid for it by loans. He owed vast sums to creditors. The money devoted to his great expeditions against Constantinople had all been wasted. The earlier results of his empire-building had been financially disappointing. The Principality of Achaea was rich enough to finance itself, but had no money to spare, especially now that Charles's whole power seemed threatened. The remnants of his Kingdoms of Albania and Jerusalem brought him nothing but expense. Their revenues were tiny; and he had to supply them not only with garrisons and arms but even with foodstuffs. Charles wanted desperately to recover Sicily, but its recovery would not be cheap.[1]

This dread of the cost of a long war helps to explain the curious suggestion that Charles made for its avoidance. Towards the end of 1282, while he was still at Reggio and Peter across the water at Messina, he sent a Dominican friar, Simon of Lentini, to the Aragonese camp, with the suggestion that the possession of Sicily should be decided by single combat between the two kings. Peter agreed, on condition that the war should continue up to the moment of the duel. After some negotiations it was decided that single combat was unsuitable; Charles was already aged nearly fifty-six and was an old man by medieval standards, whereas Peter was fifteen years younger. Instead, each king would be accompanied by a hundred knights of his choosing, to fight by his side. The meeting should take place on 1 June 1283, at Bordeaux, the capital of the French lands of King Edward of England.[2]

No one can now tell how sincere Charles and Peter were in planning their duel. It is part of human nature to like to appeal to some tribunal whose moral authority is recognized, even if the apellant has no intention of abiding by an adverse decision. Modern man appeals to an international assembly. In the Middle Ages the appeal was made to the purer verdict of God. By the thirteenth century the ordeal by battle was obsolescent; but men still believed it to be a means for assessing the justice of a cause. If equal conditions were provided, God would give victory to the righteous. It is probable that to both Charles and Peter the suggestion seemed at first sight to provide a solution of the Sicilian question without the trouble and expense of a great war. Each realized the propaganda value of showing his willingness to submit the dispute to the judgement of God. To Peter, whose prospects should the war become general were darker than Charles's, the duel was not unattractive. He was in the prime of life; he had been brought up at a gallant and chivalrous court among comrades who would relish the adventure. Charles had more to lose in submitting himself to such a risk; but, for all his harshness and ambition, he was a pious man. It is likely that he genuinely believed that his possession of Sicily, granted to him by Holy Church, would be guaranteed by God. On second thoughts each king may have doubted the wisdom of the affair; but, having once consented, neither could face the stain on his reputation that a withdrawal would bring.

Their doubts might well have been increased by the reception given to the news by their fellow-rulers. The Pope was frankly horrified. If an appeal to God was desired, he was there as the representative of God's will on earth. Showing little confidence in the direct judgement of God, he wrote to ask Charles whether it was wise to meet on equal terms an enemy who was so much weaker. Only understandable ill-temper could, he thought, have induced Charles to make such a foolish suggestion. He forbade him to fight the duel; and he forbade the King of England to allow it to take place within his dominions. King Edward himself considered the duel as frivolous.[1] The Sicilians, faced with the risk of being returned to Angevin rule by an event over which they would have no control, must have shared his views. But King Charles did not change his mind openly. It is probable that he wished in any case to visit the French court and his own lands in

France; and during his absence from the Kingdom he was glad that his son, Charles of Salerno, should promulgate measures of appeasement on his own responsibility. King Peter was similarly pleased to have an opportunity of returning for a while to Aragon, though he did not intend to leave till he had improved his military position in Calabria.[1]

On 12 January 1283 Charles issued an act investing his son, Charles of Salerno, with sovereign power in the Kingdom till he should return from abroad. Five days later he left Reggio and made his way slowly northward through the Kingdom, pausing for a few days in early February at Naples and reaching Rome at the end of the month. He was at Viterbo with Pope Martin on 9 March, entrusting his son, the Regent, to his care, and passed through Florence on 14 March, on his road to Viareggio, where Provençal galleys met him and carried him to Marseilles. In April he journeyed on to Paris, where his nephew, King Philip, gave him a cordial welcome.[2]

King Peter was in less of a hurry; he wished to follow up his military successes. In early January, before King Charles had left Reggio, an Aragonese guerilla company had raided the naval port of Catona in the suburbs and had forced its way into the hostel where the Count of Alençon was staying and killed him. The naval arsenal was destroyed. Such raids reduced the morale of the Angevin army, whose commanders tried wherever possible to replace local troops by men from France and Provence. King Peter, on the contrary, made the gesture of releasing two thousand Italians whom he had captured.[3]

On 13 February 1283 the Prince of Salerno moved the Angevin army out of Reggio and retired to a good defensive position in the plain of San Martino, some thirty miles further north. Next day King Peter crossed the Straits and entered Reggio without opposition. He issued a manifesto offering rewards to any Calabrian who would join him. There was a fair response; but his troops failed to dislodge the Angevins from their position at

San Martino and failed to give support to rebels north of the fighting line.[1] Charles of Salerno countered by summoning a parliament to his camp at San Martino and promulgating with its approval a series of ordinances to codify and complete the reforms that his father had promised the previous June. The Cardinal Gerard of Parma, papal legate to Sicily, was by his side, representing his overlord and patron, the Pope, and saw to it that a number of the ordinances were concerned with the independence of the clergy from royal control, a policy which did not command much popular support. The next group of ordinances showed that the Angevin court was nervous about its vassals. The feudatories were allowed freer rights to contract the marriages that they pleased, greater powers over their own vassals, the privilege of trial by their peers and a promise that they should never be required to perform tasks unworthy of their station. There followed a jumble of reforms, some guaranteeing the property and freedom of the innocent womenfolk of criminals and traitors, some restricting the liability of village communities to be fined for the misdeeds of one member. One clause abolished the taxes levied for the repair of the fleet; another reduced the taxes to be paid locally for the upkeep of castles. Others guarded against frivolous accusations made by the police or prison officials, against the practice of high functionaries to obtain transport animals at nominal prices, and of the royal household to pay too little for its supplies. Others reorganized the administration of the forests and of markets, and the whole currency system. As usual, the King's subjects were promised the liberties that they had enjoyed in the days of Good King William.[2]

If so many reforms were needed, the whole government of the Kingdom must have deteriorated under the stress of Charles's expensive and no longer successful imperialism. It is doubtful how many of them were carried out. Some lawyers from the Kingdom went so far as to ask Pope Martin what exactly were the famous liberties enjoyed in the days of Good King William.

They received the testy reply that he did not know; he had not been living then. As propaganda the ordinances of San Martino had little effect. King Charles's Italian subjects were as ready as before to desert his cause if the moment seemed opportune. The Angevins were better helped by the rift that was beginning to appear between the Sicilians and their Aragonese rescuers.[1]

In the early spring of 1283 King Peter sent for his queen to join him. He was pleased with himself. Letters were sent to his Ghibelline allies in the north, Guy of Montefeltro, Conrad of Antioch and Guy Novello, to tell them that the enemy army in Calabria was dying of starvation. He even wrote to Venice to urge the Doge to join the winning cause. He returned to Messina on 4 April. Queen Constance arrived there on 16 April, bringing with her their two younger sons, the Infants James and Frederick, and their daughter the Infanta Violante, and her trusted counsellor, John of Procida.[2] A parliament was held at Messina on 19 April, at which it was announced that on King Peter's death the Infant James would succeed to the Sicilian throne, while his elder brother Alfonso should inherit Aragon. Queen Constance was meanwhile named as regent, with Alaimo of Lentini as Grand Justiciar, John of Procida as Chancellor and Roger of Lauria Grand Admiral. Next day Peter left Messina to tour slowly through the island on his way to Trapani. From there he sailed on 6 May for Valencia. A fortnight later he left Valencia on his way to the meeting-place at Bordeaux.[3]

Neither he nor Charles had any intention now of fighting the duel; but the comedy had to be played out. King Edward, obedient to the Pope's command, refused to have any personal connection with the affair. He remained himself in England, and would not promise any safe-conduct to the participants. But he allowed his seneschal in Guienne, John of Grailly, to make arrangements to welcome the visitors and to prepare the tilting-ground. King Charles arrived at Bordeaux with great pomp, accompanied by the King of France and a splendid escort of French knights from whom he could choose his hundred champions. The world should see that he was still a great king. Peter adopted a different technique. He arrived modestly with his champions, carefully avoiding any ostentation, as though to show that he pinned his faith solely on God.

The date for the combat had been fixed for 1 June, but unfortunately no one had named the hour. Early in the morning King Peter and his company rode into the lists, to find themselves alone there. His heralds formally announced his presence. He then rode back to his lodging and issued a statement declaring that his opponent had failed to meet him at the proper place. His, therefore, was the victory. A few hours later King Charles arrived in all his panoply and followed exactly the same procedure. He, too, had been victorious. The rival kings left Bordeaux a few days later, each declaring the other to be a coward who had not dared to face the judgement of God.[1]

The real duel was to be fought on a wider tilting-place. King Peter and King Charles might have preferred to restrict the war to Italy. Pope Martin willed otherwise. He was already preaching the crusade against Aragon, and in so doing was preparing the downfall of the medieval Papacy.

CHAPTER XV

THE END OF KING CHARLES

It was tragic for the Papacy that at this moment of its history its destinies were guided by a patriotic Frenchman. From the outset Pope Martin had taken the Sicilian rising as a revolt against himself. A wiser Pope would have understood its cause and the Sicilians' genuine desire to place themselves under papal protection. Martin only remembered that it had been the Papacy which had placed the French prince Charles on the Sicilian throne. It would be treachery to the Church and to France to countenance the rebellion. His intransigence had driven Sicily into the arms of Aragon. His answer was to use the authority of the Church against Aragon.

Peter of Aragon had been excommunicated since November 1282. On 13 January 1283 Martin pronounced that the war against Peter and the Sicilian rebels and anyone who might aid them ranked as a crusade, and participants would enjoy privileges granted to those who fought the infidel in the Holy Land. These fulminations were not enough. Charles, when he saw the Pope at Viterbo on his way to fight the duel which he already knew to be meaningless, planned larger measures, for which he counted on the co-operation of the King of France. On 21 March, a few days after Charles had left him, Martin declared Peter to be deprived of his dominions, which would be given to good Catholics chosen by the Holy See. Neutral princes were warned to have nothing to do with the excommunicated king. Edward of England, whose daughter was betrothed to Peter's eldest son, Alfonso, was told, without result, to break off the engagement. The Doge of Venice, who was suspected of readiness to listen to King Peter and who had refused to lend any more galleys to the Angevins, was cautioned by the public reading in the Piazza of Saint Mark's, by the papal legate, of the sentence against Peter and his allies.[1]

Meanwhile in Paris and on the futile journey to Bordeaux and back, King Charles planned with his nephew King Philip how the crusade against Aragon should be directed. He wished to involve the French court as completely as possible. It was almost certainly on his suggestion that in August 1283 the Pope sent a legate, John Cholet, Cardinal of Saint Cecilia, to Paris to offer the throne of Aragon to King Philip's younger son, Charles, Count of Valois. Philip had already, in expectation of the offer, won the support of James, King of Majorca, who was desperately jealous of his brother King Peter and resented his vassalage to him. King James was, it seems, offered complete independence when the French prince should sit on the Aragonese throne. The cardinal legate further promised a tithe for three years to be paid by the clergy of France. Many of the French disapproved. Aged counsellors who survived from Saint Louis's day did not hesitate to point out that their revered master never approved of papal attacks on secular princes. The heir to the throne, the future Philip the Fair, whose mother had been a princess of Aragon, expressed sympathy with his uncle Peter. King Philip made use of these doubts to extract a promise of a longer tithe; and the Pope was irritated into making a formal declaration that the projected French expedition against Aragon would indeed be a crusade. At last, on 2 February 1284, King Philip publicly announced that he accepted the Kingdoms of Aragon and Valencia for his son Charles of Valois.[1]

The war in Italy had continued meanwhile. In central Italy the Ghibellines were kept in check. An active papal legate, Bernard, Cardinal of Porto, toured the country, encouraging the Guelfs. The war between Genoa and Pisa prevented either from giving help to the Ghibelline cause. John of Eppe, papal governor of Romagna, was provided with reinforcements and money, with which he bought back the allegiance of some towns in the Romagna and the Marches and stormed others, beginning with Forli, whose walls were razed to the ground. But the Umbrian cities remained in Ghibelline hands; and Guy of Montefeltro, in his Apennine

16-2

castle of Mendola, and Conrad of Antioch, at Saracinesco in the Abruzzi, were both unconquered, for all that their foes had been given the rights of crusaders.[1]

Further south the Pope had less cause for satisfaction. Charles of Salerno was desperately short of money. During the month of February 1282 the Papacy provided him with no less than 90,000 ounces of gold. At a synod at Melfi, the legate, Cardinal Gerard, offered the prince concessions from the ecclesiastical revenues of the Kingdom. Even so he was obliged to borrow money from the Kings of France and England, from the bankers of Lucca and Florence, from the King of Tunis and from the municipalities of the Kingdom.[2] Thanks to these efforts he was able to have a Provençal fleet equipped and brought south to Naples. There it joined a local squadron and sailed with it to Nicotera, in Calabria, to which the prince had moved his camp toward the end of April. The Aragonese army had not meanwhile advanced far beyond Reggio; but part of the fleet, under Manfred Lancia, was blockading Malta, where the Angevin garrison was hard pressed. Prince Charles sent his new fleet to the relief of the island, whose preservation was important if he were to maintain communications with Tunis and with the East. The Angevin ships, under the Provençal admiral Bartholomew Bonvin, slipped through the Straits; but Roger of Lauria, with the main Aragonese fleet, followed in pursuit and caught up with them off the Maltese coast. He easily out-manœuvred Bartholomew and destroyed almost all his vessels. He then sailed back triumphantly to make a demonstration off Naples and raid the neighbouring coasts, and to capture and garrison the islands of Capri and Ischia.[3]

After this humiliating reverse it was little consolation for Prince Charles to learn that the enemy regent, Queen Constance, was equally short of money. The queen herself and her Italian-born ministers were careful of her new subjects' rights. But the Aragonese nobles and soldiers were poor and rapacious, and it was not easy to restrain them. Hardest to control were the regiments of the Almogavars, mercenaries to whose guerrilla tactics much of King Peter's successes had been due; but, like all good mercenaries, they had little respect for other persons' property. Sicily was not rich; and many Sicilians began to wonder if the change of master was a change for the better. Before King Peter had left the island there were disquieting rumours about the great noble Walter of Caltagirone, one of the original conspirators with whom John of Procida was said to have plotted. By the end of May proof of his contact with the Angevins was provided by Alaimo of Lentini to the Infant James; who, acting as his father's deputy, sentenced him to death.[1]

Further defections were likely unless the Aragonese government could offer more than financial oppression to Sicily. Roger of Lauria's victory encouraged everyone's morale. King Peter sent congratulatory messages from Aragon, but he sent no money to pay the sailors. When John of Procida wrote to him to complain of the insubordination of the Aragonese mercenaries, he replied that John was not allowing the Aragonese officials in the island to carry out their duties. He wrote again refusing to let the Sicilian clergy take back the procurations that they had given to the laity during the crisis of the rebellion. When Queen Constance saw that her husband was going to give her no help from Aragon, where, indeed, he needed to concentrate resources against the threatened invasion, she decided, on John of Procida's advice, to appeal for subsidies from Constantinople. The Emperor there had financed the conspiracy that led to the Vespers; he would surely provide money to continue the war. In 1281 the Emperor Michael had suggested that the Infanta Violante might be sent as a bride to his widowed son Andronicus. The Court of Aragon had avoided an answer. But Andronicus was Emperor now and his help was needed. Unwisely Constance consulted her husband before sending the embassy to Constantinople. He was furious and wrote to John of Procida forbidding the project. The Greeks, he said, would insist on the marriage before providing the money;

and it would be a shame on his family if he permitted his daughter to marry such a schismatic prince. He was hurt to find that the queen was not of his opinion, he said.[1]

These praiseworthy scruples on the part of a king who was already excommunicated neither impressed the Pope nor provided the Sicilian government with the money it needed. Fighting continued in Italy only because Roger of Lauria's raids brought in enough booty to satisfy his crews. On land things were at a standstill. Fortunately for Peter the invasion of Aragon was not easy to plan. King Edward was told by his agents at the time of the French acceptance of the Aragonese crown that no one expected operations to start for a year. There was a lack of enthusiasm in France; there were delays at the papal chancery. It was not till May 1284 that the Bull investing Charles of Valois with his new kingdoms was published, and June that the crusade was formally proclaimed; and it was not till May 1285 that the crusading army set out. But in the meantime Peter did not dare to leave his Spanish dominions. Sicilian interests had to come second.[2]

The Angevin government was aware of his embarrassment. King Charles planned to recruit a new army and fleet in Provence and told his son at Naples to gather whatever troops he could in Italy but to remain strictly on the defensive till he should himself arrive. Charles of Salerno obediently gathered an army of feudal levies, of Saracen troops from Lucera, and of Guelf troops from Tuscany and sent it under the command of the Count of Artois to the borders of Calabria. His local officials were ordered to see to the defences of all the coastal towns and castles, and only to take offensive action against such points as Scalea, where the enemy had established a foothold. New ships were hastily built in the dockyards at Naples, to be ready for the great expedition which King Charles would launch on his return from France.[3]

Sicily was saved by the brilliance of the admiral Roger of Lauria. He had for the moment command of the sea, and he made full use of it. Almogavar guerrilla raiders were landed at intervals along the coasts of Calabria and Basilicata, vanishing always before the Count of Artois's troops could find them. In May Roger took his main fleet to the Bay of Naples. The Angevins had been unable to recover Capri or Ischia. Roger used the islands as a base for raids into the bay. He occupied the little island of Nisida, off Posillipo, and anchored a squadron under its shelter, with which he could blockade the harbour. Any Neapolitan boat that ventured out into the bay was promptly captured or sunk. The blockade infuriated the Neapolitans. They demanded that the government should take action, and when it delayed they murmured of revolt. Charles of Salerno was uncertain what to do. His father, of whom he was in awe, had forbidden him to attack the enemy. The papal legate, Cardinal Gerard, who was always by his side, kept repeating his father's advice. He was himself a diffident young man. An accident in early childhood had left him lame and conscious of his weakness. He was deeply worried about the effects of the blockade. He did not know when his father would arrive. It may be, too, that he was anxious to prove to the world and to himself that despite his lameness he could fight gallantly and well.

King Charles and his fleet left Provence at the end of May 1284; but his son did not know of it. In early June, in spite of the legate's disapproval, Charles of Salerno armed the galleys that his ship-yards had just completed. On Monday, 5 June he embarked with a large suite of knights, and sailed out of the harbour. He seems to have believed that Roger of Lauria's main fleet was away raiding down the coast and that he would destroy the squadron based on Nisida. But Roger, who knew that King Charles was approaching, had concentrated his forces to be ready for him. The Prince of Salerno led his ships into an enemy fleet far superior to his in numbers and in arms. The battle was brief and decisive. The Prince and his comrades fought bravely, and for a moment, when they first attacked, they had some success. But they were quickly surrounded. One or two Angevin galleys were sunk;

the majority were captured with their crews, and amongst them the Prince himself.

When the news of his defeat and capture was known in Naples riots broke out. Frenchmen found in the streets were massacred and their houses were pillaged and burnt. The legate and the members of the government who had not been captured with the prince took refuge in the citadel. Other cities down the coast followed the example of Naples. Roger of Lauria, knowing that Queen Constance was anxious to secure the release of her half-sister Beatrice, Manfred's daughter by his Greek wife, sent a message to the Princess of Salerno to say that he could not answer for the prince's life unless she were handed over to him. The Princess had to comply; and Beatrice was sent on board, to enjoy her freedom after her eighteen years of imprisonment. The Admiral, who had transferred his principal captives to his own flagship, put in next day at Sorrento; and a delegation of citizens came to present him with flowers and, more usefully, with money. As they climbed aboard the flagship they mistook the captive prince for Roger. 'If only it had pleased God to let you take the father as you have taken the son', they cried, and they declared that they had been first to change sides. Prince Charles turned laughing to the admiral. 'By holy God,' he said, 'these are good loyal sub-jects of my lord the King.' The Aragonese fleet then sailed on with its distinguished prisoners to Messina.[1]

King Charles arrived with his fleet at Gaeta, the northernmost port of the Kingdom, on 6 June, the day after the disaster off Naples. He soon heard the news; and his first reaction was fury with his son. 'Who loses a fool loses nothing', he said, and added bitterly: 'Why is he not dead for disobeying us?' He hurried on to Naples. There he found that the legate had managed to put down the riots with the help of the great barons of the neighbour-hood. His arrival completed the restoration of order. He ordered a hundred and fifty of the ringleaders in the rising to be hanged. Everyone else was pardoned. On 9 June he wrote to the Pope to give him a full account of what had happened. It was a proud letter, which showed that disaster had in no way weakened his ambition. He grieved for the loss of his son, he said, but he had numerous grandsons; and, indeed, Charles of Salerno, though he was now the king's only surviving son and none of his brothers had left issue, had thirteen children of his own, of whom eight were boys. The king went on to tell the Pope that he still had ample forces. He enumerated the thirty-four well-armed galleys and the four galiots that he had brought from Provence. Another squadron of twenty-three ships, most of them recently built, lay in Naples harbour. A larger contingent was awaiting his orders at Brindisi. He had as many soldiers and sailors as he required. He could, he said, succeed in a far more difficult enterprise than the campaign that he contemplated.[1]

King Charles had the ships and he had the men. But, though the ships were of good quality, the men were not. The levies drawn from the Kingdom were weary of the wars that the foreign king and his foreign nobles forced them to fight. The soldiers from France and Provence were finer fighters, but they despised the Italians and caused their commanders ceaseless trouble by their violence and their looting in districts whose good will was now essential. Much of the army was mercenary, professional soldiers who fought well if they were paid well. Charles boasted of his strength to the Pope, but he had to ask him for more financial help. Before the expedition could start a loan of 50,000 scudi had to be raised from Roman and Tuscan bankers. There was not enough money in the royal coffers to pay for a long campaign.[2]

Nevertheless the expedition that left Naples on 24 June was impressive. The king travelled with his army down the coast road. It was a large army; awe-struck chroniclers, exaggerating as usual, spoke of ten thousand horsemen and forty thousand infantrymen, by which they meant to indicate an unusually large force. The fleet, strengthened by a squadron summoned from Pisa, kept pace with him off the shore. Progress was slow; Charles was determined to leave no enemy nest behind him. At the end of July the expedition reached the toe of Calabria and laid siege by sea and land to Reggio. The city held out against him; but Charles, who was established at Catona close by and had been reinforced by the fleet from Brindisi, attempted a landing in Sicily itself. He was driven back and decided that the time was inopportune. Meanwhile he used his superiority in ships to bottle up Roger of Lauria and the Sicilian-Aragonese fleet in Messina harbour.

Once again Roger showed himself a better sailor than the Angevins. He waited until a storm obliged their fleet to disperse, then slipped out of harbour through the gale and began to ravage the coasts in Charles's rear. The king was unwilling to give up the blockade of Reggio, especially as a squadron of fourteen galleys sent from Aragon under Raymond Marquett of Barcelona arrived in the Straits and began to harry shipping there. He could only afford to send inadequate forces against Roger, who either outmanœuvred or destroyed them.[1]

King Charles was less than a fortnight before Reggio. He had encouraged his soldiers to believe that they would cross straight into Sicily, and his failure to take Reggio quickly lowered their morale. When Roger began to land guerrilla forces behind him, he knew that he must retreat. He left Catona with his army on 3 August. Because of the efficacy of Roger's raids on the Tyrrhenian coast he took the road along the eastern coast of Calabria. From 17 to 21 August he was at Crotone, and a week later at Brindisi. His forces abandoned the whole of Calabria and were stationed along a line across southern Basilicata, from the Gulf of Policastro to the Gulf of Taranto.[2]

To his friends Charles announced that he was putting off his expedition till the following spring, when it could coincide with the French invasion of Aragon. But even he must now have begun to lose confidence. There had been widespread desertion from his army which threats of punishment failed to deter. Fine promises of trading privileges in Acre for merchants who would lend him ships or money produced little result. More reforms were suggested; and the Pope even told his legate to find out what actually were the liberties enjoyed in Good King William's day.[1] The population remained sullen and unhelpful. Aragonese and Sicilian raiders still sailed out from Capri and Ischia to hold up communications in the Bay of Naples. On the northern frontier Conrad of Antioch led forays through the Abruzzi from his castle at Saracinesco. The king's son and heir was held in prison in Sicily; and many of the Sicilians clamoured for his death, as a just revenge for the death of Conradin whom his father had slain. Queen Constance, whose natural kindliness was strengthened by the knowledge that he was more valuable alive than dead, had difficulty in preserving him from angry crowds at Messina. She moved him for safety to the castle at Cefalù. King Charles himself could have borne with equanimity the death of a son whom he despised. But the insult to his prestige would have been intolerable.[2]

Once again some small consolation was to be found in the situation in Sicily. Hitherto the mainstay of the Aragonese government there had been Alaimo of Lentini. He had been one of the three conspirators named by legend as John of Procida's associates. He had been Captain of Messina and responsible for its gallant defence. He was now Grand Justiciar of the realm. Suddenly he fell under suspicion. The gossip of the time blamed his wife, the Lady Machalda. She had never forgiven King Peter for rejecting her amorous advances. She was furiously jealous of the Queen Constance. The Queen usually travelled on horseback; but when once, owing to ill-health, she had to make use of a litter to enter Palermo on her way to the shrine at Monreale, at once Machalda, who was in perfect health, paraded the streets of Palermo in a grander litter hung with scarlet cloth, borne on the shoulders of her husband's unwilling servitors, who were obliged to carry her all the way to Nicosia. When the young Infant James made a royal tour of the island, she insisted on riding with him and on being treated as one of the royal family. She then insulted the Queen by refusing, on an obviously inadequate excuse, Alaimo's suggestion that Constance should be godmother to their youngest child. It was commonly believed that she intended to become Queen of Sicily herself.

Alaimo may have been influenced by her; but equally he may have had sincere doubts of the value to his island of the Aragonese connection. The grand conspiracy in which he had taken part had been for the liberation of the island, and the first action of the liberated islanders had been to offer themselves to the Pope, not to Aragon. When Alaimo took command in Messina his first messages were still not sent to Barcelona but to Constantinople. Pressure of events had made him accept Aragonese intervention. But the King of Aragon and his greedy soldiery were doing little enough for the island. It may be, too, that he was jealous of his colleagues in the government; John of Procida and Roger of Lauria were Italians from the mainland, not islanders. Their loyalty was not to Sicily but to Queen Constance, the daughter of John's old patron and herself Roger's foster-sister. They were anxious for the welfare of Sicily, but only if Queen Constance and her children ruled there.

However provocative Machalda may have been, Alaimo's treason had not gone very far. He had probably done no more than criticize the lawless rapacity of the Almogavar troops and discuss with his intimates whether a better government free of Aragonese control might not be found. But the queen's government was taking no risk. He was summoned to a Council over which the Infant James presided; and the Infant suggested that it would be useful if he paid a visit to Barcelona to see King Peter. Alaimo could not refuse. He left the island in November 1284. King Peter welcomed him cordially but kept him under strict surveillance. His departure caused some disquiet in Sicily, which enabled the government to see who were its enemies. It was not long before Machalda and several of her friends were arrested.

Alaimo himself early next year was discovered to have been in correspondence with the King of France, through the agency of his Sicilian lawyer, Master Garcia of Nicosia. His nephews murdered Garcia in an attempt to suppress the evidence, but in vain. Alaimo was kept for the rest of his days in a Catalonian prison.[1]

Of the three principal Sicilian leaders, Walter of Caltagirone now had been executed, Alaimo was suffering life-imprisonment, and the third, Palmiero Abbate, had disappeared into obscurity, apparently in disgrace. All was not well with Sicily. There was, however, money enough at the moment to pay for the armed forces; for Roger of Lauria took advantage of King Charles's retreat and the dispersion of his fleet to make a raid on the African island of Jerba. It was highly profitable. A vast amount of booty was taken, and the emir himself was captured when trying to escape to Tunis. The emir, Margam ibn Sebir, was imprisoned in the castle of Mategriffon at Messina, where he soon had the Lady Machalda for company. She shocked her gaolers by her gay and immodest dress when she went to play chess with him.[2]

News of such unrest in Sicily and of the preparations for the crusade against Aragon encouraged King Charles as he planned his campaign for the coming spring. He decided to spend the winter in Apulia. It was a rich province that had been as yet un-affected by the war. Unlike Naples, which was blockaded by the enemy garrisons in Capri and Ischia, the great port of Brindisi was open, and through it he could maintain contact with his overseas dominions in the East. There was little left of them. The Principality of Achaea was for the moment peaceful and loyal enough to him so long as he appointed local magnates as his vice-roys; and they allowed neither men nor money to be sent from the principality to aid him. Further north he still held Corfu and one or two fortresses on the opposite mainland; but the cost of garrisoning them was great. Of his Kingdom of Albania only the town of Durazzo was left to him, and it too needed a strong garrison. In the Kingdom of Jerusalem his authority was restricted to the city of Acre. Soon after the disaster of the Vespers he had summoned his *bailli*, Roger of San Severino, back to Italy with what troops could be spared. The acting *bailli*, Odo Poilechien, was so little sure of himself that when he made a truce with the Mameluk Sultan Qalawun in 1283 he did not venture to sign it himself, but had it signed by the Commune of Acre and the local Templar communities. The Mediterranean Empire of the Angevins was worn down to a shadow.[1]

Charles did not despair. During the months that he spent at Brindisi orders flowed from his chancery. More measures to tighten the administration were announced. His justiciars were told to make arrangements to levy a general aid for next year's fighting. If in his privacy he compared the fiasco of his last campaign with the glorious days of Benevento and Tagliacozzo, in public his grim and vigorous determination never slackened.[2]

In December he moved to Melfi, to spend Christmas there, and on 30 December he went on to Foggia. His health was deteriorating; but he was still at work. He was shocked to learn that some of his officials had a method of alienating their goods to the Church in order to avoid taxation. On 2 January 1285 he issued a stern ordinance forbidding the practice. It was his last public action.[3]

On 17 January there arrived at Messina a delegation from the town of Gallipoli, on the Gulf of Taranto near the heel of Apulia. Its members announced that their fellow-citizens wished to put themselves under the protection of the Sicilian government. They also announced that King Charles was dead and his body had been taken for burial at Naples. Delegations from other Apulian towns followed, to make the same request and to confirm the same news.[4]

Charles had died ten days previously. On 6 January he knew himself to be sinking and made his will. If his son Charles of Salerno was not released from captivity, then his kingdom and his counties were to pass to his eldest grandson, Charles Martel. Till the boy was older, or till Charles of Salerno returned from his prison, the regency was to be exercised by Robert, Count of Artois, and the Captaincy-General by his chamberlain and friend, John of Montfort. He bequeathed the sum of 10,000 ounces of gold to be distributed by Robert of Artois amongst the members of his household, on condition that they swore fidelity to his heirs. The Pope was asked to give his approval to all these dispositions and to give to the government of the Kingdom his supervision and his protection.

He lingered through that night, fortified by the rites of the Church and confident of his salvation. 'Lord God,' he is said to have prayed with his dying lips, 'as I believe truly that Thou art my saviour, I pray Thee to have mercy on my soul. Thou knowest that I took the Kingdom of Sicily for the sake of the Holy Church and not for my own profit or gain. So Thou wilt pardon my sins.' Next morning, on Saturday, 7 January 1285, he died, at the age of fifty-eight. His body was taken from Foggia to Naples, to be buried in a marble sepulchre.[1]

For twenty years Charles of Anjou had dominated the Mediterranean stage. He had shown himself to be one of the great statesmen of his time. It had even seemed that he would build a large and lasting empire. But he died a failure. His personal assets were many. He was bold, determined and imperturbable, vigorous and unsparing of himself, capable equally of planning grandiose projects and of supervising minute details. He was a competent soldier and administrator. His piety was sincere. He had been brought up at the remarkable court of Queen Blanche and Saint Louis; he had seen for himself how a good king governs. But these assets were not quite sufficient for the role that he chose to play. He failed as a man. There was no kindliness in his make-up, no pity nor any imaginative sympathy. His personal ambition was too crude and too obvious. His piety was its servant; for he saw himself as the instrument of God and the champion of His holy Church. He was not an unscrupulous adventurer of the type that Machiavelli was to admire. He was a man of honour according to his lights, but they were narrow and selfish lights. Men could admire him; his courtiers and ministers would work for him with whole-hearted devotion and praise for his achievements. But few of them loved him, nor could he inspire any love in the bulk of his subjects. It was the lack of human understanding that was his downfall. His plans were laid with care and precision, but they failed to allow for the opposition that they roused in men's hearts. When he put Conradin to death, he did so as an act of deliberate political calculation; but, being pitiless himself, he never realized the shudder of pity that the execution would send round the world. His human weaknesses were a certain vanity that made him reach for such valueless titles as King of Jerusalem, and a certain excess of confidence that as the years went on led him to underrate his enemies. Though he had been warned, it never occurred to him that the impoverished court of Aragon would ever venture to challenge him. He could not believe that the terrified Emperor at Constantinople would weave a web of intrigue right into his own dominions. Finally and fatally, it was beyond his comprehension that the Sicilians should so care for their freedom that they would rise against the most powerful prince of the age. He was used to the people of France. There the nobles had been troublesome to the crown, but humbler folk had welcomed the officials of the king. Neither his experience nor his imagination was wide enough for him to envisage a whole people striking for its liberty.

Howsoever it may have been plotted and prepared, it was that one March evening of the Vespers at Palermo that brought down King Charles's empire. But he had prayed that God would only let him fall by little steps; and his prayer was granted. His power crumbled slowly; and, soon after his death, the decline was halted, and the Angevin house found new roads for its advancement. The Sicilians, who had forced King Charles on to the downward flight, gained little from it. Their tangled and unhappy history during the next few decades was a poor reward for their courage.

CHAPTER XVI

THE VESPERS AND
THE FATE OF SICILY

In the months that followed King Charles's death it seemed that nothing would save his kingdom. The new king was a captive in enemy hands. Calabria was lost; one by one the Apulian towns were going over to the enemy. Naples itself was simmering with rebellion. Nor did Pope Martin make things easier by refusing to accept the late king's will in its entirety. He did not admit the accession of the prisoner Charles of Salerno, merely referring to him as the late king's son. Some days passed before he recognized Robert of Artois as regent, and then he placed the legate, Cardinal Gerard, on a level with him; both were regents for the Holy See, not for any absentee monarch or any boy prince. He made it clear that there was an interregnum in the Kingdom and that meanwhile the Pope as suzerain rightfully took charge. There was some point to his attitude; for it diminished the importance of the royal prisoner and his value as a hostage or as a source of ransom money. But it demanded a number of wise administrators at the papal court and loyal servants of the Papacy to work in the Kingdom.[1]

The French court, committed now to the crusade against Aragon, was horrified by the news from Italy. With King Charles dead and his kingdom near to chaos, there could be no expedition against Sicily to coincide with the crusade; King Peter could concentrate all his forces for the defence of Aragon. But the great army which Philip III had collected could not be sent fruitlessly home. At the end of May 1285, King James of Majorca opened the campaign for his French allies by landing troops in Roussillon and sacking Elne, on the road from Perpignan to the Pyrenees.

With the way thus cleared for him King Philip led the crusading army, estimated by awed contemporaries as being over 100,000 strong, over the Pyrenean passes. On 25 June he laid siege to Gerona. The Aragonese army was hopelessly outnumbered; and King Peter received little support from his nobles, many of whom were in touch with the French or the Majorcan king. He made use of the traditional Spanish guerrilla tactics, harassing the slow-moving French army so successfully that Philip did not dare to disperse his forces. Gerona was bravely defended and held out till 5 September. It was a hot summer; and the plain of Gerona was malarial. By the time that the fortress was captured, half the crusader army was ill, and the older soldiers began to remember the horrors of the Tunisian Crusade, fifteen years before. Then came the news that the French fleet, which had been cruising down the Catalonian coast, had been annihilated on 4 September off the islands of Las Formigas, near Palamos. Roger of Lauria had been summoned from Sicilian waters and easily outmanœuvred the French admiral. After his victory Roger landed troops at Rosas, where the coast road approached the Pyrenees, thus cutting King Philip's main supply route. In the middle of September Philip ordered the army to retreat. He himself was sickening of a fever; many of his men were out of action, and all of them were impatient to be done with the baleful campaign. With the Almogavar guerrillas striking from all sides the retreat soon became a panic-stricken flight. The whole crusade proved a humiliating fiasco.[1]

Events in further parts of the Angevin world were no more encouraging. For Achaea, where trouble seemed likely, the regency at Naples had the wisdom to appoint as governor the richest and ablest of the neighbouring magnates, William, Duke of Athens. Till his death in 1287 he was in complete charge of the principality, paying little more than nominal deference to his overlords.[2] At Acre the acting *bailli*, Odo Poilechien, clung bravely to his diminishing power, uncertain who was the master that he represented. When the rightful King of Jerusalem, Henry Lusignan of Cyprus, landed at Acre in June 1286 it was clear even to the faithful Odo that Angevin rule in Outremer was ended. The festivities that marked the young king's coronation and the departure of Odo and his men showed how little popular it had been. But in fact the rejoicing was inopportune. Only five years later Acre was captured by the Mameluk Sultan of Egypt; and the royal title of Jerusalem became as empty an adornment to the House of Lusignan as it was to the House of Anjou.[1]

The Angevin cause was saved by a fortunate series of deaths. The year 1285 proved fatal for many princes. In January Charles himself had died. He was followed to the grave on 29 March by Martin IV, the Pope that he had created. Martin's pontificate had been disastrous both to the Angevins and to the Church. He had been, according to his lights, a good man. His morals were impeccable and his integrity high. But he was narrow, vindictive and devoid of understanding. His passionate French patriotism and his devotion to the House of Capet had blinded him to the Oecumenical position of his high office. His predecessor Nicholas III, a far less worthy man, had seen what sort of role the Holy See should play; to the best of his ability he had been a peacemaker and an arbiter between princes. But Martin was a bitter partisan who tried to involve the Church in a policy offensive to the legitimate wishes of its faithful congregations. Thanks largely to his own inflexibility the policy had failed, and had dragged down himself, his friends and the Holy Church into a slough of disrepute.[2]

On 5 October King Philip III of France died at Perpignan, 'fleeing and disgracing the lilies', as Dante scornfully noted; and on his death the crusading army melted away. He had been a weak and foolish man. In his last illness, as his litter bore him northward from the Pyrenees, he had time to reflect on the humiliation into which his admiration for his uncle Charles had led him.[3]

Five weeks later, on 10 November, it was the turn of King Peter of Aragon, who died at the height of his triumph. Despite his achievements his figure does not stand out clearly in history. He was gracious and full of charm; he made a good impression among the populace in Sicily. He had courage and enterprise, as his defence against the crusade had shown, but he was also cautious; he waited almost too long before he ventured to intervene in Sicily. He was neither a profound politician nor a skilled administrator. When he left Sicily to return to Aragon he soon forgot its needs and was irritated when his wife and her ministers reminded him of them. There was something frivolous about him; but his experience was widening and his prestige growing. His loss was a blow to his people.[1]

The new actors on the scene differed greatly from their predecessors. Charles of Salerno, Charles the Lame as he was called from his infirmity, had the traits usual in the son of an unloving and domineering father. He was diffident; and his diffidence had been increased by the knowledge of his folly in being captured and by the humiliation of his captivity. He was secretive and he was patient; and he had a sensitivity that his father entirely lacked. He was warm-hearted, as befitted the affectionate father of thirteen children. In the end he showed himself to be a just and prudent ruler and a shrewd diplomat. But at the moment, hidden from the world in a comfortable prison in Catalonia, there was little that he could do.[2]

The new Pope, Honorius IV, was a Roman, a member of the Savelli family and akin to the great house of the Orsini.[3] He was a man of no great spiritual quality, but a clear-sighted politician who was determined to give peace to Italy. However little he may have approved of his predecessor's policy, he calculated that the Papacy would lose more in prestige if he repudiated it entirely than if he pursued it in a modified form. He was determined to preserve the integrity of the Kingdom of Sicily for the Angevins; the Papacy was too far compromised to permit the Aragonese to keep the island itself. But he was equally determined that the Kingdom's administration should be reformed. Using his suzerain rights he issued two bulls in September 1285, which carried into effect the reforms promised by Charles I in 1282 and by Charles of Salerno at San Martino the following year. In addition he interpreted the liberties enjoyed in Good King William's time as being freedom from heavy taxation. A preamble recounted the history of the Kingdom since Frederick II's days and spoke frankly of the abuses that had come in under King Charles. The General Aid, which Charles had demanded on every possible occasion and which had been fixed at 107,892 ounces in 1282, was reduced to a maximum of 50,000 ounces and could only be raised for the four causes traditionally permitted by feudal custom. He saw to it that many other taxes and duties were abolished, and many more personal freedoms guaranteed than even the parliament at San Martino had allowed. The whole administration was to be overhauled. It was an admirable constitution, which, had it been put into practice, would have given the subjects of the Kingdom as much liberty as was enjoyed anywhere at the time. Honorius doubtless thought that by admitting that there had been misgovernment and by guaranteeing a better future he removed from the Sicilians and Calabrians their only reasons for continuing in rebellion.[1] In the meantime he made peace wherever possible with the Italians of the centre and north with whom Martin had quarrelled. Guy of Montefeltro made his submission, on generous terms. Bologna, which was on bad terms with Martin, was reconciled. The Venetians who had contemplated an Aragonese alliance, were cajoled into a friendlier attitude. He even suggested the release of Henry of Castile from the prison where he had languished since the time of Conradin's defeat.[2]

The Sicilians, however, were unmoved by the Pope's reforms. They would not submit again to Angevin rule, even if the Pope guaranteed its improvement. And, in fact, part of the reforms proved impracticable and others were easy to ignore. Nor were the rebels discouraged by the death of Peter of Aragon. As he had promised, Sicily passed to his second son, James, while

Alfonso, the eldest, inherited Aragon. The new King of Aragon was aged twenty-one. He was an intelligent and gallant youth, devoted to his mother and his brothers. He was already betrothed to a daughter of King Edward of England, who thought highly of him. The King of Sicily was two years younger. He too was able; but his character was less open and more self-seeking than his brother's. For the moment he was under the good influence of his mother, Queen Constance, and her experienced adviser, John of Procida.[1]

The new King of France was the ablest of the princes who came into power in 1285. Philip IV, surnamed the Fair, was still aged only seventeen, but he had already shown his independence of character. His mother had been Peter of Aragon's sister; and he had disapproved of his father's subservience to Charles of Anjou, perhaps because it was encouraged by his stepmother, whom he disliked. He had tried to oppose the crusade against Aragon. But when he became king his attitude began to change. It may be that he did not feel for his cousins of Aragon the respect that he had felt for their father, King Peter; and he was anxious now for the glory of France and of his dynasty. He was ready to see his brother, Charles of Valois, seated on the Aragonese throne. But, for the moment, after the defeat of the crusade, it was impracticable. With the Pope's approval he asked King Edward of England to mediate between him and Alfonso of Aragon and arrange a truce.[2]

Pope Honorius was ready to liquidate the Aragonese crusade, especially as the present King of Aragon did not claim to be King of Sicily. He was not ready to accept the secession of Sicily. King James was crowned at Palermo in February 1286, and used the occasion to promise his subjects the same liberties that Honorius had recently offered the mainlanders. It was believed that the Pope sent two Dominican friars to try to raise a revolt in Sicily with the help of a local priest. James discovered them and courteously sent them back unharmed to Italy. Immediately after his coronation he sent an embassy to Honorius to offer him homage and ask for his confirmation of the title. Honorius answered by excommunicating him, his mother Queen Constance, and all the people of Sicily. The two clerics who performed the coronation, the Bishops of Cefalù and Nicastro, were summoned to explain their misconduct before the papal court.[1]

The history of the next few years is one of abortive arrangements for making peace. The captive Charles of Salerno was willing to make sacrifices in order to obtain his freedom; and his captors would have let him go in return for the recognition of their rights over Sicily and Calabria. But the Papacy refused blankly to permit Charles to cede the island, while the French court was nervous of any too great increase in Aragonese power. A treaty signed at Paris in July 1286 established a truce between France and Aragon, to last for fourteen months and then to be replaced by a definite peace-treaty.[2] But at the same time Charles of Salerno signed at his prison in Catalonia a treaty with his captors, in which he promised to cede Sicily and the neighbouring lands including Malta, Reggio and its neighbourhood, and all his rights to the tribute paid by the King of Tunis. He would himself receive his liberty; he would see that the Papacy withdrew its excommunications and interdicts against the Aragonese princes and their subjects; and the treaty would be confirmed by the marriage of the King of Sicily to one of Charles's daughters and of the Infanta Violante to one of his sons. It would have been a just and reasonable settlement; but it needed the approval of the Pope, and Honorius would have nothing to do with it. Instead, he ordered a new offensive against Sicily.[3]

War had been going on in southern Italy, with damaging guerrilla raids along the west coast. The Pope now planned the invasion of Sicily, to take place in the spring of 1287. It was a disastrous affair. A large expedition put out from Brindisi and landed near Augusta, between Catania and Syracuse, on 1 May and settled down to besiege the town. By the end of June its supplies were running short and Augusta still held out. A fleet was equipped at Naples to reinforce it, under the leadership of the Count of Flanders. On 23 June Roger of Lauria swept into the Bay of Naples and lured the Count out to fight with him. Once again Roger was completely victorious. He captured forty-eight galleys, with some five thousand on board, including the Count of Flanders, the Captain-General John of Montfort, the Count of Joinville and many other nobles from Provence and France. The battle was watched from the shore by the ambassador of the Mongol Ilkhan of Persia, the Nestorian priest Rabban Sauma, who had come to Europe thinking to find Christendom ready to unite against the Muslims of the East. On the news of the battle the expeditionary force in Sicily gave up the struggle and capitulated. But Roger did not follow up his victory. He contented himself by freeing his captives for a very heavy ransom, which enabled him to pay his sailors wages that were long overdue to them, and to keep some money in hand for the future.[1]

Pope Honorius did not live to see the results of his obstinacy. He died at Rome on 3 April 1287. For ten months there was a vacancy; the anti-French opposition in the College of Cardinals was strong enough to block for a while the election of another pro-Angevin Pope, but eventually compromised on the person of the former General of the Franciscan Order, Jerome of Ascoli, who was installed as Nicholas IV in February 1288.[2] During the interregnum Edward of England, who was alarmed at the possibility of further war in Spain which might embarrass him and his French dominions at a time when he had worries in Wales and in Scotland, arbitrated once more between Alfonso of Aragon and Charles of Salerno. At a treaty signed at Oloron in Béarn in July 1287, Charles was to obtain his liberty in return for the payment of 50,000 marks of silver and for sending his three eldest sons and sixty noblemen of Provence as hostages in his place. He would then work for a peace which would satisfy Alfonso of Aragon and James of Sicily on the one hand and himself, the King of France and his brother Charles, and the Holy See on the other. If such a peace were not negotiated within three years, Charles was to return to captivity or else forfeit the County of Provence, to which the House of Aragon had an hereditary claim. Representatives of the College of Cardinals were present at the signing of the treaty and reluctantly gave their consent to it.[1]

Now it was the King of France who refused to co-operate. He was alarmed by the clause about Provence; and he wanted to be sure of proper compensation for his brother, the would-be King of Aragon. Charles remained in prison. The new Pope soon showed himself as intractable as his predecessors. He demanded the complete submission of King Alfonso and his brother James. He refused to listen to the Aragonese ambassadors who tried to explain to him that the rising in Sicily had been a justifiable protest against oppression and that the excesses committed against the French had shocked and distressed the majority of the Sicilians.[2] But Pope Nicholas was alarmed by the revival of the Ghibellines in central Italy. Guy of Montefeltro was on the warpath again, and even the city of Rome was showing Ghibelline sympathies. Moreover, news came from the East that the Mameluks were planning a new campaign against the remnants of Outremer.[3] He encouraged Edward of England to try his hand at arbitration once more.

At the treaty of Canfranc, signed on October 1288, Charles was to be given his liberty on the same terms as at Oloron; but Edward himself, in his desire for a settlement, offered hostages from his own Duchy of Guienne and a large sum of money to be given to King Alfonso, should it prove impracticable to send Charles's eldest son, Charles Martel, as a hostage along with his brothers. On receiving Edward's guarantees, Alfonso freed Charles and sent him to the court of France to secure King Philip's adhesion to the treaty. But he told him not to take the title of King of Sicily, as that would be an insult to his brother James.[4]

Charles had an embarrassing reception at the French court. Philip IV had no intention of making peace with Aragon just yet.

He arrested the Aragonese ambassadors who accompanied Charles; and when Charles left after a few weeks for Italy he provided him with an unwanted escort of well-armed knights. Charles was no more treated as a peacemaker when he arrived in Italy. The Guelfs everywhere gave him a brilliant reception. The Pope welcomed him as a returning hero. Nicholas himself, who had found Rome too full of Ghibellines to be a comfortable residence, had moved to Rieti, near the borders of Charles's kingdom. There he crowned Charles King of Sicily on Whit Sunday 1289, and forced him to accept a tithe on all Church property in Italy, so as to pursue the war against Aragon and Sicily. Charles, who was a man of honour, was acutely uncomfortable. The Pope attached a cardinal-legate, Berard of Cagli, to him, to see that he behaved according to the wishes of the Holy Father.[1]

To Charles's credit he still worked for peace. The opportunity came unexpectedly. Alfonso of Aragon, furious at his deception, planned with Roger of Lauria to make a descent on the coast of the Kingdom and was led to believe that the city of Gaeta would rise against the Angevins. He was misinformed. He landed near Gaeta; but the city refused to admit him. While he besieged it a large Angevin army under Charles Martel and the Count of Artois came up and entrapped him in front of the city walls. A mutual blockade lasted for nearly two months. Then Charles appeared in person. He was nervous for his captive sons. Edward of England had sent an embassy to beg him to fulfil his obligations. News had come that the Egyptians had taken Tripoli in Syria; and Edward was eager to plan a crusade. Charles offered Alfonso a two years' truce. The Pope, as soon as he heard of the English embassy, had sent two cardinals to see that Charles did nothing peaceable. He ignored them. Knights with his army complained that it was full of priests and prophecies, in contrast to the gay chivalry of Alfonso's camp; but his religiosity gave no satisfaction to the Pope. One of the two cardinals, Benedict Caetani, the future Pope Boniface VIII, never quite forgave Charles.[2]

In spite of papal disapproval Charles's policy proved wise. Though the truce of Gaeta was not to apply to Calabria and Sicily, where James of Sicily continued the war, it began to detach Alfonso from his brother. The King of Aragon began to wonder if Sicily could not now look after itself and if he should not retire with the gains that he had made and concentrate on establishing his power in Spain.

Charles's next peacemaking move was to go to France, to placate the French court and satisfy Charles of Valois. To clear his conscience with regard to Aragon he journeyed to the frontier, to the Pass of Panicar, on 1 November 1289, and officially offered himself for re-arrest. No Aragonese official appeared to take him off into custody; so, his honour satisfied, he went on to Paris. After some months of negotiation there, he signed a pact at Senlis on 19 May 1290. Charles of Valois had the previous day been married to King Charles's daughter Margaret and had received the rich Counties of Anjou and Maine as her dowry. In return he now promised to abandon any claim on Aragon when the Pope should so wish. King Philip agreed to make peace with Aragon as soon as its king was reconciled to the Papacy; and he offered the Papacy 200,000 pounds towards the reconquest of Sicily. Next winter a peace conference met first at Perpignan and then was transferred to Tarascon. An English mediator presided over delegates sent by the Pope, King Charles, King Philip, Charles of Valois, King James of Majorca and by the Kingdom of Aragon, representing the nobility as much as the king. A preliminary treaty was signed at Brignoles on 19 February 1291. The arrangement made at Senlis was confirmed. Peace was signed between France and Aragon and between Charles's kingdom, still officially called Sicily, and Aragon. Charles of Valois gave up any claim to the Aragonese throne, but was confirmed in the possession of Anjou and Maine. In compensation King Philip gave to King Charles those districts of the territory of Avignon which had been part of the County of Toulouse. King Alfonso would go as soon as possible to Rome to be reconciled with the Church, and there a definitive treaty would be signed in the presence of the Pope. There was a hitch when Alfonso refused to give back Majorca to his uncle James, who had lost it as a result of the failure of the Aragonese crusade, but he agreed to submit the question to the Pope's arbitration. Everyone was satisfied except for King James of Sicily and the Sicilians, who were left to fight their battles alone.[1]

Once again death intervened. On 18 June, just as he was about to leave for Rome, King Alfonso died of a sudden fever, aged twenty-seven. His desertion of the Sicilians in the last months of his life has stained his reputation. He was not entirely to blame. Constitutionally and financially he was largely dependent on his nobles; and they were tired of the war and the Sicilian connection. Loyalty to Sicily might well have cost him his crown. But his mother and his brother in Sicily found it hard to forgive him. His marriage to Eleanor of England had never taken place, owing to his long excommunication. His heir therefore was his brother James of Sicily. But, in conformity with his father's will, he ordered that if James became King of Aragon he must hand on Sicily to their younger brother, the Infant Frederick. The Aragonese, fearing anarchy, hastened to send a ship to fetch James from Messina. After a brief tour round the island James set sail from Trapani on 23 July.[2]

James refused to be bound by any treaty or will that his brother had made. He was heir by right to Aragon, he said, and was not obliged to renounce the Sicilian throne. He left the Infant Frederick merely as his lieutenant, not as king. He interrupted his voyage to Barcelona in Majorca and declared the Balearic Islands to be inalienable from the Crown of Aragon, whatever the Pope might say. The Treaty of Brignoles thus was repudiated. Pope Nicholas excommunicated James once more, as well as the Sicilians; and everyone prepared again for war.[3] But very soon James, as King of Aragon, found himself in his late brother's position. His subjects there had had enough of war and of Sicily.

He began to hint that if he were properly compensated he would abandon Sicily to the Angevins. An Aragonese ambassador was sent to offer the king's submission to the papal court. A few days later, Pope Nicholas died, on 4 April 1292.[1]

The ensuing papal interregnum lasted for two years. During those years Charles continued his efforts to make peace with Aragon and to detach it from Sicily. Potential allies of the Sicilians, such as the Genoese, were bribed or threatened into neutrality. King James was wooed through the mediation of King Sancho of Castile, Edward of England now being at war with France.[2] Charles was particularly anxious for a Mediterranean settlement, as he had new ideas now for his dynasty. King Ladislas IV of Hungary had died in 1290, without issue, and his sister, Charles's queen Maria, was his heiress. The Hungarians, not wanting the rule of an absentee princess, had given the throne to the last male member of the ancient House of Arpad, Andrew III, surnamed the Venetian, from his Venetian mother. Queen Maria was determined to secure her inheritance, for herself or for one of her numerous sons, and wished her husband to be free to intervene at least when King Andrew, who had no son, should die.[3] A truce between Charles and James was arranged at Figueras at the end of 1293, in which James agreed to abandon Sicily in return for suitable compensation.[4] Six months later Charles ended the papal interregnum by forcing upon the quarrelling Conclave a saintly hermit, Peter of Morone, for whose apocalyptic spirituality he had a personal sympathy. The new Pope, who took the name of Celestine V, was utterly unused to political life. He did whatever Charles told him, allowing him to raise money from papal sources in Italy, France and England, for a campaign against Sicily and encouraging him in every scheme to placate James of Aragon.[5] In the meantime Charles and Philip of France began to hold out bribes to the Infant Frederick and to his chief ministers, John of Procida and the Admiral Roger of Lauria. Neither John nor Roger were Sicilians. Roger had gained nothing for serving so impoverished a country but fame and booty that had to be spent at once on his crew. John, who was nearly eighty, longed to be back in the Italian estates which King Manfred had given him. They had avenged Manfred in humbling Charles of Anjou. The adventure could end now.[1] For the Infant Frederick Philip IV had a tempting solution. Philip of Courtenay, titular Emperor of Constantinople, was dead. By his wife, Charles of Anjou's daughter Beatrice, he had had one child, Catherine, now aged twenty and living at the French court. The Infant should marry her and console himself for the loss of Sicily with a claim to the Imperial throne of Romania.[2]

In December 1294 Pope Celestine could bear the strain of papal responsibility no longer and abdicated his office. Next day the Conclave elected Cardinal Caetani, who took the name of Boniface VIII. He had long been on bad terms with Charles II, but as the result, it was believed, of a secret interview on the eve of Celestine's resignation, he worked willingly with Charles over the Aragonese business.[3] Thanks to his readiness to confirm the plans made during the last few months, peace was signed in his presence at Anagni, in the palace of the Caetani, on 12 June 1295. James would hand over to the Holy See the island of Sicily and his mainland conquests. He would give Majorca back to his uncle James in return for Sardinia, which had hitherto been a no-man's-land. He would liberate Charles's II sons, and would marry his daughter Blanche, with a large dowry provided by the Pope; and his sister Violante would marry one of Charles's sons. His brother Frederick would be compensated by the hand of Catherine of Courtenay and a handsome subsidy for the reconquest of Constantinople. Philip of France and Charles of Valois would renounce for ever any claims on Aragon. James, his mother, his brothers and all the people of Sicily would be received back without spiritual penalty into the bosom of the Holy Church.[4]

Once again the settlement was designed to please everyone but the Sicilians. On the news of the Truce of Figueras the Sicilians had sent a mission to Barcelona to tell King James that the island would never submit again to French rule. The Infant Frederick was hesitant. Roger of Lauria and John of Procida as well as the courts of Barcelona and Naples urged him to accept. Only his mother, Queen Constance, opposed them. He did not want to desert his Sicilians; he had doubts whether, even if he married Catherine, an expedition against Constantinople would be feasible or desirable. When the actual peace-terms of Anagni were known in Sicily the Sicilians told Frederick that they wanted to have him as their king, but that they would defend their island against him or anyone else who tried to reintroduce the French. To gain time he announced that if Catherine of Courtenay would announce her readiness to accept him by September 1295, he would comply with the treaty terms. Catherine's answer solved his problem. She was a sensible girl. A princess without lands, she said, ought not to marry a prince without lands; and she refused him. Frederick, who was now being acclaimed by the Italian Ghibellines as their future Emperor Frederick, was crowned King of Sicily at Palermo on 12 December 1295. Next year he continued the war against Naples and conducted a not very successful raid into Basilicata.[1]

At the beginning of 1297 James of Aragon, already married to his Angevin bride, was summoned by Pope Boniface VIII to Rome. He sent an embassy to Sicily to suggest to Frederick that he should meet him to settle their differences at Ischia. Frederick, after consulting his parliament, refused the invitation; but he could not prevent John of Procida and Roger of Lauria's accompanying the embassy on its journey to Rome, nor did he venture to disobey his brother's order that Queen Constance and the Infanta Violante were to go with them. The Queen was unwilling, but consented in the hope that she might reconcile her two sons. At Rome, in March 1298, Violante was married to Robert, who was now Charles II's heir; for Charles Martel was dead and the next brother, Louis, had entered the Church. She made him a good wife, and even Pope Boniface could think of nothing unkind to say of her; but she died young, in 1302, leaving only one son. James during his visit to Rome was appointed Gonfalonier of the Church, received the investiture of Corsica as well as of Sardinia, was allowed to postpone the cession of the Balearic Islands, and was promised tithes from the ecclesiastical revenues. His friendship was worth buying, even at a heavy price, if only because he brought with him into the Angevin camp his great admiral, Roger of Lauria, whom the Pope rewarded with the lordship of the African islands of Jerba and Kerkena.[1]

Sicily was isolated; but the new allies, King James, King Charles II and the Pope, were curiously ineffectual. In a series of campaigns during the autumn of 1298 and the following winter they cleared Calabria of the enemy. When they tried to invade the island, Robert, Charles's heir, only succeeded in taking a few towns and villages near Messina but not Messina itself, while King James, after vainly besieging Syracuse, was severely defeated by his brother Frederick nearby, and the joint Angevin and Aragonese fleet, under Roger of Lauria's nephew, suffered heavy losses in a battle off Messina. In consequence James left the island.[2] In the summer of 1299 a new campaign was launched. For it both King Charles and the Pope had borrowed heavily from the merchants of Tuscany and the Jews of Rome. It opened well for the allies. Roger of Lauria virtually annihilated the Sicilian fleet under King Frederick on 4 July off Cape Orlando.[3] But only some desultory raids, easily driven off by Frederick, followed on the victory. In September King James, with his mother Constance, who hated to see her sons fighting each other, departed from Italy on the grounds that his presence was needed in Spain.[4] Roger of Lauria was left behind with the bulk of the Aragonese fleet to continue the war, but the Aragonese army accompanied its king. About the same time Prince Robert, with Roger's help, landed at Catania and occupied the city and its neighbourhood. In October Charles sent his fourth son, Philip of Taranto, to land at the Western end of the island, so that Frederick would be caught between two invading armies. Frederick, whose information system was good, hurried westward and fell on Philip's army just after it had disembarked, in the plain of Falconaria, on 1 November. The invaders were routed and Philip was taken prisoner with most of his staff.[1]

This victory encouraged all the Ghibellines in Italy. Many Genoese took service with the Sicilian king, including the best-known admiral of the Republic, Conrad Doria. Now there were rumours that the Republic itself was officially going to join the war. The seneschal of Provence was so anxious that he began an invasion of Genoese territory, to the embarrassment of King Charles, who hastened to send an apologetic embassy to Genoa, promising territorial concessions if the Genoese would keep out of the war. More effective than Charles's promises were Roger of Lauria's actions. He intercepted Conrad Doria and a mixed Genoese and Sicilian fleet raiding off Naples near the island of Ponza, on 14 June and destroyed it. The Genoese withdrew from the war and the Republic announced its neutrality.[2]

In spite of this victory the Angevin invasion of Sicily made no progress. Roger of Lauria failed to find a spot at which to land further troops. Robert had advanced from Catania to lay siege to Messina; but the city held out against him as firmly as against his grandfather in 1282. His troops captured a few castles in the interior but held them with difficulty against the Sicilian guerrillas. The conquest of the island would clearly be a long and painful operation. After the Angevin fleet had been severely damaged in a storm off Cape Passaro in July 1301, Prince Robert listened to the pleading of his wife, the Infanta Violante, and allowed her to arrange a truce for a year between him and her brother, King Frederick. Robert remained in possession of Catania and its district, but he withdrew his troops from the rest of the island.[3]

The court of Naples accepted the truce. Pope Boniface disapproved of it, but he had too many other worries to protest.

There had been a Ghibelline resurgence in northern Italy, led by Azzo of Este, lord of Ferrara. There were Ghibelline risings in the Romagna and the Marches. The Umbrian cities, except for Perugia, reaffirmed their Ghibellinism. To complicate matters, the Guelfs in the cities where they were dominant, such as Florence, began to split into two factions, the Blacks and the Whites. Pope Boniface felt his hold slipping. He called in a new champion for the Church, choosing Charles of Valois, whose Neapolitan wife had died and who had recently married the titular Empress of Constantinople, Catherine of Courtenay. Charles of Valois thought that it would help his future campaign against Constantinople, which some day he hoped to conquer, if he established influence in Italy. But he was an irresponsible adventurer who did the papal cause little good. When the truce in Sicily was ended, he was sent there as Captain-General of the Angevin forces. Prince Robert remained Vicar in the island for his father; but Boniface did not trust him. A private report from Cardinal Gerard of Parma, the legate, pronounced him to be under the domination of his Aragonese wife, whose death in childbirth later in the year the Pope did not therefore regret.[1]

Charles of Valois landed in Sicily at the end of May 1302, on the north coast, near Termini which he captured. Roger of Lauria made a simultaneous attack on Palermo, but only succeeded in taking an outlying fort. Charles then crossed the island to Sciacca on the south coast and laid siege to it. It was a hot summer. By the end of August the Angevin army was tired and sick, and the town still untaken. Charles of Valois then received letters from his brother King Philip calling him home to France. Philip had recently quarrelled with the Pope and had also suffered a bad defeat at the hands of the Flemish at Courtrai. He needed his brother's support. Charles II had given Charles of Valois authority to treat with the enemy if need be. In the last days of August he and Prince Robert met King Frederick at Caltabellotta, in the hills behind Sciacca. Peace was signed there on 31 August.

The Treaty of Caltabellotta gave Sicily her independence. All Angevin troops were to be withdrawn from the island, and all Sicilian troops from the mainland. Frederick was to have the title of King of the Island of Sicily, in order that the Kingdom of Sicily should officially remain with the Angevins. He was to marry King Charles's youngest daughter Eleanora, and was to be king for his lifetime only. On his death the crown would revert to the Angevins and his heirs would be compensated with the Kingdom of Sardinia or that of Cyprus, neither of which were in the gift of the Angevins, or the sum of 100,000 ounces of gold. All prisoners were to be returned.[1]

The treaty was everywhere welcomed with sighs of relief. King Charles had given up hope of reconquering the island; but he had the likelihood of recovering it peaceably when Frederick should die, and he might well die young, like his brother Alfonso. Moreover the clause returning it eventually to his House saved his face. Pope Boniface, though he disliked the loss of Sicily to an excommunicated member of an excommunicated family, could also find consolation in the clause. He merely insisted that Frederick's title should be 'King of Trinacria', so as to avoid the word Sicily, and that Frederick's reign should officially begin from this date. He gave his blessing to it and received Frederick and the Sicilians back into the Church. He reserved his anger for Charles of Valois, whom he received very coldly.[2] Soon afterwards, in May 1303, the wedding of Frederick and Eleanora was sumptuously celebrated at Messina.[3]

In fact, both to Boniface and to Charles II the Sicilian question had become of secondary importance. The former was fully involved in his dispute with Philip of France, the dispute which culminated in the humiliating scene of his kidnapping by the king's officers from his own palace at Anagni.[4] Charles II's main object now was to establish his dynasty in Hungary. His queen, the Hungarian heiress, had transferred her rights to her eldest son, Charles Martel, a youth of great promise, whose death by fever in 1296 had been a heavy blow to the Angevin cause. Charles Martel's claim to the title had not however been recognized outside of his father's dominions; and the Sicilian war had prevented Charles II from taking action in Hungary against King Andrew III, whom the Hungarians had accepted.[1]

Charles Martel and his wife Clementia of Habsburg, who died soon after him, left three small children, a son and two daughters. When Pope Boniface ascended the throne he agreed with Charles II that the king's Italian and Provençal possessions should go to his third son, Robert, the second, Louis, having entered the Church, and that Charles Martel's second son, Charles Robert, or Carobert, should have the Hungarian throne. On Andrew III's death early in 1301 Carobert was sent to Hungarian territory in Dalmatia and there crowned king. But meanwhile the Hungarian magnates offered the throne to the King of Bohemia, Wenceslas IV, whose grandmother had been a Hungarian princess. He accepted it for his son Ladislas, who was crowned with the Crown of Saint Stephen, without which no Hungarian coronation was considered valid, at Szekesfehervar in August 1301. The Pope summoned both kings to appear before him for arbitration, but only Carobert came. His rights were therefore upheld by Rome. During the next few years papal legates worked for the Angevin cause in Hungary while Rudolph, King of the Romans, Carobert's other grandfather, put pressure on the Bohemian king. Ladislas found the Hungarian throne so uncomfortable that when his father died in 1305 he renounced it on taking up the Bohemian; but he handed the precious crown of Saint Stephen not to the Angevins but to Otto, Duke of Bavaria, whose mother had been an Arpad princess. Otto had an unhappy reign. In 1307 he went to visit his most powerful vassal, Ladislas Kan, voievod of Transylvania, thinking that he was to wed his daughter. But Ladislas saw that he was not worth supporting, arrested him and only let him go when he handed over the crown of Saint Stephen. Otto then gladly returned to Bavaria. The majority of the Hungarian magnates met and at last proclaimed Carobert as their king, in October 1307, but there were still important abstentions. It was not till November 1308 that he was able to come to Pest and take over the kingdom. He was crowned the following June, but only with a diadem made for the occasion, as the voievod Ladislas refused to give up the crown of Saint Stephen. At last, under the threat of excommunication, the voievod yielded next summer; and Carobert was crowned again with the holy relic in August 1310.[1]

The anxious care with which the court at Naples watched the young King's progress diverted its interest from Sicily. The Hungarian throne offered far greater scope than did the possession of the Mediterranean island; and, in the outcome, it was in Hungary that the Angevin house reached its highest point. Charles of Anjou, when he married his son to the daughter of the Hungarian king, cannot have foreseen what glory he would thereby bring to his house; yet of all his actions it was in the long run the most successful.

King Charles II could therefore face the loss of Sicily with equanimity. To Frederick of Aragon the Peace of Caltabellotta was a fitting reward for his efforts. That he was only to be life-tenant of his island throne did not worry him; it would be possible to deal with that later on. Nor did he obey the Pope in agreeing to date his reign only from the moment of the Pope's confirmation of the treaty. His success also had the result of reconciling him with his brother King James of Aragon; who, having extracted all possible advantages from his alliance with the enemy, allowed his family affections to triumph once more.[2]

To the Sicilian people the settlement brought an even more greatly deserved reward. The war had in truth been won by their determination to be free. For twenty years, since the day of the Vespers, they had ignored the tergiversations of princes and statesmen and they had made it clear that they would accept no peace that gave them back to the hated French. They had no regret that their new king was without possessions on the mainland; he could concentrate the better on their welfare. For a century to come Sicily was a free and self-contained kingdom, not very rich and playing no great part in world politics, but, for the while, contented.[1]

The Angevins did not indeed give up hopes of reconquest. In 1314 Robert, who had by then succeeded his father Charles II at Naples, attempted to invade the island to punish King Frederick for offering help to his enemy the Emperor Henry VII. The invasion was a failure. Its main result was to make Frederick repudiate the clause of the Treaty of Caltabellotta, restricting his dynasty's tenure of the throne to his own lifetime. The Sicilian parliament recognized his son Peter as his heir. In 1328, so that there might be no further doubt, he associated Peter with him as co-monarch. At the end of his reign King Robert made several attempts to recover Sicily for his cause. He launched six various expeditions against the island; but none had more than a temporary success. There was a certain number of raids during the reign of his grand-daughter and successor, Joanna; till at last a durable peace was signed under the aegis of the Pope at Aversa in 1372. This left Sicily without question to Frederick's branch of the House of Aragon. But the King of Trinacria had to recognize not only the Papacy but also the ruler of the 'Kingdom of Sicily' at Naples as suzerains. It was a suzerainty which did not weigh too heavily on the island; and it meant an end to the attacks and threats from the mainland. Soon afterwards the decline of the Angevin kingdom under the amorous and incompetent Queen Joanna and the troubles that followed her murder reduced the suzerainty to a nominal formality.[2] Early in the fifteenth century Sicily passed by succession to the Kings of Aragon; and the vassalage was soon forgotten[3].

In 1435 Alfonso III, King of Aragon and Sicily, conquered the mainland kingdom itself from the collateral heirs of the last ruler of Charles I's house, Queen Joanna II. Thus Aragon won in the end. But, in a strange reversal of the past, the island of Sicily remained attached to the throne of Aragon while for half a century Naples enjoyed independence under a bastard line of the House.[1]

Sicily, indeed, was never independent again after the year 1409. From the Kings of Aragon she passed to their heirs, the kings of united Spain. In the eighteenth century, after brief interludes of Austrian and Piedmontese rule, she was given, together with Naples, to a branch of the French dynasty of Bourbon which was on the throne of Spain. Their kingdom was called that of the Two Sicilies; but of the two the island was the junior partner, except for a few years, when Napoleon's armies drove the royal house to take refuge at Palermo. From the Bourbons Sicily was liberated by Garibaldi, to become part of united Italy, but a part that was long neglected and resentful. Now at last she has her own parliament again; and her friends may hope that the fierce courage shown by her people throughout their history will receive its reward.

CHAPTER XVII

THE VESPERS AND
THE FATE OF EUROPE

The theme of the story is twofold. The episode of the Vespers at Palermo marked a savage and important turning-point in the history of Sicily. It also taught a lesson to the whole of Europe.

On the death of the Emperor Frederick II and the disintegration of the Hohenstaufen Empire the Papacy seemed to have triumphed over its chief rival for the oecumenical sovereignty of Europe. To maintain its triumph its policy was to prevent the concentration of too much power in any one potentate's hands. From the time of Frederick's death in 1250 to the coronation of Henry VII in 1311 there was no crowned Emperor in the West. Partly by accident but still more by papal policy the King of the Romans, the Emperor-elect, was no more than King of Germany; and the extension of his power into Italy was, whenever it was possible, hindered by the Popes' deliberate actions. But the Papacy could not in fact become the sovereign of Christendom without lay help. However many of the faithful might accept its transcendental claims, it still needed material strength. However well organized its court might be as a legal or financial centre, it needed the sanction of physical force to ensure that its decrees were obeyed and the taxes and tithes that it demanded were paid. The ideal solution would have been a subservient Emperor whose power would be at the Pope's command. Innocent III had hoped for this when he allowed his ward Frederick II to become Emperor. But he and his successors failed to understand that a proud and ambitious Emperor could not be expected to plan his policy to suit a hierarch whose interests were not always his own or his subjects'. In clashing with the Emperor the Pope divided the only centripetal force of the time. Instead, he gave his support to its chief centrifugal force, the nascent spirit of nationalism, which was to be a far worse menace to the idea of the Oecumenical Papacy. He encouraged the growth of separate secular units, without realizing that the strength of these units lay in their nationalism. There was never a more devout and conscientious son of the Church than King Louis IX of France. But Saint Louis believed that his first duty, under God, was to the people whom God had summoned him to govern. He would not sacrifice the interests of the French to please a papal empire-builder. Had all his fellow-monarchs been of the same high calibre, the government of Europe would have been smooth and the Papacy would have had time to understand the limits to its monarchy. But Louis was an exception. In the turmoil of the times the Popes never paused for reflection.

When Frederick died, the Popes' main object was to prevent the rebirth of Hohenstaufen power. It was not easy. There were still able and glamorous members of the family who commanded loyalty, while the long struggles had created among the Italians, with their passion for party politics, two rival factions, Guelf and Ghibelline, who used every phase of it for party ends. To bring peace to Italy an overriding force was necessary. In the meantime the Pope could not be sure of living safely in his own see of Rome. When Manfred acquired the Hohenstaufen inheritance in Italy, he seemed, owing to Italian politics, as dangerous as his father had been, without the handicap of his father's distractions in Germany. To crush him and to provide Italy with a more dutiful government, the Pope decided to call in a prince from abroad with enough money to pay for the military campaign that would be needed. An English prince would have been suitable, had there been a suitable English prince, and a wiser king on the English throne. But Prince Edmund's youth and King Henry III's incompetence were combined with the excessive financial demands of the Papacy to make the English candidature impracticable. Instead, salvation was sought from France.

It was unfortunate that at this moment a Frenchman should have sat on the papal throne. With the Italian cardinals quarrelling among themselves Pope Urban IV, who had been Patriarch of Jerusalem and was a man of wide international experience, had seemed an obvious choice. A century and a half before, Pope Urban II, a Frenchman likewise, had proved himself to have the widest vision and sympathies of any medieval Pope. But during the interval France had developed as a nation, and her sons were Frenchmen in their outlook. To Urban IV it was natural to call in a French prince to rescue the Church from a German-Italian dynasty, especially as there was a French prince available of outstanding ability.

The Papacy's alliance with Charles of Anjou brought it nothing but ill. Charles was a man of vast ambition; and the invitation to come to Italy gave him full scope for it. He was soon as dangerous to the independence of the Church as ever the Hohenstaufen had been. The danger, indeed, was greater because he, instead of the Pope, became the leader of the Guelfs in Italy; he could give them material help that was far more useful than the Pope's spiritual support. He could also put pressure on papal elections as few Emperors had been able to do for over two centuries. A French Pope meant the creation of a number of French cardinals, who with their Guelf allies could be trusted to fill a vacancy in the Papacy with a Frenchman or a man sympathetic to the French, especially if Charles were at hand with an army. Urban IV, who invited him to Italy, was a Frenchman, as was Clement IV, who welcomed him there. After Clement's death there was a reaction in the Conclave, which led to an interregnum lasting nearly three years. This suited Charles quite as well as a French Pope. The election of Gregory X was a defeat to him; and Gregory hindered several of his plans. The three short-lived Popes that followed, a Savoyard, an Italian Guelf, and a Portuguese, were all friendly to him. Then, largely owing to his being in retirement owing to illness, he had another rebuff with the election of Nicholas III, who, like Gregory X, had a wider conception of the Pope's duty. On Nicholas's death Charles ran no risks and secured the election of the most intransigent of all French Popes, Martin IV. Thus by 1282 Charles was sure of the backing of the Pope, whatever might befall him. It was typical of the age that Charles so greatly desired the support of the Papacy. His piety was genuine and would forbid him to go against the expressed will of the Papacy; but it did not prevent him from taking every possible step to see that the Pope whom he revered should be a creature of his own.

With his own great abilities, and with the Papacy, France and the Italian Guelfs to back him, it seems at first surprising that Charles's career should have ended in failure. He failed through his own insensitivity and his lack of understanding of the peoples with whom he had to deal. The French had shown themselves to be the most vigorous and enterprising race in medieval Europe, and they knew it. They began to see themselves as a master-race. They had organized the crusading movement and had supplied most of its manpower and its direction. They had established their way of life in Palestine and in Greece. It was their destiny to dominate Christendom. Charles was a Frenchman. He was moreover a French prince; and it was above all the Royal House of France that had given the country unity and national consciousness. It was the Capetian Kings who were bringing order and justice to the people and breaking down the arbitrary and disruptive power of the nobles. While Charles was a child his mother and his brother were busy crushing the turbulent nobility of France. As a young man he had the task of crushing the nobility of Provence. He grew up in the assumption that popular sympathies were with the centralizing power.

This pride of race and position led him into two grave errors, one of foreign politics and one of home politics. He saw himself as the heir of the crusader princes, especially in eastern Europe. The French had taken pride in the Fourth Crusade and the establishment of the Latin Empire at Constantinople. Its fall was an insult to them. They could not quite understand it, for it never occurred to them that to the Byzantines, as to the Arabs in the East, they did not represent the finest flower of civilization but were savage intruders with a liking for religious persecution. Charles believed that it would be an easy task to restore the Latin Empire, if only he were allowed to send an expedition against Constantinople. From the military aspect he was right; but he made no allowance for the passionate hatred that the Byzantines bore against the West nor for the lengths to which they would go to prevent an attack; nor did he appreciate properly the skill in diplomacy that they had acquired down the centuries. He despised the court of Aragon and never saw how effectively its claims could be used against him. He underrated all his foreign enemies and never understood that they could be dangerous in combination.

Their combination was successful because of Charles's errors in the internal government of his kingdom. He was not unaware of the forces of nationalism. He knew that he could trust his fellow-French, and he trusted no other race. It was his practice in each of his dominions as far as possible to employ officials drawn from some other of his dominions. But he took no account of the resentment that such a policy might cause. He seems to have thought that, as in France, the element dangerous to the monarchy was the nobility, and that lesser folk would automatically rally to the king. In his Italian lands he diminished the power of the local nobility and relied upon imported French nobles and knights, to whom he never allowed too much territorial power. He failed to see either that these imported noblemen did not at once become efficient and incorruptible functionaries, just because they were divorced from their ancient hereditary territories, or that a local population might dislike foreign officials even if they were efficient. Charles was a good administrator, but he could not supervise everything. It is clear from the reforms that he hastily introduced when things went wrong, that his administration had been full of flaws. In particular it failed to satisfy the Sicilians.

It is here that the Sicilian theme mingles with the European. Charles neglected Sicily. He found it poorer and less useful to him than his other dominions. The Sicilians had annoyed him by a long rebellion early in his reign. He never paid a serious visit to the island and never himself inspected its governmental machine. The officials there were more corrupt and oppressive than on the mainland where he could exercise a personal control. Yet, in spite of their earlier rebelliousness, Charles does not seem to have foreseen trouble from the Sicilians. They were of mixed racial origins. Only half a century earlier, the Greek and Arab elements could be clearly distinguished from the Latin. He may well have thought that a people of such diverse blood would never come together sufficiently closely to threaten his power for long. But in fact the misfortunes, grievances and aims of the whole island brought the islanders into union. It gives a striking example of how little national feeling depends upon purity of race. It was the revolt in the island, plotted, fostered and organized by his enemies from outside, but carried out and maintained by the angry courage of the Sicilians themselves, which pulled Charles's empire down. Some of the Sicilian leaders might waver. The intervention of Aragon and of the naval genius of Roger of Lauria might contribute to the victory; but it was the unflinching determination of the Sicilians themselves, undiminished by the desertion by their allies later on, which freed them from the hated rule of the Angevins.

Charles's failure as an empire-builder lay in his failure to understand the Mediterranean world of his time. Had he been content with the role of King of Sicily he might have had time to learn how to govern his subjects there. But he saw himself as the soldier of God, chosen by the Holy Church to be its champion. The western Empire had fallen because it had opposed the Church. He would build a new Empire under the aegis of the Church, as its secular arm. He was too late. Christendom had split into too many units with their own local interests; nationalism was growing too fast. Charles himself was affected by it. Whatever his own conception of his rôle may have been, in his actions he was partly the agent of papal imperialism, partly of French imperialism and partly of his own personal and dynastic ambition; and the parts were confused. Later the Angevin House was to find glory when seated on the Hungarian throne, but only so long as it confined its interests in central Europe. When it tried to combine its dominions in Italy with those in central Europe, the task was beyond it. The kings of the Angevin dynasty were nearly all of them men of outstanding ability who made their mark on European history. But it was an ephemeral mark and did little good to Europe.

The massacre of the Vespers ruined the experiment of King Charles's empire. But more, too, perished in the blood-bath. It was the ruin of the Hildebrandine Papacy. The Papacy had committed itself to Charles. A few wiser Popes, such as Gregory X and Nicholas III, had tried to reduce the commitment, but in vain. The Sicilians themselves did their best to offer the Papacy a road of escape. A better Pope than Martin IV might have cut the losses of the Papacy in time. But even so there would have been losses. The failure to support Charles would have been an admission that Rome had been wrong. But to support him so blindly against the wishes of a devout people and against the conscience of much of Europe, and then to be dragged by him into defeat, meant a far crueller humiliation. The Papacy threw everything into the struggle. It threw more money than it could afford. It threw the weapon of the Holy War, and all to no purpose. It emerged financially impoverished; and to recoup its finances it was forced to try to extract from the secular powers more than they would now willingly pay. It emerged with its chief spiritual weapon tarnished; for there were few Europeans outside of France and the Guelf cities of Italy who could regard the repression of the Sicilians as a spiritual aim. The idea of the Holy War had been cheapened already when it was used against the Hohenstaufen. Now it fell into utter disrepute. The high authority of the Papacy was wasted on a losing cause, without the certitude of moral right on its side. No conception in medieval history was finer than that of the Universal Church, uniting Christendom into one great theocracy governed by the impartial wisdom of the Vicar of God. But in this sinful world even the Vicar of God needs material strength to enforce his holy will. It proved impossible for the medieval Papacy to find a lay supporter whom all Christendom could trust. By crushing the Universal Empire, which alone might possibly have provided such a support, the Popes set themselves a hard problem. Their choice of Charles of Anjou is easy to understand; but it was fatal. When Charles's power was broken by the Vespers at Palermo they were too inextricably involved. The story led on to the insult offered to the Holy Father at Anagni, to the Babylonish captivity of Avignon, and through schism and disillusion to the troubles of the Reformation.

The Sicilian men who poured, with knives drawn, through the streets of Palermo on that savage evening struck their blows for freedom and for honour. They could not know to what consequences it would lead them and with them the whole of Europe. Bloodshed is an evil thing and good seldom comes of it. But the blood shed on that evening not only rescued a gallant people from oppression. It altered fundamentally the history of Christendom.

The lesson was not entirely forgotten. More than three centuries later King Henry IV of France boasted to the Spanish ambassador the harm that he could do to the Spanish lands in Italy were the King of Spain to try his patience too far. 'I will breakfast at Milan', he said, 'and I will dine at Rome.' 'Then,' replied the ambassador, 'Your Majesty will doubtless be in Sicily in time for Vespers.'

JOHN OF PROCIDA
AND THE VESPERS

The question to what extent the massacre of the Vespers was organized outside Sicily has been a matter of rather bitter controversy. The traditional view was to regard the massacre as the outcome of a great conspiracy organized by the Neapolitan exile, John of Procida, working in the interest of the House of Aragon. This is the view taken by such eighteenth-century writers as Voltaire and Gibbon, according to whom 'the revolt was inspired by the presence or the soul of John of Procida'.[1] To the Italian historian Oriani, John was 'the Great Conspirator'.[2] He appears as the chief figure in such dramatic versions of the story as the tragedies of *Les Vêpres Siciliennes* by Casimir Delavigne and *The Massacre at Palermo* by Mrs Felicia Hemans and in the absurd libretto written by Scribe for Verdi's opera, *Il Vespro Siciliano*.[3]

This view was vehemently challenged by the eminent nineteenth-century Sicilian historian, Michele Amari. His *La Guerra del Vespro Siciliano* was first published in 1842 and was the first really scholarly account of the massacre and the subsequent war. But Amari was a politician as well as a scholar. He wrote at a time when his native island was restive under the government of the Bourbon kings of Naples, and he wished to rouse the Sicilians to strike a blow for liberty. They should be made to realize that in 1282 they had taken the law into their own hands and risen against the oppressor. But the message would be ineffectual if the rising was merely the result of foreign intrigue. He was an honest man and undoubtedly believed in his own thesis, which involved the denial that John of Procida had anything serious to do with the whole movement. The rising itself was wholly spontaneous, and it was only later that the Aragonese, advised by John, took advantage of it to establish their rule in the island. Instead of featuring as the Great Conspirator, John of Procida is turned into a minor politician with a rather despicable character.[1]

Amari's view was backed by several sound arguments. He could show that John was unmentioned by several of the more reliable sources, that others deny the pre-existence of a conspiracy, and that in any case the time-lag between the Vespers themselves and the arrival of the Aragonese in Sicily argues against a conspiracy. Other sources which were unknown to him bear out part of his contentions. On the other hand it seems clear that his desire to draw a contemporary political moral led him into exaggeration. Nor did he always realize that the original sources themselves sometimes had political motives.

Amari was impressed because neither of the two original Aragonese sources mention a conspiracy. The Catalan chroniclers, Bernard d'Esclot, whose chronicle ends in 1285, and Ramon Muntaner, who wrote about forty years later, take the line that King Peter happened to be in Africa fighting the Moors at the time of the Vespers and that the Sicilians invited him a little later to come to their rescue.[2] This was obviously the official story put forward by the Aragonese court, which for propaganda purposes had to minimize its own responsibility. It cannot be held to disprove the existence of a conspiracy. It is moreover cancelled out by the French official line, which was to implicate Aragon as far as possible in order to justify the crusade against the Aragonese. William of Nangis, in his life of Philip III, says that King Peter was instigated by his wife to plot with the Sicilians; he talks of Sicilian envoys going to Aragon and of the revolt breaking out immediately on their return. An anonymous panegyrist of King Charles repeats the charge. He says that Peter equipped a fleet to use against Charles at the suggestion of the Sicilians and of his wife, and that his African campaign was intended to provide him with an excuse to give to the Pope. This story is repeated in the anonymous *Praeclara Francorum Facinora* and the chronicle of Saint Bertin. None of the French sources mention John of Procida.[1]

Details are given by the Italian and Sicilian sources; but they are not consistent. The most reliable of them is Bartholomew of Neocastro, who was living at Messina at the time and took a part in the government of his city, and who, in spite of a flowery and not always grammatical Latin style and of certain prejudices, carries conviction in what he says. He makes no mention of preliminary plots, but implies that the rising at Palermo took place as the direct result of Angevin oppression. But he mentions Queen Constance's claims as part of the story and says that the Pope and King Charles suspected that the Aragonese expedition sent against Africa was really intended for the invasion of Sicily.[2] Nicholas Speciale, who wrote his *Sicilian History* half a century later, says that the revolt broke out 'nullo communicato concilio'; but he probably wished to give the point of view of the Aragonese dynasty.[3] The anonymous chronicle which tells the history of Sicily from 820 to 1328 takes the same vague line.[4]

The story of John of Procida's conspiracy is based primarily on an anonymous chronicle in the Sicilian dialect, the *Rebellamentu di Sichilia, lu quale Hordinau e Fichi pari Misser Iohanni in Prochita, contra Re Carlu*, said to be written by a Messinese of the thirteenth century, and on two 'synoptic' works, the *Liber Jani de Procida et Palioloco* and the *Legenda di Messer Gianni di Procida*, which is attributed to an anonymous Modenese.[5] In the *Rebellamentu* John appears as a hero, in the other two as a villain. The dates at which these works were written is disputed. The attempt of their latest editor to prove that the *Rebellamentu* is exactly contemporary with the rebellion is not conclusive; it depends on one single word in the text.[6] But it seems most unlikely that they can any of them have been written after 1298, the date at which John deserted the Sicilian cause and was reconciled with the Church. After that date he could not have been quite such a hero to the Sicilians or such a villain to the Guelfs. It seems therefore that the story of

John's personal activity in organizing the great conspiracy was current in his own lifetime, though only in 'popular' writings. Early in the next century it was accepted as true by serious historians. The Florentine Chronicle of Ricordano and Giachetto Malespini, which only goes as far as 1286 but was probably completed at least a decade later, repeats the account of John's activities and makes him the ambassador who offers the Sicilian throne to Peter of Aragon. It also repeats the account of the bribing of Pope Nicholas.[1] In the first half of the fourteenth century Brunetto Latini and Villani reproduce the whole story with picturesque and gossipy details, and Francesco Pipino of Bologna, Boccaccio and Petrarch accept the full version.[2] Dante does not mention John of Procida by name, but goes so far as to condemn Pope Nicholas to Hell for accepting money for opposing King Charles.[3]

It is difficult entirely to reject a story which was firmly believed by reputable and intelligent writers, many of whom had been born while the actors were still alive. Yet we know that part of the legend cannot be true. It seems certain that John of Procida cannot have left Aragon during the period when he was supposed to have been touring the Mediterranean world in disguise. There is nothing in the exactly contemporary accounts of Pope Nicholas III or in the many papal documents of his time that survive to suggest that his policy towards King Charles deviated from a perfectly clear and logical course.[4] The time-lag that occurred between the Vespers and the intervention of the King of Aragon hardly suggests that the whole affair was organized and controlled by a politician living in Aragon. On the other hand, Amari certainly exaggerated. The legend is given with details that carry conviction; nor could John of Procida have become the great villain of the story from the Guelf point of view if there had not been good reason for believing him to have been mixed up in the rebellion. The Sicilians themselves, a proud and not a modest people, would not have allowed their legends to exalt a man of Neapolitan birth into such a position of leadership unless they had believed him to have led them. Many people alive at the time of the massacre must have heard the story before they died, and no one denied it. Moreover, a rebellion does need some organization. Amongst a people so given to secret societies as the Sicilians one cannot hope for documents describing a plotter's organization to survive; and in an island where oral traditions linger long one must place some faith in them. It is hard to believe that there was not a definite conspiracy organized by the agents of John of Procida; possibly one of his sons went on the journey attributed to him in the legend.

It is possible that historians have underrated the part played by Byzantium. In the legend Byzantine gold plays a large part, and John's visits to Constantinople are emphasized. Indeed, the title of one of the legends refers to his connection with Michael Palaeologus. This is not just to discredit him by associating him with a schismatic prince; for the *Rebellamentu* takes the same line. Various other sources talk of money subsidies going to the Aragonese, presumably to John's agents;[1] and, significantly, Michael himself in his autobiographical fragment, whose authenticity need not be doubted, boasts that it was he himself that saved the Empire from an Angevin invasion.[2]

The sequence of events bears out his claim. It is obvious that the Aragonese would have preferred to postpone a war in Sicily till Charles was fully committed in the East, with the bulk of his fleet and his army there. The actual rising seems to have taken King Peter a little by surprise. His sailing for Africa indicates that he was not sure what was happening or going to happen. The Sicilians on their part did not ask for his help till they were hard-pressed. They clearly would have preferred autonomy under a vague papal suzerainty. But it was essential for Byzantium that the rising should take place before Charles set sail for the East. It occurred, in fact, at almost the last possible moment that could save Byzantium. It is remarkable that one of the first actions of the Messinese after they had risen was to send a message to Constantinople, long before they had made any contact with Peter of Aragon.[1] Pope Martin in his bull of excommunication against King Peter and the Sicilian rebels had no doubt about Michael's complicity.[2]

It is impossible to ascertain the complete truth. But the story seems to be that the Sicilians had been driven desperate by a sense of mixed oppression and neglect; that Aragonese agents, organized by John of Procida, fanned their resentment, and with the help of Byzantine gold and Byzantine agents, organized it into a definite rebellion. Meanwhile, again largely owing to John, a diplomatic alliance was built up against King Charles, largely financed by Byzantine gold. Pope Nicholas III was induced, also by Byzantine gold, not to break off relations with Byzantium entirely and not to give permission to Charles to attack the Empire, again, probably, through John's agents. When Nicholas died and the new Pope proved to be Charles's creature, more direct action was needed. The actual date of the outbreak may have been fortuitous; but it was so convenient for the Byzantines that the Emperor Michael almost certainly had something to do with it, as his own words and the message sent him from Messina suggest. It was a little early for Aragon, and the Aragonese alliance was not at first entirely welcome to the Sicilians; nor, as the sequel showed, were they prepared to maintain it if it threatened their independence.

The main credit, if a massacre deserves credit, should go to the Sicilians themselves who provided the motive force. The organization of the conspiracy and the alliances that enabled it to succeed was chiefly due to John of Procida; but the financing and the dating were the work of the Emperor at Constantinople.

NOTES

PAGE 1

1 For the history of Sicily in Greek and Roman times, see the relevant passages in the *Cambridge Ancient History*. There is no good general history of ancient Sicily.

PAGE 3

1 See Bury, *History of the Later Roman Empire*, vol. I, pp. 254–8, 333, 410; vol. II, pp. 129, 171, 215–16, 255–60.

PAGE 4

1 Ostrogorsky, *History of the Byzantine State*, pp. 109–10, with references.

PAGE 5

1 Vasiliev, *Byzance et les Arabes*, vol. I, pp. 61–88, 127–37, 187–8, 204–8, 219–22, 260–4; vol. II (original edition in Russian), pp. 20–5, 43–6, 58–68, 84–7, 122–30, 258–62, 302–9. Amari's *Storia dei Musulmani in Sicilia* (3 vols. in 4), published 1854–72, remains the best full history of the period.

2 Ostrogorsky, *op. cit.* pp. 293–4.

PAGE 10

1 For the Norman conquest of Sicily see Chalandon, *Histoire de la Domination Normande en Italie*, vol. I, pp. 189–211, 327–54. For Norman rule in Sicily, vol. II *passim*.

PAGE 11

1 Chalandon, *op. cit.* vol. II, pp. 439–91. See also Jordan, *L'Allemagne et l'Italie aux XIIe et XIIIe Siècles*, pp. 150–60.

2 Kantorowicz, *Kaiser Friedrich der Zweite*, vol. I, pp. 11–12.

PAGE 12

1 Jordan, *op. cit.* pp. 160–6.

2 *Ibid.* pp. 172–3; Kantorowicz, *op. cit.* pp. 20–1.

PAGE 13

1 For Frederick's minority see Bäthgen, *Die Regentschaft Papst Innocenz III im Königreich Sizilien*; Van Cleve, *Markward of Anweiler*; Luchaire, *Innocent III*, vol. III; *Rome et l'Italie*, pp. 153–204.

PAGE 15

1 Jordan, *op. cit.* pp. 204–6; Léonard, *Les Angevins de Naples*, pp. 29–34; Cohn, *Das Zeitalter der Hohenstaufen in Sizilien, passim*; Schipa, *Sicilia ed Italia sotto Federico II, passim.*

PAGE 16

1 Innocent IV, *Registres*, no. 5345, vol. II, pp. 244–5; Boehmer, *Regesta Imperii*, new ed. by Ficker and Winkelmann, no. 13783, vol. v, 2, p. 1990.

PAGE 20

1 The best brief summary of Frederick's character is in Jordan, *L'Allemagne et l'Italie*, pp. 219–21, and of his career in the succeeding chapters. Kantorowicz's life, *Kaiser Friedrich der Zweite*, is throughout rather too adulatory and romantic. For the origins of the Guelf and Ghibelline parties see Jordan, *op. cit.* pp. 272–4. See also Hefele-Leclercq, *Histoire des Conciles*, vol. VI, 1, pp. 6–9.

PAGE 22

1 For Papal policy and polemics see Jordan, *op. cit.* pp. 251–5.

PAGE 24

1 For the collapse of Byzantium see Ostrogorsky, *History of the Byzantine State*, pp. 356–70.

2 See Hitti, *History of the Arabs*, pp. 484 ff., 652–8.

PAGE 25

1 See Runciman, *History of the Crusades*, vol. III, pp. 237–54.

PAGE 27

1 Besides the children mentioned here, Frederick had one legitimate daughter by Isabella of England, Margaret, who married Albert of Thuringia, Margrave of Misnia. For their son Frederick, see below, pp. 122–4. Of the Emperor's illegitimate daughters, one, Selvaggia, married Ezzelino III, tyrant of Verona; another, Violante, married Richard, Count of Caserta; and two, whose names are unknown, were married to Jacob, Marquis of Carretto and to Thomas of Aquino, Count of Acerra.

2 Boehmer, *Regesta Imperii*, no. 3835, vol. v, 1, p. 693; *M.G.H., Constitutiones*, vol. II, p. 382. His grandson Frederick was, if he were surviving, to inherit Austria from his mother.

3 See Runciman, *History of the Crusades*, vol. III, pp. 182, 220–1, 275.

PAGE 28

1 *Cambridge Medieval History*, vol. VI, pp. 109–13; Jordan, *L'Allemagne et l'Italie*, pp. 289–96.

PAGE 29

1 Italian history during this period is described in detail by Jordan, *Les Origines de la Domination Angevine en Italie*, book I, chapters I to VIII, with a brief summary in the preface, pp. ix–xii. See also Jordan, *L'Allemagne et l'Italie*, pp. 317–19. For German affairs see references in previous note.

2 Jordan, *Les Origines*, pp. 173–82, 235–40.

PAGE 30

1 Nicholas of Carbio, *Vita Innocentii IV* (Muratori, *R.I.S.*, vol. III, pp. 592); Rymer, *Foedera*, vol. I, p. 302; Jordan, *Les Origines*, pp. 238–9; Léonard, *Les Angevins de Naples*, p. 38.

2 Matthew Paris, *Chronica Majora*, vol. IV, p. 542; Paulus, *Geschichte des Ablasses im Mittelalter*, vol. II, p. 27.

3 Baronius-Raynaldi, *Annales Ecclesiastici*, vol. II, p. 505. Manfred was accused by the Guelfs of murdering Conrad by means of a poisoned clyster administered by John of Procida as Court physician. See Salimbene de Adam, *Cronica* (*M.G.H.*, *Scriptores*, vol. XXXII, pp. 444, 472).

PAGE 31

1 Hampe, *Geschichte Konradins von Hohenstaufen*, pp. 4–7; Runciman, *History of the Crusades*, vol. III, p. 281.

PAGE 32

1 Jordan, *L'Allemagne et l'Italie*, pp. 321–2.

2 Nicholas of Carbio, *Vita Innocentii IV*, pp. 592, v–ξ; Boehmer, *Regesta*, no. 4644d, vol. V, 1, p. 855.

PAGE 33

1 Nicholas of Jamsilla, *Historia de rebus gestis Friderici II, Conradi et Manfredi* (Muratori, *R.I.S.*, vol. VIII, pp. 513–41). See Hefele-Leclercq, *Histoire des Conciles*, vol. VI, 1, p. 18.

2 Nicholas of Jamsilla, *loc. cit.*; Jordan, *L'Allemagne et l'Italie*, pp. 322–3.

PAGE 34

1 Hefele-Leclercq, *op. cit.* p. 18, n. 3. For Innocent's character see Jordan, *Les Origines*, pp. lxxix–lxxxi.

2 Nicholas of Carbio, *op. cit.* p. 592; Salimbene de Adam, *op. cit.* pp. 453–4.
Salimbene calls Pope Alexander scholarly and pacific. For a harsher judgement
see Jordan, *L'Allemagne et l'Italie*, p. 323.

PAGE 35

1 Nicholas of Jamsilla, *Historia*, p. 543; Jordan, *Les Origines*, pp. xiii–xiv. For
Manfred's arrangement with Conradin's party, Boehmer, *Regesta*, no. 4771,
vol. I, p. 882.

2 Nicholas of Jamsilla, *Historia*, p. 584: Baronius-Raynaldi, *Annales Ecclesiastici*, vol. III, pp. 24–5; Capasso, *Historia Diplomatica Regni Siciliae*, pp. 167–8
(for the Pope's denunciation of the coronation). Manfred's complicity in the
rumour of Conradin's death is discussed fully in Schirrmacher, *Die letzten
Hohenstaufen*, p. 449.

PAGE 36

1 Dante describes Manfred as 'blond and handsome and gentle of aspect'
(*Purgatorio*, III, l. 107), and calls him an illustrious hero and patron of letters
in *De Vulgari Eloquentia* (book I, §12). The Guelf chronicles all accuse him
of every possible vice, but the troubadour Raymond Tors, who was a friend
of Charles of Anjou, praises him for his probity, justice and elegance, while
an anonymous troubadour, after his fall, when nothing was to be gained by
praising him, calls him a valorous, joyous and virtuous prince. De Bartholomaeis, *Poesie Provenzali Storiche relative all'Italia*, vol. II, pp. 212–15, 234.
Modern historians judge him more severely. To Previté-Orton (*Cambridge
Medieval History*, vol. VI, p. 184) he was 'indolent and undecided', 'a child
of the harem', 'loving the imagination of his own greatness', and showing
an 'oriental mixture of self-confidence and enervation'. The summing-up
of Léonard, *Les Angevins de Naples*, p. 40, is temperate and just.

2 See Libertini and Paladino, *Storia della Sicilia*, pp. 444–5.

PAGE 37

1 For the 'double election' see Jordan, *L'Allemagne et l'Italie*, pp. 304–10, with
references, and Hefele-Leclercq, *Histoire des Conciles*, vol. VI, 1, pp. 23–6.

PAGE 38

1 Jordan, *Les Origines*, pp. 241–2; Hampe, *op. cit.* pp. 15–19.

2 Jordan, *Les Origines*, pp. 94–142, 179–211, 242–4; Dante, *Inferno*, X, l. 86,
refers to Montaperti, 'Che fece l'Arbia colorata in rosso'; G. Villani, *Cronica*
(1823 ed.), vol. II, pp. 108–9.

PAGE 39

1 See Longnon, *L'Empire Latin de Constantinople*, pp. 178–86, also Wolff, 'Mortgage and Redemption of an Emperor's Son', in *Speculum*, vol. XXIX, pp. 45–54, containing a valuable discussion of Baldwin II's debts.

PAGE 40

1 Vasiliev, *History of the Byzantine Empire*, pp. 506–7; Ostrogorsky, *History of the Byzantine State*, p. 378.

2 Ostrogorsky, *op. cit.* pp. 384–91.

3 *Ibid.* pp. 371–95.

PAGE 41

1 Miller, *The Latins in the Levant*, pp. 91–8; Norden, *Das Papsttum und Byzanz*, pp. 332–3; Longnon, *op. cit.* pp. 217–23.

PAGE 42

1 Sufficient emphasis has not, I think, been given to Manfred's aim of embarrassing papal opposition to his rule by appearing as the champion of Latin Christianity in the East. See below, pp. 51–2. For Innocent IV and Richard of Cornwall see Powicke, *King Henry III and the Lord Edward*, vol. I, p. 197, n. 2.

2 For Constance, who was rechristened Anna by the Byzantines, see Gardner, *The Lascarids of Nicaea*, pp. 169–71. Michael Palaeologus was said later to have wished to divorce his wife to marry Anna, but was prevented by the Patriarch of Constantinople (Pachymer, *De Michaele Palaeologo*, pp. 181–6).

PAGE 43

1 Gardner, *op. cit.* pp. 197–231; Ostrogorsky, *op. cit.* pp. 395–7.

2 For William's marriage and dowry see Geneakoplos, 'The Battle of Pelagonia', *Dumbarton Oaks Papers*, no. VII, pp. 111–12. For Manfred's, *ibid.* pp. 103–5. Its date is given in the anonymous Trani chronicle. Manfred's prior possession of various Epirot and Albanian towns, Durazzo, Avlona, Velegrad and Sphinaritsa, seems proved by a private Greek notarial act dated 23 February 1258, which refers to him as lord of these districts (Miklosich and Müller, *Acta et Diplomata*, vol. III, pp. 239–40). The document is further dated the eighth year of Conrad II, King of Sicily, but the phrase is not entirely clear. Conrad II must be Conradin; and it is anyhow possible that a Greek provincial lawyer did not know the difference between him and his father, whose eighth year it would have been were he alive. It has been suggested that the cession was made at the time of Manfred's betrothal to

Helena, the date of which is not known. But Manfred's first wife, Beatrice of Savoy, seems only to have died in 1258. See del Giudice, 'La Famiglia del Re Manfredi', *Archivio Storico per le Provincie Napoletane*, pp. 55–6.

PAGE 44

1 Gardner, *op. cit.* pp. 231–40; Ostrogorsky, *op. cit.* pp. 397–8.

PAGE 45

1 Dölger, *Regesten der Kaiserurkunden des Oströmischen Reiches*, vol. III, p. 31; George Acropolita, *Historia* (ed. Heisenberg), p. 165; Norden, *op. cit.* p. 382.

PAGE 47

1 The battle of Pelagonia is described in the *Chronicle of the Morea*, ll. 3602–900 (Greek version, ed. Kalonaros); by Acropolita, pp. 165–70; Pachymer, *op. cit.* pp. 83–6; Nicephorus Gregoras, *Historia Byzantina*, vol. I, pp. 71–5, a late and muddled account, which makes Manfred be present at the battle. There is a good modern account in Geneakoplos, *op. cit.* pp. 120–36; but see Nicol, 'The Date of the Battle of Pelagonia', *Byzantinische Zeitschrift*, vol. XLVIII, 1, pp. 68–71, proving convincingly that the date of the battle was July 1259, at the latest, not in the late autumn as Geneakoplos, following previous historians who relied on Gregoras, has assumed.

PAGE 49

1 Gardner, *op. cit.* pp. 254–60; Ostrogorsky, *op. cit.* pp. 399–400. For the Treaty of Nymphaeum, Dölger, *op. cit.* vol. III, pp. 36–8.

PAGE 50

1 *Chronicle of the Morea* (Greek version), ll. 4324–48; Pachymer, *op. cit.* p. 88; Longnon, *op. cit.* pp. 228–30; Dölger, *op. cit.* vol. III, pp. 38–9.

2 Pachymer, *op. cit.* p. 89. Strategopulus was handed over to Manfred and subsequently exchanged for the Empress Constance (Anna), Manfred's sister.

PAGE 51

1 Durazzo, though mentioned in the Deed of February 1258 (see above, p. 43, n. 2), was not mentioned in the dowry and was presumably returned then to the Despot.

2 Wolff, 'Mortgage and Redemption', pp. 65–6; Miller, *Latins in the Levant*, pp. 114–15.

PAGE 54

1 Hefele-Leclercq, *Histoire des Conciles*, vol. VI, 1, p. 28.

2 Jordan, *Les Origines*, pp. 293–6, an account of Urban's past and a good appreciation of his character. Urban's life was written in bad verse by Thierry of Vaucouleurs (published in Muratori, *R.I.S.*, vol. III, 2, pp. 405 ff.).

PAGE 55

1 For Constance's marriage see Carini, *Gli Archivi e le Biblioteche di Spagna*, vol. II, pp. 185–6. The betrothal took place on 28 July 1258 at Barcelona, and the actual marriage four years later (13 June 1262).

2 Jordan, *Les Origines*, pp. 297–307, a full account of the new Cardinals.

PAGE 56

1 *Ibid.* pp. 336–55.

2 Libertini and Paladino, *Storia della Sicilia*, pp. 444–5.

PAGE 57

1 Innocent IV, *Registres*, ed. Berger, vol. II, pp. cclxxvi–cclxxxv; Matthew Paris, *Historia Anglorum*, vol. III, p. 126, saying that Richard asked about Conrad's rights, but hinted that he might accept if well paid; and *Chronica Majora*, vol. V, pp. 346–7, when Richard is said to have refused outright and spoken about the moon.

2 For Saint Louis's scruples, see Jordan, *Les Origines*, pp. 376–7.

PAGE 58

1 Rymer, *Foedera*, vol. I, 14 (1816 ed.), pp. 297, 301.

2 *Ibid.* pp. 301–2; Matthew Paris, *Chronica Majora*, vol. V, p. 410.

PAGE 59

1 Powicke, *King Henry III and the Lord Edward*, vol. I, pp. 236–8.

PAGE 60

1 *Ibid.* pp. 239–42.

PAGE 62

1 *Ibid.* pp. 370–5.

PAGE 63

1 *Ibid.* pp. 376–8.

2 *Ibid.* pp. 385–7; Boehmer, *Regesta*, no. 9178, vol. V, 2, p. 1423.

PAGE 65

1 Urban IV, *Registres*, ed. Guiraud, vol. I, p. 145 (letter to John Mansel).

PAGE 66

1 Hefele-Leclercq, *Histoire des Conciles*, vol. VI, I, p. 38, n. 1; Jordan, *Les Origines*, pp. 374–8.

PAGE 67

1 Jordan, *op. cit.* pp. 378–90. See also Wolff, 'Mortgage and Redemption', pp. 66–7.

2 Boehmer, *Regesta*, no. 4737 *a*, vol. V, I, pp. 874–5.

3 Pachymer, *De Michaele Palaeologo*, p. 88.

4 Jordan, *op. cit.* pp. 389–92.

PAGE 68

1 *Ibid.* pp. 392–6.

2 *Ibid.* pp. 397–401.

PAGE 69

1 *Ibid. loc. cit.*

2 Baldwin's letter to Manfred and Urban's letter commenting on it are given in Martène and Durand, *Thesaurus novus Anecdotorum*, vol. II, pp. 23 ff. Queen Margaret had made her seven-year-old son, the future Philip III, swear never to ally himself with his uncle Charles. King Louis was furious when he heard of it; and the Pope had recently sent a letter absolving the boy from his oath. See Wolff, *op. cit.* pp. 66–8.

PAGE 70

1 The terms of the treaty are given at full length in Jordan, *op. cit.* pp. 20–6.

PAGE 71

1 The story of Beatrice's ambition is told in detail by Villani, *Cronica*, vol. II, pp. 129–30.

PAGE 72

1 Charles has been judged very severely by German historians, who cannot forgive him for the death of Conradin, and by Italian historians such as Amari, who have to emphasize his oppression to justify the Sicilian revolt. Jordan, *op. cit.* pp. 410–19, gives a well-reasoned if perhaps rather too kindly an account of his character. A balanced assessment is given in Léonard, *Les Angevins de Naples*, pp. 41–7. See also below, pp. 255-6. Charles's nose is mentioned by Dante.

2 Léonard, *op. cit.* pp. 47–8.

PAGE 75

1 *Ibid.* pp. 48–9. The story of Charles's rule in Provence is told in detail in Sternfeld, *Karl von Anjou als Graf der Provence*.

PAGE 76

1 Léonard, *op. cit.* pp. 50–1.

PAGE 78

1 Jordan, *Les Origines*, pp. 458–60, with full references about the rather obscure negotiations.

2 *Ibid.* pp. 478–9.

PAGE 79

1 *Ibid.* pp. 460–2. The Pope explained his view in a letter to Albert of Parma, given in Martène and Durand, *Thesaurus*, vol. II, p. 50.

2 Jordan, *op. cit.* pp. 465–8. For the actual correspondence see Martène and Durand, *Thesaurus*, vol. II, pp. 33–43.

PAGE 80

1 *Ibid.* pp. 468–75, giving Charles's counter-proposals.

2 *Ibid.* pp. 486–90; Urban IV, *Registres*, vol. IV, pp. 807–9, 816–36.

PAGE 81

1 Jordan, *op. cit.* pp. 495–500. For Gantelme in Rome, see Sternfeld, *Karl von Anjou*, p. 229.

2 Jordan, *op. cit.* pp. 490–5, 506–9.

PAGE 82

1 Thierry of Vaucouleurs, *Vita Urbani IV*, p. 420; Potthast, *Regesta Pontificum Romanorum*, vol. II, p. 1540.

2 Sternfeld, *op. cit.* pp. 214 ff.

PAGE 83

1 Jordan, *op. cit.* pp. 516–17.

PAGE 84

1 *Ibid.* pp. 299–303. See above, p. 79.

2 *Ibid.* pp. 521–2.

PAGE 85

1 *Annales Januenses* (*M.G.H., Scriptores*, vol. XVIII, p. 249); Pachymer, *op. cit.* pp. 167–8; Caro, *Genua und die Mächte am Mittelmeer*, vol. I, pp. 142–57, 167; Jordan, *op. cit.* pp. 570–5.

2 Sternfeld, *op. cit.* pp. 242–6.

3 Jordan, *op. cit.* pp. 524–6. Martène and Durand, *Thesaurus*, vol. II, pp. 141, 264, 324; Boehmer, *Regesta*, no. 4760, vol. V, 1, p. 879.

4 Boehmer, *Regesta*, no. 4763, vol. V, 1, p. 880. Saba Malaspina (Muratori, *R.I.S.*, vol. VIII, pp. 815–16), says, however, that Manfred was nervous at the news, though he had recently been reassured about his position by his astrologers.

PAGE 86

1 Jordan, *op. cit.* pp. 526–33.

2 *Ibid.* pp. 534–5.

PAGE 87

1 The finances of the campaign are discussed at length in Jordan, *op. cit.* pp. 536–58.

PAGE 88

1 *Ibid.* pp. 592–8.

PAGE 90

1 *Ibid.* pp. 593–6; Léonard, *op. cit.* pp. 55–6.

2 Boehmer, *Regesta*, no. 14276, vol. V, 2, p. 2060; the Bull accrediting the Cardinals was dated 29 December; *ibid.* nos. 9622–3, p. 1479; Villani, *Cronica*, vol. II, pp. 142–3, reporting the coronation.

PAGE 91

1 Léonard, *op. cit.* p. 57; Hefele-Leclercq, *op. cit.* vol. VI, 1, pp. 49–50. The bridge was supposed to be defended by Richard of Caserta, whose wife Violante, Manfred's own half-sister, Manfred was supposed to have seduced. Dante's reference to the treason is in *Inferno*, XXVIII, ll. 16–17.

2 Léonard, *op. cit.* pp. 57–8; Oman, *A History of the Art of War in the Middle Ages*, vol. I, pp. 498–9.

1 Contemporary accounts of the Battle of Benevento are given by Andrew of Hungary, *Descriptio Victoriae a Karolo reportatae* (*M.G.H., Scriptores*, vol. XXVI), containing letters of participants such as Hugh of Les Baux; Charles's own reports to the Pope, in Baronius-Raynaldi, *Annales Ecclesiastici*, vol. III, pp. 188–9; Saba Malaspina, pp. 825–30; Ricordano Malespini (Muratori, *R.I.S.*, vol. VIII, pp. 1002–5); Villani, vol. II, pp. 147–55, a slightly later and over-picturesque account. There are shorter mentions in almost every chronicle of the time. A good summary is given in Oman, *op. cit.* pp. 500–5. Dante refers to Manfred's grave in *Purgatorio*, III, ll. 124–32.

1 Del Giudice, 'La Famiglia del Re Manfredi', pp. 69–70, establishing the date; Villani, vol. II, pp. 155–6 describes the royal entry into Naples.

1 Martène and Durand, *Thesaurus*, vol. II, p. 319.

2 Hampe, *Geschichte Konradins von Hohenstaufen*, pp. 65–7; Jordan, *L'Allemagne et l'Italie*, pp. 366–7; Léonard, *Les Angevins de Naples*, p. 60.

1 Del Giudice, 'La Famiglia del Re Manfredi', pp. 71 ff. See also Wieruszowski, 'La Corte di Pietro d'Aragona', *Archivio Storico Italiano*, Anno 96, vol. I, pp. 142–3, and notes, in which she gives convincing reasons for believing Manfred's three sons to have been illegitimate.

2 Jordan, *L'Allemagne et l'Italie*, pp. 366–7, with references.

3 See Trifone, *La Legislazione Angioina*, pp. 5 ff.

1 See above, p. 36, n. 1.

2 Boehmer, *Regesta*, nos. 9667, 9713, 9730, 9761–2, vol. V, 2, pp. 1484, 1488, 1490, 1493.

1 Jordan, *op. cit.* pp. 370–1.

2 Saba Malaspina, pp. 833–4; del Giudice, *Don Arrigo, Infante de Castiglia*, *passim*.

PAGE 100

1 Jordan, *op. cit.* pp. 375–7; Léonard, *op. cit.* p. 372.

PAGE 101

1 Léonard, *op. cit.* pp. 372–5.

2 Salimbene de Adam, *Cronica*, p. 473. Her body was taken to Aix for burial.

3 Hampe, *op. cit.* pp. 21–41, and 176 (for Frederick of Austria).

PAGE 102

1 *Ibid.* p. 24.

2 *Ibid.* pp. 68–9.

PAGE 103

1 *Ibid.* pp. 95–100.

2 Martène and Durand, *Thesaurus*, vol. II, pp. 456–8, 525, 574; Jordan, *op. cit.* pp. 377–9.

PAGE 104

1 Hampe, *op. cit.* pp. 111–50. Henry's poetical welcome to Conradin is given in d'Ancona and Comparetti, *Le Antiche Rime Volgari*, vol. II, pp. 305–7.

PAGE 105

1 Jordan, *op. cit.* pp. 386–90; Léonard, *op. cit.* pp. 65–6; Hampe, *op. cit.* pp. 189–95.

PAGE 106

1 For Conradin's manifesto see Hampe, *op. cit.* pp. 346–50. For his departure from Germany, *ibid.* pp. 172–4. He said goodbye to his mother at the castle of Hohenschwangau.

2 Jordan, *op. cit.* pp. 385–6; Saba Malaspina, *op. cit.* pp. 834–6.

PAGE 108

1 Hampe, *op. cit.* pp. 211–69, a detailed account of Conradin's journey. Saba Malaspina, *op. cit.* pp. 842–4, gives a vivid picture of his reception at Rome.

2 Jordan, *op. cit.* pp. 392. Pope Nicholas III's Bull, *Fundamenta Militantis Ecclesiae*, issued in 1278, refers to the papal disquiet of this time.

PAGE 109

1 Hampe, *op. cit.* pp. 270–82.

PAGE 113

1 The fullest contemporary source for the Battle of Tagliacozzo is the chronicle of the French monk Primatus, of which extracts are given by John of Vignay, *M.G.H.*, *Scriptores*, vol. XXVI, pp. 655–67. Saba Malaspina gives a good account, *op. cit.* pp. 845–8. Charles's own report to the Pope and to the people of Padua gives further details. Baronius-Raynaldi, *Annales Ecclesiastici*, vol. III, pp. 242–3; *Annales S. Justinae Patavini* (*M.G.H.*, *Scriptores*, vol. XIX, pp. 190–1). Villani's account is as usual rather too picturesque (vol. II, pp. 181–9). For modern accounts see Hampe, *op. cit.* pp. 288–95, and Oman, *op. cit.* vol. I, pp. 505–15. The actual site of the battle is difficult to identify, owing to the draining of the plain. The modern Via Valeria avoids the direct valley leading from the pass to Tagliacozzo, but curves down to the east. Conradin seems to have crossed over the north-east flank of Monte Bove, past Tremonti and Sante Marie.

PAGE 114

1 Saba Malaspina, *op. cit.* pp. 848–50.

PAGE 115

1 Hampe, *op. cit.* pp. 305–6, 314.

PAGE 116

1 *Ibid.* pp. 312–27, 358–65. Most contemporary chronicles mention Conradin's death with some sympathy for the victim, though Salimbene, p. 476, says blithely and incorrectly that after his death his name vanished like smoke.

PAGE 117

1 See Genealogical Table IV. For Constance's claims, see below, pp. 201–2.

2 De Bartholomaeis, *Poesie Provenzali*, vol. II, p. 230.

PAGE 118

1 Margaret was the daughter and co-heiress of Matilda of Bourbon, Countess of Auxerre, Nevers and Tonnerre, and of Eudes, eldest son of the Duke of Burgundy. She inherited the County of Tonnerre and parts of Auxerre, and the baronies of Montmirail, Alluyes, Torigny and Brugny, all in north-eastern France. Charles gave her the town of Le Mans for her dowry. See Léonard, *Les Angevins de Naples*, pp. 72, 75–6.

2 Potthast, *Regesta Pontificum Romanorum*, vol. II, p. 1648.

PAGE 119

1 De Boüard, *Le Régime politique et les Institutions de Rome au Moyen Âge*, pp. 76–9, 137–8, 162–3, 172–5; Gregorovius, *Geschichte der Stadt Rom im*

Mittelalter, ed. Schillmann, vol. II, pp. 64–5, 1411; Jordan, *L'Allemagne et l'Italie*, pp. 401–2. For his projected university, see del Giudice, *Codice Diplomatico*, vol. I, p. 68.

2 Sternfeld, *Cardinal Johann Gaetan Orsini*, pp. 152 ff.; Jordan, *op. cit.* pp. 394–5.

PAGE 121

1 Jordan, *op. cit.* pp. 403–5.

2 *Annales Placentini Gibellini* (M.G.H., *Scriptores*, vol. XVIII, pp. 542–5); Jordan, *op. cit.* p. 414.

PAGE 122

1 Jordan, *op. cit.* pp. 411–14.

PAGE 123

1 *Annales Placentini Gibellini*, pp. 535–9; Jordan, *op. cit.* pp. 411–13.

PAGE 124

1 Jordan, *op. cit.* pp. 395–6. A Provençal troubadour, Galega Panzano, reproved Charles for being far kinder to the Muslims than to the Christians. Monti, *Gli Angioini di Napoli nella Poesia Provenzale*, p. 418.

2 Jordan, *op. cit.* pp. 396–7; Léonard, *op. cit.* pp. 72–3.

PAGE 125

1 Del Giudice, *Codice Diplomatico*, vol. II, pp. 239, 250, 258, 322.

PAGE 126

1 Léonard, *op. cit.* pp. 80–2, with useful references.

PAGE 127

1 *Ibid.* pp. 82–3. A full list of the higher officials is given in Durrieu, *Les Archives Angevines de Naples*, vol. II, pp. 189–213.

PAGE 129

1 Jordan, *op. cit.* pp. 398–400; Léonard, *op. cit.* pp. 83–9. Such fiscal records as survive are given in de Boüard, *Documents en Français des Archives angevines de Naples, Règne de Charles Ier: I, Les Mandements aux Trésoriers; II, Les Comptes des Trésoriers.*

2 Charles's movements have been fully traced by Durrieu, *Les Archives Angevines*, vol. II, pp. 163–89.

PAGE 130

1 Durrieu, *op. cit.* pp. 267–400, lists the Frenchmen employed by Charles. For the use of the French language, see del Giudice, *op. cit.* vol. I, p. 17.

PAGE 131

1 For the island of Sicily see below, pp. 211–12. It was divided into two administrative provinces, separated by the river Salso.

PAGE 133

1 Léonard, *op. cit.* pp. 75–7.

PAGE 134

1 *Ibid.* pp. 77–80.

PAGE 136

1 See above, pp. 41–2, 51–2.

2 Pachymer, *De Michaele Palaeologo*, p. 508; Miller, *The Latins in the Levant*, pp. 125–6; Léonard, *Les Angevins de Naples*, pp. 103–4.

PAGE 137

1 The text of the treaty is given in Buchon, *Recherches et Matériaux pour servir à une Histoire de la Domination française*, vol. I, p. 33; Miller, *op. cit.* pp. 126–7.

2 Miller, *loc. cit.*

PAGE 138

1 Runciman, *History of the Crusades*, vol. III, pp. 313, 331–2.

2 Léonard, *op. cit.* pp. 105–6.

PAGE 139

1 The claims of Baldwin II's daughter, Helena, Queen of Serbia, who, though married to a schismatic prince, was a zealous missionary for the Latin Church, seem to have been ignored at Viterbo.

2 Miller, *op. cit.* pp. 129–30, and pp. 252–3 for the alleged will in favour of Margaret.

PAGE 140

1 Martène and Durand, *Thesaurus*, vol. II, p. 469 (Clement's letter to Michael); Pachymer, *op. cit.* pp. 359–61; Norden, *Das Papsttum und Byzanz*, pp. 448–57.

2 Pachymer, *op. cit.* pp. 361–2; *Annales Januenses*, p. 264; Norden, *op. cit.* pp. 265–6.

PAGE 141

1 Sternfeld, *Ludwigs des Heiligen Kreuzzug nach Tunis und die Politik Karls I von Sizilien*, pp. 164 ff.

PAGE 142

1 Sternfeld, *op. cit.* pp. 201 ff.; he is unconvincing in stating that Charles did not know of his brother's African project. Saba Malaspina (*op. cit.* p. 859) says outright that he arranged that Africa should be attacked; Joinville, *Histoire de Saint Louis*, ed. de Wailly, pp. 398–400.

PAGE 144

1 Sternfeld, *op. cit.* pp. 237–48; Runciman, *op. cit.* vol. III, pp. 291–2; Hefele-Leclercq, *Histoire des Conciles*, vol. VI, 1, pp. 64–6. The main source is William of Nangis, *Gesta Sancti Ludovici* (Bouquet, *R.H.F.*, vol. XX), pp. 440–62. See also *Annales Januenses*, pp. 267–9.

2 Villani, vol. II, pp. 203–4, reports the dissatisfaction of the Crusaders. For Edward's part, see Powicke, *King Henry III and the Lord Edward*, vol. II, pp. 598–9.

3 William of Nangis, *Gesta Philippi III* (Bouquet, *R.H.F.*, vol. XX), pp. 476–8, 482–4; Hefele-Leclercq, *op. cit.* vol. VI, 1, p. 66.

PAGE 145

1 For Queen Margaret, see above, p. 69. King Philip remarried in 1274; and his second wife, Maria of Brabant, ended her mother-in-law's influence. See below, p. 193.

2 Hefele-Leclercq, *op. cit.* vol. VI, 1, pp. 66–7; Pinzi, *Storia della Città di Viterbo*, vol. II, pp. 280–92.

PAGE 146

1 Powicke, *op. cit.* vol. II, pp. 609–610.

PAGE 147

1 Léonard, *op. cit.* pp. 107–8; Miller, *op. cit.* pp. 516–17, and *Essays on the Latin Orient*, pp. 432–3; Bourcart, *L'Albanie et les Albanais*, p. 98; Norden, *op. cit.* pp. 477–80.

2 Longnon, *L'Empire Latin*, pp. 240–2; Diehl, Oeconomos, Guilland and Grousset, *L'Europe Orientale de 1081 à 1453*, pp. 204–6; Miller, *The Latins in the Levant*, pp. 131–3; Norden, *op. cit.* pp. 480–5.

PAGE 148

1 *Gregorii X Vita Auctore Anonymo Scripta* (Muratori, *R.I.S.*, vol. III, 1, pp. 599 ff.); Throop, *Criticism of the Crusade*, pp. 12–15; Hefele-Leclercq, *Histoire des Conciles*, vol. VI, 1, p. 67; Potthast, *Regesta Pontificum Romanorum*, vol. II, pp. 1651–2.

2 Gregory X, *Registres*, ed. Guiraud and Cadier, vol. I, p. 55–6; Hefele-Leclercq, *loc. cit.*

PAGE 150

1 *Annales Januenses*, pp. 262, 272–3; Caro, *Genua und die Mächte am Mittelmeer*, vol. I, pp. 213–33; Jordan, *L'Allemagne et l'Italie*, pp. 407–11.

PAGE 151

1 *Annales Placentini Gibellini*, pp. 554–5; *Annales Januenses*, pp. 273–4; Potthast, *Regesta*, vol. II, p. 1456.

PAGE 152

1 Gregory X, *Registres*, pp. 129–32, 328–9; Jordan, *op. cit.* pp. 406–7.

2 Gregory X, *Registres*, pp. 65–7. Alfonso's letter has not survived, but its sense is clear from Gregory's answer.

PAGE 153

1 Hefele-Leclercq, *op. cit.* vol. VI, 1, pp. 68–9; Jordan, *op. cit.* p. 416. It was believed at Genoa that Ottocar was the Pope's candidate. A Bohemian chronicle, *Annales Ottokariani* (*M.G.H.*, *Scriptores*, vol. IX), says that Ottocar was offered the crown by the German princes, but refused.

2 Champollion-Figeac, *Lettres des Rois, Reines et autres Personnages*, vol. I, p. 652.

PAGE 155

1 Hefele-Leclercq, *op. cit.* vol. VI, 1, pp. 69–71; Jordan, *op. cit.* pp. 417–20. The documents concerning the election are published in *M.G.H.*, *Constitutiones*, vol. III, pp. 7–15, and by Krammer, *Quellen zur Geschichte der Deutschen Königswahl*, vol. II, pp. 1–12.

2 Ottocar seems to have hoped, even after the election, that Gregory would still support his claim. The Crusading memoir presented to the Pope by Bruno of Olmutz just before the Council of Lyons next year was really a skilful advocacy of Ottocar's cause. See Throop, *op. cit.* pp. 105–6. For Ottocar's own protest, *M.G.H.*, *Constitutiones*, vol. III, p. 19.

3 See below, p. 163.

PAGE 156

1 Caro, *op. cit.* vol. I, p. 319, giving the text of the Venetian *démarche*.

2 *Annales Januenses*, pp. 280–2; Caro, *op. cit.* vol. I, pp. 265–78.

PAGE 157

1 Norden, *op. cit.* pp. 471–2, 491–2; Hefele-Leclercq, *op. cit.* vol. VI, I, pp. 159–60; Chapman, *Michel Paléologue*, pp. 113–14.

PAGE 158

1 Norden, *op. cit.* pp. 499–520, a detailed account of the negotiations, with full references; Hefele-Leclercq, *op. cit.* vol. VI, I, pp. 161–3, 167–8.

2 Potthast, *Regesta*, vol. II, p. 1672; Longnon, *op. cit.* pp. 242–3.

PAGE 159

1 Pachymer, *De Michaele Palaeologo*, pp. 317–18, 342–55.

PAGE 160

1 *Ibid.* pp. 308–9, 322–4, 410.

2 *Annales Placentini Gibellini*, p. 553; Caro, *op. cit.* vol. I, p. 288; Chapman, *op. cit.* p. 96.

3 Gregory X, *Registres*, vol. I, p. 123; Norden, *op. cit.* p. 518 and n. 2.

PAGE 161

1 Powicke, *op. cit.* vol. II, pp. 609–11. See above, p. 146.

2 Villani gives a detailed story of the poisoning of Thomas (vol. IV, p. 195), and Dante, *Purgatorio*, XX, ll. 68–9, accepts it.

PAGE 163

1 Hefele-Leclercq, *op. cit.* vol. VI, I, pp. 168–72; King James of Aragon's lively and boastful account of his part at the Council is given in the *Chronicle of James I of Aragon*, translated by Forster, vol. II, pp. 639–54. Hefele-Leclercq gives the Canons, *op. cit.* vol. VI, I, pp. 181–209.

PAGE 165

1 Pachymer, *op. cit.* pp. 384–96; Norden, *op. cit.* pp. 520–2; Hefele-Leclercq, *op. cit.* vol. VI, I, pp. 172–3; Chapman, *op. cit.* pp. 109–12.

2 Pachymer, *op. cit.* pp. 396–9; Norden, *op. cit.* pp. 520–36; Hefele-Leclercq, *op. cit.* vol. VI, I, pp. 172–8.

PAGE 166

1 Hefele-Leclercq, *op. cit.* vol. VI, 1, pp. 178–80.

2 Gregory X, *Registres*, pp. 207–9; Léonard, *op. cit.* pp. 118–20.

PAGE 167

1 Gregory X, *Registres*, p. 123; Léonard, *op. cit.* pp. 116–17; Norden, *op. cit.* pp. 537–53. Pachymer, *op. cit.* p. 410, says that Charles was so angry at being forbidden to attack Constantinople that he bit the end of his sceptre.

2 Potthast, *Regesta*, vol. II, p. 1693; Léonard, *op. cit.* pp. 121–2.

PAGE 168

1 Fournier, *Le Royaume d'Arles et de Vienne*, p. 230; Léonard, *op. cit.* pp. 118–19.

2 *Annales Placentini Gibellini*, pp. 558–9; Monti, *La Dominazione Angioina in Piemonte*, pp. 45–6.

3 *Annales Placentini Gibellini*, pp. 559–60; Monti, *op. cit.* pp. 50–2.

PAGE 170

1 For Maria of Antioch and her claims, see La Monte, *Feudal Monarchy in the Latin Kingdom of Jerusalem*, pp. 77–9; Hill, *History of Cyprus*, vol. II, pp. 161–5; Runciman, *History of the Crusades*, vol. III, pp. 328–9, 342.

2 Potthast, *op. cit.* vol. II, pp. 1702–3.

PAGE 171

1 Potthast, *Regesta Pontificum Romanorum*, vol. II, p. 1704. Charles remained at Rome throughout the whole pontificate. Durrieu, *Les Archives Angevines de Naples*, vol. II, p. 179.

PAGE 172

1 Potthast, *Regesta*, vol. II, p. 1705.

2 *Annales Januenses*, p. 283; Caro, *Genua und die Mächte am Mittelmeer*, vol. I, pp. 367–380; de Boüard, *Actes et Lettres de Charles Ier concernant la France*, p. 302; Potthast, *op. cit.* vol. II, p. 1708.

PAGE 173

1 Potthast, *op. cit.* vol. II, pp. 1709–10. Saba Malaspina, *Historia Sicula*, pp. 871–2, describes Charles's illicit intervention in Adrian's election.

2 Potthast, *op. cit.* vol. II, pp. 1710–11; Durrieu, *op. cit.* vol. II, p. 180.

3 John XXI, *Registres*, ed. Cadier.

4 Léonard, *Les Angevins de Naples*, pp. 121–3.

5 *Annales Placentini Gibellini*, pp. 564–5; Villani, vol. II, pp. 224–5.

PAGE 174

1 Hefele-Leclercq, *Histoire des Conciles*, vol. VI, 1, pp. 234–5; Redlich, *Rudolf von Habsburg*, pp. 268–84.

2 Redlich, *op. cit.* pp. 420–1.

PAGE 175

1 Pachymer, *De Michaele Palaeologo*, pp. 398–402; Chapman, *Michel Paléologue*, pp. 120–1.

PAGE 176

1 Norden, *Das Papsttum und Byzanz*, pp. 563–680; Hefele-Leclercq, *op. cit.* vol. VI, 1, pp. 209–12.

2 Norden, *op. cit.* pp. 546–8. Narjot of Toucy was forced to ask for reinforcements from Italy.

PAGE 177

1 Pachymer, *op. cit.* pp. 324–36; Sanudo, *Istoria del Regno di Romania*; Hopf, *Chroniques Gréco-Romanes*, pp. 120–1; Miller, *The Latins in the Levant*, pp. 134–6; Longnon, *L'Empire Latin de Constantinople*, pp. 243–4.

PAGE 178

1 Pachymer, *op. cit.* pp. 410–13; Sanudo, *op. cit.* pp. 125–6, 136; Miller, *op. cit.* pp. 136–40; Dölger, *Regesten der Kaiserurkunden des Oströmischen Reiches*, vol. III, pp. 68–9.

2 Miller, *op. cit.* pp. 141–2.

PAGE 180

1 Runciman, *History of the Crusades*, vol. III, pp. 345–8.

PAGE 181

1 *Ibid.* pp. 346–7, 387.

2 Hill, *History of Cyprus*, vol. II, pp. 174–5. See Nicholas III, *Registres*, ed. Gay, vol. I, pp. 336–7.

PAGE 182

1 Potthast, *op. cit.* vol. II, p. 1718.

PAGE 183

1 For Nicholas's previous career see Sternfeld, *Der Kardinal Johann Gaetan Orsini, passim.* For his appointment of Cardinals, see de Mas Latrie, *Trésor de Chronologie,* col. 1193. Villani, vol. II, pp. 226–7, reports the story of his marriage-scheme with the Capetian house. Dante's severe judgement of him is to be found in *Inferno,* XIX, ll. 98–9. The story of his corruption is part of the legend of John of Procida. See below, pp. 207–8.

2 *Ibid.* pp. 1719–20. Charles's movements throughout the summer and autumn of 1277 were more restricted than usual (Durrieu, *op. cit.* vol. II, pp. 180–1), and Nicholas's letter of early December (Potthast, *op. cit.* vol. II, p. 1720) condoles with him on his illness.

3 Nicholas III, *Registres,* p. 332.

PAGE 184

1 Redlich, *op. cit.* pp. 307–20; Fournier, *Le Royaume d'Arles et de Vienne,* p. 230. See Rymer, *Foedera,* vol. I, 2, p. 599.

2 Nicholas III, *Registres,* pp. 369–76; Fournier, *op. cit.* pp. 233–4; Léonard, *op. cit.* pp. 126–7.

PAGE 185

1 Nicholas III, *Registres,* pp. 378–9; Fournier, *loc. cit.*; Léonard, *loc. cit.*

PAGE 186

1 Léonard, *op. cit.* pp. 127–8.

2 *Ibid.* pp. 128–9.

3 The evidence for Charles's finances at this time is negative; he makes no special appeals for financial aid.

PAGE 187

1 Nicholas III, *Registres,* pp. 127–37. See Geneakoplos, 'On the Schism of the Greek and Roman Churches', *Greek Orthodox Theological Review,* vol. I.

PAGE 190

1 Pachymer, *op. cit.* pp. 449–66; Norden, *op. cit.* pp. 589–601; Hefele-Leclercq, *op. cit.* vol. VI, 1, pp. 211–16.

2 Pachymer, *op. cit.* pp. 462–3; Norden, *op. cit.* pp. 605–6. For the question of money, see below, pp. 205–8.

PAGE 191

1 Potthast, *op. cit.* vol. II, pp. 1754–7; Hefele-Leclercq, *op. cit.* vol. VI, 1, pp. 268–9; Léonard, *op. cit.* pp. 130–1. Villani, *op. cit.* vol. II, p. 237, accuses Charles roundly of having rigged the election.

2 For Martin's past career see above, pp. 79-82.

3 Potthast, *op. cit.* vol. II, p. 1758; Léonard, *op. cit.* p. 131.

PAGE 192

1 Villani, *op. cit.* vol. II, pp. 264-7.

2 Monti, *La Dominazione Angioina in Piemonte*, pp. 58-60.

PAGE 193

1 Fournier, *op. cit.* pp. 248-55. In January 1282, Martin tried to make peace between Margaret and Charles (Rymer, *Foedera*, vol. I, 2, p. 601).

PAGE 194

1 Pachymer, *op. cit.* p. 505; Hefele-Leclercq, *op. cit.* vol. VI, 1, p. 216.

2 The text of the treaty between Charles, Philip and the Venetians is given in Tafel and Thomas, *Urkunden zur ältern Handels- und Staatsgeschichte der Republik Venedig*, vol. III, pp. 287-97. See Norden, *op. cit.* pp. 625-9. For Pisan participation, Kern, *Acta Imperii, Angliae et Franciae*, pp. 15-17. The Emperor Michael and King Peter of Aragon both asked the Pisans to abstain.

PAGE 195

1 Potthast, *op. cit.* vol. II, p. 1763; Pachymer, *loc. cit.* The full text is given in *Annales Altahenses* (*M.G.H.*, *Scriptores*, vol. XVII, p. 409).

2 See below, pp. 205-8.

PAGE 196

1 Pachymer, *op. cit.* pp. 508-19; Sanudo, *op. cit.* pp. 129-30; Norden, *op. cit.* pp. 621-3; Miller, *op. cit.* pp. 171-3; Chapman, *op. cit.* pp. 140-2.

2 Pachymer, *op. cit.* pp. 518-19.

PAGE 197

1 Miller, *op. cit.* pp. 161-4.

2 Sanudo, *op. cit.* pp. 130, 132.

PAGE 198

1 Pachymer, *op. cit.* pp. 430-49; Jireček, *Geschichte der Bulgaren*, pp. 275-80.

2 Jireček, *Geschichte der Serben*, vol. I, pp. 326-31.

PAGE 199

1 Léonard, *op. cit.* p. 134.

PAGE 200

1 Pachymer, *op. cit.* pp. 472–4; Chapman, *op. cit.* pp. 150–1.

PAGE 201

1 The prophecy is given by Jordan of Osnabruck, *De Prerogativa Romani Imperii*, ed. Waitz, p. 79. Sanudo, *Istoria del Regno di Romania*, p. 138, says of Charles that 'aspirava alla monarchia del mondo', and Nicephorus Gregoras, *Historia Byzantina*, vol. I, p. 123, says that he contemplated rebuilding the Empire of Julius Caesar and Augustus. Charles was descended from Charlemagne through his grandmother, Isabella of Hainault.

PAGE 202

1 For Constance's claim to the Sicilian throne and her use of the title of Queen see Wieruszowski, 'La Corte di Pietro d'Aragona', pt. I, pp. 142–6. She seems to have used the title from the time of Manfred's death, but only within the ambiance of the Court.

2 *The Chronicle of James I of Aragon*, which is almost certainly his own work, gives the most vivid picture of this vain but vigorous prince.

3 Wieruszowski, *op. cit.* pt. I, pp. 147–52; Cartellieri, *Peter von Aragon und die Sizilianische Vesper*, pp. 23–6. Amongst the other exiles from Manfred's court was Constance's aunt, Constance-Anna, former Eastern Empress (for whom see above, pp. 26, 42, 45). She had been at Naples at the time of the Angevin conquest, but Charles allowed her to retire to Spain in 1269.

PAGE 204

1 For John's early life see Sicardi's introduction to *Due Cronache del Vespro* (Muratori, *R.I.S.* new series, vol. XXXIV). He was one of the witnesses to sign Frederick II's Will (see above, p. 27, n. 2). The history of his earlier life is given very fully in de Renzi, *Il Secolo decimo terzo e Giovanni da Procida*. For the accusation that he poisoned King Conrad, see above, p. 30, n. 3. His letter of recommendation from Cardinal Orsini to King Charles is given in Martène and Durand, *Thesaurus*, vol. II, p. 298. Villani, vol. II, pp. 234–5, tells the story of his wife's and daughter's maltreatment. For his negotiations with Frederick of Misnia see Busson, 'Friedrich der Friedige als Prätendant der Sizilianischen Krone und Johann von Procida', *Historische Aufsätze dem Andenken an Georg Weitz gewidmet*. The detailed arguments about his whole career given by Sicardi in his introduction to *Due Cronache del Vespro*, though well referenced, are somewhat uncritical, as Sicardi will not hear a word against his hero.

PAGE 205

1 Cartellieri, *op. cit.* pp. 28–53.

2 See below, pp. 206–9 and appendix, pp. 288–93.

3 Carini, *Gli Archivi e le Biblioteche di Spagna*, pt. II, pp. 2–4, 190.

PAGE 207

1 *Lu Rebellamentu di Sichilia*, in *Due Cronache del Vespro*, pp. 5–11; *Liber Jani de Procida et Palialoco*, ibid. pp. 49–52; *Leggenda di Messer Gianni di Procida*, ibid. pp. 65–8. The *Rebellamentu*, written in the Sicilian dialect, treats John as a hero, the *Liber Jani* and the *Leggenda*, both in Italian and the latter probably by a Modanese Guelf, as a villain. Ricordano Malespini, *Storia Fiorentina*, ed. Follini, pp. 180–1, Brunetto Latini, *Tesoro*, ed. Amari, in *Altre Narrazioni del Vespro Siciliano*, pp. 60–89, and Villani, *Cronica*, vol. II, pp. 233–7, 239–42, give brief résumés of the legend.

PAGE 208

1 *Rebellamentu*, pp. 14–17; *Liber Jani*, pp. 52–5; *Leggenda*, pp. 68–71.

2 Wieruszowski, 'Der Anteil Johanns von Procida an der Verschwörung gegen Karl von Anjou', pp. 230 ff., giving John's itinerary as shown by the charters issued or signed by him, and showing that it would have been impossible for him to have journeyed even as far as Rome. For Nicholas's bribes, see above, pp. 182, 190.

PAGE 209

1 For the Sicilian nobles, see *Due Cronache del Vespro*, introduction, p. xxxvii, n. 1. For Andrew of Procida, see Cartellieri, *op. cit.* p. 90.

2 D'Esclot, *Cronica del Rey en Pere*, in Buchon, *Chroniques Etrangères relatives aux Expéditions Françaises*, p. 624; Muntaner, *Cronica*, ed. Coroleu, pp. 86–8; William of Nangis, *Gesta Philippi III*, p. 514; Cartellieri, *op. cit.* pp. 63–4, rejecting the story, told by Muntaner, of Peter's rudeness to Charles of Salerno. But the story is told with convincing details; the kings of France and Majorca remind Peter that Charles had married his first cousin. Moreover, William of Nangis suggests that there was some unpleasantness. Peter's letter to Milan, of which copies were sent to the other chief Ghibelline communes in Lombardy, is given in Carini, *op. cit.* vol. II, p. 41.

PAGE 210

1 See above, p. 194. For the Sardinian tithes, Martin IV, *Registres*, no. 116.

2 D'Esclot, *op. cit.* pp. 626; Muntaner, *op. cit.* pp. 100–1; Cartellieri, *op. cit.* pp. 80–1, 149.

3 Ptolemaeus of Lucca, *Historia Ecclesiastica* (Muratori, *R.I.S.*, vol. XI, pp. 1186–7); Martin IV, *Registres*, p. 112; Sanudo, *Istoria del Regno di Romania*, p. 133; Cartellieri, *op. cit.* pp. 87–9; Dölger, *Regesten der Kaiserurkunden*, vol. III, pp. 74–5. The Emperor asked for the hand of an Aragonese princess for his son and heir Andronicus.

PAGE 211

1 Carini, *op. cit.* vol. II, p. 45.

PAGE 212

1 Bartholomew of Neocastro, *Historia Sicula* (Muratori, *R.I.S.* new series, vol. XIII, iii, p. 10), a chapter entitled 'How King Charles oppressed the people'; Nicholas Specialis, *Historia Sicula* (Muratori, *R.I.S.*, vol. X, pp. 924, 930). See also, Libertini and Paladino, *Storia della Sicilia*, p. 442: Pontieri, *Ricerche sulla Crisi della Monarchia Siciliana nel sec. XIII, passim*; Léonard, *Les Angevins de Naples*, pp. 143–4.

2 Norden, *Das Papsttum und Byzanz*, pp. 626–9. Charles spent January at Rome and Orvieto, but was at Capua and Naples in February, and remained at Naples throughout March. We do not know whether he actually intended to command the expedition himself. Durrieu, *Les Archives Angevines de Naples*, vol. II, p. 187.

PAGE 213

1 Villani, *op. cit.* vol. II, p. 242, says that Charles was warned by King Philip but was too arrogant to take notice. He adds a popular proverb as comment: 'If someone tells you that your nose has gone, put up your hand to see.' Charles neglected such a precaution.

PAGE 214

1 Amari, *La Guerra del Vespro Siciliano* (9th ed.), vol. I, pp. 193–4.

2 *Ibid.* p. 193, n. 1. The date, Monday the 30th, is given by Bartholomew of Neocastro and other contemporary Sicilians. The church is today lost in the exuberance of a large Sicilian cemetery.

PAGE 215

1 Descriptions of the actual massacre are given by Bartholomew of Neocastro, *Historia Sicula*, pp. 11–12; Nicholas Specialis, *Historia Sicula* (Muratori, *R.I.S.*, vol. X, pp. 924–5); continuation of Saba Malaspina, *Rerum Sicularum Historia* (Muratori, vol. VIII); *Annales Januenses*, p. 576; Ricordano Malespini, *Storia Fiorentina*, pp. 182–3; Villani, *Cronica*, vol. II, pp. 242–3; *Rebellamentu*, pp. 19–20; *Leggenda*, pp. 72–3; D'Esclot, *Cronica del Rey en Pere*, pp. 628–9; Muntaner, *Cronica*, pp. 94–5; William of Nangis, *Gesta Philippi III*, p. 516.

There are shorter references in most of the chronicles of the time. The account in Amari, *op. cit.* vol. I, pp. 193-200, is an excellent summary.

2 The cry 'Death to the French' is mentioned in all the accounts. Even Dante later refers to it, *Paradiso*, VIII, ll. 73-5.

3 Amari, *op. cit.* vol. I, p. 301, combining the various sources.

PAGE 216

1 Nicholas Specialis, *Historia Sicula*, pp. 924-5. See Egidi, 'La "Communitas Siciliae" del 1282', in *Annuario dell'Università de Messina*. 1914-15.

2 *Ibid.* pp. 201-2.

PAGE 217

1 *Ibid.* pp. 203-20.

2 Bartholomew of Neocastro, *op. cit.* pp. 12-15. Bartholomew was living in Messina and playing a prominent part in its public life. His account of what happened there is full and convincing.

PAGE 219

1 *Ibid.* pp. 18-22.

2 *Ibid.* pp. 21-2.

PAGE 220

1 *Ibid.* pp. 36-7; Michael Palaeologus, *De Vita Sua Opusculum*, ed. Troitsky, *Christianskoe Chtenie*, vol. II, pp. 537-8. Bartholomew, pp. 10-11, cites as one of the grievances of the Sicilians Charles's assumption of a 'robber's cross' against 'our friends the Greeks'.

2 Bartholomew of Neocastro, *op. cit.* p. 22.

3 *Ibid.*; Villani, *op. cit.* vol. II, p. 244, quoting what were believed to be Charles's actual words.

PAGE 221

1 Bartholomew of Neocastro, *op. cit.* p. 15; Villani, *op. cit.* vol. II, pp. 245-6. See Amari, *op. cit.* vol. I, pp. 228-31, and Cartellieri, *op. cit.* pp. 162-4.

2 Potthast, *Regesta*, vol. II, pp. 1769-70.

3 Villani, *op. cit.* vol. II, pp. 244-5.

4 Champollion-Figeac, *Lettres des Rois, Reines et autres Personnages*, vol. I, p. 285. See Cartellieri, *op. cit.* pp. 169, 187. Maurice of Craon wrote on May 19 and Ferdinand of Aragon-Majorca on May 26 to Edward of England to tell him the news; Rymer, *Foedera*, vol. I, 2, p. 609. It was presumably known in France by the first half of May.

PAGE 222

1 D'Esclot, *op. cit.* pp. 626–7; Muntaner, *op. cit.* pp. 103–8; Cartellieri, *op. cit.* pp. 192–3.

2 D'Esclot, *op. cit.* pp. 631–2; Cartellieri, *op. cit.* p. 199.

3 D'Esclot, *op. cit.* pp. 628, 630–1; Muntaner, *op. cit.* pp. 108–11.

PAGE 223

1 Bartholomew of Neocastro, *op. cit.* pp. 23–5; Amari, *op. cit.* vol. I, pp. 232 ff.; Léonard, *Les Angevins de Naples*, p. 147.

2 Potthast, *op. cit.* vol. II, p. 1771; Bartholomew of Neocastro, *op. cit.* p. 27.

3 Trifone, *Legislazione Angioina*, no. LVIII, pp. 92–3.

PAGE 224

1 Bartholomew of Neocastro, *op. cit.* pp. 24–5.

2 *Ibid.* pp. 29, 67.

3 *Ibid.* pp. 33–6.

PAGE 226

1 *Ibid.* pp. 26–9.

PAGE 227

1 *Ibid.* p. 29; D'Esclot, *op. cit.* pp. 632–4; Muntaner, *op. cit.* pp. 112–13, 116–18, Peter also wrote a justificatory letter to Edward of England, Rymer, *Foedera*, vol. I, 2, p. 612.

2 Bartholomew of Neocastro, *op. cit.* p. 30; D'Esclot, *op. cit.* pp. 635–6; Muntaner, *op. cit.* pp. 119–20.

PAGE 229

1 D'Esclot, *Cronica*, pp. 636–7; Muntaner, *Cronica*, pp. 112–13, saying wrongly that Peter was crowned at this time; Bartholomew of Neocastro, *Historia Sicula*, p. 30.

2 Bartholomew of Neocastro, *loc. cit.*

3 *Ibid.* pp. 30–2.

PAGE 230

1 *Ibid.*; D'Esclot, *op. cit.* p. 638.

2 Bartholomew of Neocastro, *op. cit.* pp. 33, 37; D'Esclot, *op. cit.* pp. 638–9; Muntaner, *op. cit.* pp. 125–6.

PAGE 231

1 Bartholomew of Neocastro, *op. cit.* pp. 38–42.

PAGE 232

1 *Ibid.* pp. 42–3; D'Esclot, *op. cit.* pp. 639–42; Muntaner, *op. cit.* pp. 130–2. A letter from Peter to Guy of Montefeltro telling of his victories is quoted in Carucci, *La Guerra del Vespro Siciliano*, p. 114.

2 Bartholomew of Neocastro, *op. cit.* pp. 45–6; Villani, *Cronica*, vol. II, pp. 260–1. Various of Charles's orders putting the south of the kingdom into a state of defence are given in de Boüard, *Les Comptes des Trésoriers*, pp. 204 ff.

PAGE 233

1 Villani, *op. cit.* vol. I, pp. 267–70; Gregorovius, *Geschichte der Stadt Rom im Mittelalter*, vol. II, pp. 86–8.

2 See Caro, *Genua und die Mächte am Mittelmeer*, vol. II, pp. 1–31. The Genoese may have foreseen that the Catalans, under Aragonese protection, would oust them from their favoured position in Sicily. See Heyd, *Histoire du Commerce du Levant*, vol. I, p. 475. Bartholomew of Neocastro pays tribute to the friendly attitude of individual Genoese (*op. cit.* pp. 36–7).

PAGE 234

1 Pachymer, *De Michaele Palaeologo*, pp. 531–2, *De Andronico Palaeologo*, pp. 87–8 (the marriage of Irene of Montferrat, which took place in 1284). Pachymer remarks that she was not of a royal family, but that she was the grand-daughter of the King of Castile; but the real point of the marriage was that the Montferrats claimed the Kingdom of Thessalonica, set up by Boniface II of Montferrat in 1205 and lost to the Angeli in 1222. William VII of Montferrat now transferred his claim to his son-in-law. Irene became eventual heiress of Montferrat and transferred the marquisate to her son, who thus founded a dynasty of Palaeologi in northern Italy. For Andronicus II's foreign policy see Vasiliev, *History of the Byzantine Empire*, pp. 603 ff.

2 For Rudolph's relations with the Papacy and Italy see Hefele-Leclercq, *Histoire des Conciles*, vol. VI, I, pp. 268–70. Pope Martin did not consider King Edward sufficiently neutral, as he did not break off the betrothal of his daughter Eleanor to Peter's eldest son, Alfonso. See Rymer, *Foedera*, vol. I, I, pp. 613–14.

3 Léonard, *Les Angevins de Naples*, pp. 149–50.

PAGE 235

1 Potthast, *Regesta*, vol. II, pp. 1773–4.

PAGE 236

1 See Léonard, *op. cit.* p. 153.

2 D'Esclot, *op. cit.* pp. 642–4; Muntaner, *op. cit.* pp. 138–41; Villani (*op. cit.* vol. II, pp. 274–5), wrongly says that the accord was signed in front of the Pope, but gives a shrewd explanation of both kings' motives. See Amari, *La Guerra del Vespro Siciliano*, vol. II, pp. 19–21.

PAGE 237

1 Potthast, *Regesta*, vol. II, pp. 1774–8; Rymer, *Foedera*, vol. I, 2, pp. 621–8.

PAGE 238

1 See Léonard, *op. cit.* p. 150. Peter's brother urged him to return to Aragon at this time. Bartholomew of Neocastro, *op. cit.* pp. 47–8.

2 Durrieu, *Les Archives Angevines de Naples*, vol. II, p. 188. Villani, *op. cit.* vol. II, pp. 275–6, tells of his passage through Florence, where also the chronicler Paolino di Piero saw him (see Léonard, *op. cit.* p. 533).

3 Bartholomew of Neocastro, *op. cit.* p. 44; D'Esclot, *op. cit.* p. 645; Muntaner, *op. cit.* pp. 133–6. He is the only source to say that Alençon was killed in this raid.

PAGE 239

1 Bartholomew of Neocastro, *op. cit.* pp. 45–6; D'Esclot, *op. cit.* pp. 645–7; Muntaner, *op. cit.* pp. 145–7. See Carucci, *op. cit.* pp. 117–19.

2 The text of the reform is given in Trifone, *La Legislazione Angioina*, pp. 93–105.

PAGE 240

1 Potthast, *Regesta*, vol. II, p. 1780.

2 Bartholomew of Neocastro, *op. cit.* pp. 46–7; D'Esclot, *op. cit.* pp. 647–8.

3 Bartholomew of Neocastro, *op. cit.* pp. 47–51; D'Esclot, *op. cit.* pp. 648–9; Muntaner, *op. cit.* pp. 147–50.

PAGE 241

1 D'Esclot, pp. 649–52, giving the Aragonese version; William of Nangis, *Gesta Philippi III*, pp. 522–4, giving the Angevin version; Muntaner, *op. cit.* pp. 170–185, based on d'Esclot; Villani, vol. II, pp. 276–80 (he makes Charles appear on the field before Peter); Amari, *op. cit.* vol. II, pp. 24–6.

PAGE 242

1 Martin IV, *Registres*, nos. 220, 221.

PAGE 243

1 *Ibid.* nos. 292–9; Rymer, *Foedera*, vol. I, 2, pp. 634–9; *Grandes Chroniques de France*, ed. Viard, vol. VIII, pp. 93–4, 97; Petit, *Charles de Valois*, pp. 5–6; Léonard, *Les Angevins de Naples*, pp. 155–6.

PAGE 244

1 Villani, *Cronica*, vol. II, pp. 270–2.

2 See Léonard, *op. cit.* p. 153.

3 Bartholomew of Neocastro, *Historia Sicula*, pp. 55–6; D'Esclot, *Cronica*, pp. 658–9; Muntaner, *Cronica*, pp. 158–9.

PAGE 245

1 Bartholomew of Neocastro, *op. cit.* pp. 49–50.

PAGE 246

1 King Peter's letter is given in Carucci, *op. cit.* p. 122.

2 Martin IV, *Registres*, no. 304. See above, p. 243, n. 1.

3 Carucci, *La Guerra del Vespro Siciliano*, pp. 127–169, quoting extracts from the Angevin registers.

PAGE 248

1 Bartholomew of Neocastro, *op. cit.* pp. 57–8; D'Esclot, *op. cit.* pp. 663–8; Muntaner, pp. 227–34; Villani, *op. cit.* vol. II, pp. 286–8, giving the story of the citizens of Sorrento.

PAGE 249

1 Villani, *op. cit.* vol. II, pp. 268–70; Bartholomew of Neocastro, *op. cit.* pp. 58–9, a fanciful account of the consolation offered to Charles by his queen.

2 See Léonard, *op. cit.* p. 158.

PAGE 250

1 Bartholomew of Neocastro, *op. cit.* pp. 60–1.

2 *Ibid.*

PAGE 251

1 *Ibid.* pp. 61–2. For the dating, Durrieu, *Les Archives Angevines de Naples*, vol. II, p. 189.

21-2

2 Bartholomew of Neocastro, *op. cit.* p. 59, saying that the Prince's life was saved by Queen Constance; Muntaner, *op. cit.* pp. 234–6, saying that his life was saved by the Infant James. It was apparently saved through the good offices of a Neapolitan gentleman called Adenulf of Aquino. See Léonard, *op. cit.* p. 158, n. 2. Villani, *op. cit.* vol. II, pp. 292–3, gives Constance the credit.

PAGE 253

1 Bartholomew of Neocastro, *op. cit.* pp. 67–9.

2 *Ibid.* pp. 62–3, 66, 70.

PAGE 254

1 Miller, *The Latins in the Levant*, pp. 174–5; Runciman, *History of the Crusades*, vol. III, pp. 392–4.

2 Durrieu, *op. cit.* vol. II, p. 160. The order for the general levy is dated from Brindisi, 5 October 1284.

3 See Léonard, *op. cit.* p. 159.

4 Bartholomew of Neocastro, *op. cit.* p. 70.

PAGE 255

1 Villani, *op. cit.* vol. II, pp. 290–1; Salimbene de Adam, *Cronica*, pp. 564–5, describing visions seen on the occasion of his death. For his will, see Léonard, *op. cit.* pp. 159–60.

PAGE 257

1 Cadier, *Essai sur l'Administration du Royaume de Sicile*, pp. 112 ff.; Léonard, *Les Angevins de Naples*, pp. 161–3.

PAGE 258

1 The Crusade of Aragon is described from the Aragonese angle by D'Esclot, *Cronica*, pp. 677–727, and Muntaner, *Cronica*, pp. 246–86, and from the French by William of Nangis, *Gesta Philippi III*, pp. 528–34. See Lavisse, *Histoire de France*, vol. III, 2 (by Langlois), pp. 113–17.

2 Miller, *The Latins in the Levant*, pp. 164–5; Longnon, *L'Empire Latin de Constantinople*, pp. 264–5.

PAGE 259

1 Runciman, *History of the Crusades*, vol. III, pp. 396–7.

2 Potthast, *Regesta Pontificum Romanorum*, vol. II, p. 1794; Villani, *Cronica*, vol. II, p. 306. He died of indigestion. Dante, *Purgatorio*, XXIV, ll. 20–4, says

that it was of indulging himself during a fast with eels from Bolsena and muscadel from Vernaccia.

3 William of Nangis, *op. cit.* pp. 534-5; D'Esclot, *op. cit.* pp. 727–732; Villani, *op. cit.* vol. II, pp. 298–305. Dante, *Purgatorio*, VII, l. 105, tells of him 'dying in flight, dishonouring the lilies'.

PAGE 260

1 Bartholomew of Neocastro, *Historia Sicula*, p. 80; D'Esclot, *op. cit.* pp. 732–6; Muntaner, *op. cit.* pp. 296–300. Dante, *Purgatorio*, VII, ll. 112–14, calls him 'robust of limb' and 'girdled with every virtue'.

2 For Charles's character, see the excellent summary in Léonard, *op. cit.* pp. 172–4. He had been moved from Sicily to Catalonia not long before King Peter's death, against the wishes of the Sicilian vice-regal government; Bartholomew of Neocastro, *op. cit.* pp. 78–9.

3 Potthast, *op. cit.* vol. II, pp. 1795–6. See Honorius IV, *Registres*, ed. Prou, introduction, for a summary of his history and character. He appointed his brother, Pandolfo Savelli, as Senator of Rome. See Gregorovius, *Geschichte der Stadt Rom im Mittelalter*, vol. II, pp. 90–1.

PAGE 261

1 Honorius IV, *Registres*, pp. 72–86, and introduction, pp. xxii–xxxv.

2 *Ibid.* introduction, *loc. cit.*

PAGE 262

1 Bartholomew of Neocastro, *op. cit.* p. 81; Muntaner, *op. cit.* pp. 300–1. D'Esclot's chronicle stops with King Peter's death.

2 Rymer, *Foedera*, vol. I, 2, pp. 662–7. The Pope was shy of having anything to do with the negotiations; Honorius IV, *Registres*, pp. 938–9.

PAGE 263

1 Bartholomew of Neocastro, *op. cit.* pp. 78, 81; Honorius IV, *Registres*, pp. 348–9, 548.

2 Rymer, *Foedera*, vol. I, 2, pp. 670–1.

3 Honorius IV, *Registres*, p. 572.

PAGE 264

1 Bartholomew of Neocastro, *op. cit.* pp. 81, 86–8, 93–101; Budge, *The Monks of Kublai Khan*, p. 171 (a translation of Rabban Sauma's narrative). Rabban

Sauma thought that the war was conducted in a very gentlemanly manner as non-combatants were not involved.

2 Potthast, *op. cit.* vol. II, pp. 1823–6. For Nicholas IV, see the article by Teetaert in Vacant and Mangenot, *Dictionnaire de théologie catholique*, vol. XI, I.

PAGE 265

1 Rymer, *Foedera*, vol. I, 2, pp. 677–9.

2 *Ibid.* pp. 680–1; Digard, *Philippe le Bel et le Saint-Siège*, vol. I, pp. 43 ff.

3 Nicholas IV, *Registres*, vol. I, p. 114; Runciman, *op. cit.* vol. III, pp. 405–6.

4 Rymer, *Foedera*, vol. I, 2, pp. 685–97; Muntaner, *op. cit.* pp. 327–9; Digard, *op. cit.* vol. I, pp. 63–6.

PAGE 266

1 Villani, *op. cit.* vol. II, pp. 331–2; Nicholas IV, *Registres*, vol. I, pp. 212–16, 247; Digard, *op. cit.* vol. I, pp. 66–70.

2 Bartholomew of Neocastro, *op. cit.* pp. 102–11; Villani, *op. cit.* vol. II, pp. 343–4; Carucci, *La Guerra del Vespro Siciliano*, p. 199.

PAGE 268

1 Muntaner, *op. cit.* pp. 337–40; Digard, *op. cit.* vol. I, pp. 100–10, and *Pièces justificatives*, no. XII (for the text of the Senlis agreement), vol. II, pp. 279–80.

2 Bartholomew of Neocastro, *op. cit.* p. 126; Muntaner, *op. cit.* pp. 340–1; Villani, *op. cit.* vol. III, p. 25.

3 Nicholas IV, *Registres*, vol. II, p. 892; Carucci, *op. cit.* pp. 252–282; Digard, *op. cit.* vol. I, pp. 136–140.

PAGE 269

1 Potthast, *op. cit.* vol. II, p. 1914.

2 See Digard, *op. cit.* vol. I, pp. 155–60.

3 For the Hungarian succession, see below, pp. 275–6.

4 Carucci, *op. cit.* pp. 349 ff.

5 Potthast, *op. cit.* vol. II, pp. 1915–16; Hefele-Leclercq, *Histoire des Conciles*, vol. VI, 1, pp. 333–7. For the gossip about his election, see Villani, *op. cit.* vol. III, pp. 11–12.

PAGE 270

1 Digard, *op. cit.* vol. I, pp. 119–20, 190–1; Léonard, *op. cit.* p. 186; Carucci, *op. cit.* pp. 81 ff. Neither Carucci nor Sicardi, whose introduction to the

Rebellamentu is a long apologia for John of Procida, will hear of anything to his discredit. Bartholomew of Neocastro, *op. cit.* p. 120, says that John went himself to Rome to open negotiations.

2 Digard, *op. cit.* pp. 190–1.

3 Potthast, *op. cit.* vol. II, pp. 1921–4; Hefele-Leclercq, *op. cit.* vol. VI, I, pp. 338–9, 348–51; Boase, *Boniface VIII*, pp. 49–51. For the gossip, see Villani, *op. cit.* vol. III, pp. 13–16.

4 Boniface VIII, *Registres*, ed. Digard, vol. I, pp. 68–70; Nicholas Specialis, *Historia Sicula*, p. 961 (saying that John of Procida and Roger of Lauria came with King James); Digard, *op. cit.* vol. I, pp. 222–4.

PAGE 271

1 *Acta Aragonensia*, ed. Finke, vol. III, pp. 49 ff.; Digard, *op. cit.* vol. I, pp. 217–18, 258, 263; Carucci, *op. cit.* pp. 427–9; Léonard, *op. cit.* pp. 184–6. For Catherine's answer, see Boniface, *Registres*, vol. I, p. 290.

PAGE 272

1 Boniface VIII, *Registres*, vol. I, pp. 68–70, 272–3, 925–35; *Acta Aragonensia*, vol. I, pp. 33, 40; Nicholas Specialis, *op. cit.* pp. 985–6; Carucci, *op. cit.* pp. 546 ff.; Digard, *op. cit.* pp. 290–2. For Violante's qualities see the anecdote in Finke, *Aus den Tagen Bonifaz VIII, Quellen*, p. xxxvi, when Boniface grudgingly agreed with Charles II's praise of her. For her influence, see below, p. 273.

2 Nicholas Specialis, *op. cit.* pp. 962–5, 995–6.

3 *Ibid.* pp. 999–1001.

4 *Acta Aragonensia*, vol. I, pp. 55, 70; Finke, *op. cit.* p. xiv.

PAGE 273

1 Nicholas Specialis, *op. cit.* pp. 1015–19; Boniface VIII, *Registres*, vol. II, pp. 913–25.

2 Nicholas Specialis, *op. cit.* p. 1027. For relations with Genoa see Léonard, *op. cit.* p. 189.

3 Nicholas Specialis, *op. cit.* p. 1035; *Acta Aragonensia*, vol. III, pp. 107, 113; Finke, *op. cit.* pp. xx, lv. The defence of Messina had been conducted by Blasco of Alagona, a Catalan admiral who had remained faithful to the Sicilian cause.

PAGE 274

1 Petit, *Charles de Valois*, pp. 52 ff.; Léonard, *op. cit.* pp. 190–3; Finke, *op. cit.* p. xx.

PAGE 275

1 Nicholas Specialis, *op. cit.* pp. 1037–43; Finke, *op. cit.* pp. xxxv, xlvi, lii, liii, lvi; *Acta Aragonensia*, vol. I, pp. 106, 108, 111; Léonard, *op. cit.* pp. 194–6; Boase, *op. cit.* pp. 289–92.

2 Boniface VIII, *Registres*, vol. III, pp. 847–64; Villani, *op. cit.* vol. III, pp. 75.

3 Nicholas Specialis, *op. cit.* pp. 1048–50.

4 Digard, *op. cit.* vol. II, pp. 175–85; Boase, *op. cit.* pp. 341–51.

PAGE 276

1 Léonard, *op. cit.* pp. 196–7. See Schipa, *Carlo-Martello Angioino, passim.*

PAGE 277

1 Léonard, *op. cit.* pp. 197–9.

2 Caggese, *Roberto d'Angiò e i suoi Tempi*, vol. I, p. 20. Pope Benedict XI in 1303 reproved Frederick for the dating of his acts (Potthast, *op. cit.* vol. II, p. 2027).

PAGE 278

1 The internal government of the island during the next century seems on the whole to have been conducted without disturbances other than the periodical wars with Naples.

2 Léonard, *op. cit.* pp. 224, 243–5, 252–5, 326–9, 433–6.

3 King Frederick's great-granddaughter and ultimate heiress Maria was succeeded on her death in 1402 by her husband Martin, son of King Martin of Aragon. On his death the Sicilian crown passed to Ferdinand, younger son of King John I of Castile and of Princess Eleanora of Aragon whose mother had been a princess of Sicily. His son Alfonso inherited Aragon as well as Sicily and was in 1420 adopted by Joanna II of Anjou, Queen of Sicily (Naples), thus reuniting the 'Two Sicilies'. See genealogical table at end of volume.

PAGE 279

1 Aragon also for a while triumphed in Greece, where owing to the activities of the freebooting Catalan Company its Sicilian branch provided a line of Dukes for Athens.

PAGE 288

1 But Gibbon adds (*Decline and Fall*, ch. LXII, ed. Bury, vol. VI, pp. 476–8) that 'it may be questioned whether the instant explosion of Palermo were the effect of accident or design'.

2 Oriani, *La Lotta Politica in Italia*, in *Opere Complete*, vol. I, p. 77.

3 Early historians who wrote about the Vespers include F. Mugnos (1669) and J. C. Meyer (1690).

PAGE 289

1 See the criticism of Amari in Carucci, *La Guerra del Vespro Siciliano*, pp. 67 ff. Carucci is perhaps over-zealous in rehabilitating John from Amari's attacks.

2 See above, pp. 226–7.

PAGE 290

1 William of Nangis, *Vita Philippi III*, p. 514, saying that Peter acted 'consilio uxoris'. Charles's panegyrist, reproduced by William of Nangis (*M.G.H. Scriptores*, vol. XXVI, p. 687) says that Peter equipped his fleet 'Siculorum monitu et uxoris'. Salimbene de Adam, representing the extreme Guelf view, calls Queen Constance in a symbolical passage an oriental hen clucking at the eagle (Charles), *Cronica*, p. 545. See also the *Praeclara Francorum Facinora*, Duchesne, *Historiae Francorum Scriptores*, vol. V, p. 7, and the *Chronicon Sancti Bertini*.

2 Bartholomew of Neocastro, *Historia Sicula*, p. 13, says that Constance was always begging her husband to avenge Manfred's death.

3 Nicholas Specialis, *Historia Sicula*, p. 925.

4 *Anonymi Chronicon Siciliae* (Muratori, *R.I.S.*, vol. X, p. 830).

5 Edited by Sicardi (Muratori, *R.I.S.* new ed., vol. XXXIV).

6 *Rebellamentu*, introduction, pp. xlvii–xlix. Talking of the Messinese at the time the author on one occasion uses the first person plural of the present tense ('putirini') in the older MSS. It has been changed to the impersonal 'putirisi' in later editions.

PAGE 291

1 Ricordano Malespini, *Storia Fiorentina*, pp. 180–1.

2 Villani, *Cronica*, vol. II, pp. 233–42; Pipino, *Chronicon* (Muratori, *R.I.S.*, vol. IX, pp. 686–7); Boccaccio, *De Casibus Illustrium Virorum*, bk. IX (Berne ed. 1539), p. cx; Petrarch, *Itinerarium Syriacum* (Basle ed., 1554), vol. I, p. 620.

3 For Dante's references see *Rebellamentu*, introduction, p. xxxi.

4 See above, pp. 182–5, and Léonard, *Les Angevins de Naples*, pp. 124–5.

PAGE 292

1 See above, p. 210.

2 See above, pp. 219–20. Bartholomew of Neocastro's phrase, 'amicos nostros Danaos' (see above, p. 220, n. 1) suggests that the Sicilians were in close touch with the Greeks.

PAGE 293

1 See above, pp. 219–20.

2 See Bull cited above, p. 221, n. 2. The Guelf writers all mention the Emperor as being implicated with the Aragonese. Ptolemy of Lucca (see above, p. 210, n. 3) cites him as the principal instigator of the plot, together with 'quidam alius magnus inter principes cujus nomen ignotum', by whom he perhaps means to suggest Pope Nicholas.

BIBLIOGRAPHY

I. ORIGINAL SOURCES

1. COLLECTIONS OF SOURCES

Acta Aragonensia, aus dem diplomatischen Korrespondenz Jaymes II (ed. H. Finke), 3 vols. Berlin, 1908–.

AMARI, M. *Altre Narrazioni del Vespro Siciliano*, appendix to *Guerra del Vespro Siciliano*, see Bibliography II.

d'ANCONA, A. and COMPARETTI, D. *Le Antiche Rime Volgari*, 5 vols., Bologna, 1875-88.

BARONIUS, C. *Annales Ecclesiastici*, continued by O. Raynaldi. 15 vols. Lucca, 1747-56. Cited as Baronius-Raynaldi.

DE BARTHOLOMAEIS, V. *Poesie Provenzali Storiche relative all'Italia*. 2 vols. Istituto Storico Italiano. Rome, 1931.

BOEHMER, J. F. *Regesta Imperii*, vol. v, *Regesten des Kaiserreichs* (ed. J. Ficker, and E. Winkelmann), 3 parts. Innsbruck, 1881–1901.

DE BOÜARD, A. *Actes et Lettres de Charles Ier concernant la France*. Paris, 1926.

DE BOÜARD, A. *Documents en Français des Archives angevines de Naples, Règne de Charles Ier*. Vol. I, *Les Mandements aux Trésoriers*. Paris, 1933. Vol. II, *Les Comptes des Trésoriers*. Paris, 1935.

BOUQUET, M. and others. *Recueil des Historiens des Gaules et de la France*, 23 vols. Paris, 1738–1876. Cited as Bouquet, *R.H.F.*

BUCHON, J. A. *Chroniques étrangères relatives aux Expéditions françaises pendant le XIIIe siècle*. Paris, 1840.

BUCHON, J. A. *Recherches et Matériaux pour servir à une Histoire de la Domination française en Grèce*, 2 vols. Paris, 1840.

CAPASSO, B. *Historia Diplomatica Regni Siciliae, 1250–1266*. Naples, 1874.

CARINI, I. *Gli Archivi e le Biblioteche di Spagna, in rapporto alla storia d'Italia in generale e di Sicilia in particolare*, 2 vols. Palermo, 1884–97.

CHAMPOLLION-FIGEAC, J. J. *Lettres des Rois, Reines et autres Personnages des Cours de France et d'Angleterre*, Collection de Documents Inédits. Paris, 1839-47.

DÖLGER, F. *Regesten der Kaiserurkunden des Oströmischen Reiches*, 3 vols. Munich-Berlin, 1924-32.

DUCHESNE, A. *Historiae Francorum Scriptores*, 5 vols. Paris, 1636-49.

FINKE, H. *Aus den Tagen Bonifaz VIII: Quellen*. See Bibliography II.

Fonti per la Storia d'Italia. Istituto Storico Italiano. Rome, 1887– (in progress).

DEL GIUDICE, G. *Codice Diplomatico di Carlo I e Carlo II d'Angiò*, 3 vols. Naples, 1863–9, 1902.

HOPF, K. *Chroniques Gréco-Romanes inédites ou peu connues.* Berlin, 1873.

KERN, F. *Acta Imperii, Angliae et Franciae, 1267–1313.* Tubingen, 1911.

KRAMMER, M. *Quellen zur Geschichte der deutschen Königswahl und des Kur-furstenkollegs,* 2 vols. Leipzig, 1911.

MARTÈNE, E. and DURAND, U. *Thesaurus novus Anecdotorum,* 5 vols. Paris, 1717.

MIKLOSICH, F. and MÜLLER, J. *Acta et Diplomata Graeca medii aevi sacra et profana,* 6 vols. Vienna, 1860–90.

Monumenta Germaniae Historica (ed. G. H. Pertz, T. Mommsen and others). Hanover, 1826– (in progress). Cited as *M.G.H.*

MURATORI, L. A. *Rerum Italicarum Scriptores,* 25 vols. Milan, 1723–51: new series, ed. by G. Carducci and V. Fiorini. Città di Castello-Bologna, 1900– (in progress). Cited as Muratori, *R.I.S.*

POTTHAST, A. *Regesta Pontificum Romanorum, 1198–1304,* 2 vols. Berlin, 1874–5.

Registres des Papes, Écoles Françaises d'Athènes et de Rome. Paris:

Alexander IV (ed. C. Bourel de la Roncière), 2 vols. 1902–17.

Boniface VIII (ed. G. Digard and others), 4 vols. 1884–1932.

Clement IV (ed. E. Jordan), 2 vols. 1893-1945.

Gregory X and John XXI (ed. J. Guiraud and L. Cadier), 2 vols. 1892–1906.

Honorius IV (ed. M. Prou). 1888.

Innocent IV (ed. E. Berger), 4 vols. 1884–1921.

Martin IV (ed. various), 3 vols. 1901–35.

Nicholas III (ed. J. Gay and S. Vitte), 2 vols. 1898–1938.

Nicholas IV (ed. E. Langlois), 2 vols. 1886–1905.

Urban IV (ed. J. Guiraud), 4 vols. 1892–1929.

RYMER, T. *Foedera* (ed. A. Clarke and F. Holbrooke), vols. I and II. London, 1816.

TAFEL, G. L. and THOMAS, G. M. *Urkunden zur ältern Handels- und Staats-geschichte der Republik Venedigs,* 3 vols. Vienna, 1856–7.

TRIFONE, R. *La Legislazione Angioina.* Naples, 1921.

2. INDIVIDUAL SOURCES

ACROPOLITA, GEORGE. *Opera* (ed. A. Heisenberg), 2 vols. Leipsic, 1903.

ANDREW OF HUNGARY. *Descriptio Victoriae a Karolo, Provinciae Comite, repor-tatae* (ed. G. Waitz). (*M.G.H., Scriptores,* vol. XXVI, 1882.)

Annales Altahenses (ed. G. H. Pertz). (*M.G.H., Scriptores,* vol. XVII, 1861.)

Annales Cavenses (ed. G. H. Pertz). (*M.G.H., Scriptores,* vol. III, 1839.)

Annales Januenses Cafari et Continuatorum (ed. G. H. Pertz). (*M.G.H., Scriptores,* vol. XVIII, 1863.)

Annales Ottokariani (ed. G. H. Pertz). (*M.G.H., Scriptores,* vol. IX, 1851.)

Annales Placentini Gibellini (ed. G. H. Pertz). (*M.G.H., Scriptores,* vol. XVIII, 1863.)

Annales Sanctae Justinae Patavini (*Monachi Patavini Chronicon*), (ed. P. Jaffe). (*M.G.H., Scriptores,* vol. XIX, 1866.)

Anonymi Chronicon Siciliae. (Muratori, *R.I.S.*, vol. x.)

BARTHOLOMEW OF NEOCASTRO. *Historia Sicula* (ed. C. Paladino). (Muratori, *R.I.S.*, new series, vol. XIII, 1922.)

BOCCACCIO, GIOVANNI. *De Casibus Illustrium Virorum.* Berne, 1539.

Chronicle of James I of Aragon (Chronica o commentari del rey En Jacme) (translated J. Forster). London, 1883.

Chronicle of the Morea. Greek version (ed. P. Kalonaros). Athens, 1940. Italian version (*Cronaca di Morea*), in Hopf, *Chroniques Gréco-Romanes.* French version (*Livre de la Conqueste de la Princée de l'Amorée*) (ed. J. Longnon). Paris, 1911.

Chronicon Sancti Bertini (ed. O. Holder-Egger). (*M.G.H.*, *Scriptores*, vol. xxv, 1880.)

DANTE ALIGHIERI. *Opere* (ed. E. Moore and P. Toynbee), 4th edition. Oxford, 1924.

D'ESCLOT (DESCLOT), BERNAT. *Cronica del Rey en Pere*, in Buchon, *Chroniques Etrangères.*

ELLENHARD. *Gesta Rudolfi et Alberti Regum Romanorum.* (*M.G.H.*, *Scriptores*, vol. XVII, 1861.)

Gestes des Chiprois (ed. G. Raynaud). Geneva, 1887.

Grandes Chroniques de France (ed. J. Viard, vol. VIII, Paris, 1934).

GREGORAS, NICEPHORUS. *Byzantina Historia* (ed. L. Schopen), 2 vols. Bonn, 1829–30.

Gregorii X Papae Vita Auctori Anonymo Scripta. (Muratori, *R.I.S.*, vol. III.)

GUIDO OF CORVARIA, *Fragmenta Historiae Pisanae.* (Muratori, *R.I.S.* vol. XXIV.)

DI JACI, ATHANASIO. *La Vinuta e lu Suggiornu di lu Re Japicu in la Gitati di Catania, L'annu MCCLXXXVII.* (ed. E. Sicardi). (Muratori, *R.I.S.* new series, vol. XXXIV: *Due Cronache del Vespro in Volgare Siciliano.*)

JOHN OF VIGNAY, *Ex Primati Chronicis per J. de Vignay translatis.* (*M.G.H.*, *Scriptores*, vol. XXVI (1882), ed. Brosien, H.)

JOINVILLE, JOHN, SIEUR OF. *Histoire de Saint Louis* (ed. N. de Wailly). Paris, 1874.

JORDAN OF OSNABRUCK. *De Prerogativa Romani Imperii* (ed. G. Waitz, *Abhandlungen der Königliche Gesellschaft der Wissenschaft zu Gottingen*, vol. XIV, 1868–9.)

LATINI, BRUNETTO. *Libri del Tesoro*, in Amari, *Altre Narrazioni.*

Leggenda di Messer Gianni di Procida (ed. E. Sicardi). (Muratori, *R.I.S.* new series, vol. XXXIV: *Due Cronache del Vespro in Volgare Siciliano.*)

Liber Jani de Procida et Palioloco. Ibid.

MALASPINA, SABA. *Historia Sicula.* (Muratori, *R.I.S.*, vol. VIII.)

MALATERRA, GAUFREDUS. *Historia Sicula, 1099–1265.* (Muratori, *R.I.S.*, vol. v.)

MALESPINI, RICORDANO and GIACHETTO. *Historia Fiorentina* (ed. V. Follini). Florence, 1816.

MATTHEW PARIS. *Chronica Majora* (ed. H. R. Luard). (Rolls Series, 7 vols. London, 1872–84.)

MATTHEW PARIS. *Historia Anglorum, sive Historia Minora* (ed. F. Madden). (Rolls Series, 3 vols. London, 1866–9.)

MICHAEL VIII PALAEOLOGUS, EMPEROR. *De Vita sua Opusculum* (ed. J. Troitsky, in *Christianskoe Chtenie*, vol. II). St Petersburg, 1885.

MUNTANER, RAMON. *Cronica o Descripcio fets e hazanyes dell inclyt Rey Don Jaume* (ed. J. Caroleu). Barcelona, 1886.

NICHOLAS OF CARBIO (CURBIO). *Vita Innocentii IV.* (Muratori, *R.I.S.*, vol. III.)

NICHOLAS OF JAMSILLA. *Historia de rebus gestis Friderici II Imperatoris ejusque filiorum Conradi et Manfredi: adnectitur Anonymi supplementum de rebus gestis ejusdem Manfredi, Caroli Andegavensis et Conradini Regum.* (Muratori, *R.I.S.*, vol. VIII.)

PACHYMER, GEORGE. *De Michaele Palaeologo; De Andronico Palaeologo* (ed. I. Bekker), 2 vols. Bonn, 1835.

PETRARCH, FRANCESCO. *Itinerarium Syriacum.* Basle, 1534.

PIPINO, FRANCESCO. *Chronicon.* (Muratori, *R.I.S.*, vol. IX.)

PTOLOMAEUS OF LUCCA. *Historia Ecclesiastica.* (Muratori, *R.I.S.*, vol. XI.)

Praeclara Francorum Facinora, in Duchesne, *Historiae Francorum Scriptores*, vol. V.

PRIMATUS. *See* John of Vignay.

RABBAN SAUMA. *History.* Translated by E. Wallis Budge, and published as *The Monks of Kublai Khan, Emperor of China.* London, 1928.

Rebellamentu di Sichilia (ed. E. Sicardi). (Muratori, *R.I.S.* new series, vol. XXXIV: *Due Cronache del Vespro in Volgare Siciliano.*)

SALIMBENE DE ADAM. *Cronica* (ed. O. Holder-Egger). (*M.G.H.*, Scriptores, vol. XXXII, 1905–13.)

SANUDO MARINO. *Istoria del Regno di Romania*, in Hopf, *Chroniques Gréco-Romanes.*

SPECIALIS, NICHOLAS. *Historia Sicula.* (Muratori, *R.I.S.*, vol. X.)

VILLANI, GIOVANNI. *Cronica*, 8 vols. Florence, 1823.

WILLIAM OF NANGIS. *Gesta Sancti Ludovici: Gesta Philippi III.* (Bouquet, *R.H.F.*, vol. XX.) Extracts, additions to Andrew of Hungary, in *M.G.H.*, Scriptores, vol. XXVI.

II. MODERN WORKS

AMARI, M. *La Guerra del Vespro Siciliano*, 9th ed., 3 vols. Milan, 1886.

AMARI, M. *Storia dei Musulmani di Sicilia*, 3 vols. in 4. Florence, 1854–72.

BÄTHGEN, F. *Die Regentschaft Papst Innocent III im Königreich Sizilien.* Heidelberg, 1914.

BOASE, T. S. R. *Boniface VIII.* London, 1933.

DE BOÜARD, A. *Le Régime politique et les Institutions de Rome au Moyen Âge.* Paris, 1920.

BOURCART, J. *L'Albanie et les Albanais.* Paris, 1921.

BURY, J. B. *History of the Later Roman Empire, A.D. 395–A.D. 565,* 2 vols. London, 1923.

BUSSON, A. 'Friedrich der Friedige als Prätendent der Sizilianischen Krone und Johann von Procida', in *Historische Aufsätzen dem Andenken an Georg Waitz gewidmet.* Hanover, 1886.

BUSSON, A. *Die Doppelwahl des Jahres 1257 und der römische König Alfons X von Castilien.* Münster, 1866.

CADIER, L. *Essai sur l'Administration du Royaume de Sicile sous Charles I et Charles II d'Anjou.* Paris, 1891.

CAGGESE, C. *Roberto d'Angiò e i suoi Tempi,* 2 vols. Florence, 1922–31.

Cambridge Medieval History, vol. VI, *Victory of the Papacy;* vol. VII, *Decline of the Empire and Papacy.* Cambridge, 1929–32.

CARABALLESI, F. *Saggio di Storia del Commercio della Puglia.* Trani, 1900.

CARO, G. *Genua und die Mächte am Mittelmeer,* 2 vols. Halle, 1895.

CARTELLIERI, O. *Peter von Aragon und die Sizilianische Vesper.* Heidelberg, 1904.

CARUCCI, C. *La Guerra del Vespro Siciliano nella frontiera del Principato.* Subiaco, 1934.

CHALANDON, F. *Histoire de la Domination Normande en Italie,* 2 vols. Paris, 1907.

CHAPMAN, C. *Michel Paléologue, restaurateur de l'Empire Byzantin.* Paris, 1926.

CIPOLLA, C. *Compendio della Storia politica di Verona.* Verona, 1899.

COHN, W. *Das Zeitalter der Hohenstaufen in Sizilien.* Breslau, 1925.

CROCE, B. *Storia del Regno di Napoli,* 2nd ed. Bari, 1931.

CUTOLO, A. *Gli Angioini.* Florence, 1934.

DAVIDSOHN, R. *Geschichte von Florenz,* 4 vols. Berlin, 1896–1927.

DIEHL, C., OECONOMOS, L., GUILLAND, R and GROUSSET, R. *L'Europe Orientale de 1081 à 1453.* (G. Glotz, *Histoire Générale, Histoire du Moyen Âge,* vol. IX, Paris, 1945.)

DIGARD, G. *Philippe le Bel et le Saint-Siège,* 2 vols. Paris, 1934.

DURRIEU, P. *Les Archives Angevines de Naples,* 2 vols. Paris, 1887.

EGIDI, P. *La 'Communitas Siciliae' di 1282.* Messina, 1915.

FAWTIER, R. *L'Europe Occidentale de 1270 à 1328* (G. Glotz, *Histoire Générale, Histoire du Moyen Âge,* vol. VI, 1). Paris, 1940.

FINKE, H. *Aus den Tagen Bonifaz VIII.* Münster, 1902.

FOURNIER, P. *Le Royaume d'Arles et de Vienne.* Paris, 1891.

GARDNER, A. *The Lascarids of Nicaea.* London, 1912.

GENEAKOPLOS, D. 'Greco-Latin relations on the eve of the Byzantine Restoration; The Battle of Pelagonia, 1259'. *Dumbarton Oaks Papers,* no. VII. Cambridge, Mass., 1953.

GENEAKOPLOS, D. 'Michael VIII Palaeologus and the Union of Lyons', *Harvard Theological Review*, vol. XLVI. Cambridge, Mass., 1953.

GENEAKOPLOS, D. 'On the Schism of the Greek and Roman Churches', *Greek Orthodox Theological Review*, vol. I (1954).

GIBBON, E. *The Decline and Fall of the Roman Empire* (ed. J. B. Bury), 7 vols. London, 1896–1900.

DEL GIUDICE, G. *Don Arrigo, Infante de Castiglia.* Naples, 1878.

DEL GIUDICE, G. 'La Famiglia del Re Manfredi', *Archivio Storico per le Provincie Napoletane.* Naples, 1878.

GREGOROVIUS, F. *Geschichte der Stadt Rom im Mittelalter* (ed. F. Schillmann), 2 vols. Dresden, 1926.

HALPHEN, L. *L'Essor de l'Europe. Peuples et Civilisations* (ed. L. Halphen and P. Sagnac), vol. VI. Paris, 1940.

HAMPE, K. *Geschichte Konradins von Hohenstaufen.* Innsbruck, 1894.

VON HEFELE, C. J. *Histoire des Conciles* (revised and translated by H. Leclercq), 8 vols. in 16. Paris, 1907–21. Cited as Hefele-Leclercq.

HEYD, W. *Histoire du Commerce du Levant au Moyen Âge* (translated by F. Raynaud), new edition, 2 vols. Leipzig, 1923.

HILL, G. *History of Cyprus*, 3 vols. Cambridge, 1940–8.

HITTI, P. K. *A History of the Arabs.* London, 1937.

IORGA, N. *Brève Histoire de l'Albanie.* Bucarest, 1919.

JIREČEK, C. *Geschichte der Bulgaren.* Prague, 1876.

JIREČEK, C. *Geschichte der Serben*, 2 vols. Gotha, 1911–18.

JORDAN, E. *L'Allemagne et l'Italie aux XIIe et XIIIe Siècles* (G. Glotz), *Histoire Générale: Histoire du Moyen Âge*, vol. IV, 1. Paris, 1939.

JORDAN, E. *Les Origines de la Domination Angevine en Italie.* Paris, 1909.

KANTOROWICZ, E. *Kaiser Friedrich der Zweite.* Berlin, 1927.

KARST, A. *Geschichte Manfreds vom Tode Friedrichs II bis zu seiner Kronung.* Berlin, 1897.

KEMPF, J. *Geschichte des Deutschen Reiches während des grossen Interregnums, 1245–1273.* Wurzburg, 1893.

KRETSCHMAYR, H. *Geschichte von Venedig*, 2 vols. Gotha, 1905–20.

LA MONTE, J. L. *Feudal Monarchy in the Latin Kingdom of Jerusalem.* Cambridge, Mass., 1932.

LANGLOIS, C. V. *Le Règne de Philippe III le Hardi.* Paris, 1877.

LÉONARD, E. G. *Les Angevins de Naples.* Paris, 1954.

LIBERTINI, G. and PALADINO, G. *Storia della Sicilia.* Catania, 1933.

LONGNON, J. *L'Empire Latin de Constantinople et la Principauté de Morée.* Paris. 1949.

LONGNON, J. *Les Français d'Outremer au Moyen Âge.* Paris, 1929.

LUCHAIRE, A. *Innocent III*, 6 vols. Paris, 1905–11.

DE MAS LATRIE, L. *Trésor de Chronologie d'Histoire et de Géographie*. Paris, 1889.

MERKEL, C. 'La Dominazione di Carlo I d'Angiò in Piemonte e in Lombardia'. *Memorie della Reale Accademia delle Scienze di Torino*, new series, vol. XLI. Turin, 1891.

MERKEL, C. *Manfredo I e Manfredo II Lancia*. Turin, 1886.

MILLER, W. *Essays on the Latin Orient*. Cambridge, 1921.

MILLER, W. *The Latins in the Levant*. London, 1908.

MINIERI RICCIO, C. *Genealogia di Carlo d'Angiò, prima generazione*. Naples, 1857.

MINIERI RICCIO, C. *Genealogia di Carlo II d'Angiò, re di Napoli*. Archivio Storico per le Provincie Napoletane. Naples, 1882-3.

MINIERI RICCIO, C. *Il Regno di Carlo I di Angiò*, 2 vols. Florence, 1875-81.

MINIERI RICCIO, C. *Saggio di Codice Diplomatico di Napoli*, 2 vols. Naples, 1878-83.

MONTI, G. M. *La Dominazione Angioina in Piemonte*. Turin, 1930.

MONTI, G. M. *Nuovi Studi Angioini*, including *Gli Angioini di Napoli nella Poesia Provenzale*. Trani, 1937.

MÜLLER, E. *Peter von Prezza, ein Publizist der Zeit des Interregnums*. Heidelberg, 1913.

NICOL, D. M. 'The Date of the Battle of Pelagonia', in *Byzantinische Zeitschrift*, vol. XLIX, 1. Munich, 1956.

NORDEN, W. *Das Papsttum und Byzanz*. Berlin, 1903.

OMAN, C. *A History of the Art of War in the Middle Ages*, 2nd ed., 2 vols. London, 1924.

OSTROGORSKI, G. *A History of the Byzantine State* (translated by J. Hussey). Oxford, 1956.

PAULUS, N. *Geschichte des Ablasses im Mittelalter*, 2 vols. Paderborn, 1922-3.

PAWLICKI, B. *Papst Honorius IV*. Münster, 1896.

PETIT, J. *Charles de Valois*. Paris, 1900.

PINZI, C. *Storia della Città di Viterbo*, 2 vols. Rome, 1887-9.

PONTIERI, E. *Ricerche sulla Crisi della Monarchia Siciliana nel secolo XIII*. Naples, 1942.

POWICKE, F. M. *King Henry III and the Lord Edward*, 2 vols. Oxford, 1947.

REDLICH, O. *Rudolf von Habsburg*. Innsbruck, 1903.

DE RENZI, S. *Collectio Salernitana*. Naples, 1854.

DE RENZI, S. *Il Secolo decimo terzo e Giovanni da Procida*. Naples, 1860.

ROHDE, H. E. *Der Kampf um Sizilien in den Jahren 1291-1302*. Berlin, 1913.

RODENBURG, C. *Innocenz IV und das Königreich Siziliens*. Halle, 1892.

RUNCIMAN, S. *A History of the Crusades*, 3 vols. Cambridge, 1951-4.

SCHIPA, M. *Carlo-Martello Angioino*, 2nd ed. Naples, 1926.

SCHIPA, M. *Sicilia ed Italia sotto Federico II.* Archivio Storico per le Provincie Napoletane. Naples, 1928.

SCHIRRMACHER, F. W. *Die letzten Hohenstaufen.* Göttingen, 1871.

DE STEFANO, A. *Federico III d'Aragona, Re di Sicilia.* Palermo, 1937.

STERNFELD, R. *Cardinal Johann Gaetan Orsini (Papst Nikolaus III).* Berlin, 1905.

STERNFELD, R. *Karl von Anjou als Graf von Provence.* Berlin, 1888.

STERNFELD, R. *Ludwigs der Heiligen Kreuzzug nach Tunis und die Politik Karls I von Sizilien.* Berlin, 1896.

STHAMER, E. 'Aus der Vorgeschichte der Sizilischen Vesper', in *Quellen und Forschungen aus Italienischen Archiven und Bibliotheken,* vol. XIX, 1927.

TEETAERT, A. 'Nicolas IV', in A. Vacant and E. Mangenot, *Dictionnaire de Théologie Catholique,* vol. XI, 1. Paris, 1931.

TENCKHOFF, F. *Papst Alexander IV.* Paderborn, 1907.

TERLIZZI, S. *Codice Diplomatico delle relazioni tra Carlo I d'Angiò e la Toscana.* Florence, 1914.

THROOP, P. A. *Criticism of the Crusade.* Amsterdam, 1940.

VAN CLEVE, T. C. *Markward of Anweiler and the Sicilian Regency.* Princeton, 1937.

VASILIEV, A. A. *Byzance et les Arabes,* vols. I and II, 2, ed. and trans. by H. Grégoire and M. Canard. Brussels, 1935, 1950. Original Russian ed., 2 vols. St Petersburg, 1900–2.

WIERUSZOWSKI, H. 'Der Anteil Johanns von Procida an der Verschwörung gegen Karl von Anjou', *Gesammelte Aufsätze zur Kulturgeschichte Spaniens,* vol. V. 1930.

WIERUSZOWSKI, H. 'Conjuraciones y alianzas políticas del rey Pedro de Aragón contra Carlos de Anjou antes de las Vísperas Sicilianas', *Boletín de la Academia de la Historia.* Madrid, 1935.

WIERUSZOWSKI, H. 'La Corte di Pietro d'Aragona e i Precedenti dell'Impresa Siciliana', 2 parts, *Archivio Storico Italiano,* anno 96. Florence, 1938.

WOLFF, R. L. 'Mortgage and Redemption of an Emperor's Son: Castile and the Latin Empire of Constantinople', *Speculum,* vol. XXIX. Cambridge, Mass., 1954.

YVER, G. *Le Commerce et les Marchands dans l'Italie méridionale au XIIIe et au XIVe Siècles.* Paris, 1903.

INDEX

NOTE. The names of countries and peoples occurring frequently in the text, such as France, Germany, Italy, Sicily, Spaniards, Byzantines, etc., are not given in the index